WATERLOO SUNSET

Published by

Librario Publishing Ltd

ISBN: 978-1-904440-83-3

Copies can be ordered via the Internet
www.librario.com

or from:

Brough House, Milton Brodie, Kinloss
Moray IV36 2UA
Tel /Fax No 00 44 (0)1343 850 178

Printed by Biddles Ltd., Kings Lynn, Norfolk

Waterloo Sunset

An autobiography by

Howard A. P. Fisher

Librario

The Author

Howard Fisher was born in Leigh-on-Sea, Essex in 1940. After studying agricultural chemistry at Glasgow University he joined Tony Benn's Ministry of Technology. After twenty years in Whitehall he moved from the Civil Service to local government and Grampian Regional Council.

Howard now lives with his wife Fiona in rural Aberdeenshire, with their son and daughter nearby.

To my dear Fiona
for her support through the good and bad times

ACKNOWLEDGEMENTS

I am grateful for all the support I have received in writing this book from my good friends, Roy Cunningham and David Kennedy. Both spent many hours reading and correcting my earlier drafts.

CONTENTS

Chapters:

Chapter I

The Dangerous Years

There is a long established television based research project which tracks a group of individuals from various social backgrounds and dips into their lives every seven years. I envy the youngsters from middle class backgrounds with their prep schools to match, who have a crystal clear plan for life. The plan usually specifies the public school they will attend after 'Common Entrance', and then Oxford or Cambridge of course, but often the particular college is named. After university the vision remains confident and further defined with either a commission in the Guards or direct into one of the 'professions'. When I was seven I had no idea what I wanted or expected of life, and indeed this did not begin to become clear until twenty years later. I suppose what I really regret is that I was not encouraged or given that confidence or poise by my parents to think in that way and be unashamedly ambitious. My father would have labelled this behaviour as 'cocky'.

Although my father was public school educated, the values associated with that education were not overtly proclaimed at home. We were rarely involved or encouraged to join in adult discussion either at meals or any other time. My father, probably reflecting his own upbringing before the Great War, preferred children to be seen and rarely heard. Right to the end my father had very little patience for debate and especially if you were coming from a point of view different from his own. Although not in any way a political animal he was a conviction Tory and some good friendships foundered on his unwillingness to be generous in debate.

One of the reasons for putting on record something of my career experiences is the paucity of information on my father's career and early life experiences. Although my father died at ninety-five when I was fifty-seven, rarely could he be persuaded to talk about his past. For example I have no idea how he got into the building business. Certainly his entry to the industry was not via a craft route or by serving any apprenticeship, in the wider sense of the term. My father was an entrepreneur and simply set up his own business, with some financial help from his father. But why the choice of this industry rather than say the City, where his own father finished his career, remains a mystery. Any success at school was confined to the sports field and he left school without any paper qualifications. He was sent on the equivalent of the 'grand tour' to Australia, New Zealand and the South Pacific. Through contacts perhaps from school, or from my grandfather who worked for the Bank of Australia and New Zealand, my father undertook farm related jobs in both Australia and New Zealand but also with a spell working for the Samoan Crown Estates Board in Western Samoa. I have a personal reference from the Secretary of the Board recalling his arrival in Samoa on the SS *Tofua* on 21 November 1921 and reporting "his services were quite satisfactory and his character excellent".

Had his elder brother, Cecil, not died at an early age from cancer I wonder whether my father would have returned to England. I know very little of the gap between these early years and when he met my mother in 1936. I do know that in about 1928 he married a Gladys Poole but she died young of TB leaving me a half sister, Pamela. From what I could glean this first marriage was not a particularly happy one.

My father was antagonistic to those he saw as 'intellectuals' and this no doubt hampered his further success as an entrepreneur and in dealing with architects, accountants and various senior officials in local government with responsibility for planning and building control matters. Nonetheless he was successful in running his own business. He sent my sister and me to public schools, me to university for seven years and ensured that the family enjoyed a comfortable, if oddly spartan, life style. Although luxuries were rationed, we did travel extensively in Europe during the summer holidays and, like my experience later in the public service, large requests were always considered and often met. However ask for the proverbial roll of sellotape then any sense of relative values deserted my father. My father would lose all reason if he caught my mother wasting food.

Leigh-on-Sea was a delightful and safe environment in which to grow up, and especially when reaching the age where freedom to roam was granted to my sister and myself. Although my mother was obsessive about risk and 'accidents' and, yes, clean knickers in the event of an accident were also part of our regime, she was surprisingly relaxed about us going off on 'expeditions' with our friends. However these were different times. Southend and its constituent communities had that relaxed and colourful atmosphere of seaside towns of yesteryear. The annual influx of five million largely day trippers to the county borough gave rise to an all pervasive informality to everyday life and this was reflected in dress codes of grown-ups as well as us kids. I think this is still the case in Southend.

Leigh was at the west end of the county borough, tended to attract the more discerning visitor and particularly families, and was relatively quiet compared with Southend's 'golden mile' sea front. Leigh is recorded in the Domesday Book of 1086, and has a strong seafaring tradition. There is reason to believe that the *Mayflower* used by the Pilgrim Fathers was built or owned in Leigh. There remains an 'Old Town' beside the sea and below the cliff top where the later town developed. The Old Town is still home to a fleet of small boats, locally called 'smacks', trawling the outer Thames estuary for cockles, whelks, shrimps, crab and other sea food delights. Jellied eel remains a delicacy on offer at the row of 'cockle sheds' sandwiched between the railway and the sea shore in Old Leigh and where the shellfish caught by the 'smacks' is processed. There can be few experiences as a grown-up more delightful than a trip to the cockle sheds on a Sunday morning, and settling down at a trestle table in the open to a plate of cockles, a crab-filled roll with a pint of bitter collected from the Crooked Billet pub that sits hard by the rail line. With the sun sparkling on the estuary and a collection of like minded sybarites, I can not imagine its equal anywhere in the world, and all to be had some forty minutes from London's Fenchurch Street station. As an old publicity slogan for the town used to say: 'Five million people can't be wrong'.

My only sibling, Helen, is eighteen months younger than me. She never moved from south-east Essex, marrying a local man and producing two sons and a daughter. My sister remains the traditional stay-at-home housewife, and I do not imply any criticism here. As small children we got on well enough but drifted apart in our late teens and this was not helped by both of us being at boarding schools some 200 miles apart. Helen went on to attend the same Methodist school as my father's sister, Edgehill College in Bideford, North Devon. On leaving school Helen had her own set of friends in Leigh and Southend and I, after one year at home when I was working on the farm, was soon to disappear to Glasgow for seven years. Although our respective houses were within a mile or two of each other in the early years of marriage the gap in our relationship has, in my view, widened over the intervening years. The death of my parents did nothing to rebuild relationships. I regret this and wish for the close links my wife has with her two brothers.

As children we probably perceived father as tight fisted, but in much later years I realised it was my mother who capped so many an idea that might have expanded the family's horizons and collective experience. It is strange how little one understands one's own parents, and for me that process of understanding and perspective did not mature until my mid fifties. I saw my father as a stern and somewhat unforgiving figure with a short fuse to a considerable temper. My mother appeared, and championed herself, as the peacemaker. I have never seen my mother lose her temper. For most of my life I saw my father as the dominant partner with my mother in a support role. However I now realise, far too late in life, that this was not the case. To see my father as a soft touch might be stretching a point, but compared with mother he was so. Mother's character was shaped by her upbringing as an only child by a single parent, and survival and security dictated her relationships with family and friends alike. I have met few women with the determination and strength of mind that my mother had. Rarely did father undertake anything including taking business decisions without mother's blessing. If he had taken counsel elsewhere, there is no doubt in my mind that he would have been a very successful businessman, rather than one moderately so. Above all father was scrupulously honest and rarely told a lie. I respected him for this. On the other hand mother was the original spin doctor.

Although my parents could never have been described as intellectually ambitious both gave some priority to good education. Measles at five either gave rise to or was coincidental to the onset of my asthma. As a result I did not start schooling until I was six years old. My first school was Highfield College, a small private boys' school nearby in Leigh-on-Sea. This was a short-lived experience as was my next school. Here I was the only boy in St Michael's Convent School (CofE) although I probably set a trend, as later boys were taken in the junior school. At both schools my attendance record was poor. Highfield College has long gone from the education scene although St Michael's still exists but not as a convent school. Both remain clearly in my mind and so must have made an impact. The only credible private alternative in the Southend area was the traditional boys' preparatory school Alleyn Court, which fed Felstead public school in mid Essex, amongst others. I suspect that finances at the time may have been a factor why I was not sent to Alleyn Court but perhaps equally important in the decision was my parents' antagonism to those in Southend 'society' that patronised this school. So I was sent to West Leigh School which was a local authority school and no more than five minutes' walk from our house. My father referred to such schools in a disparaging tone as Board or Council schools.

In fairness I remember the experience of West Leigh School as a happy one, in all ways. I remember the teaching as good and staff dedicated. Strictly speaking the title was West Leigh Schools in the plural since the complex also housed the senior or then secondary modern option. This did not have a good reputation which somewhat slopped over to the junior department, which had its own Head, Mr Gibbs.

I do not remember any bullying to speak of although the playground offered the confrontations necessary to growing up. There were teachers I still remember fondly and with respect including Mr Wakefield, and Miss McKissock who gave me private coaching to overcome my continuing poor attendance. West Leigh School got me through the 11-plus examination and entrance to the local grammar school, Westcliff High School for Boys.

I was at Westcliff for two years before sitting the Common Entrance for Cranleigh, my father's old school in Surrey. Again I remember the 'High School' with affection and respect, although my record of attendance remained abysmal. The school had (and still has) a prestigious record of academic achievement. The Headmaster, Mr Cloke, I remember welcomed us as young gentlemen rather than boys and the ethos of achievement and learning was, at that time, stronger than that of the public school I transferred to at thirteen. I remember the equal emphasis on sport but Westcliff seemed to have the balance well tuned. Drama was important as were after school clubs. Indeed it was the Gardening Club that started a life long interest. This was run by one of the tougher masters and he ensured one took out only what one put in. For example the amount of vegetables distributed amongst members to take home at the Friday harvesting session reflected the time you put in digging and weeding. This was my first insight into practical socialism.

It was plain to both my parents that I was dropping seriously behind with my school studies and perhaps my father more than my mother realised things could not go on as they were. The decision to send me to boarding school was the right one as I suspect that my mother's over protective approach was actually making my health worse. At the same time I liked staying at home rather than going to school, and the more I dropped behind in class the more reluctant I was to go to school. There is no doubt that I did have a serious asthma problem with attacks that were of real concern to our local doctor. On one occasion I was hospitalised. For me the idea of boarding school was not attractive but not one that filled me with horror.

Although I sat the Common Entrance examination there was little likelihood that I would 'pass' it in any formal sense of the term. My parents took me for an interview with the Headmaster, David Loveday. Loveday was intimidating. He was tall, thin and lacked that easy charm so prized by the English public school educated. He was a bachelor and also a cleric but unlikely of the Anglican High Church tradition. David Loveday left Cranleigh about a year after I started there and was appointed first as Archdeacon of Dorking and then as Bishop of Dorchester in Oxfordshire. Many years later and well after Loveday's death I visited Dorchester and its beautiful church and met a lady who ran the excellent tea shop in support of the church fabric and still remembered Bishop Loveday. Her memories were of a man difficult to get on with. Although I had very little time with him as my Head I met him a number of times at Old Cranleighan events over the years until his death at the age of 89. He remembered without fail my name and addressed me always, of course, as 'Fisher'. The photograph in a 'History of Cranleigh School' (Collins, 1983) of the Bishop's last occasion back at School before he died was of him talking to me in the Reading Room. It was not that I was in any way a 'mover and shaker' in the OC (Old Cranleighan) hierarchy, but a coincidence that has some poignancy for me.

With barely nine years since the end of the Second World War Cranleigh was a somewhat spartan and tough place for a thirteen-year-old with no Prep school apprenticeship. With nearly sixty boys sharing one 'Houseroom' which was the focus of life during the periods not spent at lessons or on the playing field, and with the same sixty boys sharing one large dormitory there was little or no privacy or creature comforts. The House was organised on a rigidly hierarchical basis from top to bottom.

Teenage years are a time to experiment with ideas and thoughts and Cranleigh, and the public school system generally, prided itself on the opportunity it provided to develop 'character' and self-reliance. Many contemporary OCs would be appalled to see their school described as an intellectual straitjacket or as intellectually suffocating but I found it so. I chose science at the time of streaming decisions and this tended to cut one off from the more thoughtful school clubs and societies. However, I did always speak from the floor at the debating society although only once was asked to speak from the platform and that was in a debate with a motion along the lines that 'This house would rather vote Labour'. Needless to say the motion was lost but I was heard politely and I think I got respect from some masters who turned out for the debate. At least I was taken more seriously after that debate. I was later to follow up this initiation into public speaking at university.

With so much academic work to catch up on my progress up the lower rungs of the academic ladder was slow. Those doing moderately well in the Common Entrance examination came straight into the Fourth Form and to the then O level syllabus. My arrival in the Fourth Form took another eighteen months but by that time I was well into my stride and achieving top marks in my class in most subjects. I can remember very clearly the all-important choice between arts and sciences that in those days put me on tram lines that took me through to the end of university days, when I was able to step off and pursue another direction. It was early in the 7.30 to 9 o'clock prep session where we all sat together (in order of seniority) on rows of benches at large oak tables in the Houseroom. Laurie Tanner the Housemaster was moving around the benches and leaned over and said, "You will wish to do science?" There was no forewarning of this important decision or discussion of the options. At that stage I was getting top marks across the range and so was not limited by weaknesses to one area rather than another. Without thinking I said, "Science, Sir" and that was that for the next ten years or so. Looking back I am not sure I would have changed my mind but I would have liked to have discussed it more and even discussed it at home.

I enjoyed science at school and it brought me into contact with a couple of masters that I admired and one that I found inspirational. This was important to me in the final years of school when the relationship with masters strays a little more towards friendship rather than one of pupil and authority. Many teachers at Cranleigh were adequate, a few were good but rarely, for me, inspirational. True, it was a bad time for the school in the post-war aftermath when many good teachers were lost and those returning found it difficult to settle with enthusiasm to their pre-war role. The academic record of the school went through a bad spell in the post-war years as a result. However at the time we pupils were not aware of this, but we were aware of bad teachers, even when in the lower reaches of the school. Only in one subject did I really suffer as a result of bad teaching and that was mathematics. I never fully overcame that handicap and my maths ability prevented me from becoming a vet or doing medicine. I know now I would have made a poor vet and a terrible doctor.

Cranleigh was also the inspiration for my lifelong interest in farming. The school had a farm within the estate and this, with a herd of Friesians, supplied the school milk requirements. The manager, Claude Gravell, was also an Old Cranleighan. He and his Finnish wife made those boys interested in farming very welcome. A relatively small group of enthusiasts regularly helped with the milking, mucking out the pigs, hay and silage making and other routine jobs around the farm. I learnt to drive on the farm's Fordson Major tractor and then its Land Rover.

I learnt a lot from Claude and it was this experience together with visits as a child with my parents to farming friends in Weathersfield and Blackmore End in north Essex that kindled my interest in a living from the land. Spare time spent at the Cranleigh's Upfold Farm also provided a refuge from the pressures of boarding school life and was somehow seen as at best instructive and at worst harmless by authority in its many guises, and particularly during my younger years. Claude Gravell gave me encouragement to choose agriculture as my course at university. Alas, the farm is no longer and neither is Claude who died in 2002. The former farm buildings were used later as a sixth form study centre and a riding stables, with some of the land providing room for the school's continuing growth and development.

My A level subjects were Zoology, Botany and Chemistry. Although I ended my university time undertaking research in chemistry it was not the strongest of my sciences. It was not until university when one was able to get to grips with organic chemistry did I find the discipline absorbing. It was about this time that the intimate chemistry of photosynthesis and the fixing of carbon dioxide by plants was being unravelled. The master teaching me Zoology and Botany was first class. Our class for both subjects was very small at about six to eight boys. We had the advantage of new biology labs with excellent facilities. With a small class and all anxious to learn the relationship with our master, Tony West, was a close one. He was able to be frank when conversation strayed, as it inevitably did, beyond the academic subject in hand. I cannot say he became a friend in the sense we would use the term in adult life, but there was an easy partnership where both parties felt secure enough in their respective roles to relax and drop guard. He was an excellent teacher, always well-prepared and always managing to transmit the atmosphere of a research lab rather than a classroom. I suspect I shared with him a disdain for the more petty aspects of boarding school life where the Common Room often mirrored life in the Houseroom.

Unfortunately university entrance application was left to my Housemaster rather than to Tony West who responsible for most of my A level teaching apart from Chemistry. My relationship with my Housemaster was one of mutual but wary peaceful coexistence. The process of application was a strangely remote process. I was aware in broad terms what was going on but felt somewhat removed from it. There was little discussion with me (or with my parents) of the pros and cons of the institutions approached and which institutions would best be suited to my needs. It was in the approach to only one Cambridge college, and a less than prestigious one, that I feel I was damned by faint praise. I remember my father expressing diplomatic concern to my Housemaster, hoping that the school's recommendations would be supportive. His reply to my father was that he would 'tell the truth'. Well, I did not make Cambridge and to this day I feel a sense of failure every time I pass through that town. This may say more about me than my Housemaster and Cambridge. I feel that with a fair wind I could have made the grade. My A levels were certainly up to the mark and I took the school prizes in Zoology and Botany besides coming top of the class in almost all examinations throughout the last four years of school life.

Applications were made on my behalf to study agriculture at London's Wye College, Bristol, Reading and also Scottish universities via the then Fitness Board. Glasgow accepted me and I plumped for this 'dear green place' on the basis I had never been to Scotland and saw the opportunity to pursue my newly discovered love affair with hills and the great outdoors, thanks to a school Combined Cadet Force camp in the Lakes. If I had had an uncomplicated choice at the time I would have chosen Wye or Reading because even then I was aware of their reputation in agriculture. I remain of the view that the school was far from helpful in the whole process of my university application. My unwillingness to yield and fit the Cranleigh and public school mould counted against me in the school character reference which was then (and perhaps still) so important in securing a place at those first division universities with strong links to the independent school sector. My outspokenness was resented rather than channelled and encouraged and I guess I reaped what I sowed at least in terms of my Housemaster.

Although not finding a place in Cranleigh's own university league table, Glasgow was an excellent university. Few of my Cranleigh contemporaries at the time were aware that Glasgow was Scotland's second oldest university, founded in 1452 at a time when Scotland had four universities to England's two. It was a graduate of Glasgow University, Bishop Elphinstone, that founded King's College, the forerunner of the present Aberdeen University in the city where I ended up in 1988. The north-east of Scotland had a little known and quirky situation when there were three universities in this part of Scotland at the time there were not many more than that in England. There was Kings College (1492), Marischal College (1593) and for a short time Fraserburgh University (1592). Kings and Marischal came together as late as 1860 to form the single University of Aberdeen. Fraserburgh University, although formally established and with some buildings, never recruited any students as such and eventually foundered.

Leaving Cranleigh in the July of 1959 was an emotional experience. For years I had looked forward to this event and had savoured a Mr Chips style exit where I would make the last trip down the imposing drive from the school to the lane that led across Smithwood Common to the main road to Guildford and what I imagined as freedom. In the event the feeling was not one of elation but of loss. In many ways I had become institutionalised in spite of all my protestations over the years, although these had been a lot more muted in the latter years. Leaving was a cliff edge experience with not much lead in and little trailing of the event with farewells and goodbyes. In the tradition of the last night of any term there was some alcohol illicitly consumed and I had got little sleep. Breakfast was, I remember, somewhat unreal with a feeling of detachment from all going on around me. Hurried goodbyes were said and most of the school had left within the hour after breakfast with the majority being picked up in parents' cars. My parents had to travel a longer distance than most and did not arrive until mid morning and so I had the school almost to myself. There is nothing as lonely as an empty school. I wandered the corridors and other colleagues' studies. Most of the posters, and small items of equipment which personalised each of our studies had gone leaving rather sad and now seemingly very small and depressing rooms. I do not recall talking to anyone or being able to share the experience of leaving school. I have tried hard to remember but I cannot recall a few kind words of farewell and good wishes from my Housemaster, Laurie Tanner.

There was a British film made in the 1950s about teenagers called 'The Dangerous Years' and starring Frankie Vaughan as a rebellious young man. I pasted on my houseroom locker a photograph from a newspaper depicting the young Vaughan resplendent in the long draped jacket, drainpipe trousers and thick crepe soled suede shoes of the 'Teddy boy' culture featured in the film. I suppose being at Cranleigh removed many of the risks of going astray during these difficult and potentially dangerous years. For me rebellion was to sport a pair of crepe soled suede shoes, slim jim tie and a tapered trousers on the morning of the last day of term.

The journey home by car through Guildford to London, then the Eastend and the suburban fringes of Essex that follow the District Line of the Underground to Hornchurch did nothing to lift the feeling of emptiness. There is no more depressing entrance to London than from the east. The A127 or Southend Arterial Road stretches through some notably unspectacular open countryside to the boundary of the then County Borough of Southend-on-Sea at Leigh. I did not say much during the two and a half hours it took to drive from Cranleigh to home. There was none of the elation usually associated with the beginning of holidays and being back at home, but more than just an emptiness and even an anticlimax. I felt a foreboding of the responsibilities of being an adult but without the support of a very protected world. It was not only the school but I missed so much the Surrey countryside of Cranleigh, its surrounding richly wooded hills, its delightful villages with their village greens and the mellowness of the indigenous handmade brick and tiles of the older buildings including the Woodyer designed nucleus of the school itself. It had been a long journey from Westcliff High School and those early days at Cranleigh when I hated everything the county stood for.

I was privileged to attend Cranleigh and how much so was just dawning during that summer of 1959. I now appreciate and am grateful for the education my parents provided but I still feel Cranleigh, at the time, had many shortcomings. My son subsequently attended Cranleigh (both the preparatory and the senior school) some twenty years later. Most of the petty rules had gone, there was more privacy, more visits home, access to the village was unfettered in anyway and there were girls, although only then in sixth form. The school in the eighties was more open, less of a hothouse, and with more overseas students was much more cosmopolitan and outward looking. Teaching was clearly so much better and so were the examination results. One can argue the pros and cons of the admission of girls but I suspect the decision had more to do with economics than any consideration of improving the wholeness of the end product and its fitness for life. Such schools cannot now afford to ignore customer wishes and gone are the days when they neither had to market themselves or compete on results and facilities.

Chapter 2

To be a farmer's boy

I had been accepted to study agriculture at Glasgow University and to start in the September of 1959. The course chosen and leading to a Bachelor of Science in Agriculture also required the student to undertake an additional year working on a farm. The theory was that it is unreasonable for any student to graduate with such a degree with no practical experience of farm life. In their wisdom the university authorities judged that the experience should include the complete cycle of seasons and so seeing a farm year through from beginning to end. Normally students chose to undertake this year's 'practical', as it was known, between the first and second year of study at university but there was the option to undertake the practical year before going up to university. Having just completed six years at boarding school I opted for the latter. As I was the only person to take the option of doing this before going up to university it resulted in me losing my first year set of colleagues and joining a new set for my second year with those freshly returning from their year on the farm. I have great difficulty now in placing my first and second year colleagues and to remember which set they belonged to. I felt there were advantages, for me anyway, in undertaking the practical year before going up to Glasgow.

This decision having been made the next and much more difficult task was to find a farmer who would take me as a student. This was an easier task for students in Scotland where the Colleges of Agriculture that work in association with the universities had a list of recommended farmers in each area. In the case of Glasgow the college concerned was the West of Scotland College of Agriculture at Auchincruive, a few miles from Ayr in the heart of Robert Burns country. The then three agricultural colleges in Scotland, namely West, East at Edinburgh and the North of Scotland in Aberdeen were, in effect, part of Scotland's agriculture department and provided the advisory services to farmers and government. At the time in England these services were provided by a separate advisory agency. So the Scottish colleges had excellent contact with local farmers. Having said that, many of the student placements were on very small farms and in the west of Scotland usually on dairy farms and so the experience for the student was often unsatisfactory and disillusioning. Many of my colleagues saw little of farming outside the byre and the dung heap and were used as cheap labour by the farmers they were assigned to. Accommodation was often a farm worker's 'bothy' or loft room. I used to visit a friend during his year on a farm near Tarbolton in Ayrshire and his bothy, apart from electric light, would not have changed much since Burns' time some 200 years earlier. Tarbolton was the location of Burn's beloved St James's Masonic Lodge and it was in and around this area that I and my family were to spend many happy summer holidays in the years to come.

There was no help offered by the college for my location in south-east Essex. Happily my mother had a contact who worked locally for the Milk Marketing Board. He was very helpful and gave my mother the names of a couple of large farms that he knew took students (likely for the Essex County Council's college at Writtle near Chelmsford). My mother accompanied me to the first interview which was at a large farm at Sutton, between Southend-on-Sea and Rochford. The farm specialised in growing vegetables for the local and London markets and was well known. I can remember the farmer looking me over like one would look for conformation in a beast at market. He asked my mother, in my presence, "Is he strong?" I had just left school and was in a pretty healthy state and looked reasonably so. I was never the stocky type but perhaps at best and at six feet tall might be described as wiry. Anyway, he was not impressed and the feeling was mutual. My next interview, and this time without my mother, was with Mr Worrin Squier who farmed Doggetts Farm at Rochford. This was altogether a different interview. Mr Squier was an educated and sophisticated man and wholly understood the experience I was looking for. He had had students before and I think he got a lot of satisfaction from the teaching experience involved.

I was accepted at Doggetts. Although with no experience the terms agreed were that I should join the twenty-strong work force on a farm labourer's minimum wage of then £8 and 9 shillings a week. Any overtime would be at the appropriate rate. The arrangement was a generous one and far in excess of the pocket money my fellow students in Scotland received. I was thrilled since this was a fortune to me at the time and was my first wage.

The Squier family farmed about a thousand acres just north east of Rochford with land spread between three farms – the main house at Doggetts and subsidiary operations at Little Doggetts and Apton Hall. The farm stretched from the very edge of Rochford to the church at the village of Canewdon. The soil was the heavy clay associated with this part of Essex. If one times cultivations correctly it produces high yields of cereals and potatoes but get it wrong and any working of the soil can become a nightmare. A few paces into the field tells all that is needed. If boots pick up a thick additional sole of clay then leave it alone. The countryside in that tongue of land between the Rivers Roach and Crouch is flat but with enough trees to make it very attractive. The skies are big as are many of the fields and there are likenesses to the countryside that Constable painted further north in Essex. However, as one travels eastwards to Wallasea Island it does become a little bleak with few trees, larger fields of even heavier clay than Doggetts Farm and wide marsh ditches and sea walls. Further east still is Foulness Island where at one time it was proposed to build a third London Airport. A lot of the land here is salt marsh fringed but cereal growing is still important. To many, including myself, this part of Essex has its own beauty. It is a strange mystical beauty and relatively untouched by the large conurbation of Southend-on-Sea just a few miles to the south on the Thames estuary. When I was on the farm the rivers and estuaries of east Essex were still used as commercial waterways. The Stambridge flour mill on the upper part of the Roach was served by big flat-bottomed barges of the type still used to take London's rubbish down river. These barges were able to come within a few hundred yards of Rochford itself. Within memory these same barges would have been powered by big black or maroon sails although today the remaining sail barges are in the hands of preservation societies. I have seen similar barges under sail in Holland and also the smaller relatives used on the Norfolk Broads where they are known as wherries.

Rochford, which takes its name from the River Roach, even today retains many of its historic buildings, some domestic, quaint with gables and overhanging upper stories but some also rather grand and befitting Rochford's long history as a market town. I used to cycle from Leigh as an eleven year old to watch the sheep and pigs being driven along West Street to the market held in the square. One shop in the square occasionally featured in those list of curious or sometimes coincidentally apt names. The shop in question was an ironmongers' called 'Rome and Bishop' and was still there during the time I lived in Rochford at the end of the sixties. Just outside the town and by the magnificent 14th-century St Andrew's church, with a tower which is considered a masterpiece of Tudor brickwork, there is what is left of Rochford Hall which was associated with Anne Boleyn, one of Henry VIII's wives.

My trips to Rochford as a young boy fed my growing interest in farming and country life. Although only four miles north of Southend with its links to London and particularly East London culture, Rochford saw itself as a rural community and even the accent of locals was shared with those living in the county's rural heartland further north and east, rather than with what is known now and colloquially as 'estuarine' Essex. A trip to Southend by my farm labourer mates was a visit to the big city and the bright lights although their outlook was distinctly parochial to the Rochford area and remarkably little influenced by its big neighbour to the south. I remember one occasion when I and the rest of the farm hands were having our breakfast break in an old grain store and someone was telling of a former worker at Doggetts who had gone to the Falkland Islands on a two year farm work contract. One interested colleague asked, "Which way did he go?" The reply was, "He went off up Ashingdon way." It took a second or two until we all realised the funny side to this story. Ashingdon was, and still is, a small village some two miles up the road!

The Squiers had moved to Doggetts a generation earlier from Stanford-le-Hope on the borders of Essex and East London. The family lived in a comfortable but not ostentatious style in Doggetts farmhouse which was the manor house built by Robert Doggett in about 1305. In a long history the house came into the ownership of the Earl of Warwick in 1619. It was bought by a Shropshire man, William Taylor Meeson, in 1867 who then worked the farm for half a century until the Squier family bought the farm in 1917. Mr and Mrs Worrin Squier had three sons, Jeremy, Dan and the youngest being Humphrey. There was a daughter but I do not remember meeting her. All the family were well educated. During my time Jeremy acted as the foreman and was very much 'hands-on', with his father looking after the business side with some clerical help. Father Squier also took a keen interest in the livestock side of the operation which included two Friesian dairy herds, fattening bullocks, a small number of pigs and a flock of sheep. This left Jeremy to oversee the field operations. The farm supported two Suffolk work horses as well as two hunter horses which Mr Squier rode and occasionally took to the local hunt. The Suffolks, 'Marion' and an ageing 'Joe', were an indulgence but they did earn their keep by taking feed out to the livestock in winter as a horse-drawn cart can often get in and out of a muddy cattle court where a tractor would invariably become bogged down. It was a real bonus and privilege for me to have handled and worked with these gentle giants.

Mr Squier would grow one field of oats, mainly for the his horses, and he would arrange that us workers would cut the oats with an old reaper and binder, then stack the sheaves into stooks (or shocks) to further dry. When fully dry the sheaves would be loaded onto a turntable haywain with ladders at the rear to cope with an overhang load and all this pulled by the two Suffolks. Back at the farmyard we would then unload and stack the sheaves into a neat cornstack and top this off with some straw thatching. At the appropriate time later in the cycle a contractor's threshing machine would appear towed by one of those marvellous Marshall tractors with a chimney or exhaust more like a North American early steam engine than a tractor. The Marshall would manoeuvre the threshing machine by the stack to be threshed and a wide and long webbing drive belt was placed over the tractor's large power take off wheel at one end, and at the other to the threshing machine. There was a platform on top of the thresher for men to stand and fork sheaves into the top of the machine, after cutting the strings of course. Near a dozen men were required to dismantle the stack, pass sheaves to the man on the thresher, place the empty corn sacks and remove them when full of grain or chaff emerging from various chutes around the machine, as well as deal with the straw emerging from the back end. There was a real sense of occasion to the whole operation and with so many of us working together there was a lot of banter. In contrast much of modern farming is made up of somewhat lonely and solitary chores and none more so than tractor driving. Whether we the farm labourers or Mr Squier, the Gov'nor, got more out of this genuflection to earlier skills and times is a moot point but a good time was had by all notwithstanding the work was hard and dirty. I would have foregone wages to have experienced this exercise in nostalgia although in practice we were all paid at a higher 'dirty money' hourly rate. I can recall clearly the thump thump of the Marshall, the flapping noise of the drive belt and the smell of dust and tractor vaporising oil.

I commuted to the farm from my parents' home in Leigh-on-Sea using a Vespa scooter that had been bought by my father some years earlier with the idea that my mother should use it. I never understood how my father could have thought that there was any chance of seeing my mother drive a scooter a few yards let alone pass a driving test. To my knowledge she never sat on the saddle let alone started it. I think it was an excuse for my father to buy a bigger boy's toy as he did ride it for a short time. He once rode it to the family's holiday property on the Norfolk Broads. This was over 100 miles from home and I think this cured any wish to further recapture his motorcycling youth in the 1920s. This very early Vespa sat unused for a couple of years in an outhouse at home until I was allowed to ride it. Unfortunately it had a habit of cutting out in wet weather but apart from that snag it was reasonably reliable and served me well for the year spent at Doggetts. I did come off twice but apart from some dents in the very vulnerable side wings or blisters of the Vespa I suffered no more than dented pride. These machines were notoriously unstable in icy or slippery conditions. This has been my only experience of motor bikes but like many men of a certain age I have a wish to get back on a bike, but this time a proper bike. However I restrict myself to reading bike reviews in the specialist magazines and motoring columns of the daily newspapers. I remember what seemed a good piece of advice and that was to buy a big bike to recapture youth rather than have the mid-life affair. A bike was cheaper, safer and much more fun. Meanwhile I will remember the exhilaration of setting out for the farm in the cool air of a summer morning before the temperature had risen and while there was little traffic on the roads. True, the Vespa was at full throttle at thirty-five miles an hour but to me that was fast enough to feel the wind on your face. The other bonus of being on a bike was to be able to smell the early morning and particularly rain after a dry spell. As a spectator I can understand the attraction of biking and also the camaraderie of the biking fraternity. I am old enough to remember the heyday of British bikes with names like Vincent, Velocette, and Sunbeam. I can remember as a child my father taking me to a bike garage in Southend called Ticketts where he knew the owner from the time when they were both young and bike enthusiasts. I wish he had indulged himself with a real bike rather than the Vespa, but perhaps his mid-life crisis was a matching small one.

Work on the farm started at seven o'clock with a half an hour break for breakfast at 8.30. Some men went home as most of the tied cottages were nearby and on the farm, but the majority stayed and breakfast was taken in an old grain shed at the centre of the farm buildings complex. The shed was wooden and supported on large mushroom-shaped legs which were so shaped to prevent access by rats. There was no heating although there was a single light bulb. We sat on piles of sacks and some bags of grain and other bits and pieces that found their way into the compound rations for the dairy herd. Breakfast here was the social highlight of the day since it was the one time most of us got together. Once we were settled down, the flasks were out and sandwiches in hand the gossip and leg pulling started. It was all good-natured and I cannot remember any real unkindness. The younger lads took the brunt of the leg pulling usually aimed at their love life or more often the absence of the same. The staff were very loyal to the Squier family and any criticism was kindly disposed and little different from that we all received in turn. There was an element of the 'its the rich wot gets the pleasure and the poor bloody workers wot gets the blame' but it was rarely very personal or bitter. It helped that Jeremy Squier was usually out in his boiler suit getting cold and dirty with the rest of us, although stopping short of breakfasting with us in the grain shed. Some of the men were members of the then National Union of Agricultural Workers but in no way militant. Doggetts workers' attitudes epitomised the problems of trade union organisation of farm workers.

Each morning at seven o'clock we assembled outside a large general purpose barn known as the 'Homestead' and awaited Jeremy Squier to arrive and give us our jobs for the day. Much depended on the weather with wet weather jobs being found if necessary. In winter this was not as difficult as it might seem as there was always potato riddling and bagging up as well as some dressing of grain and grass seed. Whatever the weather stock had to be seen to and provided with fresh litter and food as well as the cattle yards tidied. With twenty staff there was some division of labour. The two cowherds had their dedicated hands as milking and cleaning up is a more than full-time job. We general hands would occasionally be involved in taking feed out to the dairy herds in winter when there would be little or no grazing available. Then there were one or two tractor drivers who rarely did other than tractor-linked operations and a driver of the farm's only tracked vehicle who never appeared for general duties.

There was a distinct pecking order or hierarchy amongst the tractor drivers which generally reflected age and experience. The more or less full-time drivers would have their dedicated machines and woe betide anybody who might innocently use their tractor. At the same time there were three or so tractors for general use and were fair game. There were two lorries but only an ex-army four-wheel drive model was available to the likes of me and other younger staff. This was a forward control vehicle with a gear change that involved reaching almost from behind and required a double declutching technique. It took me some time to master this and I used to rather dread having to take this lorry out and suffer the ribbing as I crunched through the unforgiving gearbox. However having mastered double declutching the lorry was great fun and would often go where tractors could not. The one exception was the tracked Fordson which never got stuck. The driver of this machine relished his call out and rescue role and particularly having to get us younger drivers out of trouble. This was before the days of the now ubiquitous four-wheel drive monster tractors.

Happily I had learnt to handle tractors on the school farm and so gained early access to the rank of tractor driver although without a dedicated vehicle of my own. My first vehicle was the now legendary 'little grey Fergie', the tractor with the revolutionary hydraulics system invented by Harry Ferguson and used in all subsequent tractors. The model had a starter operated by the gear stick and so was impossible to start in gear but also for the novice difficult to learn the knack of starting at all. Again lots of leg pulling and the humiliation of having to get someone to start the Fergie for me. Needless to say I spent some time in private practice to master this technological challenge. I undertook most of the mechanised field operations and became quite proficient including gaining the ability to reverse a tractor with coupled trailer and even reversing a four-wheeled trailer with an articulated front axle. The latter is a manoeuvre that even old hands can find a challenge. Over forty years later these skills were to be called upon when we bought a caravan. Like riding a bicycle the skills are quickly summoned up again.

I regret that I was never given the opportunity to plough although I was quite proficient in harrowing, rotavating and could keep a decent line across a large field. Ploughing was still seen as a task reserved for the time-served farm hand and not for the likes of boys fresh out of school, and quite right too. Combine harvester driving was the pinnacle as so much was at stake: not only the most expensive piece of machinery on the farm but the loss of time and harvesting opportunity that would result in a breakdown or blockage of the combine's innards by careless or unskilled handling. However I was content to trail the combine and then drive along side as it emptied the contents of the on board tank into the trailer behind my tractor. Get this manoeuvre wrong and the grain would land on the ground or on one's head. Either way you would receive a cursing from the combine driver who never took any responsibility for the synchronising of the speed between the two vehicles. The analogy is refuelling ships at sea. In between emptying procedures and until my trailer was full I would sometimes ride on the platform of these ship-like machines. They were noisy brutes with the throttle necessarily set at full speed to drive the cutter bar, the sails and all the internal threshing machinery as well as drive the vehicle forward. The driver sat outside right above the cutter and sails and so in the thick of a permanent dust cloud. Nowadays combine drivers sit in air-conditioned cabins with radios and on-board computers telling them of the yield per acre at any point.

Some of the farm work was quite hard and much of it was undertaken in conditions that were physically uncomfortable. The winters in south-east Essex can be harsh with no significant hills between Essex and Russia to break the east and north-east winds. Notwithstanding my many years in north-east Scotland I still remember the cutting east winds experienced in that peninsula running eastwards from Rochford to the marsh fringes of Essex. At seven o'clock on a cold and dark winter's morning with one of the infamous east winds blowing, the youthful enthusiasm for tractor work evaporates in preference for, ideally, an indoor job but otherwise any manual job that works up a little body heat, such as a spot of hedging and ditching. The tractor driver's winter uniform was usually an old army great coat and gauntlet gloves. However when additional insulation was required we tied the big two and one quarter hundredweight capacity corn sacks around the waist and occasionally over the shoulders. In wet weather waterproofs were useful but these could be very cold and unless one had a full suit with trousers then the rain merely ran off the top 'mac' on to the legs and feet. Wellingtons were rarely used by my professional colleagues as it is difficult to keep feet really warm in these although for some jobs there was no alternative. The cowmen were never seen out of their wellies. The army boot was the norm with a couple of pairs of thick socks. As CQMS at school I had left with a good supply of boots and army issue clothing. These stood me in good stead and was popular working attire. I remember one colleague, Bob, who wore exactly the same work clothes whatever the weather and the season. His uniform was blue jeans (actually not good in wet weather in my experience), a check shirt, khaki battle dress jacket and a flat cap. One Saturday afternoon I had to go to the farm to feed the livestock and in doing so passed this man in the lane dressed in grey flannels and a smart sports jacket. It was not until he called back to me that I realised it was Bob but without the work uniform. It was the first time I had seen Bob in any other clothing be it for work or leisure.

Most new work colleagues were kind and helpful. I spent more time with some than others. I mentioned Bob and I guess I learnt more from him than almost any other member of the farm staff. I would judge Bob's age to be about twenty-five at the time I joined the farm. He was already a skilled and valued general farm worker and could turn his hand to most tasks including some useful, although I suspect not expert, thatching. He was patient, thoughtful but certainly not slow, either in mind or in any of the practical skills. He was very methodical in all he did and took a great pride in a job well done, be it a highly skilled task such as hedging or thatching to something more mundane like unloading ten tons of cattle concentrates from a lorry. I remember this latter chore very well. I would be standing with two or three colleagues chatting, usually just before lunch, when the cattle cake delivery lorry would be spied making its way down the long chase or lane leading to the farm, and when returning my gaze to the colleagues I had just been speaking to there was, suddenly, nobody to be seen. So, there I was with just the delivery driver to unload ten tons of knobbly bags each weighing 140 pounds. The bags were heavy and awkward to handle as they were made of hessian and they leaked the smaller and dustier bits of the contents which always found their way under the collar and down the back, and remained there for the rest of the day. However Bob was one of the few that stayed at post and assisted. It was not that the others were lazy, as they were not, but this was a chore they saw as rightly delegated to the student. Looking back I would not argue and it was probably good for me and even may have been 'character forming', if that is the interpretation of colleagues' comments such as 'Do the young bugger some good to learn about hard work', or something very similar and in a tad more colourful English.

Bob was a very skilled hedger and could tame the wildest of overgrown hedgerows and produce a neat, trim and stockproof hedge using not much more than a bill hook and a sickle. The most important point I learned about hedging could be summed up in Mao's phrase about victory being the first step in a long march. In other words one has to make a start and not be deterred by the apparent enormity of the task. I learned also that there is tremendous satisfaction to be obtained in taming a nine to twelve feet high row of impenetrable thorn and forest and producing a neat-sided and level-topped hedge that would be as at home around the suburban garden as around a farm field. Half the battle is starting and method but there is a skill to be acquired in using a billhook (so described as in profile it looks like a bird with a large bill) and sickle. Part of this skill is maintaining a keen edge on the blade using a carborundum stone, and the same goes for effective hoeing. It would be some years of much practice before I could have produced a result anything like Bob's but over the years his tuition in hedging, like so much else he taught me, has stood me in good stead. Hedges are now cut with tractor-mounted cutters which commonly work on the flailing chains principle. The result is an ugly collection of what I describe as chewed stumps and shredded smaller branches. The hedgerow does recover quite well but of course the tractor is not able to undertake the layering of branches to infill gaps and make the hedge impenetrable and thus stock proof without resorting to sheep netting and barbed wire as back up.

Another skill acquired then that has provided lifelong value is the roping of a load on a trailer. Bob would maintain that a well stacked trailer of straw or hay bales should need only the minimum of roping. The key is the interlocking and cross binding of bales, and the same applies to the successful stacking of sacks, be they sacks of potatoes or cattle feed. One of our regular migrant workers, old Bill Cundy, also believed in the help of the supernatural! Late one summer evening we had completed loading a large trailer with straw bales in a field by historic Canewdon church, an area well known for witches and witchcraft over the preceding centuries. We had just put on the tarpaulin, since we were not going to get the load back to the stack yard before the next morning, when old Bill urges us to stop and take the tarpaulin off as he says we have trapped a witch under the cover. Of course there were great guffaws all round, with the consensus that Bill was a 'silly ol' bugger' and off we all go back to the farm and home for the evening. We go back with a tractor next morning to hitch up and take the load back and what do we find? The trailer has shed its load and we have to start again. Bill is delighted to be proved right and saw this as a lesson to all of us to heed his advice and respect things we did not understand and notwithstanding 'all your larning'. I do not think for one moment that this old man disturbed the load overnight, and vandals or kids were not suspected from the manner in which the load shifted. Bob was in charge of stacking and his loads did not shift or shed. At that stage I shared the 'silly old bugger' view and joined in gently cursing him, but now I am not so sure I have an explanation and maybe he was wiser and more knowledgeable than all of us.

Horses, except the hunters, were Ernie's responsibility. Ernie was about sixty and a lifelong farm hand with a wicked but gentle sense of humour. Ernie took tasks at his own pace as befitted the handling of horses. One of the Suffolks, Joe, was an old boy at over twenty years and needed a little extra consideration. His younger companion and in her teens, Marion, was a little more forgiving to my inexperienced handling. Under Ernie's tuition I learned to harness and hitch up to a cart. I learnt the voice commands and rein control and the surprisingly difficult technique of driving a horse and cart. Carts are heavy timber vehicles with iron clad wheels and should a wheel catch on a gate post not only would the post be badly damaged there is a real risk of serious injury to the horse. The responsibility is much greater than driving a tractor and more skills are required as well as the responsibility for another life apart from your own. A tractor radiator can be repaired but not so the front leg or chest of a horse. I had never been a 'horsey' person but the experience with these two Suffolks changed my attitude. I had never before realised how intelligent horses are. They have a keen sense of what was not possible and would let you the driver know this. I am not saying they could judge the width of a gateway but they could well judge unsuitable terrain. A horse and cart is able to manoeuvre in tighter spaces than a tractor and trailer, and the horse can turn in its own length and in the deep muck of a cattle court. You can 'work' a horse by remote control by commanding it from a distance. For example one can command it to move forward a few paces or more and then stop, and the horse will do exactly as it is ordered. This is particularly useful when single handed and taking a load of kale or silage out to cattle in a field. Once in the field you can get down from the cart, tell the horse to 'walk on' and get on with forking off the feed for the cows and so obtaining an even line of food distribution across the field. Once the cart was empty or a perimeter fence was coming up all you had to say to get the horse to stop was 'whoa there' and it stopped. Try that with a tractor (and I have done) and one can get into a lot of trouble. A horse will maintain a straight line whereas a tractor rarely will with all the bumps and ruts of a winter field.

I talk of the privilege of working at Doggetts, and the opportunity to work with these Suffolks was truly a privilege as was working with Ernie. I was not allowed to have a go at horse ploughing but I accompanied Ernie in the ploughing out of the headland rows of sugar beet to ease access for the tractor-pulled beet harvesting machine. I can understand why I was not allowed to undertake this exercise as it requires years of experience to not only control the horse but at the same time the plough and keep one's footing in a heavy and sticky clay soil. Unfortunately the sugar beet factory at Felstead waited for no one and you had to meet your delivery slots, and hence the reason for ploughing out the headland beet to hasten access of the tractor.

We had no foreman apart from the elder Squier son but one of our number, Big Frank, seemed to see himself in a sort of management role. Frank looked after the large grain dressing and silo storage facility and drove the farm's roadworthy lorry. He would oversee weighing out of grain and the dispatch of the same. If there was a sharp card and slightly roguish member of the team then Frank filled the bill. Frank was not lazy as such but never missed a chance to chat and yarn. Having said that he was intelligent and as far as I was aware ran the grain and seed facility well. He understood the technical side and had an air of authority aided by a stout build and a large ruddy face. Frank always treated me well and like all my colleagues taught me much. His wife, Gwen, was a delightful woman who was always cheerful. I can never remember Gwen being anything but helpful, kind and positive. Latterly she looked after one of the milking herds and the cattle at the subsidiary Little Doggetts site and I used to visit regularly with supplies of feed, to assist in mucking out and cattle movements. Gwen was in the Women's Land Army during and after the war and she used to regale us with stories of the Land Army. All this might explain my weakness for the Land Army uniform and books and films on the subject. Anyway that's my story and I am sticking to it!

Glasgow University required that farm students keep a full diary of their year on the farm. I was meticulous in keeping my diary as well as a detailed description of the farm and field plans. Here father Squier was very helpful and gave me access to all his field plans. He ensured that I experienced every aspect of the farm operation and would often take me aside and explain some aspect of the season or field operation. His approach was paternalistic but at the same time a little stern. I am not so sure that his son would have had the patience or would have been willing to devote the time to this rather green student. Happy to say I got the top mark for my diary when going up to university.

My year at Doggetts was one of the happiest of my life, and this is not a rosy nostalgic view massaged over the intervening years as I remember clearly enjoying life at the time. I enjoyed the feeling of physical tiredness at the end of the day and the feeling of a job well done with congenial workmates. At the same time I had no responsibilities and therefore no worries. I looked forward to each day on the farm although the memory of rain and cold east winds has certainly dulled over the years. I am so glad that I decided to undertake my year on the farm before going up to Glasgow. I am sure I grew up in that year and was the better fitted and the more mature to tackle university.

Chapter 3

Dear green place

My mother and father drove me up to Glasgow in their car. I cannot remember if we stopped for an overnight or not but I do remember that the journey in those days was a long and tiresome one with then little dual carriageway on the main route. We would have made our way through the attractive north Essex countryside to Cambridge and then on to the A1, eventually turning left at Scotch Corner to make the slow haul over the moors to Penrith and then over Beattock summit in Scotland's southern uplands to Hamilton and the eastern approaches to Glasgow. This was a first time visit to Scotland for all of us and indeed my first encounter with the North of England, except for my outward bound course in the Lakes whilst at school. The entry to Scotland via Gretna and the bleak hills of Dumfries and then Lanarkshire is pleasant enough but is not the Scotland of calendars. Worse was the approach to Glasgow's centre through its eastern suburbs and then Bridgeton and the Gallowgate did little to inspire. I do not believe it was raining on arrival but I do remember that all of us found the experience a depressing one. The name Glasgow is said to be derived from the Celtic glas(green) and cu (place) and had I known this on that first visit then I would have been sceptical, as indeed some academics are, to this explanation. We stayed in the Bath Hotel on Bath Street which lies just behind and parallel to Sauchiehall Street in the heart of the central shopping area.

Next day I checked into Maclay Hall, a grand Victorian town house overlooking Kelvingrove Park, with views to the Gilbert Scott designed buildings of Glasgow University. Maclay Hall was the largest of then four halls of residence for men operated by the university. I was to share a room with two others. So much at Maclay was like being back at boarding school and so suited me fine, and indeed I stayed there for my four years as an undergraduate. The hall was no more or less comfortable than school and the food was on a par. Meals were taken together and dinner was at a set time with waitress service. Lunch and breakfast were less formal and taken on a self-service basis. The emphasis on communal eating was important and gave Maclay its character and a sense of belonging to a community. The warden was an elderly former naval officer and somewhat dour and forbidding. Here again the similarity with school and a headmaster was striking. The analogy went further as the warden was supported by a matron-like figure who oversaw the office and household, and dealt with student day-to-day inquiries. Maclay was a happy and well run place. There were rules but only those of common sense and good manners and this approach was always outlined by the warden in his pep talk to new students at the beginning of each academic year. He would point out that our new found freedom was more illusory than real and the difference between school and university discipline was that at university the emphasis was on self-discipline and 'freedom' was in fact as constrained. Of course we all sniggered and publicly dismissed his advice, although I suspect most, like myself, took to heart the central tenet of this guidance to achieving a smoother path into and through student life.

Matriculation was a mystery and the first task for a 'fresher' student. The mystery was to be revealed in one of the Gilbert Scott building's large halls, which was later to become more associated with examinations. Matriculation was a drawn out and bureaucratic registration process but also included a chest X-ray. In subsequent years the routine was less forbidding but nonetheless still time consuming. Matriculation was also the opportunity for the numerous university societies to sell their wares including membership of the Union, then a men only institution and where membership was optional. I have never been a joiner of political parties, Rotary or the like and it was not until my third year that I joined the Union as in my early years at university I felt I had little need for its facilities. In retrospect I regret this, as it was not just meals and bar facilities that the Union provided but also the opportunity to attend and participate in the Union debates. Contemporaries of mine at the university included Donald Dewar, the First Minister immediately following Scotland's devolution from England, John Smith, former leader of the Labour Party and Menzies ('Ming') Campbell, later to become leader of the Liberal Democrats. They and many others first made their mark in the Union's famous debating chamber. Thus the Union had a very serious side as well as a meeting the day-to-day needs of students and not least in its 'beer bar'. The other attractions were the weekly dances and the opportunity to engage with the opposite sex on the dance floor and perhaps, if fortunate, in the discreetly lit lounge area known as the 'squeezy'.

Glasgow in 1960 was a culture shock but not an unpleasant one. Most challenging was the climate and learning to accept its copious quantities of rain, fog and grey skies. It took me all of my first year to come to terms with Glasgow's climate, but it did have its compensations and one of these was that Glasgow was rarely very cold and what snow there was lasted a very short period. Glasgow is windier than south- east England but winds are generally from the west and appropriately mild and wet. On the pleasant side was the legendary friendliness of Glaswegians. I encountered this from the first day when asking directions from a postman. Not only did he oblige, he went out of his way to accompany me a hundred yards or so to set me on course. Glasgow remains the most welcoming city that I have experienced. The city has much in common with New York, and Glaswegians continue their love affair with all things American. They talked of going to the 'movies' when the rest of us went to the 'pictures' and the city centre is, unusually for British towns, laid out on a grid pattern like New York. It shares also that dynamism and excitement. Rough and tough Glasgow can be, and especially in the sixties, but it could never be described as boring. Where it is so different from New York is in the street friendliness of its citizens and whereas Glasgow has changed over the last forty years, and much for the better, it remains a welcoming city, and even its enemies not too far away to the east would concede this.

As a student the one feature of the Gilmorehill campus that surprised was that the majority of fresher students wore the university black blazer with its gold crest, and for the men often with flannel trousers. These blazers were not the garments of the cricket club or of the variety seen in the Surrey pub (usually accompanied by mushroom coloured cavalry twill trousers) but the thicker and less sophisticated material of the school uniform. The blazer convention may have been something to do with the Scottish education system where students often started at 'Uni' at the tender age of seventeen and the blazer reflected that students were then a privileged minority with parents still fitting out their offspring for university as for school. My wife-to-be sported a similar blazer but in the deep purple of the Glasgow & West of Scotland College of Domestic Science (now part of Glasgow Caledonian University) which was just down the road from Glasgow University, by Kelvingrove Park. By the end of my final undergraduate year in 1964 the black blazer had started to disappear and by 1967 when I finally left Glasgow it had more or less disappeared. We never wore blazers at Cranleigh but rather tweed jackets and I continued this as my uniform throughout my university career. I was kitted out for university by my parents and this may support my theory about the reasons for the Glasgow black blazer.

The Faculty of Agriculture was a strange hybrid creature with close links to the West of Scotland College of Agriculture and some shared academic staff. The Professor at the College was also the Professor of Agriculture at the University. The College's main campus was at Auchincruive near Ayr but with a building in Blythswood Square in the centre of Glasgow. Blythswood Square is respectable office land but then famous for its ladies of the night. However for those ending up as other than 'pure' agriculture graduates our studies were based on the main campus at Gilmorehill with only occasional forays to Blythswood Square and even rarer visits to Auchincruive, except for the College's excellent dances and with their better than average chance of meeting a lady. Not only did the College have a significant roll of female students but the nearby student nurses from Ayr were often included.

Honours degree courses at Scottish universities take four years reflecting a quite different system of education where there is a broader based curriculum at school, but stopping short of the standard of the English A level, and with pupils often leaving school without a sixth form year. Therefore I found the first year at university easy with much repetition of the A level syllabus. However I was always a bit of a workaholic and found it difficult to 'coast' this year, and so came out with top marks in the class examinations at the end of the year and at the same time picking up class medals in Botany and Zoology. My Physics was always a bit weak and I welcomed this first year to better understand and finally master the basics of the subject. The quality of lecturers was high and often better than the teaching at my school. This is not the norm at universities, as I was to find out many years later although not in a study context.

I think all my colleagues were anxious to get onto the second year of the B.Sc. Agriculture course as no lectures in that first year had any agricultural slant but were aimed at providing a good grounding in basic science. In this context we shared many lectures with medical students and others intent on graduating in some aspect of science. I can recall particularly the lectures in Botany and Chemistry to first year science students because they took place in very large ranked lecture theatres of the type seen in the televised Royal Institution's Christmas lectures. Such occasions were a stringent test of any lecturer and all the skills of classroom teaching were required. One Botany lecturer in particular failed miserably to hold his audience and all his classes were interrupted by pranks and high jinks. Happily I knew most of the content but I suspect that many students would have assembled the sparsest of notes if relying on the lecture format as the only means of knowledge assimilation.

The second year was far more interesting with all subjects set in an agricultural science context. This was a crucial year since at its end one had to decide whether to take the Honours course or settle for a three year course leading to an Ordinary degree. Very few took this latter option voluntarily although the award of an Ordinary degree was occasionally the lot of the unfortunate who, for one reason or another, failed to secure a Honours classification. At the end of second year the results of class examinations would make quite clear what options were on offer. Most of my class wished to end up in some branch of practical agriculture and opted for the Honours course in 'straight' agriculture which would be undertaken in the third and fourth years at Auchincruive. The rest of us split fairly evenly between Chemistry, Botany, Zoology or Economics and all in an agricultural context. I chose Agricultural Chemistry as I thought it offered the widest choice of employment on graduation and even today I feel that is true. Over the next forty years Chemistry graduates were to cross my path more frequently than those from any other scientific discipline, and this was long after I had left the field myself where my job bore no relation to the world of Chemistry.

Female company for me in my first year was in short supply, notwithstanding I was one of a select group of students that then had their own car. On arriving in Glasgow I went out with the daughter of friends of my mother and father. The family had lived in the Southend-on-Sea area and returned to their native Bearsden later in life together with their only daughter, Sheila. I liked Sheila and her mother and father were very hospitable but clearly had me marked out as 'suitable' for their daughter and as a result I found the situation rather oppressive. I remember another occasion when I asked a girl in my class out to lunch. I thought this would be a low key thing to do and without any obligation or subsequent embarrassment if the occasion was not a success. I believe the lady found the invitation to lunch at best amusing but bordering on the bizarre. We went to one of a small chain of restaurants or tea rooms called Wendy's which, at the time, were a bit of an institution in Glasgow. Wendy's was very respectable, somewhat 'mumsy' and even bordering on the twee. I do not know if it was my 'patter', as they say in Glasgow, but I did not feel any interest I had in her was reciprocated. It was all terribly civilised but we were not to go out again.

It was not until the Easter term of my second year in 1962 that I met Fiona Munro, whom I was later to marry in 1967. Her brother Ronald was in my class and was one of five in that year, including myself, to make Chemistry their Honours course choice. Ronald was a very open and likeable colleague and obviously by manners and speech from a traditional middle class west of Scotland family. It was not an instant friendship but one that grew from casual chat at the dissection bench in Zoology and other practical laboratory work where there was the opportunity for quiet exchange. Eventually Ronald asked me home to 'tea', but not to his lodgings in Springburn but rather to his parents' house in Hamilton. This was in no way arranged to facilitate his sister access to a friend of her brother as at the time Fiona had plenty of boyfriends. However Fiona was in attendance having been roped in by her mother to help with the tea, although I have no doubt there was an element of curiosity about this public school boy from the south of England that her brother had spoken about.

I remember fish pie was on the menu and this had been made by Fiona's fair hand. The Munro's had a large detached red sandstone villa in a quiet and pleasant residential road not far from the centre of town. The furnishings were traditional and obviously of quality but for me so was the lady. It was not until well into the first term of my third year that I was to be taking Fiona out on a regular basis. When we first met, Fiona was seventeen although within weeks of her eighteenth birthday at the end of May and she had yet to leave school at Hamilton Academy.

With just five of us taking Chemistry as our Honours subject we were to get to know each other very well over the next two years. Agricultural Chemistry was part of the main chemistry department, then under the direction of Professors Monteith-Robertson, Raphael and Cruickshank, with Dr Rees as our Head of Department and also a Reader within the Department. Rees was a small and stocky Welshman and with an accent that could have been from central casting. Like many of his countrymen he was a natural orator and so a good lecturer and able to inject a passion and enthusiasm into even the most boring parts of chemistry. His own research area was in plant sugars or saccharides. However, he rarely seemed to publish much and the same went for the rest of the research staff who worked for him. Rees was engaging but he was difficult to get to know really well. He was supported by Harry Duncan at lecturer level and then by a number of Ph.D. students. My fellow students were Ronald Munro (brother of Fiona), Bob Stark who was to become my best man, Jennifer Adam and Penny Herford. Bob was from a working class Glasgow south side family and Penny from a middle class family of English origin. Jennifer was from Perthshire farming stock in the Aberfeldy area. So we were a pretty mixed bunch with seemingly little in common. I suppose Penny and I had the most in common and perhaps for this reason I did go out with her for a while. On the whole all of us got on very well in the laboratory and occasionally socialised together.

The focus of the third year was the so called 'double Chemistry' course where we joined the pure chemists for lectures and a large part of our practical work. This was a demanding course and had to be successfully completed before Dr Rees would allow us into the final year of the agricultural chemistry course. The lab work was time-consuming and rigorous. We also had an excellent lecturer in Organic Chemistry, Dr Will Parker, who subsequently died at a young age. By the end of this year we could provide a theoretical synthesis to most routine organic compounds. His aim, he said, was that we should arrive at ICI and be useful in an organic lab on the first day. At the same time we undertook some 'agrichem' lab work as well as lectures, but the double course syllabus did not leave much spare time for additional work. It was a great feather in Dr Rees's cap that we all did rather well and indeed I topped the end of term examinations which was a first time for an agrichem student. In fact we were always known in a dismissive tone as 'bucket chemists' by our mainstream chemist colleagues. This was because much of the research work included isolation of chemicals from vast amounts of animal or vegetable material, and were often observed lugging pails of unpleasant 'sludges' along the main corridors in dirty and stained lab coats. Secretly we envied those who had spotless lab coats and 'minded' clean analytical machines with apparently no sweat or mess.

Our final year was no less demanding with similar emphasis on lab work alongside a full programme of lectures. The content was more biochemistry than the more traditional agricultural chemistry with its associated study linked to soil, crop and feed analysis. The syllabus more reflected the research work of the department. and its work on sugar compounds and metabolic intermediates in plants, although it did include the role of most of the key elements in nutrition, soil and plants. There was clearly competition amongst the five of us to achieve a first class degree and although we enjoyed ourselves and played hard there was a lot of hard work put in.

At the beginning of my final year I had not given a lot of thought to a future career but neither had my colleagues. During that year we were lucky to have a visiting Professor from the State University of South Dakota in Vermillion. Dr L. C. Smith came with his family and settled well to his secondment year in Glasgow. We students took to this big bear-like man and his stay was a great success but whether he achieved any research success I am not sure. His research field was very different from that of Glasgow's 'agrichem', as we were later to find out when he asked the five of us to South Dakota after our finals in June. Although this trip dominated our thoughts we had to address the life after 'finals'. Some of us were inclined to a research career and therefore a higher degree. Dr Rees had sounded me out about a research studentship and put in hand inquiries that led to an offer of a research post at Oxford University. I was flattered but this presented me with a dilemma as by that stage I was very involved with Fiona. There was little likelihood that she could move to Oxford with me for a number of reasons and not least her mother, but also her own studies. At the same time Dr Rees made the offer of joining his own department to work with one of the assistant lecturers, John Edmond, on a low molecular weight calf spleen ribonuclease enzyme. This material offered possibilities for molecular structure studies using the X-ray crystallography expertise built within the chemistry department by Professor Robertson. Further options secured by Dr Rees were Agricultural Research Council funded research studentships at the University of Wales at Aberystwyth or Rothampstead Experimental Station.

At the time my four colleagues were going through the same procedure. One, Jennifer Adam, took what seemed at the time the easy route and intended to get married to an auctioneer in Perthshire, but the others were set on a research career. Penny Herford successfully applied to Aberdeen to undertake her PhD and Bob Stark stayed to undertake his research with Dr Rees in 'agrichem'. I am not sure what Ronnie Munro's ambitions were at that stage and I suspected he was keeping his powder dry until he knew his degree grading. For all of us the target had to be a minimum 'upper second' before being eligible for acceptance to studies towards a research degree.

None of the five of us were disappointed as three of us, including myself, achieved 'firsts' and the other two gained 'upper seconds'. Dr Rees was as pleased as any of us since this represented one of his best harvests. By this time I had made up my mind to accept his offer of a place in the 'agrichem' department and all that remained was to secure a research grant. Funding materialised quickly in the form of a Department of Scientific and Industrial Research (DSIR) grant held by Professor Robertson and reflecting his interest in the potential for X-ray crystallographic structure study of the small molecular weight enzyme I was to be working with. All things being equal, and they were not, I regret not having taken up the offer of a research place at Oxford. If I had I guess that Fiona and I would have drifted apart and my life and career would have taken a very different turn. I think it is very likely that with the better research supervision and intellectual stimulation of Oxford I would have continued with an academic career.

With the preparations to travel to South Dakota, taking my Austin Mini loaded with all my belongings back to Leigh-on-Sea and making arrangements for my return to the agrichem department in October, the end of term was hectic. I do not remember much post-examination euphoria and celebration. Three of us did go out for an evening meal at a more formal restaurant in Glasgow's west end. Even in 1964 good restaurants were a scarce commodity in Glasgow except from one or two prestigious and well known restaurants in the centre of town such as the Malmaison at Central Station, Shandon Buttery and the still very stylish Rogano's. Apart from the pioneering work of Reo Stakis and his Olde Worlde Inns there was little within student reach and so the arrival of the likes of the Courtyard off Great Western Road, where we celebrated, were sought out and prized. Fiona also attended this celebration dinner.

Although I was very pleased about my 'first' I recall a sense of foreboding which overshadowed the examination success. I guess the sense of anticlimax after all the adrenaline of the past few weeks played a part. At the same time I was uncertain where my relationship with Fiona was going. I had made no proposal of marriage although I think it is fair to say that both of us had been facing the possibility that it would all end in marriage.

Chapter 4

Intermission

Through the good offices of the British Universities' North America Club the five of us from 'agrichem' flew from Prestwick in June 1964 to Toronto where we negotiated the purchase of a black '55 Pontiac. After two days of preparation we set off on the long journey west to Vermillion in South Dakota, crossing the border into the United States at Windsor Bridge and Detroit, Michigan and then through Illinois, skirting around Chicago to Iowa and Sioux Falls in South Dakota, and finally to Vermillion. We took two tents and camped along the way. In Michigan we did run into trouble with the local police after being reported by a farmer as trespassing. We were 'moved on' with the warning that 'folks in these parts usually shoot first and ask questions afterwards'.

Vermillion was very like one of the small towns described in Bill Bryson's book "The Lost Continent". Indeed Bill Bryson grew up in Des Moines, Iowa which is not far from Vermillion. Situated on the Missouri River in the south-east corner of the State, Vermillion at that time had a population of about 6,000, which I guess swelled to around 10,000 during term time at the State University. It had a film set Main Street with a couple of small supermarkets, a 'laundromat', cinema, two or three bars, a hardware store, a general store (a branch of J.C. Penney) and a sheriff's office together with businesses such as a local real estate office and other professional services. There was the usual gas station, not on Main Street but rather on the main road connecting Vermillion to the Interstate 29. The town was divided into two parts with the poorer residents living down by the Missouri and up above the flood plain and within walking distance of Main Street was the middle class residential area with the university at its edge. This part of town was very attractive with most houses of wooden clapboard construction and painted white or a pastel shade. Churches were large, prosperous and in colonial style with wedding cake-like steeples. The university buildings were mostly traditional in style and pleasantly laid out in campus form set in acres of the coarse bluish amenity grass much used in America's suburbia. The overall impression was one of a secure, prosperous, protestant and white community reflecting the area's largely Scandinavian earlier settlement. I could see that tenure at the State University of South Dakota could be very attractive, if one could settle in this small and somewhat isolated midwest community. Ronnie Munro, who was to become my brother-in-law, did succumb and stayed on in Vermillion for the year to undertake his MSc.

I think the culture shock that we experienced was matched by our hosts. Vermillion, notwithstanding its university town status, saw few Europeans and a even fewer Scots. We were a curiosity and especially Bob Stark with his carrot red hair. Although we were young I think the image we presented was beyond our years. Dr Smith confirmed this by indicating his experience in Scotland was that students grew up faster. This may say more about Glasgow students than British students in general?

The biggest cultural difference and one that even the more conservative of our group found disturbing was the political beliefs of new colleagues in the Medical School where we worked and of friends we made over the ten weeks in Vermillion. Our visit in 1964 coincided with the period when Senator Barry Goldwater was making a bid to become President. Vermillion was obviously a cell of disciple-like Goldwater support, or so it seemed to us. I remember during one morning coffee break in the biochemistry department's office the Director was proposing that the only solution to the threat from China was to "nuke 'em". The look on our faces must have been one of confusion and shock. Happily we all recognised as visitors it was not our place to question the stance of the Director and held our tongues. However on subsequent occasions we did venture to explain and support the concept of a health service 'free at the time of need'. I am sure we were seen as at best misinformed and at worst as communist sympathisers. An amusing aspect of our induction to a very different political system was the requirement of the University that we all sign a declaration swearing our allegiance to the State of South Dakota and confirming that we were not members of the Communist Party. There were the echoes here of McCarthy and 'Are you, or have you ever been a member...' but most amusing was the apologetic way in which Dr Smith introduced this requirement to us. Two of our group were committed socialists with the other three passive Conservatives, or Unionists as they used to be labelled in Scotland. The latter were forced to think where they stood and for perhaps the first time. I guess we all had to recalibrate our political antennae as a result of our stay in Vermillion.

As I have found many times since and in very different parts of this strange and foreign country, regardless of how abhorrent and despicable one might find US foreign policy, at an individual level one will find no friendlier, hospitable and thoroughly decent people. During our stay in the Midwest we experienced nothing but kindness and generosity at all levels from lab colleagues to casual meetings in bars and along the way. One of our overnights on the journey from Toronto was spent in the house of a young family that we met during a refreshment stop. Their house was opened to the five of us and nothing more was expected than our company. This experience was not an isolated one and was to be repeated on many subsequent occasions.

Dr L.C. Smith, our sponsor, worked as a full professor in the Biochemistry Department that formed part of the Faculty of Medicine at 'USD'. His field of research was the lipid compounds associated with cancer cell growth and metabolism and by way of this topical area of research he had access to what seemed to us as generous research budgets. These were generous enough to find $200 a month for each of us and in return for this money we undertook a necessarily small research project. I really have my doubts whether Dr Smith got value for money but most of us took the set tasks seriously. To say we worked hard might be a tad on the strong side but we did our hours at the bench and with enthusiasm. I am sure we left the better as potential research scientists and better fitted to what awaited our return. I suppose that is as much as a summer school, in these circumstances, might achieve. Nobody could have been more helpful and hospitable than 'L.C.' and his wife where our visit coincided with the delivery of their fifth son. Mrs Smith coped with a new baby but also regularly entertained us, made us hotpots (or the equivalent) and had these delivered to our lodgings as she was concerned about the quality of our diet, and rightly so I should add. To save money for travel we would scour the supermarket free sheets for the week's bargains. I remember a lot of beans, sweet corn, pasta and potatoes with the occasional burger and chicken at weekend barbecues. When we were invited out to a colleague's house it was a treat to eat meat. I only hope that this did not add to the list of strange ideas that many South Dakotans had of life in Scotland.

With bar-served beer in the State of Dakota regulated at 3.2% alcohol and daytime temperatures often in the high eighties, and made much worse by the saturation humidity created by the damming of the Missouri River, needless to say that side of our diet did not suffer. We became old hands at taking our beer with a pinch of salt as was the local custom. 'Carey's Bar' on Main Street became a social centre for us, and for some more than others. I was a bit concerned for our image since few of our lab colleagues patronised Main Street bars as 'respectable' folk tended to drink at home or the country club. However I think we were seen as different and strange enough to enable our different drinking conventions to be tolerated as mere eccentricity. I am sure the students at the university did enjoy a beer but this was a conservative area in all senses and young 'USD' undergraduates probably never indulged to the extent that Glasgow students did at that time. This may explain Dr Smith's comment about the greater 'maturity' of Scottish students although I am not so sure of the logic here.

At the end of our summer school in South Dakota our group split three ways with Ronnie Munro staying in Vermillion. As events turned out he was to make the rest of his life in North America and specifically in Canada, after starting his PhD at Michigan University and spending some time with the Smith Kline pharmaceutical company in New Jersey as a research assistant. The others went west in the now struggling '55 Pontiac to Yellowstone whilst I took the Greyhound bus from Omaha via Chicago to Boston and Cambridge, Massachusetts. My mission here was to look over biochemistry laboratories at Harvard University and to find out what was the state of the art in DNA sequencing equipment. I was fortunate in meeting on the Greyhound the son of a Harvard professor who kindly offered me accommodation in the family home and I once again experienced the kind of hospitality that is rare, in my experience, in the UK. The family were able to point me in the right directions and I spent a very pleasant and educational two days in the Boston area. From Boston I took the Greyhound to New York and found accommodation in the down town YMCA hostel not too far from the main Greyhound bus station. I did the usual tourist things in New York and also visited the World Trade Fair which was in place at the time. The YMCA was a bit grim but I never experienced any problems here or during my time in New York. I am not a natural loner and did miss company, although I am glad I took the route east rather than go to Yellowstone. I felt I had seen enough spectacular scenery in Dakota from the Black Hills, Mount Rushmore, and the Badlands in the west of the State to the Indian reservations with protected buffalo herds in the centre, and to the miles and miles of maize crop in the east. The memories of this State are vivid and clear and it is still my intention to return as a tourist. I doubt if the State has changed much since the sixties. To my knowledge it has not seen the influx of population that the South and the sunshine belt has. One of the most evocative memories I retain is dancing in the Blackhills town of Hot Springs with a large Sioux lady, Elizabeth, from the nearby Pine Ridge Reservation. I am no dancer and so any dancing is memorable but the bar in this small town was as near a Western film set as one could imagine but short of the tourist contrived experiences in places like Deadwood. The evening was hot and steamy and the bar was crowded and rowdy. What impressed us was that the bar was patrolled by the local sheriff complete with gun. Disney could not have improved on this. I remain a closet cowboy!

I arrived back in Toronto via Niagara Falls for the flight home, but with a quick diversion to Ottawa and a visit to the Federal parliament. My three colleagues arrived safely back from Yellowstone with the Pontiac now ready for the breakers yard. It had served us well and had, like a dying person, held on to life until all commitments were honoured and farewells made. After arriving back at Prestwick the four of us went our separate ways. I was never to see Jennifer Adam again. Penney Herford went to Aberdeen to study for a PhD, and Bob Stark and I were destined to see a lot of each other as we were to share a lab back in Glasgow University's Chemistry Department, with the hope of achieving our PhDs in the three years financed by our respective research student grants.

Chapter 5

Fit for purpose

From the start of my research project with Dr Rees I was aware of the politics of his lab. It seemed to me that individual research projects dragged on with little pressure to publish results and at the same time a reluctance to write up PhD studies and move to examination and graduation. As a lecturer to undergraduates Rees had a remarkable ability to inspire but this seemed to fail him in handling his research students. Few seemed to challenge the boss although others must have been aware of the low productivity of the agrichem unit.

I was assigned to John Edmond, one of the assistant lecturers, as my immediate supervisor. The nub of our endeavours was to extract and crystallise a low molecular weight enzyme from calf spleen. The enzyme was a ribonuclease enzyme which acts upon RNA (ribonucleic acid) breaking the RNA chain into its constituent nucleotides. The impetus for the line of research was that the molecular weight of this spleen enzyme was thought to be small enough to offer the opportunity of X-ray crystallographic study. This was an area where Professor Monteith-Robertson, the Director of the Chemistry Department, had made his name using heavy atom shadowing techniques in unravelling the structure of complex molecules.

The extraction process, starting with calf spleens freshly collected from the abattoir, was a long, messy and laborious process and hence the description of us as 'bucket chemists' by our more mainstream professional colleagues. Little fresh veal was produced in Scotland at the time and so a university car was arranged for me to collect about two buckets of spleens packed in ice from a small abattoir in Girvan, on the Ayrshire coast. Due to some oddity of the slaughterhouse scheduling, calves were dispatched at the end of the day's work and so it was about nine o'clock before we returned to the Chemistry Department in Glasgow's west end. Like most protein molecules the one we were after was likely to denature and degrade quickly once the host body is dead, and so speed was of the essence. On arrival back at the lab work on the extraction process had to start immediately, and to minimise the risk of protein degradation all work had to be carried out in a refrigerated room at four degrees centigrade. During the next three years I was to spend a significant portion of my time shut in this big windowless butcher's-like cold room with only the roar of large fan blowing a blast of cold air to maintain that four degree maximum. Early extraction was more like a kitchen process with use of a mincer and blender to produce bucket quantities of a pink slurry with the consistency of porridge. I suppose it could have been used as a stage substitute for vomit and did not smell a lot better. Only after the first crude extraction step had been undertaken and the first 'cut', as they say in distilling, had been salvaged could one go home to bed.

There were many subsequent purification stages, the whole operation taking some months rather than weeks, finally ending up with grams of the sought material and even then one was not entirely sure whether the material collected was indeed the same as that of an earlier extraction process. Subsequent work using various chromatographic procedures followed in order to purify and characterise the enzyme. Much of the work was repetitive and involved handling hundreds of test tubes all of which had to be washed individually, and meticulously so. Even if we had a washing-up machine or person (and we had neither)) I would not have jeopardised months of work by risking the possibility of a dirty or chemically contaminated tube. In such situations you can only wholly trust yourself. Then there were hours spent at a UV spectrophotometer taking readings of the contents of similar hundreds of test tubes. Technology has moved on a bit since and a lot more of biochemical analytical work is now automated. However I suspect that the old rule that work is 90% perspiration and 10 % inspiration still holds good.

My immediate supervisor was friendly enough but played his cards close to his chest. Perhaps it was more my own limitations but I do not remember many off-the-wall and stimulating discussions about the challenges of the project. One occasion I do remember is together considering the idea of deviating from the literature in enhancing the efficacy of column chromatographic separation techniques by using the amino acid leucine as part of an elutant, in the quest to obtain as pure enzyme end product as possible. Our theory was that the leucine molecule would act like a detergent molecule but without the deleterious effect a straightforward detergent would have on the target protein. It is not so much the science here that is important but more the reaction of our Director, Dr Rees. He was apoplectic when told of this and accused John and myself of going behind his back and presumably trying to cut him out of any success and a scientific paper that might have arisen had we been especially successful. As it turned out we were not, although the diversion was interesting enough. It was a curious outburst and did cause me to begin to consider whether the life of a research chemist was right for me. I have always found it frustrating to deal with a person if I cannot work out where they are coming from and their motives, be these obvious or more devious and obscure. This was a case in point and to this day I did not understand what had fired up Rees to such an outburst. I suspect there were lab politics involved of which I was not aware.

After examination, in September 1967, of my thesis for the degree I did not see Dr Rees again, and heard little of him until he left Glasgow University Chemistry Department not so very long after I did. He was said to have given up academic life and returned to his native Wales. This has never been confirmed to me and as far as I am aware no colleague in the Department at the time had any idea what happened to Dr Rees. In spite of the laboratory's then rather pedestrian record, I still believe the man had considerable talent and certainly as a teacher. Such ability to inspire students was, and is still, only too rare in university teaching. Subsequently in 1997 the National Committee of Inquiry into Higher Education (the Dearing Report) addressed the need to improve training of higher education teachers. I remain of the view that if Dr Rees did leave the academic world prematurely then his departure was a sad loss, but I do hope he found peace and satisfaction wherever he found refuge.

John Edmond facilitated my access to a side of Glasgow life I would not have had the privilege to experience but for him and, more specifically, his mother-in-law Mrs Smith. John married Lorna sometime during his PhD studies. If I remember rightly John had met Lorna when she was a horticultural student at the West of Scotland College of Agriculture. Lorna was a quiet and sweet newly-wed, but Lorna's mother was anything but quiet or sweet. Mrs Smith was the landlady of the Majuka Bar just off Bridgeton Cross and a few yards down the Dalmarnock Road. As a part of Glasgow it did not come much tougher and Bridgeton in the sixties still lived on its reputation of territorial gang wars, religious bigotry, debt, squalor and housing to match. The Majuka was a mean bar with a small lounge bar and an equally small public bar. I do not know how the pub came to be so-named but I do know that the Majuka is a type of beetle and perhaps in a curious way rather apt. For anyone to run such a bar in this area they needed to be tough, bloody tough but for a woman exceptional qualities would be part of the job description. Mrs Smith was a tough woman and woe betide anyone who stepped out of line. It was a toss up who the clientele most feared, Mrs

Smith or the arrival of Glasgow's finest 'polis', and these boys did not even go through the pretence of politeness but were quickly in with the knee to the groin of any rowdy customer exhibiting the merest hint of resistance or bravado. I have witnessed such very efficient removal from the Majuka of 'tired and emotional' customers and it is not for the squeamish. However I must admit to taking the view that the means justified the ends since if such customers were left 'unattended' the likely end result was some greater injury to themselves at best.

The Majuka was hardly my local and besides it was at the opposite end of town in Glasgow's east end but I visited it many a time, not only because of the link via John Edmond but also because my lab colleague, Bob Stark, did become a part time barman. I cannot say I ever felt quite at home in the Majuka, whether it was in the public or lounge bar. There were some conventions that I never came to terms with such as the discouragement of unaccompanied men using the lounge bar and especially at weekends. Another weekend taboo was the serving of pint measures in the lounge bar, although half pint measures were served. This was all aimed at maintaining what is referred to in Glasgow as a 'well-run shop' and that is one without violence or social unrest. As in most Glasgow working men's pubs, discussion of religion was banned, especially in those pubs which catered for both sides of the religious divide, as indeed the Majuka did although with a slight Protestant or 'blue' undercurrent. I must have seemed very much a fish out of water with my background but although fellow drinkers were curious to establish my religious credentials (a Church of England member was viewed suspiciously and as somewhat of a failed Catholic) I was always treated politely and with generosity. On a number of occasions Bob Stark and I were invited back to homes in nearby Bridgeton tenement buildings. Most were poor with wives struggling to keep a respectable home on very little money. Often the problem was not so much a shortage of money earned but too little finding its way to the family and the struggling woman of the house. No doubt considerable amounts of family income found its way to the tills of the pubs and betting shops. Drugs were available in the sixties but not to the extent they are now and were little in evidence in the society that inhabited the Bridgeton area. Besides drink and betting, the tally man and debt were the scourge of the time and place.

Already Glasgow was making enormous strides to rehouse people from some of the worst slums of Europe and had created a number of huge new housing estates on the periphery of the city of which Easterhouse and

Castlemilk are perhaps the best known. These estates created more problems than they solved. They are surely a testament to the darkest hour of planners and local politicians. Who could design a housing estate with 60,000 inhabitants with no pubs and few amenities and then be surprised that there was mayhem on the late-night buses? Castlemilk was known locally as the 'Ponderosa' after the cowboy ranch in a sixties television series. It does not require much imagination to fathom the derivation of the nickname. Naively I would ask many of the regulars at the Majuka why they and their family did not opt for one of these new housing estates. One unexpected reply was that the rental costs were much higher and the poorer but cheaper property was preferred, but also and understandably many quoted the loss of friends and the close knit community of Bridgeton as the reason for staying put. However the authorities were to have other ideas and that end of Dalmarnock Road around the Majuka Bar and most of the neighbouring tenements were razed to the ground in the decade that followed.

During these forays into the heart of Bridgeton I experienced the same generosity and hospitality as I found elsewhere in the city. Whatever the circumstances always, on going back to somebody's home after closing time, one was made welcome even if the circumstances only stretched to putting on the chip pan, and what was in that house was shared without stint. On one occasion this was extended to a viewing of the man of the house's proudest possession and that was his Hibernian Order sash. This was somewhat the equivalent to the sash of the Orange Order. My mate Bob was with me at the time and as a 'bluenose' (a Glasgow Rangers supporter) he was more aware than me that we were in a situation that required very delicate handling. The slightest hint of disrespect would have seen an immediate evaporation of any goodwill and hospitality. I was never ever able to balance the occasion, in the interests of social research, with a similar close inspection of an Orange Order sash and indeed I never sought a repeat of the experience. I have always been nervous of joining organisations from the benign of the Rotarians, through Freemasonry to a political party, and I put some of this nervousness down to my Glasgow experiences and finally a trait confirmed in what used to be part of the Civil Servant's ethos or trade craft and that is a demonstrable and strict neutrality.

Settling down to a research project was not so very different to being an undergraduate student and indeed the laboratory shared with Bob Stark was the same one that the five of us shared until our Finals scarcely three months before. The routine for me was to arrive at the lab by nine o'clock and work until about five o'clock when we would either go out for scotch pies to heat in the lab oven or adjourn to the 'Roma', a small cafe in Byres Road owned by an Italian family. Again pies would feature although augmented with baked beans and chips. John Edmond and other colleagues from agrichem would often join us in the Roma and these 'teas' became quite a social highlight of the day. Bob and I would usually return to the lab for an hour and a half or even more, and particularly towards the end of our project when we were scrambling to assemble last pieces of data and at the same time begin the task of writing our results into the thesis required for examination for our degree. A number of us would often lunch together either in the new and large student refectory just up University Avenue or at the Research Club in University Gardens. The refectory was cheaper and had the bonus of a spot of girl-watching. This was the mid-sixties and mini skirts had found their way to Glasgow as soon as anywhere in London. Glasgow was always a little avant garde even then, although now much more so with Glasgow currently seen as a national focus of experimentation in youth fashion, art, music and much else.

The Research Club occupied one house in a terrace in University Gardens and was primarily a private luncheon club for research staff although mainly at the research studentship level as there was another club for established academic staff in the main Gilmorehill buildings. The Research Club employed a manageress and was run by a member Management Committee. For a year I was a member of the Management Committee as the Club's Entertainments Convener. The club was mainly patronised by scientists and as such was particularly well supported by chemists and especially so the parties that various interest groups held at the Research Club. In my view the 'liveliest' of parties were those under the aegis of the Alchemist Club whose parties were the stuff of legends. In fairness the Alchemists were not only about partying, although they did their fair share of this, as they also arranged learned lectures within the very broad discipline of chemistry. I met many colleagues outside my own small subdivision of chemistry at the Research Club and for me it was a breath of new air and a chance to break away from the often claustrophobic politics of agrichem.

It was not until the last year of my research project that I began to seriously consider my future after, hopefully, obtaining my PhD. The assumption was that it should be research based in some way and likely university or similarly based. This was the time of rapid expansion of the universities and those such as East Anglia at Norwich were already establishing a reputation in biological sciences and lab colleagues and I were beginning to pay attention to the many lectureships advertised. However there was always a vague notion at the back of my mind that somehow the life of a university lecturer and research scientist was not for me. What I was clear about was I did not wish a job in industry with the likes of ICI or Shell which then had large commitments to the agricultural sector via pesticides and herbicides research and manufacture, and so a natural provider of employment to agrichem graduates, and the ultimate destination for some of my lab colleagues.

Politics were of continuing interest although not to the extent of committing myself to the institutional party politics of the Glasgow University Union. I found the Union debating chamber posturing of my contemporaries at Glasgow such as Donald Dewar and John Smith unattractive. It was not so much that I disagreed with their politics but rather I had little idea of where they were coming from or going to. I suppose I was searching for something more radical and idealistic. Donald Dewar was never left-wing or idealistic in any sense of the word and that remained the case through his time as Scotland's First Minister until his untimely death. I do not buy into the idea that somehow he carried a torch for a Scottish parliament but rather what he did was to add form to Labour's political expediency in Scotland. A politician, perhaps, but never a visionary and torch carrier. I could have joined one of the fringe parties and at the time there was the vestige of the old Independent Labour Party with its magnificent hand crafted posters which were to be seen around the university precincts in my earlier years as a student. I have never been motivated sufficiently to join any political organisation and over my life I have cast a vote for every one of the mainstream parties including one protest vote as a student for the Communist Party. Contrary to popular belief our ballots are not secret and I would have expected my vote on this occasion to have been picked up by my future employers. So, I eschewed the chance to establish the necessary credentials to rise to the top of the Labour Party by having a "youthful flirtation" with the Communist Party. Idealistic I remain but never, I hope, unrealistic. If politics are the art of the possible, even in 1966 the CP was not the answer to our country's challenges.

Without any clear idea how I might further my interest in politics I thought I ought to make some preparation and so joined a public speaking skills evening class at Glasgow's Woodside Schools. As so often with evening classes the participants were a mixed bunch. I did not pick up much information on the motivation of my class mates but I suspect the reasons were as varied as the class number and would have included those with job, trade union and social needs. The class was likely largely working class in background with much emphasis by the lecturer on overcoming the glottal stop so prevalent in the Glaswegian accent. Time was given to techniques such as building a phrase sequence to finish with a flourish on the third point, which is a technique much loved by politicians. Expression, use of hands, tone and pattern of speech were all explored. As the only person with a South of England and public school accent I was given a particularly hard time in the regular peer group appraisal sessions. In retrospect this was to my advantage. Although in later years I undertook training courses in radio and television techniques I have not had any tuition since Woodside Schools in the art of public speaking as such. I think it stood me in good stead. The most valuable piece of advice that my evening class teacher gave was to take every opportunity to inflict yourself on an audience. Most audiences are pretty forgiving and, if not, do not worry and use them as a training vehicle.

In 1967 I applied to join the Canadian Scientific Civil Service and was accepted. At the same time I was far from sure that the life of a research biochemist was my ideal. I was beginning to see life at the bench as a somewhat lonely one with few responsibilities except the maintenance of one's integrity. Neither did the teaching side of academic life provide a counter balancing interest to work at the bench. My experiences with supply teaching in Basildon, Essex in the summer holidays as an undergraduate had soured me to school teaching for life. Maybe I was unlucky in being allocated to a large all-girl secondary school. I enjoyed the classroom experience but it was rather teaching colleagues that I found tiresome. There was only one other male on the staff and life with the female staff in the common room was claustrophobic, small-minded and gossipy. I do not think I would have enjoyed life in the common room of a public school any more although two of my close friends spent their careers very happily in such schools.

I saw myself on the same tramlines which were determined one evening during 'prep' some twelve years earlier, when my Housemaster, after a full minute of discussion on the matter, suggested I specialise in science rather than 'arts'. I said 'yes' and had not been able to leave the tramlines since. I owe the *Observer* for my disentanglement from a straitjacket fitted back in fourth form. I was in the lab one Sunday morning attending to the needs of a temperamental fraction collector used in column chromatographic separation procedures. More specifically I had been for some time in the cold room and had come upstairs to thaw out to find my colleague Bob Stark reading the *Observer* appointments' section. He drew my attention to an advertisement and suggested that this might be one for me with my interest in politics. The advertisement was for the then Administrative Class of the Civil Service. I knew something of the Scientific Civil Service but nothing of this senior policy making side of government employment. Like most, my impressions of civil servants other than 'boffins' were restricted to Post Office counter staff, tales of the 'labour exchange' and images from post-war films and what amounted to bowler-hatted buffoons. I was aware my father never had a good word to say for any official although his experience was largely confined to local authority officials and, of course, his local tax office. The advertisement painted a glamorous picture of working alongside Ministers and being in the thick of Government policy formulation. It all sounded so much more interesting and challenging than being stuck in a lab coat all my life, notwithstanding that I would have enjoyed Canada.

I went to the careers office at the university to see if I could obtain some further information. Surprisingly they had little to offer except the lady at the desk was aware that somewhere in a classical studies department there was a lecturer who provided some sort of link with the Civil Service. I went to see him and to say he was unenthusiastic would be an understatement. He advised that few Glasgow graduates found their way into the Administrative Class and there was no tradition of this means of entry to the Civil Service at Glasgow. Edinburgh and St Andrews supplied most of the Scottish entrants he helpfully informed. His parting shot was that as a scientist to boot I stood no chance. Happily I was not too deterred and anyway I had little to lose. Canada was in the bag and it was the time when graduates had the world at their feet and jobs were not a problem. Subsequently and after many years in the Civil Service I deduced the Glasgow University contact man was not there to advise on general recruitment but more likely to act as a talent scout for the Security Service (MI5) and the Secret Intelligence Service (MI6).

I filled in the application forms and gave little thought to whether I would be successful or otherwise. It was a surprise and a little destabilising to receive an invitation to attend the Civil Service Selection Board (CSSB – pronounced 'sisbee' in Civil Service jargon). This was a very thorough two-day process involving psychometric tests, case analysis, appraisal interviews and observed joint exercises with fellow applicants. The process is a rigorous one and has been a bench mark for recruitment elsewhere together with the Armed Services' somewhat similar procedures. In latter years a good friend of mine chaired many CSSB

Boards and I realise now how much effort is put in to giving candidates of varying aptitudes a chance to demonstrate the full range of their abilities, and at the same time to ensure the Civil Service recruits not only the ablest but also those that will meet its idiosyncratic requirements. During the interview process I could not but think of the advice from the Glasgow 'link man'. Most of the candidates on this CSSB batch were from Oxford or Cambridge but also a number from the Armed Services that had reached that career bar at Lieutenant Colonel level or the equivalent and were being encouraged to transfer to the Civil Service. Applicants would ask which 'college' one attended and the reply 'Glasgow University' ensured that was as far as interested conversation progressed. In spite of the fact I shared a public school attendance with the majority this did little to make me feel at home. The written papers seemed geared to the arts graduate and those better read than myself. I cannot say the exercise was unpleasant as the Civil Service Commission staff did all they could to make the occasion as civilised as possible. In one interview I was challenged as to why I was wasting the money provided by the taxpayer to complete seven years of very expensive training to become an administrator instead of applying that training to a career in science. The reply here had already been provided by then Prime Minister Harold Wilson's 'white hot technological revolution' statements and the growing concern over the lack of scientific training amongst the ranks of the policy making cadre, namely the Administrative Civil Service, which at that time numbered only 2,000 to 3,000 individuals. Also I made the case forcefully that a scientific training was as good and rigorous training of the mind as was a degree in history, 'greats' or politics and economics. As I was to find out when I started work in Whitehall the arguments and the political requirements of the time ensured that a fair sprinkling of those with science based studies were accepted and like myself a number were assigned to Tony Benn's Ministry of Technology.

However the two day CSSB Board was only the first hurdle. After this ordeal I put the likelihood of a Civil Service career from my mind and resettled to the task of writing up my thesis and in the margins playing the prospective groom's limited role in planning my marriage to Fiona in the September of 1967. Again, it was a surprise to be called to a final selection Board a few weeks hence. I cannot remember much about this but I do remember that this was a conventional Board with a large number of people arrayed in front of me with a chairman. Each in turn would ask a question, with the occasional and sometimes challenging supplementary. The only exchange I do remember was a question about my research and did I think science would ever develop to the stage we could synthesise a protein from its constituent amino acids. I said that I thought this unlikely as the conformation or shape was also a complex challenge, apart from the mechanics of linking a chain of amino acids together. If asked that now I would not have given as certain an answer, although we are still a long way from synthesising all but the simplest protein chains like insulin, for example. I was elated when I received notification that I had been selected to join the Administrative Class and then asking me to express a choice of Departments but with no guarantees, of course, that my choice would or could be met.

I told Dr Rees immediately. His response was a mixture of pride and betrayal. Whilst he was aware of the coup for Glasgow's Agricultural Chemistry Department at the same time I think he felt I was betraying my calling and all the effort he had spent in producing this chemist, for all this input to be tossed aside and lost to a bureaucracy. I am not sure he quite forgave me. Certainly our relationship was not to improve in the months left to me in agrichem. Coincidentally and uniquely another contemporary Glasgow University chemist had applied at the same time and been accepted to the Administrative Class. As I sat occasionally with this chap at coffee in the Department's common room this may not have been the coincidence I initially thought it to be. He joined the Scottish Office and was expected to have a brilliant career, but fate took a hand and he was to die relatively young. I never met him after we had hung up our respective lab coats but heard of his death by a chance remark to a Scottish Office colleague some years after.

Up until this stage Fiona and I had given little thought to the practicalities of life after marriage and where we might live. Canada was still a dream but the likelihood of a career in the UK Civil Service and a job in London, or possibly in Edinburgh as part of the Scottish Office, jolted us back to reality and the need for some far reaching decisions. At the same time I had to complete my thesis and extricate myself from agrichem and Glasgow. I had to concentrate on this as my main priority and somehow let other events take their course. I decided very quickly after the CSSB result to accept the Civil Service offer although this was a leap into the unknown with a total change of planned career and a move away from the world of science, at least in a hands-on sense.

My four hundred-page thesis had to be professionally typed as these were times before word processors although the Xerox photocopying machine had arrived. Fiona had a friend in Hamilton who undertook such private commissions and this lady did a splendid job with a text that was necessarily technical with a lot of formulae and chemical jargon. Corrections by traditional typewriter were a nightmare, with the options of white correction fluid, or a paper insertion (Tippex) that when typed over deposited a white letter masking using the same principle as 'Letraset'. A typewriter rubber could also be used but care had to be taken not to create a hole in the paper. So one did not, in practice, have the luxury of several retypes of a paragraph since this often meant a retype of a complete page and then with the danger that the spacing for subsequent work is thrown out of kilter. So often compromises had to be made between maintaining the patience and goodwill of the typist and a perfect text. Word processing has since enabled the amateur to produce a respectable and clean text every time.

Finally, everything came together in a rush and so much so that much of that August and September in 1967 remains a blur. The thesis was completed, printed and submitted, we were married on 26 September in the University Chapel, a flat in Rochford in Essex was provided by my father for us to return to after our honeymoon in the then very small village of Torremolinos, and it was agreed with the Civil Service that I should start in October in the Ministry of Technology in London. My only preparation for life in Whitehall was a copy of C. P. Snow's novel 'Corridors of Power' which I took to Spain to read. Snow had been a junior Minister in the early Wilson government.

One definition of a quality product is one that is 'fit for purpose'. I was far from sure I was that quality product when I left Glasgow with Fiona after our wedding on an overnight train to London and onwards to Spain and married life.

Chapter 6

Whitehall introduction

I reported to Mr Blanks (truly his name) in Est.1(b), Ministry of Technology, in Shell Mex House, a fine art deco building next to the Savoy Hotel by the Thames. Est.1(b) was a branch of 'Establishments' dealing with Assistant Principal postings in what now we would call a personnel or human resources department. It was also my introduction to the convention of using initials for just about everything, and particularly so in a Ministry that had strong links with the Armed Services, or at least the part I was about to join. 'Mintech', as it was known in Whitehall, was on my list of Departments of choice but was not top of the list. I had asked to be posted to the Ministry of Agriculture (MAFF) in view of my training and interests. A little later and on a training course I met a lady from the same intake who had been posted to MAFF. This featured nowhere on her wish list. Her degree was in classical studies and her first job was to deal with some aspect of kipper colouring. Although we both understood that one's degree subject was of minor relevance to the eventual assignment to a Department there did seem a perversity about our respective positions. However I was not too fussed about this as Mintech was very much at the centre of Harold Wilson's strategy to build our technology base and better equip us to compete in a very different and more technology driven world. Although often held up to ridicule, the 'white hot technological revolution' was what the country desperately needed and the Ministry of Technology was created to be the powerhouse for this change, backed by the Department of Economic Affairs (DEA) and the, by 1967 discredited, National Plan. With Tony Benn as the senior Minister life in Mintech would never be dull and the department would never be far from the headlines.

After signing the Official Secrets Act I was taken to meet the Principal I had been assigned to in my first training post. My new boss Eric Wood had an office in the same Shell Mex House and worked in a branch of the aviation secretariat called Central Secretariat. His boss, our Assistant Secretary, Harvey Orchard or referred to in correspondence and minutes as AS/CS, had an office in the Ministry of Defence's 'Main Building', just off Whitehall. Although introduced to this Assistant Secretary on my first day I was to see very little of him over the next year. Eric was very kind and welcoming. He had never had responsibility for an Assistant Principal (AP) before and in his late fifties was obviously flattered to have assigned to his care and tutelage a fast-track trainee. Eric had risen to Principal grade via the Executive stream of the Service which is not quite the same as the distinction between officer and NCO in the Armed Services but there were parallels. The Administrative Class was the crème de la crème and membership ensured access to posts that were policy dominated with frequent contact with ministers whereas the Executive Class tended to posts more concerned with implementing policy. There are hints here of the old snobbery which distinguishes between profession and 'trade'. However, like so many British institutions the distinctions were more subtle than this and a lot less crude. There is no avoiding the fact that there were two career paths and at least the distinctions were overt, with separate structures reaching to the very upper levels with parallel equivalents to be found at just below a department's highest rank. As with the army and officers rising from the ranks, many Principals had Executive backgrounds and had crossed over to the Administrative Class at the Chief Executive Officer (CEO) grade which is the Executive stream equivalent of Principal. All this was to change in the next few years and following the 1968 Fulton Report on the Home Civil Service such distinctions would be swept away to be replaced by a unified grading structure. What we have now appears more egalitarian but I suspect less so in practice and certainly a less transparent system.

I do not think all this bothered my new boss too much as this was the system he had grown up with. What did frustrate him, and obvious after only a few weeks, was that this was as far as he was going to get before his retirement. Eric relished the informality and access that membership of this small class of Whitehall's elite provided. My first instruction was into the etiquette of this club. He explained how that use of surnames amongst the Administrative Class was the norm but at the same time use of Christian names was acceptable. What was taboo was to address such equals as 'Mr'. That was a title reserved for the Executive Class. I was, of course, instructed never to address an envelope to anyone using the designation 'Mr', but rather use 'Esq.' unless another title was more appropriate. I still abide by this rule although these days some see it as a little quaint. Eric advised that we were paid and expected to give honest advice and not to compromise when advice might be perceived as unpalatable to the recipient. Again I have stood by this and seen it as core to my professional integrity. In those early days as a Civil Servant and for some years after I believed that this approach was welcomed and would stand me in good stead. I might be accused of being a little naive to believe the Service had more integrity then. For me the watershed was about the mid seventies, with any doubts as to the beginning of a politicisation of the Civil Service confirmed with the election of Margaret Thatcher in 1979.

The staff kitted me out with a black leather 'dead lock' briefcase complete with an imposing EIIR crest in gold lettering on the front. I was later to learn that there was a whole world of complex status and symbolism attached to these official briefcases. The most sought after were brown leather ones which tended to be reserved for very senior officials. Black leather was the norm for most of the Administrative Class but the older and the more battered the model the greater the status. Lesser mortals such as 'HEOs' and 'EOs' (Higher Executive Officer and Executive Officer) made do with black plastic briefcases unless they could make the case on security grounds of the need for a dead lock leather briefcase. A few colleagues rejected the image branding of an official briefcase and preferred to remain more anonymous on the train from Guildford. I have got myself out of a few difficult situations by judicious display of my official briefcase and often on overseas forays as well. I still have my official briefcase although not the original one. Another nice sign of the times was the issue of a towel and soap which one kept in one's desk and took along to the toilets as necessary. I cannot remember when personal towels were withdrawn but I guess in about 1970.

Eric Wood was a portly man with high colour, sandy and greying as well as thinning hair and a moustache. He dressed in a suit, as we all did, but in the style of a country squire and more the gentleman's weekend suit rather than the dark grey or blue suit of the average senior official. In fact 'central casting' would have welcomed Eric as an archetypal retired major with a house in Surrey, where indeed Eric and his wife did live in a comfortable detached house on the north side of Guildford. In keeping with his suits the hat choice was a trilby. The bowler hat was still to be seen but in Mintech at least it was notable by its rarity. One of our Deputy Secretaries, a Scotsman from Lanarkshire, wore a bowler but perhaps here was a Scotsman trying too hard to hide his roots. My next Principal, Andrew Moat, also wore a bowler. My father was never enthusiastic about my choice of career but he was anxious that I presented myself in the right light and so I was taken to Locks, a hat shop for gentlemen in Pall Mall, and fitted for a bowler. I have never had the confidence to wear it other than in jest but I still have it and in pristine condition. Apart from at Orange Lodge parades and official stewards at the more prestigious county shows one would be hard pushed to spot a bowler hat even in the City of London these days let alone the Civil Service. To complete the picture of the comfortable country gentleman Eric was a pipe-smoker, which was to cause him a lot of grief when later we moved offices to Abell House, just off Horseferry Road. I could tolerate Eric's pipe but my always sensitive nose found his choice of a pungent aftershave more of a challenge. As someone who has never worn aftershave of any sort I have no idea of its provenance. All I could say that it was suitably manly and, knowing Eric, likely expensive as well.

Eric had a love of the good things in life although this was confined to food and wine rather than any vulgar show of wealth. A Principal's salary enabled a comfortable lifestyle but not an extravagant one. As was common at the time members of the Administrative Class would often have other sources of income, either inherited or earned by hobbies and often quite learned interests outside their life in public service. Eric's income was supplemented by returns as the author of the 'Collins Field Guide to Archaeology in Britain' series. He was a Fellow of the Society of Antiquities and a respected expert in his field. I was to come across a number of senior colleagues with reputations established in fields quite separate from their 'day time' professional life. My first Assistant Secretary, Eric Wood's superior, was a Cornish bard, and others met included a writer of BBC plays (not so far away from the day job perhaps), and Richard Adams, the writer of 'Watership Down' who I was to work with in the early seventies. However, for Eric the boundaries between his two careers became somewhat blurred. Many a long lunch break was spent in research for his books in the nearby library of King's College. Whether this was a factor in Eric's lack of promotion in later life or more that his archaeological interest began to compensate for his loss of interest in the Civil Service was unclear. What was clear was he always hoped for promotion and did not give up until our Under Secretary explained to him towards the end of my period with Eric that he would go no further. Eric told me this and seemed to take the news stoically. I had never seen him lose his temper or sulk, and he seemed, as is often the case when people are dealt with honestly, relieved to be able to give up the hope of advancement.

Eric was often a figure of fun and I suspect he was well aware of this, but he was always the gentleman. At worst he could get flustered but no more than that. His various layers of superiors would often ring in exasperation of the lateness of a piece of work and Eric's reply would be a calming "It's in the pipeline, Richard," or whoever. His work when delivered was good and painstakingly correct in every detail. He was a hard task master in that every piece of my written work was crawled over and every mistake, including the grammar, corrected. I cursed to myself at the time but in retrospect I am grateful for the training he gave me.

The work we did was not very typical of the average Principal's lot. Central Secretariat served some of the central administrative needs of the eighteen research establishments brought together under the Mintech banner. Nine of these were ex Ministry of Aviation research establishments such as the very large and prestigious Royal Aircraft Establishment (RAE) at Farnborough, the Royal Radar Establishment at Malvern (RRE) and the National Gas Turbine Establishment (NGTE) but including also small establishments like the station dealing with torpedo testing. The civil laboratories included the National Physical Laboratory (NPL) at Teddington, and Water Pollution Research Laboratory (WPRL) and Warren Spring Laboratory (WSL) both at Stevenage. This was a rag bag mixture but represented some of the best scientific brains in the country working at the frontiers of their particular scientific specialism. The collection was mixed in that the aviation establishments were heavily defence oriented, although not entirely, whereas the work of NPL had a strong regulatory role as even more so did the Laboratory of the Government Chemist (which I was to get to know a lot better at a later stage in my career). Mintech had a chief scientist or more correctly a Controller Research in Dr George Macfarlane and it was his job to make some strategic sense from this diverse and enormous resource. Capital investment, research direction and priorities were controlled by numerous review procedures, panels and boards of one sort or another together with a Headquarters hierarchy of Directors, Heads and Deputy Heads of this and that function or discipline. This was very confusing for a newcomer, and not only in coming to terms with the myriad of posts and initials but trying to work out the pecking order, which was not always clear from the nomenclature. For example RAE at Farnborough had a Director, as did every Establishment or Laboratory (there is really no difference between these two modes of address except that MOD convention tended to call its research stations 'Establishments' and this convention was retained) but Farnborough was so large and prestigious that its Director stood apart and as a forceful man was rarely challenged in a hierarchical sense. Often specific disciplines, over and above responsibilities at the level of the individual establishment or laboratory also had Directors or Controllers. Here again the initials proliferated – DCA(RD) was Deputy Controller Aircraft, Research and Development and D.Eng. was Director of Engines and their development, and DGWL was Director Guided Weapons and Electronics. Life on the civil laboratory side was a little less complicated and also less bureaucratic.

Our team's job was to service the many top level meetings which were needed to run this empire and this included arranging meetings, consulting numerous people on the make-up of the agenda, minuting the meeting and circulating formal minutes or records of the meetings. Eric was excellent at the drafting of minutes and I left his care with a reasonable ability to produce the sort of minutes required by the Civil Service. These were certainly not the almost verbatim record analogous to that of a courtroom stenographer but more a summation of the sense of the meeting, even if that was far from clear to the participants at the time. Action had to be clearly recorded and if possible an indication as to the officer responsible for the action, and again even if at the time the officer concerned was not aware the action was to subsequently land on his desk. Writing minutes of this sort is far more skilled as the writer has to have a good grasp of the subject and the mood of the meeting. He has also to have a feel for the politics of the organisation and how much weight should be given to, maybe, an outburst from an individual which might have occupied a significant part of the meeting. This requires knowledge, instinct as to the will of the mainstream (as distinct from the majority) and above all judgement. Often a lot will ride on the formal minutes of a meeting and so rather than a boring and low level task the minute taker can exercise substantial, although seldom acknowledged or admitted, influence over events that follow. This was something I learnt from Eric and have since rarely shirked taking on the task when volunteers are sought to 'take the minutes'. I am always amazed how infrequently minutes of meetings are challenged. Most people are grateful to have a piece of paper that seems to make perfect sense out of a discussion that to those present often seemed chaotic.

For the first six months I used to dread the next big meeting which came along as soon as I had finished the task of polishing to Eric's exacting standards my draft of the previous meeting. The subject matter seemed daunting and highly technical, which it often was. Eric had no technical bent and I wondered how he coped. A parallel that might be helpful is the skill of a minicab driver with his radio on, receiving a constant stream of messages and chatter, but being able to immediately hear his own call sign amidst the background noise when necessary.

However it does become a professional skill in the Civil Service to be able to change from one job and one subject matter to another with the ability to cope seamlessly in a very short space of time. There was an old Whitehall phrase that experts should 'always be on tap but never on top' and that was generally the case when I started and for some years afterwards. So the senior administrator had to quickly master the art of being able to debate the issues with the experts even if he did not understand all the scientific details. Ministers refer to this as 'mastering their brief'. Part of the skill is knowing what to focus on. Since leaving the Civil Service I have been conscious of the general low standards of not only formal records of meetings but also the quality and style of papers submitted to meetings compared with those in the Civil Service.

Eric's responsibilities included the assembly of what was known as the 'Pink Book'. This was an annual summary of the Department's research programme. It gave an overview of the priority areas and the main thrust of research with costs, budgets and time scales. It was printed in spreadsheet form and had a pink cover. Soon after my arrival I was assigned responsibility for assembling the Pink Book which was a laborious exercise involving contact with the laboratories and headquarters staff and all at senior levels. It enabled me to become familiar with the key individuals including many of the Directors in the field. This was further assisted by my travels around the laboratories with Eric and the endless round of producing the minutes of the meetings which were the justification for our travels. A bonus of travelling with Eric was that I was able to travel First Class. Eric ensured the hotels we stayed in were up to standard and at the same time we were well received by the out-station directors and especially so those with the MOD traditions which often operated 'mess' arrangement for eating with acceptable food. However the assembly of the Pink Book itself was very definitely the 90% perspiration part of the job, with endless chasing of tardy individuals and consultation when information was incomplete or unintelligible. Even the simple procedure of mailing a letter or minute was laborious as we were dealing with material that usually warranted the classification of 'Secret' and so all correspondence had to be placed in double envelopes and dispatch and reception recorded by each end of the communication link.

I had the assistance of two delightful female Executive Officers (EOs). One was very smart and trendy with a flat in Holland Park not so very far from our then Minister, Tony Benn. It was a happy office and although Eric was not a high flyer his staff were very protective and fond of him. I think we all worked hard but there was never a question of working overtime. If Eric saw you around when he left the office he would suggest that you did the same. Even at that time there was peer group pressure to stay late in the office even if the work did not dictate these hours. Some offices dealt with subject matter that needed officials to be around after five o'clock or so because of Parliament's and so Ministers' timetables. Even when one's work did not require this cover to Ministers there was a macho and competitive element in staying late. However at the same time many senior officials did not arrive until ten o'clock, and morning starting times then mirrored those working in the City of London. These are changed days now for both groups of professionals. Eric would arrive at about ten o'clock in the tradition of the time for many senior staff but would leave about five o'clock. There was certainly no need for any of us to work late to cover possible Ministerial requirements. I decided at an early stage to arrive at about nine or just after and this was my pattern through out my time in the Service.

The work was 'sensitive' and so some form of security clearance was the norm. There were two types of security clearance and the most basic of these was referred to as 'negative vetting' which is a fairly straightforward and routine check on your background and an ability to answer, in essence, the court question 'Anything known?' I assume some check was made on me before joining as the Civil Service Commission referred in one of their early letters to me "that our inquiries have been satisfactorily completed". It was not until about two years later that I was to receive the more in depth 'positive vetting', but in the meantime I had access to a lot of sensitive information about the nation's aerospace and weapons research. I had no particular worries about colleagues working with me but I was concerned that we worked in an 'open' building with no entrance security, although we were able to lock our rooms. However I would often come back from a lunch break to find the EOs' office unlocked and the components of the Pink Book scattered over desks and sometimes the floor whilst the occupants were out to lunch . I would voice my qualms from time to time but nobody seemed particularly concerned. However a visit to our Assistant Secretary in the MoD Main Building on Horseguards was much better controlled with a pass issued on entry, an escort to the officer to be visited and he, or she, had to escort you back to the front door where you handed in your pass. Eric had a pass and so was excused all this. By the time I left the Service all buildings had pass control although most were slack on control once within the building. I suspect this improvement across Whitehall had more to do with IRA threats rather than security of sensitive information and documents.

The training an Assistant Principal or 'AP' received was a privileged one with a dedicated officer in Establishments and regular monitoring of progress. This puts some considerable responsibility on the Principal to which the AP is attached as well as the knowledge that the supervising Principal is almost as much on trial as the trainee. Eric was particularly aware of this. It is important that the AP is aware if not always directly involved in all the challenges of the job of his Principal. It is the Principal's duty to expose his AP to a wide a range of experiences and contacts as he can. Eric did a good job in this respect. What, I suppose, I missed was more contact with superiors in our own Division, or in other words Eric's immediate bosses. This reflected the not very typical job he had and in turn that he had long been passed over in terms of promotion and plum jobs. Although I learnt a lot from Eric and he was good for me as a first posting, at the same time I wonder why I was so posted. At the time I never thought to query this. Towards the end of this first year I had a sufficient handle on my new environment to fuel some concern. The Department ran a very enlightened system whereby APs could make their views known at a more informal level and with less fear that their records may be adversely marked by any formal approach through Establishments. We had an Under Secretary, Patrick Shovelton, who acted in addition to his line responsibilities as the AP 'uncle'. Patrick provided a sympathetic ear and, if not tea and sympathy, then certainly something stronger in his office. He had an easy manner and indeed had many of the attributes of a friendly uncle. You could confide in Patrick without too much fear your indiscretions would be reported back, at least not without some helpful filtering. I regret I did not talk more with him in my first two years in Mintech.

At the same time our Permanent Secretary, Sir Richard 'Otto' Clarke took a great interest in the Department's newest AP intake. Incidentally, his son, Charles, was a Cabinet Minister in the Blair-led Labour government. To enable him to observe us at first hand Otto requested that a pair of APs plan and execute the twice yearly visit to the Department by groups of university students who were considering a career in the Civil Service. I wish I had been able to avail myself of this opportunity but it was not brought to my attention by the Glasgow University 'friend' or Civil Service link man. The senior of the pair would take the lead and in the subsequent student visits his or her deputy would assume a lead role with the help of a new deputy and, a bit like jury service, you were not called upon again for this duty. If I remember correctly the visits would take place over two days and so a programme that presented the broad range of the Department's responsibilities was required but with an emphasis on meeting practitioners at all levels rather than lectures on departmental structure and Ministerial duties. A programme had to be submitted for Otto Clarke's agreement and after the visit there was a debriefing meeting with him. This all sounds a bit tame but for a new recruit, however laid back he or she might be, this was a daunting exercise. Clarke took this seriously and would challenge small points of detail in the programme and offer criticism. It was a clever vehicle and enabled him to meet all his APs and for us to meet the top man on a one-to-one basis rather than from afar at a large meeting. I passed my scrutiny well enough I believe and regrettably was never to meet this or any future Permanent Secretary again on a personal basis.

The experience of an office in the splendour of Shell Mex House was not to last for long since research policy administration was reorganised and Eric and our team were transferred to an office in Abell House, behind Horseferry Road. Here Eric and I were to share a large office with a disagreeable Principal colleague from another section of the new Research Planning Division. I suspect the interloper to our rather civilised office life style had a Armed Services background. He was a non-smoker and his clean air requirements were pursued with a particularly aggressive zeal. It was uncomfortable for me as both would seek my support of their case. Eric was the archetypal public servant and always sought a negotiated solution to any problem, and one where ideally all were winners, and in this case would have responded similarly to our new colleague if the man had approached the matter with a modicum of tact. This colleague's work included some responsibilities for the fledgling electronics industry through the National Electronics Council which was chaired by Lord Mountbatten. Once I was unfortunate enough to take a telephone call from one of Mountbatten's imperious secretaries who seemed a bit upset that I asked for details as I had not a clue who she was. I got the haughty reply "I work for Lord Mountbatten". I was irritated by her dictatorial manner and replied that I worked for Her Majesty and put the phone down. I fretted after doing this fearing Mountbatten himself would complain but I heard no more. I must admit that when years later Mountbatten made the television series about his life I was already prejudiced by this pompous and seemingly unattractive man. Here was my first practical experience of the importance of the first point of contact with an organisation, be it the doorman or the front desk. Louis

Mountbatten might have been a splendid fellow but for me his staff failed him. The TV series was clearly self assassination.

I was moved to my second Assistant Principal posting just twelve months after joining Mintech and this was par for the course. Eric was never assigned a replacement AP although I spoke glowingly to Establishments of my experience with him. We did not keep in touch but I tracked him in office notices until he retired a year or two after my time with him. Fiona and I did enjoy a visit to his house in Guildford for dinner one summer evening in 1968. Mrs Wood was rather as we expected, gracious, intelligent and a good cook. If this had not been the case it would have been a waste of all that produce that Eric regularly purchased from Jacksons of Piccadilly during his long lunch breaks.

Looking back I do not feel I was ready on joining Mintech for the very bright and extrovert Principal boss that was clearly a rising star and with a job much more centrally placed in the Department. After a year I was in a position to compare my first posting to those gained by my AP contemporaries and even now I fail to understand why Eric was chosen to host a trainee so late in his career. I would like to think it was enlightened action by Establishments where both Eric Wood and I by some process of symbiosis would emerge the better for the experience. If so I am sure we did, but this was not reflected subsequently by similarly inspired postings and I never recovered status in the eyes of my peers. I was to know by the end of this year there were 'good' and 'not good' jobs and my first posting was not a 'good' job. However I will be ever grateful to this thoroughly decent man and it was a privilege working for Eric.

Millbank Tower was to be my base for the next eleven months and here I was to join 'IP' or Industrial Policy Division with Andrew Moat as my new Principal. IP was also a bit of a rag bag collection of functions and responsibilities which resulted in a heavy load of Ministerial briefing and an endless stream of Parliamentary Questions (PQs) to be serviced. My new section had responsibility for appeals against eligibility for Selective Employment Tax and a similar adjudication role with respect to applications for Investment Grants. The section also briefed on aspects of Value Added Tax which was then only a cloud on the horizon for UK businesses.

Andrew Moat was as different from Eric Wood as one could imagine. Andrew was very cerebral and enjoyed every twist and turn of a Whitehall battle over some obscure interpretation of one of the Acts of Parliament that governed our work. Once a dispute was resolved then Andrew lost interest. It was not that he was in any way aggressive in character, demeanour or in negotiation, and indeed quite the reverse. He would argue and press his point in a delightfully entertaining manner and not without some considerable degree of wit and humour. Andrew, unlike Eric, was gregarious and enjoyed company and indeed a stage, but at the same time he was not crudely extrovert. His physical appearance belied his character. If Eric was 'central casting's' country squire then Andrew was the stereotype stage civil servant. It was not so much his height at over six feet, nor his very slim build and a gaunt grey complexion that made Andrew look the part but it was the combination of all these attributes together with his dress style. He was one of the last wearers of a bowler hat and this period appearance was complemented by a very long, formal and dark grey or black wool overcoat. He favoured lighter grey pinstripe suits which, although showing their age a little, were obviously of quality. The ensemble was completed by a gold pocket watch and chain. He did get his leg pulled but appeared to almost welcome this attention. His image was, I suspect, carefully cultivated to be so archetypal as to be unconventional and invite comment. Once you knew him, it was difficult to see him as conventional. He had a very lively mind and with a sense of humour to match, he was always good company and never pompous or intimidating, although this was not a first impression.

On this occasion I was not to share an office with my new Principal although it was custom for an AP to share. Millbank Tower was a prestigious building and was at the time the base for Tony Benn and a number of other Mintech Ministers but its shape resulted in curved rooms and sub division had resulted in some small coffin shaped single occupancy rooms. There was just no way that we could have shared without falling over each other. For a while I had a similar 'coffin' to myself along the corridor to Andrew. We were on the seventh or eighth floor and overlooking the river and on to what would now be the MI6 'chateau'. The view was spectacular and truly inspirational. Millbank Tower was one of the early high rise office buildings (along with Centrepoint at the foot of Tottenham Court Road) and even today remains one of the capital's more pleasing examples of post war architecture. We shared the building with Vickers, the engineering company. A game played by our younger males whilst killing time in the reception area on the ground floor was to bet whether the woman (usually young of course) coming through the main entrance worked for Vickers or Mintech. It was easy to verify which were Vickers' staff as they took a different set of lifts to the upper floors of the Tower. The theory was that Vickers' ladies were better dressed, more glamorous and better looking. In joining in this game on a number of occasions my experience was to guess correctly for the great majority of female entrants to the building. I am not sure what this says about the respective employees but at the time we in Mintech would ascribe the difference to pay differentials, although I suspect the reasons are a little more complex, if our observations had any reliability and validity at all.

My move to IP in 1968 coincided with the final stages of Fiona's pregnancy and the safe arrival of our daughter Kathleen some three weeks later on the fourth of November. We managed to see the 'Forsyte Saga' which was being shown on Sunday evening television before I had to dash up to the Market Square in Rochford to telephone the hospital to say that we were on our way. Rather stupidly we had decided against putting a telephone in our new flat to cut down on our outgoings. Marriage on an AP salary needed some tight personal budgeting even with Fiona's housekeeping set at just £5 per week. We arrived at the hospital about eleven o'clock that evening and I left shortly afterwards. Even at the end of the sixties the NHS discouraged husbands from attending a birth and to suggest such was treated as something bordering on perversion. Neither was there any paternity leave and both of us were reluctant to use up my annual leave allowance. So I was on the platform at Rochford station the next morning as usual and while I was negotiating the District Line from Liverpool Street to Westminster I had become a father. It was not until I arrived home at the normal time did I see my new daughter and a tired but happy wife. I look back now and think I must have been irresponsible to give the office such priority at such a time. By the evening Fiona's mother had arrived from Hamilton to take charge of new baby and mother after their very short stay in hospital.

Commuting to Westminster from Rochford by the slower rail line from Southend was a tiresome process. Had I worked in the City of London then the Liverpool Street terminus would have been fine but riding the Circle Line round to Westminster added significantly to the journey. Liverpool Street was a rail bottleneck with frequent delays outside the station as an incoming train had to wait for a platform berth. The Circle and District line at Liverpool Street had a redeeming and I suspect rare feature in that it boasted a bar which served customers standing on the platform itself. Sloane Square beyond St James's and Victoria on the same line also had a station bar and although the bar entrance was from the platform it was a separate and self-contained bar. It did mean that one could dash straight from the bar on to the train when you saw it arrive at the platform. I was, a number of years later, to hold one of my office farewell parties in this Sloane Street Underground station bar. However in those first years of commuting I had yet to develop the patience or fatalism of the time served commuter. My job then was not generating the type of work that required a lot of background reading or that could be securely undertaken on the train. But more importantly I had yet to establish that balance between consciousness and napping that comes with years of experience. On the homeward journey to Rochford I was afraid that I would sleep and miss my station. I did this three times and ended up at Southend Victoria but these occasions were always after partaking of some refreshment after work with new office friends. In later years, when missing my station would have meant ending up perhaps as far away from Guildford as Portsmouth Harbour, I had developed the experienced commuters' built in alarm system, and could read for the first half of my journey, sleep the second half and wake without fail as my InterCity slid by Surrey University into Guildford station. This routine was robust enough to cope with the same train journey after the most challenging bouts of office socialising. At least in Rochford our flat was within walking distance of the station. The walk took about six or seven minutes but it remains in my memory as involving some of the coldest walks of my life. Although South East Essex has warm and dry summers its winters can be as cold and with a wind as cutting and disabling as anything that rural Aberdeenshire was to offer me twenty years later.

My new office routine was not particularly challenging but different from the strongly defence-influenced atmosphere of my previous post. There was little by way of travel to break the routine of office procedure and convention. There were occasional meetings in other Government Departments and especially Department of Employment and the Treasury. Very rarely we would visit a firm in dispute with us as our policy was to avoid this if at all possible because it made us vulnerable to pressure from the firm or the individual. I think the furthest I travelled in the first six months was to a meeting with a large corporation with prestigious offices at the other end of the Strand. Most of my work for the eleven months I was with Andrew was case work and again most of this was conducted within the context of a paper-based file. Our filing was quite efficient. As soon any correspondence was received it was placed on a file and all subsequent action was conducted with reference to that file. Whether the correspondence was passed up or delegated it would travel around Mintech on its file and comments by officials would be entered on the left side of the file as 'minutes'. These would more often than not be handwritten. Within the Department a complete file may be circulated for comment although extensive consultation more usually took the form of separate minutes to individuals. Such a file should be able to be picked up by somebody totally unfamiliar with the case and should contain a complete set of correspondence relating to the case or subject. All 'enclosures' on the right side of the file would be numbered in the top right hand corner and all branch level comment and handling 'minutes' would be on the left hand side with cross referencing to the enclosure side. That was the theory but as I moved through the next twenty years of my career in the Service I noted a slackening of filing discipline with the result that files were often incomplete or duplicated elsewhere by a colleague in the same office. Pressure on individuals did grow as did the pressure on clerical staff who were so essential to make the system viable. Often files were not returned to the central file registry, partly because retrieval took so long as pressure on clerical staff increased and partly because handling everything in the context of a file was psychologically daunting as even a few items in an in tray assumed the proportions of a mountain on one's desk. However it was a reasonably foolproof system and especially if some sort of audit or case review was needed, as well as for archival reasons in important cases involving policy development. I understand much of the correspondence within Whitehall now is conducted via computer and electronic transfer but I guess the need for paper records still exists in some sensitive areas of public service. Many outside the public sector would see what I have described as wasteful bureaucracy and paper-chasing. In a public sector context it can be justified as at any time case-handling and records can be challenged, and rightly so. By comparison my experience in local authority employment was very different, with a slack attitude to filing and records. Advantage was taken of poor records by unscrupulous officials and elected politicians alike. There was no central control over filing, and records would often go missing and disappear when they were most needed. Conducting any form of 'audit trail' in such circumstances was nigh impossible.

I should perhaps say a word or two here about the quality of staff that then manned the coal face of Whitehall and key amongst these were the Executive Officer (EO) and Higher Executive Officer (HEO) grades. But first I should single out the next grade up the Executive chain, namely the Senior Executive Officer or SEO. In my experience these were the equivalent of the experienced Sergeant Major and could be relied upon to guide the young and inexperienced Commissioned Officer or, in the Civil Service context, the Principal or even a rash Assistant Secretary. The SEO was often mature in years and one would be unwise not to heed his or her advice. As often as not the SEO would 'have seen it all before' and more importantly would be able to dig out the files that would illustrate the precedent. The SEO, like the Sergeant Major, was essential in maintaining office discipline and would monitor for example timekeeping, sick leave and annual leave. He or she would not flinch at reminding a whippersnapper AP that leave in government service was a privilege and not a right and the exigencies of the Service took precedence. Some of the very best drafting of letters in my experience was from this valued senior NCO cadre of the Service. However I would place the HEO as the key grade in terms of keeping the machine going and the business of government moving. He, or very often she, was well educated, if not always formally so then through the in-service training offered by movement through the ranks and thus regular change of jobs. The good HEO was well-rounded and would be willing to tackle most tasks. Much of the day-to-day correspondence in a policy branch was dealt with at this level.

I would be less than honest to say that I had no problems with staff over the next twenty years but in the seven years that were to follow in local government I had many more staff problems than in the whole of my Civil Service career. What was rare in the Service was a lack of commitment by staff and any discipline problems were more health-related including alcohol-linked problems. There were the usual problems met in dealing with young staff such as personal relationships intruding into professional life down to petty problems such as dress code. Once only did I have to invoke any formal disciplinary procedure and that concerned my decision not to renew a clerical officer's appointment after the initial probationary period had expired. Here, and the only time, there was a temptation to use the apocryphal route of promoting an unsatisfactory staff member rather than use the formal disciplinary procedure. In other words transfer the problem to someone else. The temptation was placed in my way by the faint heart of Establishments Division because the staff member in question was female and black, and my personnel colleagues did not wish to risk a race relations case being brought against the Department. I was leant on to confirm the lady's permanent appointment but I stuck to my guns and her employment was terminated. Needless to say there were no repercussions.

I mentioned in passing the lower rungs of the Civil Service hierarchy, namely the Clerical Officer or CO and the bottom rung, the CA or Clerical Assistant. Again many of these colleagues were of a high calibre and included the very young starting out on their Civil Service careers but also those at the other end of the spectrum, and some of the latter often came into the Service late in life after full and interesting careers elsewhere, in both the public and private sectors. Indeed some of the most interesting characters I met over the years were COs and CAs. One of my COs was a Jewish lady, Violet Cohen, who unusually was to follow me through two consecutive posts. Violet was splendid at her job and fiercely loyal to our small office group. She was also a lady freemason and during my time with her became the equivalent of the Worshipful Master (or is it Mistress?) of her Lodge which was City of London based and had a largely professional membership. I was honoured to attend her 'gentlemen's night' and speak in reply to a toast to the guests. Fiona and I got to know Violet and her family quite well during the five years she was with me. A visit by Violet and her husband to our house for dinner required Fiona to research the relevant Jewish cook books to be able to serve a kosher meal or at least as near as we could get as gentiles. Other COs and CAs met included ex-colonials returning to the 'old country', ex-servicemen, and former and usually failed businessmen. In one job we drew heavily on the expertise of a former businessman CO. Although there was a hierarchy in the office it has to be remembered that the offices that I worked in were not those of the local DHSS or local Inland Revenue but were usually small policy making operations with close working contact at all levels. The word 'team' has been devalued somewhat by the sort of books on management theory often seen on airport bookstalls but it is appropriate here since the team approach was the only one that made sense. The image from the outside is perhaps of a more formal and hierarchical office with clear lines of division reflecting rank and social status. There were senior officers that were overt snobs and tried to run their office staff more along the lines of the Indian Army of the old Empire, but these types were few and far between and for the most part relationships were very civilised and pretty informal.

The office relied also on the Messengers who delivered and collected the mail from each office, as well as performing many other duties such as escorting visitors, looking after visitors in Ministers' offices and marshalling them between the waiting room and the Minister's office. Occasionally some would offer a visitor a coffee or tea if an unexpected delay in the appointment occurred. Again many were former armed forces personnel, but rather the men than women. A bit like the janitor in a school one relied on these people and it was essential in moving to a new office to make your number at an early stage with the Messengers. Most were extremely good natured and very supportive work colleagues and would often stray out with their job description to be helpful. During my time in Millbank Tower I got to know one of the Messengers well. She was a mature lady from the west of Ireland and in her quieter office moments between postal collection and delivery rounds was a prolific and excellent knitter. She put her talents to good use and took on a little bespoke garment work. For a very modest price I commissioned an Aran sweater for Fiona. This was done in a remarkably short time and to a very high standard. She had been brought up in a tradition that was common to both the west of Ireland and the Scottish Isles where youngsters were taught to knit at a very young age by their mothers and the skills learnt would be put to use though the long winter nights to supplement the family income. In no way was our Messenger's formal work compromised as she could also deal with any inquiry as well as gossip at the same time as knitting. She had no need to consult a pattern and like a concert pianist all was committed to memory. In a strange way it was the Messenger Service and characters like my Irish knitter that I missed as much as any other group when I left the Civil Service.

I must be honest and admit that try as I did I could not generate the fascination for the subject matter of our work as Andrew did. Selective Employment Tax, inevitably abbreviated to SET, was an unpopular tax with business but it was very efficient and relatively cost-effective to collect. The idea behind the tax was to discourage investment of resources into service industries by taxing employment in these industries and hopefully encouraging the channelling of scarce resources into manufacturing industry in preference. As one could imagine much depended on how a particular business was classified (we used the Standard Industrial Classification) and our job was concerned with sorting out disputes and appeals against placement in a category that attracted SET. Many business operations involved staff that were clearly engaged in a manufacturing process and others that were not, and some less clearly so and sometimes all on the same site. Many cases were delegated to me to deal with by myself and in others I was asked to give my views and provide Andrew with a draft reply to either the firm or the Department of Employment. Often the arguments were finally balanced and the file would shunt backwards and forwards between us and quickly filling the 'minute' side of the file. Finding against a supplicant firm could be a drawn out affair as often many employees were involved and so the potential tax implications for the firm could be decisive in any calculation of the firm's profitability. The skill was to cover all the angles and draft a reply to the firm that discouraged a long drawn out exchange of correspondence or, even worse, a series of meetings. Andrew was very patient with the naivety demonstrated in my early drafting of such letters. He was an excellent teacher and would go to great lengths to explain and illustrate a point without a hint of condescension. Sometimes cases would be elevated to Ministerial level but the skills involved were the same. Ministers could not possibly be experts on the minutiae of SET and so always took our advice. I do not remember one face to face meeting with a Minister on the topic of these SET cases.

The other main task also concerned interpretation of legislation. The Investment Grant Scheme employed a large number of people in three or four regional centres including Bootle, Cardiff and Southend-on-Sea and all processing claims by business. The scheme included provision for grants to cover the costs of developing scientific prototypes and here borderline cases and disputed applications were referred to Mintech for resolution and specifically to Andrew Moat and his staff. The parent department for the scheme was the Board of Trade but that department did not have the necessary technical expertise to investigate, evaluate and resolve disputes involving scientific prototypes. We would consult appropriate expertise across Mintech including that residing in our eighteen research laboratories. Occasionally we had to go further afield. Somebody once said to me in those early days that the beauty of the Government machine was that however obscure or exotic the topic there would be an expert somewhere within the bureaucracy. However, the skill was to be able to locate it. Andrew had no technical qualifications but with his agile mind and some input of science from me it was uncommon that consultation added much to our enlightenment. We consulted of course, and extensively so, but more to back up our conclusions and to ensure that should any case be the subject of some form of arbitration or legal action we had covered all the angles. Some of the cases were entertaining either intellectually or for straight amusement. We used to receive a steady trickle of applications for what were in effect perpetual motion machines and had no veracity as scientific prototypes. As with SET cases, for Andrew the thrill was the chase and not the end result and there would be occasions when Andrew seemed genuinely disappointed when we wrapped a case up or an applicant unexpectedly conceded defeat. This enjoyment of the chase was a trait that I came across frequently and comparisons of the Civil Service at this level with life at an Oxford or Cambridge college were apt. In the late sixties there was still time for a more cerebral approach and the disease of measuring everything (and valuing nothing) and setting spurious targets for the often not measurable had yet to be detected outside textbooks written by Americans with German names. By the mid seventies the clouds were gathering and life would change.

Occasionally debate would include consultation with our Assistant Secretary, Chris Herzig, who was of a similar character to Andrew although I suspect he lacked Andrew's analytical intellect. Chris was the epitome of the laid back and always charming public school boy. He was at the same time up front and honest in his dealings and what you saw is what you got, without the deviousness that I was to meet on many occasions. Career ambition is always held up during our formative years as an incontrovertible 'good' that should be cultivated. I doubted this even then and now I am even more doubtful about the role of ambition and its contribution to a happy and fulfilled life. I suppose 'naked' ambition was more frowned upon then than now and was unacceptable in a society where effortless ease was prized. The Thatcher years saw a reversal where raw ambition and 'balls' were prized and this lingers on at the turn of the century although with some clothing.

I recall no highlights to my time with IP Division apart from a false dawn when I was asked to draw up a scheme to better market the civil applications of research and development undertaken by Mintech's research laboratories. The British Productivity Advisory Service was the umbrella name for the body contemplated. The pressure, perhaps from the Treasury, was to encourage spin-off from Government research (or more cynically referred to in the office as 'slop over') and not only get some return on enormous government investment in these eighteen laboratories but to try and improve the efficiency and better use of technology in British industry, which was at the heart of the 'white hot technological revolution' and the justification of Mintech. I got no guidance or terms of reference and I suspect that I was a handy quiet siding for this idea until another initiative came along that found more support from senior officials. The idea withered but to be resurrected in other guises in the years ahead. Other manifestations in later years of the need to capture spin-off from government research include the various UKAEA (atomic energy) spin-offs, and the privatisation or part privatisation of some of these facilities.

I was rarely privy to any high level discussion during my time in IP but I was aware of the antagonism then shown at senior levels towards Ministers and particularly to Tony Benn. This does not come through strongly in the Benn diaries where officials are spoken of with respect. Amongst the rank and file Tony Benn was a popular and charismatic

Minister. It was the small things like his willingness to pass the time with staff sharing the lift that impressed us. Tony Benn would also hold large meetings with staff and this was an innovation. He started the tradition of celebrating the forthcoming weekend by wearing a pink shirt on Fridays and a number of colleagues, including myself, adopted the Pink Shirt on Friday convention. One must remember even in the swinging sixties a white shirt was the office norm with some of the more flamboyant sporting shirts with broad stripes, although these tended to have political connotations and were and still are, at least vestigially, linked to Tory grandees. Whatever one's views of Tony Benn, life with him as Minister was never boring and most of us enjoyed the high profile Mintech had as a result. I can remember only one other Minister in Mintech and its successor departments that ever raised much interest at grass roots level and that was Sir Keith Joseph, although for quite different reasons. I suppose Lord Young as Secretary of State at DTI had a high profile but I do not remember much more than cynicism amongst grass roots staff at the time.

As with my time with Eric Wood I remain grateful to Andrew Moat for not only what he taught me and especially in terms of drafting skills and dealing with the public, but also for his warmth and encouragement. Occasionally he would invite me to his home in Battersea for lunch. It was these occasions that introduced me to an excellent source of draft cider from Stoke Bromyard in Herefordshire. Although no rebel I feel he found the Civil Service a little claustrophobic. His intellect was wasted in the job we had. He did achieve promotion but by the time he was told of this he had secured a job in Brussels working for the European Commission. I have no idea whether he was successful in Brussels and lost contact when he left Mintech. I would expect him to have had a very successful career.

Chapter 7

Continuing Professional Development

For those who sought training it was always available and line managers were generally sympathetic to the aspirations of their staff. During my time in the Service most training was self-elective and was rarely part of an agreed improvement strategy to meet both the needs of the individual and the needs of the Service. However in the case of APs there was a required training programme in the early years provided centrally by the Treasury, and later by the Civil Service College consisting of the facility at Sunningdale and a grim building in Victoria's Belgrave Square. In the early days there was also a College outpost in Edinburgh where I was to attend a course on the European Community, but this Scottish satellite operation was short lived.

In my first year I attended a short introductory course at the Treasury's Centre for Administrative Studies in Cambridge Terrace on Regents Park. At the end of my second year I attended a three-month course split between the Regents Park Centre and the Civil Service College at Sunningdale Park near Ascot. The Sunningdale facility, a former Civil Defence Staff College, was centred around a rather grand mansion in substantial grounds together with a number of newer study/bedroom accommodation blocks scattered in manicured parkland. For the most part I found the three month course interesting and some of it subsequently useful. Lecturers were expert in their field and usually recruited from outside government circles. For example we had lecturers from Ashridge College (a private management college) on psychology with some valuable advice on the conduct of meetings. This material was derived from RAF briefing with guidance on how to put your opposition at a disadvantage. Tricks included sitting at meetings with your back to the light so that your adversary finds it difficult to see your face in detail, but also advice on creating a friendly environment rather than a hostile one. An interesting technique I once experienced but not covered on the course is to conduct a meeting in a near whisper so that all have to strain to hear what you say. My experience of this was some years later when visiting a British arms trader resident in Venezuela. It tends to work better in small meetings where there will unlikely be a clamour to 'speak up'.

The three-month course examined local government in a number of European countries including a field study visit by small groups of four to five of us. My assigned country was West Germany and the Bonn area. We made study trips to also look at UK local government and here my target was Hull and the part of Yorkshire which then had Beverley as its administrative centre. The thrill for me here was my first visit to the marvellous Beverley Minster. Over the period we had lectures on every aspect of government and the government machine as well as economics. The Civil Service did a good job on the whole in training us administrators but they did not always get it right. One private training organisation commissioned caused a minor revolt. The organisation sold a package on leadership skills through team participation in a number of exercises such as building a fire and 'Lego' towers and then learning about leadership through peer analysis of the process. All of us thought the Service had been sold a pup and our co-operation was withdrawn. The boss of the firm was dispatched to try and rescue the situation and we made our views quite clear. It was some time before the services of this firm were dispensed with but the delay may have reflected a contractual obligation or our masters wanted to ensure that we were representative and not a bunch of troublemakers.

It was during the three-month course that I was summoned to my 'Positive Vetting' interview which took place in the Regents Park Centre, lasted for about two hours and was conducted by a former Rhodesian policeman, or so he said. This was no interview by a suave interrogator from one of the unmentionable government departments featured in the likes of the 'Ipcress File' film and other Harry Palmer (Michael Caine) adventures but more like your routine 'Met' plainclothes and "Just a few routine inquiries, Sir". I was not asked whether I was a homosexual but most of the other expected questions were put with emphasis on political affiliations and sympathies. I was to frustrate him in this respect as I had never been a joiner of any organisation. He admitted some confusion and found it difficult to believe that my beliefs, like most people, were a 'pick 'n' mix' from the spectrum of political thought rather than a set of beliefs tied to a manifesto. Life for most of us is a little more sophisticated. He asked whether I had a car and then how did I afford this. I said it had been bought by my father and then, no doubt to raise the adrenaline level, he makes a snide remark about being a rich kid. The fact that the car I had at the time was French (a Renault R10) also raised doubts about my loyalty. I suspect much of this was deliberately petty and almost hostile in style and it was only when we got on to race issues did I begin to think this man cannot be for real. His tack was to volunteer his background and go on to question whether it was fair for immigrants to flood our country and take our jobs. I said I had little experience of immigrants of any kind except for my Kashmiri neighbours in Glasgow and I had no strong views and was not antagonistic to any immigrant group. His parting shot was something to the effect that he could not fully understand me. The experience was not a pleasant one and was very like the experience of any innocent contact with the police and the misplaced feeling of guilt. I had nothing to hide and presumably this interview, with linked inquiries, resulted in a clean bill of health, and the necessary security clearance as I was to have access in the years ahead to very sensitive information.

Sunningdale has happy memories, not only for the stimulation provided by much of the course material but also for the beauty of the grounds and the surrounding countryside. My time there coincided with a glorious autumn with Sunningdale's magnificent trees, lawns and shrubs at their richest. On the estate they grew tennis ball sized chrysanthemums and I took a bunch of these home to Fiona. A bonus was really quite good food in some very civilised surroundings.

Just north of Steyning and set into the Sussex Downs is Wilton Park. This beautiful and ancient house complete with its own church and extensive grounds was used by the Foreign and Commonwealth Office (FCO). I understand it was used after the war as a denazification centre. My introduction to this slightly mysterious place was as a participant on a two-week residential course for about fifty carefully chosen Europeans. The aim was to influence European leaders of tomorrow, be they in the private or public sectors. I had no idea how the selection process was conducted but I assume the criteria were similar to those used in inviting VIPs to this country as guests of Her Majesty's Government. Some invitations were overtly commercial but some were less obvious and probably little more than a 'good bet' that the person may at some point in the future be useful, in one way or another. Apart from the lecturing staff and various minders I was one of the very few British participants on the course. I was representing my then Assistant Secretary, Phyllis James, who was unable to attend and the FCO agreed I should attend in her place.

The two weeks were aimed at presenting our institutions and British way of life in the best light. With a little imagination one might detect an element of the previous use of Wilton Park here as what was on offer was a 'soft sell' propaganda exercise. The food was excellent and served in formal and rather grand surroundings. Interspersed with meals were lectures and discussions on a wide range of topics and some quite surprising as to their relevance, other than to get the group to debate together and bond, but also providing the opportunity for FCO observers to assess participants. I remember lectures on game conservancy (I learnt almost all I know about partridges from this talk), museums access, and a visionary performance by Tony Benn on the exponential pace of change in the years ahead. His predictions on the effect of computers were not the job loss fear of the time but rather that job opportunities would expand. What he did not predict in 1970 was the loss of white collar and financial services jobs rather than manufacturing jobs. The most heated debate was on Willy Brandt's 'ost politik' and here the German contingent almost came to blows, with passions running high and one side seeing Brandt as irresponsible with the suggestion he was a traitor to his country. The other saw him as a saviour with an initiative that surely would lead to German reunification. However in 1972 there were few of the group that saw any prospect of German reunification in our lifetimes. How wrong we all were, although it did take another generation to see the Berlin wall come down. It would be interesting to reconvene this group and see how many of us would now see Brandt as a traitor, although he did leave his country in its darkest hour.

Wilton Park provided a very enjoyable two weeks. It was not only the surroundings and company but also the opportunities to see aspects of British life that even I was unfamiliar with. For example we were taken to lunch in the House of Lords, visited New College, Oxford for afternoon tea with the Master and enjoyed a night in the Randolph Hotel before returning to Wilton Park. It was late autumn and the weather was not always the best but I know our visitors enjoyed the setting as well as the opportunity for walks on the Downs and to Chanctonbury Ring. Whether the FCO got value for money and there was an eventual pay back I will never know as government is very secretive about such things, but the truth is more likely that government have never attempted any true cost/benefit study. What is clear to me now is Wilton Park would have cost a fortune to maintain and provide the standard of accommodation and hospitality that was offered.

Even more spooky than Wilton Park was a short course that I attended at GCHQ, the modern day successor to Bletchley Park, the wartime code-breaking establishment that featured in the film 'Enigma'. At the time I was on the Latin America desk and had access to the services offered by GCHQ. In those days we were not even allowed to acknowledge the establishment in Cheltenham existed, although like MI6

(Secret Intelligence Service), then south of Waterloo station, every minor Eastern Bloc embassy official and driver would have known exactly where and what these places were. My first recollection of public and published acknowledgement of GCHQ, MI6 and MI5 and the London telephone tapping centre affectionately known as 'Tinkerbell' and more jewels was by reading articles in the *New Statesman.* It says a lot about our national character and love of secrecy that the British public were last to know of the whereabouts of these agencies. Such knowledge in no way compromises their effectiveness. At the time MI6 was at Century House and I had a friend working in the Central Office of Information building across the street. She had a visit from a very attractive Russian lady who fronted a BBC TV programme at the time on learning Russian. Unfortunately the lady had left her car in the Century House car park. There was a panic amongst the security guards. This Russian lady had no idea of the nature of the cigarette packet shaped block opposite but the daftness of the situation was hugely enjoyed by COI staff.

The GCHQ course was not exciting and gave little clue to the capabilities of its vast computer complex and large site in Cheltenham as well as at satellites elsewhere in the UK and overseas, nor how closely it was tied to the bigger American equivalent, the National Security Agency. The course did explain better the front shop services it offered to certain Whitehall officers and, surprisingly, to elements of British business, although suitably filleted. The trouble with much of the information was that in practice it was difficult to use, because of the dangers of compromising the source. Sometimes the information was titillating but the more so the less the practical use. In my experience there were very few occasions that this source of information was able to influence our commercial relations with a Latin American country to British advantage and that would not have happened otherwise through normal commercial procedures. In South America to know, for example, someone was taking a bribe was no great revelation and the more senior the person the less one could affect any outcome. GCHQ was customer responsive and would tailor its research to your particular requirements if given sufficient warning.

A friend working in a London-based South American embassy (not Argentina) shortly after the Falkland Islands saga was in charge of sending telegrams. One evening the Ambassador had asked that an urgent message be sent to their capital. My friend asked whether it should sent in code. The Ambassador's reply was not to bother as 'they' (GCHQ) would have decoded it before their own people at the other end had received it. This story illustrates just how well-known were GCHQ's capabilities by all those in the 'communications' business

As exotic, but in a very different sense, was the month-long residential course I spent with the General and Municipal Workers Union (GMWU) at their southern college at Woodstock near Surbiton. This came about by a rather odd route involving then Labour Parliamentary Under Secretary of State for Industry, Les Huckfield. Huckfield had become engaged in an argument with David Basnett, then General Secretary of the GMWU, as to whether civil servants had sufficient knowledge of trade unions. Huckfield's response was to challenge Basnett to correct that by taking a civil servant on one of GMWU's internal training courses. So Basnett was to offer two places on their residential course for senior shop stewards, shop conveners and newly-appointed full-time officials. This was the first time that officials had been offered such an opportunity outside the Civil Service's own unions. The idea was to promote a better understanding in Whitehall between trade union activists and civil servants. I am not sure how I was chosen although by that time I was becoming active in my own union, the Society of Civil and Public Services (SCPS) and no doubt this was known to Establishments Division either via routine annual assessments by my superiors or by sources within the union itself. I was delighted to be chosen, along with another young man who had achieved the grade of Principal via promotion from the Executive stream. He did not to my knowledge have much of a trade union commitment and so I am not sure how his name was pulled from the hat. There were occasions that I imagined that he might have been chosen to keep an eye on me. Here was the archetypal bright young man enjoying unexpected promotion and who would take great care to see nothing inhibited his further advance. By the end of four weeks I knew that this colleague saw me as naive, impulsive and not only a danger to myself but to him also in the charged atmosphere of the Woodstock group.

Woodstock was one of two colleges the Union owned, the other one being in the north of England at Hale in Cheshire. The facilities at Woodstock were of a high standard and as good, if not better, than the Civil Service in-house equivalent. True, the buildings were likely post war, functional and with none of the grandeur of Sunningdale but accommodation was adequate with good food and, of course, a good bar which was the centre of so much animated debate and often into the wee hours. There were eighteen course members including myself and my Civil Service colleague, with most from industrial backgrounds although the white collar wing of the union, MATSA, was represented by a couple of members. As one GMWU colleague described, all political opinion was present from Karl Marx to Reg Prentice (a Labour MP of the time who later crossed the floor of the House). One colleague Mick, a shop steward, was an active Trotskyite, but not in the loose sense of the term now used to label anyone with far-left views. I spent a lot of time talking to Mick about his beliefs, which were not in anyway shared by the majority of his colleagues on this course and he was very obviously at odds with the 'moderate' GMWU hierarchy of the time. The Union's executives included then Larry Whitty as a Research Officer, later a Blairite Minister as Lord Whitty. By coincidence I had come across Larry earlier in Mintech as he was a fellow AP before he left to join the trade union movement. Mick was never slow to challenge senior office-holders in the Union, including both Larry Whitty and David Basnett in our presence, and usually to the amusement of the rest of us. Mick introduced me to Robert Tressel's "The Ragged Trousered Philanthropist", a book that has encouraged so many to take up the socialist cause. I remember one other piece of guidance from Mick and that was never resign as one can do so much more working within an organisation than wasting opportunity on what is likely a useless gesture. Maybe there were shades of Militant's philosophy here and its choice to work within the old Labour Party.

I found the month at the GMWU College one of the most enjoyable and stimulating courses of any in my public service career. The content was predictable enough bearing in mind the needs of the participants. The quality of debate was as good if not often better than experienced on any Civil Service courses, notwithstanding that few of the GMWU participants had much formal education beyond secondary school level. I learnt to respect and appreciate the often trying and difficult job of the trade union official, be that at shop steward, shop convener or full time union official level. Before I had little idea of the breadth of the shop steward's job and how demanding a job it is if done well. A good shop steward must be a combination of diplomat, social worker, educationalist, administrator, lawyer and advocate. I started at Woodstock with impressions tainted by Peter Sellars' portrayal of a shop steward in the film 'I'm Alright Jack'. There is also a difficult balancing act for trade union officials between representing their members' interests as perceived by members, and representing the overall interests of the union and the trade union movement as a whole. The role involves considerable emotional maturity and tact and a willingness to take responsibility and offer leadership not only to the members but often to employers and their managers, although few managers would recognise this fact.

One has to be aware of the mood of the time in that autumn of 1977 with the Labour government under James Callaghan losing its grip on the country. Many of our discussions at Woodstock reflected this mood with membership of a trade union seen by the majority of participants as being more than just a co-operative society with member benefits as the raison d'être. During the course we had a visit by delegates from the German OTV public services union. Whilst many of us saw trade union membership as an extension of the commitment to socialism and the vision of a fairer society, our German colleagues made no such connection and found the additional emotional baggage that course members carried confusing and a likely barrier to achieving better pay and workplace conditions. The chaos that was to bring the Callaghan government down was regrettable, but rather than blame the unions alone I would put a large part of the blame at the feet of a Labour movement that had raised, intentionally or otherwise, expectations of a genuine socialist state with real worker involvement. I am sure there were those on both sides of the political divide that welcomed a phoenix solution, and here I would include both sides of the divide within the Labour movement itself. Many of my colleagues on the course were strongly opposed to the Government's attempts at 'planning agreements' with individual firms and also the idea of compulsory trade union representation on company Boards. Opposition to closer involvement of unions in running the country or a firm came both from Labour 'right' and 'left'. There was still a strong wish to retain the traditional confrontation between management and workers, and anything short of this smacked of selling out. Again our German union colleagues did not share this view. Later I will explain something of this conflict within the context of the different world of Civil Service unions.

I drafted a report to the Minister, Les Huckfield, of our experience with the GMWU and made recommendations that such exchanges should continue, but also we should offer places to industrial trade unionists on Civil Service courses. Further I recommended that there should be short-term secondments of industrial trade unionists to the Department to shadow a Principal and so provide a better understanding of the Civil Service. Needless to say the Minister accepted the recommendations with enthusiasm and due lip service was paid by senior departmental officials. The GMWU welcomed a repeat of the experiment and also endorsed my recommendations. Shortly after the course I was to join the Iron and Steel Division within the Industry Department and I did manage to follow up with a secondment of Iron and Steel Trades Confederation's (ISTC) Roy

Bishop to my office for one week. I was not aware of any further Civil Servants being sent on external trade union courses or vice versa during the rest of my time at DTI. This was a pity as both 'sides' had so much to learn from each other. My lasting memento is an essay I wrote at Woodstock that looked at Britain's recent economic decline compared with other mixed economies and how we might arrest this. I often return to my Woodstock thesis and treasure the passion of the time I was privileged to share with a splendid bunch of colleagues, including my Civil Servant colleague. A bonus for me is that even 25 years later I am not too embarrassed by what I wrote in the heat of the enthusiasm of that four weeks' sabbatical.

Part of Harold Wilson's 'white hot technological revolution' was to see more administrators in the Civil Service with some technical or scientific training. I was recruited in the heat of this 'revolution' together with a number of others with scientific degrees, but most of my colleagues recruited then or just after continued in the mainstream tradition of the Administrative Class with degrees in the arts and here I would include politics and economics. This obviously remained of concern in Mintech and its successor DTI as in our early years we were sent on a course run by the prestigious Royal Institution. The Royal Institution is perhaps more widely known for its excellent annual Christmas lecture series for children which is televised. I watch these if I can as the standard is usually very high and the content quite challenging even for one with a scientific bent. The course arranged for us was demanding for the non-scientist. All found it interesting but nobody could pretend that such a brief introduction could achieve much except that the department was able to claim, if challenged, that it had addressed the problem of a lack of understanding of basic science amongst its senior administrators.

Over the years I volunteered for a number of courses on economics including understanding company accounts during the period I had DTI responsibility for oversight of the British Steel Corporation's overseas investments. Maybe at the time I was not that motivated as I learnt little that I was able to use. Many years later I had to return to the challenge of company accounts and try to get a better grip on the skills involved in reading a balance sheet. Happily in DTI we had help from the Department's professional accounting staff and BSC's intentions were transparent enough.

As part of my trade union work I became a member of my local health and safety committee which was a statutory provision under the Health and Safety at Work etc. Act 1974. The Act provides for joint committees representing both management and trade unions with provision for plant and building inspection by local committees. If there is resistance from local management over access to facilities or necessary information the Act provides for intervention by the Health and Safety Executive and, if necessary, an improvement order or finally a fine for non-compliance. Unfortunately in those days most Government departments pleaded Crown exemption from the Health and Safety at Work Act provisions. However the Health and Safety Executive still had a role in Crown-owned facilities and could issue notices that could be very embarrassing to Ministers and local management.

My local branch of the Society of Civil and Public Services sent me on an excellent course on the Act and its implications for our members. Armed with this in 1980 I became Chair of the staff side of my local health and safety committee. Before the course a large and modern office block in Victoria Street seemed unlikely to be much of a health or safety threat to our staff, apart from the occasional kettle scald in making the office coffee. How wrong I was. My first formal inspection of the building, which housed about a thousand people, involved a brief visual inspection of every room in the building. Most of the hazards worth reporting involved trailing wires, faulty electrical insulation and loose connections and unsafe furniture, including overloaded shelving and filing cabinets. All important and regularly giving rise to minor and even a few serious accidents. A common office accident involved filing cabinets toppling over when too many drawers are opened at the same time, but this is the fault of the user and not the furniture itself. The more senior the person in the office visited the less helpful they were. Some senior staff were positively hostile even though we bent over backwards to be polite and explain why we were inspecting their office, including an offer to return at a more convenient time. A lot of this hostility, I suspect, was rooted in hostility to trade union membership and a resentment of the trade union inspection rights given under the Act. However we were accompanied by a representative of the 'official' side or the employer or, in shop floor speak, a representative of 'management', and so proper decorum was observed. Hostility was the exception and not the rule and many staff as well as many at senior levels were polite and even appreciative. Most of the work was tiring and routine and there was a risk of becoming careless and overlooking a problem.

On one occasion we inspected a large printing operation in the DTI headquarters building. We expected this area to be well covered by those who worked on the litho printers and large copying machinery with a greater operator awareness of hazards than the white collar workers that filled the rest of the building. Even on cursory inspection we found many shortcomings in safety procedure including the lack of eye wash bottles, poor ventilation and sloppy disposal of waste materials and many other minor matters. Much more important I discovered that supervisors and operatives had no idea of the hazards associated with many of the solvents they were using in the print process. Relevant data sheets on each chemical were not available and so there was little idea of the safe limits to skin contact or inhalation levels. These 'safe' limits are the Threshold Limit Values and are the maximum exposure levels permitted but are regularly reviewed in the light of new data and the trend is usually downwards. The chemical hazards involved were not those leading to a spot of minor skin irritation but chemicals that were known carcinogens. My chemistry background came into its own and I spent some time researching the chemicals used and using the provisions of the Act to prize the data out of the manufacturers and then checking against published data, mainly from US sources, and especially the carcinogenic risk. I produced a learned and well-researched paper that I remain proud of. I knew if we submitted anything but a comprehensive and well-researched view it would be brushed aside. My report went to the Health and Safety Executive and caused a stir not only in DTI but in Her Majesty's Stationery Office (HMSO) who arranged purchase of chemicals centrally.

My efforts resulted in a change in the whole regime of such chemicals usage throughout the Civil Service and the substitution of safer and less carcinogenic chemicals. Oddly, we received less co-operation from the print staff concerned who claimed that they had worked for years with these chemicals. The official side in my own department were grudging at best in their appreciation of this major piece of trade union-led work. Shortly after, I remember coming into the office of the official side co-chairman of the health and safety committee (my counterpart on the joint committee) when he was being asked whether Dr Fisher was a 'real' doctor. His reply was "No, just a troublemaker". There are some remarks in life that remain at the front of the memory and slowly ferment. That was one such comment!

When asked that difficult question 'what have you done in life you are most proud of?', it is that change I brought about in print chemicals throughout the Service, and particularly so as it was not part of my mainstream role and also I was able to use my scientific training to real advantage.

Chapter 8

Saints and Sinners

After a long training course I was posted in October 1970 to Industrial and Commercial Policy Division (IC Division) and my first post at Principal level. Mintech had merged with the Board of Trade to become the Department of Trade and Industry following the election in June of that year of a Conservative government under Prime Minister Edward Heath. Once more Millbank Tower was to be my base and for the first time I was to work for a woman. Phyllis James was my Assistant Secretary who was very much in the tradition of strong and colourful Whitehall ladies. Underneath a bluff exterior was a genuinely caring person and, although she would pretend not to suffer fools gladly, I never witnessed any unkindness to staff although she was temperamental and when under pressure her language would be more at home on a shop floor than in the rarefied atmosphere of a Whitehall office. Her black moods never lasted long and she would soon return to that relaxed and apparently effortless approach to her work that was the prized mark of those often destined for greater things in the Service. She had a good if somewhat bawdy sense of humour with an infectious and totally unrestrained full laugh. I never saw Phyllis as an intellectual but obviously a bright lady, and neither did I think she saw herself or would have wished to be seen as a bluestocking. She enjoyed the good things in life including her wine, with a preference for a good Beaune, loved the gossip of Whitehall and was a regular at the Cabinet Office mess. She was a serious collector of graffiti and that interest gives a clue to her sense of humour. She could not stand the prissy and consciously correct and I suspect in her younger days had lived life to the full. Indeed was still to since she was later to marry Lord Bowden when, on promotion to Under Secretary, she became Director of DTI's North West Regional Office in Manchester.

Of all my bosses in the Service I liked Phyllis the most. She was motherly (she would hate that description) and looked out for my interests in my first Principal level posting. When she spotted opportunities that she saw as good for my experience and training she bullied me into accepting the challenge. One example of this was packing me off to New York in September 1971 for a UN Preparatory

Environment Conference two days after I had moved house to Surrey with our second child, Andrew, only four months old. Her decision was the right one although I and Fiona saw it as a little unfeeling at the time. The change of gear from the training grade Assistant Principal to Principal was a significant one. For the first time one had direct responsibility for staff and what left your desk was your responsibility. There was also a significant uplift in status and income.

IC Division was another of those ragbag collections of policy issues which tended to attract work that had no clear theme unlike the DTI Divisions dealing with the steel industry or motor vehicles for example, but more catering for across-the-board industrial policy, and no less important for that. My new responsibilities were to co-ordinate DTI's interest in the environment which was, at last, being taken seriously by the Government and the population at large. It was the time of the television series "Doomwatch" which featured a fictional Government agency with glamorous operatives sent to deal with a series of environmental disasters. The format was more "Avengers" than a day in the life in your local environmental health inspector. However it did focus public interest and the nearest we got to a Doomwatch unit in Whitehall was the new Department of the Environment's Central Unit on Environmental Pollution, headed up by a distinguished scientist, Dr Martin Holdgate. DTI was very much a saints and sinners department with statutory responsibilities for environmental controls such as the Nuclear Installations Inspectorate and the air pollution monitoring role of the Warren Spring Laboratory at Stevenage. At the same time the Department had what was termed a 'sponsorship' role for most of UK manufacturing industry, with one or two exceptions such as the agricultural industry which continues to be one of the biggest threats to our environment. Later the Thatcher government and DTI under Sir Keith Joseph (often then known as the Mad Monk) tried to move away from the concept of 'sponsoring' this or that sector of industry but it failed to achieve any significant change. At its mildest, sponsorship was a paternal interest by government in the health of a particular sector of industry, but most of the time it was more interventionist and included the concept of actively championing winning sectors such as the then emergent silicon chip industry. However, more often than not, sponsorship was about supporting failing and uncompetitive industry sectors, or more popularly referred to as the lame duck policy. In the circumstances much of my responsibility was to ensure new environmental legislation coming from the Department of the

Environment (DoE) did not undermine the profitability and international competitiveness of British industry.

I spent time at many meetings with DoE fighting an indefensible corner rather than working with the DoE brief to clean up our land, rivers and air. On the whole colleagues at DoE were understanding and even sympathetic but the reality was I was nearly always pursuing a policy on behalf of my Department that was against the grain and unpopular. Often a strange bedfellow was the Foreign and Commonwealth Office (FCO) which had its own Science and Technology Department. This was headed up by diplomat Ronald Arculus, who I was to come across again some years later when he was our Ambassador in Rome. The FCO were concerned to maintain the competitive position of UK firms and avoid adopting new legislation that would give our competitors an 'unfair' (whatever that is) advantage. For example, and this is but one of many, our European neighbours had a really pressing problem with pollution by industry of major rivers such as the Rhine and Danube. The policy line went something as follows: The UK might have polluted rivers but none of the problems of say the Rhine and its tributaries. The continental Europeans need to do something to clean up their rivers whereas most of our rivers are relatively short and we are surrounded by seas that would quickly disperse and dilute any effluent put into our rivers. To accept European permitted pollutant levels would put our chemical industry, for example, at an unnecessary disadvantage to the German, Swiss and Dutch chemical industries.

Ronald Arculus in his dry manner was very helpful and supportive. As time went on I appreciated that underneath a rather formal exterior was a sense of humour and perspective. It took a visit to the 'gents' during a break in an OECD meeting in Paris before I was able to appreciate this. The meeting had been one of a regular series of OECD meetings to try and co-ordinate a developed (rich) country line on major pollution issues and the Australian delegate had been going on at great length that morning. We adjourned for coffee and the three of us in the UK delegation, myself, Martin Holdgate from DoE and Ronald Arculus visited the small gents which led directly off the main meeting room. Martin Holdgate was a very pleasant and outward going scientist but never 'turned off' and had little time for small talk, and it was so at the stalls in the gents. As the three of us stood in a row he asked Arculus what he had made of the Australian contribution but Arculus, like myself, really wanted a respite and turned to Holdgate and said, "I think it's all a lot of fucking nonsense, Martin". Holdgate was speechless as he saw

Arculus as a dry, prim and proper FCO man and this was about the last comment he expected to hear. Holdgate quickly recovered his composure and saw the amusing side of their exchange and returned to his analysis of the session in the meeting chamber. I warmed to Arculus and was able to detect a gentle sense of humour that was often lost on the more intense of my colleagues.

I had many exchanges with Holdgate but I cannot remember one that demonstrated any interest in me as a person, although he was always polite and pleasant. My stance often in support of the industry case, in effect to continue to pollute the environment, must have been frustrating for him. From later feedback I think my role was respected. I did establish good relations with other officials in the Central Unit on Environmental Pollution and particularly so with Dr Ian Presst who was one of Holdgate's scientific deputies. Presst went on to become the Director of the Royal Society for the Protection of Birds at their headquarters in Bedfordshire but unfortunately ran into health problems and died a relatively young man. My credibility as a very young and inexperienced Principal was helped by my scientific training and by that time my title as 'Doctor' which I was to use throughout my professional career. However some of my Administrative Class colleagues coming into Mintech or DTI with scientific doctorates were advised that retention of the handle would do their careers as administrators no good and so most dropped the title. I suspect that they took the right decision.

New legislation on both air and water based pollution was beginning to cascade out of DoE. This involved much internal consultation within DTI and it was my job to draw proposed changes to the attention of the numerous interests in the Department and bring together a single DTI view to new legislation proposals. In some sectors my Department was the focus of government technical expertise on the subject and particularly on the detection and measurement of air pollution. We were also the experts on domestic sewage disposal via our Water Pollution Research Laboratory, also at Stevenage with the Warren Spring Laboratory dealing with air pollution monitoring. However DTI was not responsible for statutory control of air or water borne pollutants. At the same time DTI did have statutory clean up responsibilities for marine pollution and particularly oil pollution, although counting the number of agencies involved then in an oil spill clear up was the stuff of many a training exercise. This range of DTI environmental interests, spanning the statutory control of nuclear installations, mining and petroleum installations to the protection of UK industry interests via the many industry sponsor divisions within the Department, made the distillation of a departmental view a tricky balancing act. One might have thought that I would have been regularly challenged as to the balance and veracity of the final line I fed to the likes of DoE and used in negotiations in the various international bodies we dealt with. In fact it was very rarely that any DTI colleague challenged the line I was pursuing. Naturally I kept my Assistant Secretary informed, initially Phyllis James and later Tony Woolmer, but they seemed happy enough to leave me to get on with the job, although were supportive when a problem did occasionally arise. The degree of responsibility was not unusual for a Principal but in the first year I would often feel hesitant in putting forward a view at one of the regular round of interdepartmental meetings including some at Cabinet Office level. The phrase in such meetings 'that my Department could not agree to this' sounded self-consciously pretentious in my early days in the job. It was all a matter of confidence and as soon as I saw my intervention actually affected the flow and even the outcome of the meeting then my delivery caught up with the reality of my role.

It was not all plain sailing and I was soon to experience Whitehall turf wars or games which often had more to do with personal ambitions of officials than Ministers. As I said I got on pretty well with most DoE officials but occasionally there would be misunderstandings and we would cross swords. One such example involved the now very successful author Richard Adams who was one of DoE's Assistant Secretaries dealing with pollution matters. He had circulated two separate drafts covering legislation dealing with air pollution and water pollution respectively and I had studied these in detail, consulted DTI colleagues and had made detailed points arising in a letter back to him. I had pointed out some inconsistency as between the proposed legislation dealing respectively with the water and air aspects. I have never understood what upset him but upset him I did. He made this quite clear in a very heated telephone call to me. I was a bit put out and did not quite know how to handle the matter and so decided that the best line was to lie low and keep out of Mr Adams' way for a while. This turned out for the best as a couple of weeks later he rang and invited me to come round to his office 'for tea'. This was a slightly odd request in so far as the description 'tea' went, but I turned up at his office, not in the awful DoE Marsham Street triple towers (thankfully now demolished) but in an older office block near St James's Underground station. I was ushered into a large office with many pot plants but not so very different from any other Whitehall office. He was very polite and 'tea' was indeed brought in but in keeping with the invitation his secretary had prepared a tray with a real china tea pot and cups to match. Adams poured and tea was sipped with no mention of our cross words on the telephone. I never did find out how I upset him but we maintained the best of professional relationships from that point on. I saw Richard Adams being interviewed not so long after he left the Civil service in 1974 to concentrate on his writing career and at this point he was very scathing of the Service and commented to the effect that it was the only organisation that could put a knife in your stomach while at the same time smiling. I can relate to that but a few years later he had mellowed and seemed almost nostalgic about his Civil Service career. The memory can be surprisingly kind to those that trespass against us.

It was a period of intense international activity, lead by the United Nations Conference on the Environment held in Stockholm in the summer of 1972 . This provided me with the opportunity to experience firsthand being party to international negotiations. The Stockholm Conference was preceded by a Preparatory Conference held at the UN Headquarters in New York. Quite a large UK delegation was dispatched under DoE's leadership with myself representing DTI interests. To sit behind the UK nameplate in the main UN Chamber was quite a thrill and especially on one occasion where I was left by myself to hold the fort. I had to find an opportunity to speak and did so but have no recollection of the topic. Countries were seated in alphabetical order and so the United Kingdom sat next to the United States. A member of their delegation was Shirley Temple Black who sat on my immediate right. I and an information scientist from DoE used to chat to her in the quieter moments of the debate. She was warm and charming in response to our no doubt rather gauche chat lines.

Dr Holdgate was a master at drafting in committee and made a significant contribution to the preparation of the concrete proposals that would go forward to Stockholm. His example taught me the power of making the proposal rather than responding to the proposals of others, which is the lazy way. It takes a lot of effort and sweat to take the lead but one is in a more powerful position and more likely to end up with a deal that is suitable to your needs. Most of the wheeling and dealing takes place in working groups, leaving the plenary session in the main chamber to essentially political debate. With individuals deployed in different rooms with subsets of negotiations to pursue taking the initiative requires a good understanding by all the team of the over-all strategy, and what is the fall back position and at what point must you say 'that is as far as we can go'. Briefing before setting out is important but perhaps more important is the briefing each morning and debriefing at the end of the day. Most senior Whitehall officials now will be well versed in the tactics of international negotiation because of the need to service the European Union and the Brussels machinery. As with Brussels, so much useful discussion is 'off the record' and takes place in the 'margins' of the meeting. This can mean a snatched word in the corridor, the gents, over coffee or over a meal and something stronger.

The successful outcome of a large international negotiation is very much dependent on team effort, but leadership is also important. Even the bit player must be aware of the big picture, and that this is regularly updated so all can make best use of the hand he or she is dealt. Where the stakes are high the HMG machine can provide access to an impressive array of intelligence as to the likely position of the 'opposition'. This can include the more exotic sources of information but analysis of other delegations' positions and options from overt material can be very useful. Much information is available from published sources but needs intelligent collation, and Whitehall and its various agencies are very good at this. The saying that only a fool goes into negotiation without knowledge of his opposite number's position is so true. With the best of preparation the unexpected will occur, and often the unexpected comes from your own carefully coached team. Add the introduction of politicians to the negotiating table, then predicting the outcome can be as accurate as reading a daily horoscope. Nonetheless preparation is everything and when the unexpected does crop up, and it surely will, at best you will have a strategy that can be adapted or at worst you have a team that can think on its feet without going to pieces. Watching the likes of Martin Holdgate in action and seeing him emerge with a document all have signed up to, and ideally one that is not too far away in content from the proposal initially tabled, is a joy. I felt privileged to be a part of such international negotiating teams.

Conferences away from home, like those in New York and Stockholm, were not all work, or not for the majority of us. The delegation that DoE's Secretary of State, Peter Walker, took to Stockholm was a large one which not only included key officials but also some political window-dressing with the likes of Lady Dartmouth (now Countess Spencer) who I think had a culture and arts interest but also other well-known public figures in environmental circles at the time. Lady Dartmouth turned out to be brighter and more intelligent than we officials expected and we had underestimated the contribution she was able to make. However, she had clear ideas as to the role of younger Civil Servants as when I escorted her to a reception for delegates on entering the venue she handed me her stole to mind. The handover was made with grace and I, almost, felt honoured to be of such use. I admired her style.

Although a lot of effort was put into that first UN conference on the environment in Stockholm it is doubtful whether much changed for the better, but there is no such thing as a 'failed' conference and this one was, of course, hailed by Environment Minister Peter Walker as a great success. In the words of Mandy Rice Davies 'He would, wouldn't he'.

Some of the toughest international negotiations were with our partners in the European Community and these discussions were taking place before our formal accession. I accompanied a DoE Assistant Secretary, Richard Bird (why do parents do this?) to Brussels and was party to agreeing the Community's 'Polluter Pays' approach to environmental clean-up. I like to think that Richard and I were instrumental in framing this policy, notwithstanding that with my industrial sponsorship hat on this policy would not have been welcomed by our 'clients'. However the greater good was for the UK government who did not wish to be left with clean-up bills for countryside ravaged or polluted by industry.

Few would admit it but it has been the European Community (or now the European Union), with all its imperfections, that has been responsible for the more significant advances towards a cleaner environment, and often in spite of the UK and not because of it. In a number of areas we dragged our feet rather than led the way and this approach typified so much of subsequent British engagement with the Community. Whereas I could live with the argument that the UK did not need to impose the strict limits on effluent disposal to our rivers that our neighbours sought, I found some of the UK policy of the time short-sighted, disingenuous and not in the overall interest of the UK, be that the long term competitiveness of our industry or the health of our population. A live issue at the time was the case of lead in petrol. The government argued that this source of lead in the environment was not a significant health hazard and the greater risk to the population could be laid at the door of lead piping within the older housing stock in areas with soft water. The campaign against use of lead tetra-ethyl, which was added to petrol to eliminate 'knocking' during fuel combustion, was championed by a chemist who, as a result, suffered a campaign of public vilification for his efforts. Much was made of the fact he was not medically qualified and his warnings of the risks that lead in petrol posed to children's health and intelligence levels were regularly ridiculed and rubbished. I suspect much of the campaign was government inspired, but at a level far above my level of responsibility. If I understood the internal debate at the time, and I tried, the reasons were not so much that the health risks from lead in exhaust fumes were not a reality, but rather that the Germans had a vested interest in seeing the use of unleaded petrol because they had the competitive edge on the catalytic converter technology needed if the move was made to lead-free fuel. So our motor manufacturing industry was said to face higher costs and its competitive position vis-à-vis the Germans put at further risk. If only the future competitive position of our motor industry had been as simple as that. As usual it was only a case of delaying a change that was clearly inevitable but few would acknowledge that, although I guess most of my colleagues in DoE saw the future clearly, but kept their heads down. Dr Holdgate gives his own account in his memoirs (*Penguins and Mandarins,* The Memoir Club 2003).

There were a number of interesting parallel nonsenses being peddled at the time. I remember sitting through an exposition by the electricity generating industry justifying the sulphur emission levels from our power stations as really being 'quite good for us' because many British agricultural soils had sulphur levels below that required for optimum plant growth. The arguments over acid rain were beginning to rage as well as the accusations from our northern European neighbours that British power station emissions (including emissions from other industries to a lesser degree) were killing their forests and lakes. Notwithstanding that we still struggle to understand why forests die and lakes become dead, it was obvious to all balanced views we must try and reduce sulphur emissions from fossil fuel fired electricity generation. Again, instead of conceding this or even leading the move for change, we dig in and defend the indefensible. Other seemingly pigheaded UK stances that I observed at the time included the question of safe levels for asbestos, although most would now accept that there are no safe levels for some forms of asbestos fibres. We handled in a much better way the worrying level of mercury in some rivers and estuaries arising as a by-product of caustic soda manufacture, but here the leadership appeared to come from industry itself and one chemical firm in particular. Some firms were less upfront about their problems and I remember incidents involving PCBs and both water and airborne heavy metal pollution. I do not remember the DoE Central Pollution Unit being part of any disinformation campaign but I did worry about some of the senior scientists in the various public sector agencies involved and some of these were core to government advice. I am happy to recall that I was never 'leant on' or called upon to take a line other than I considered, on balance, to be honest and reasonable. My experience of the government machine is it is far more sophisticated than that, and I was but a foot soldier in the scheme of things. I can see parallels in the government's recent approach to BSE (and new variant CJD) and some of its approaches to the environment during my time in IC Division at the beginning of the seventies, although I believe our handling of BSE was so much worse with implications we may have still to realise. By a coincidence when we lived in Surrey, the Ministry of Agriculture veterinary scientist who was to characterise the prion organism causing BSE lived across the road from us.

My job looking after DTI's interests and responsibilities in environmental pollution matters was the beginning of my realisation that a government assurance should always be received with a large measure of scepticism. Following the BSE disaster I suspect that a large minority of the population would not place much credence on a government assurance that this or that is 'safe' or unlikely to affect your health. That is sad but at the same time a welcome reminder to government and its agencies that the public is now much more sophisticated, as are the lobby groups which were easy targets in the seventies for snide remarks from officials and Ministers about the beards, sandals and the 'veggie' brigade.

Having said that, the DoE team I worked with was not overtly cynical and, on the whole, would judge a case put forward by any interest group on its merits. An example of this was the handling of the debate in 1972 arising from the 'Blue Print for Survival' proposals published in the E*cologist* magazine, which provided us all with an opportunity to revisit the policy of pursuing continuing growth in the economy. The thesis was that our very survival was threatened by the western world's constant striving for greater and greater growth measured in terms of growth in GNP per capita, and we should examine the case for a simpler and more environmentally sustainable lifestyle. Interestingly the same thesis had a short-lived outing in the aftermath of the 2001 Foot and Mouth disease outbreak when it was realised the spread of the disease was aided by the focus of livestock sales on a very few centres, with cattle trucks criss-crossing the length and breadth of the country, rather than the use of smaller local marts and slaughter facilities. After the funeral pyres some brave souls suggested that we should take the opportunity provided by large scale farm destocking to think afresh whether there was a 'better way' and how we might return to more environmentally friendly farming units. Examples of farming activities in Sweden and New Zealand were examined. The price of change was acknowledged as more expensive food to the consumer, but 'so be it' said some pundits, in the interests of more sustainable living. Needless to say we have heard little more of this, either from the re-badged Ministry responsible for agriculture or the food distribution and retail industry. Big business interests are at risk but to be fair how much public support would there be for dearer food? In my view leadership is required and this would need to come from government itself and in turn from Brussels and the Community.

I had three and a half years in IC Division and enjoyed it immensely. I had good bosses and an excellent small staff. Although I had a change of Assistant Secretary from Phyllis James to Tony Woolmer this was a change over for me as smooth as baton change in a relay race. Tony Woolmer had entered the Civil Service as a direct entry Principal from the army. I came across a number of former army officers (and one ex navy man) during my own career. All I met were impressive in their own way and all showed the qualities of man management and leadership that is promoted in Ministry of Defence recruitment posters and advertisements. Also they had what we now describe as 'good interpersonal skills' and were excellent in consulting staff and running a happy and motivated office. Maybe I was lucky as I found them all direct, honest and uncomplicated which is more than I could say for many of my colleagues entering the Service via the usual graduate recruitment route.

On moving to my next posting in October 1973 I felt good about the Civil Service and good about my career choice. After a bit of badgering of Establishments Division I even got the posting I wanted and that was to one of the Commercial Relations and Exports Divisions (CRE) dealing with overseas trade policy and relations. This work was very much at the heart of the former Board of Trade which had been amalgamated with Mintech to form the new Department of Trade and Industry (DTI). Past Board of Trade staff included the former Prime Minister Harold Wilson and for years after amalgamation to become DTI former Board of Trade staff continued to identify themselves as 'Trade' people and often their careers remained on the trade side of the new Department. Jobs in CRE were sought after, considered to have a modicum of mystique and prestige, dealing as they did with the FCO and our embassies overseas. Perhaps more by accident than any plan either by myself or my personnel officers I was to spend most of the rest of my Civil Service career on internationally linked policy work.

Chapter 9

Exporting is Fun

Encouraging British firms to export was always a government priority during my years in DTI and its predecessors including the Board of Trade, a name which continued to be used in a formal sense. In later years one Secretary of State, Michael Heseltine, was to assume the old title of President of the Board of Trade. This venerable title is not to be confused with the British Overseas Trade Board (BOTB) which was the body composed of business people and officials charged with directing the government's export services at home and overseas. Over my twenty years in the job I have seen just about every approach possible to raising the UK's export game. These have ranged from the threatening approach of 'Export or Die' to the exploits of a cartoon character called 'Export 'Enry'. We even had 'Superman' advertisements with a BOTB Clark Kent clutching a small bowler hatted British businessman in his arms as he soared skywards. Some will remember the 'Exporting is Fun' campaign but most were earnest and slightly dull, backed by numerous video presentations featuring successful businessmen with a view *pour encourager les autres,* including the use of broadcaster Brian Redhead exhorting us to export to Europe. I had the pleasure of meeting Mr Redhead at one of our export conferences and was able to see him in action with an audience. He was impressive and could do a piece to camera that was word perfect after only a brief look at a script. I am sure the likes of 'Export 'Enry' and 'Exporting is Fun' will feature in future export campaigns although I seriously doubt their efficacy.

In October 1973 I joined the Commercial Relations and Exports Branch 2 (CRE2) and spent three years here dealing with Latin America. In March 1980 I was to return to exports policy with the Exports to Europe Branch and to spend the last nine years of my civil service career on export policy and export services, ending up as Director of Exports for the sixteen counties that constitute the south-east of England. During this time I was involved in every type of export campaign or gimmick imaginable and a few of these of my own making. I would be very surprised to witness a fresh and new idea that had not been tried over my years of close involvement in exports services to British industry. Passing on this experience to the north-east of Scotland in the '90s was a challenge I will return to later.

CRE2, based in DTI Headquarters at 1,Victoria Street, was headed up by Assistant Secretary Mike Treble, who had supervisory responsibilities for Australasia and the Caribbean as well as for me and Latin America. In the jargon of the Foreign Office I was the Latin America 'desk officer' and as such was the focus of expertise within DTI for all the countries concerned. For most of my time I was responsible for only those countries in the subcontinent south of the border between Panama and Colombia, although for a short time I had responsibility for the Central American countries in addition. I had no choice in the geographical patch I was assigned to but I could not have been more delighted as I knew hardly anything about this part of the world and it was a wonderful opportunity to learn. I had a staff of about ten and all were excellent, enthusiastic and well informed. On taking up the post I felt a bit nervous about meeting my predecessor, Charles Cammell, as he was very reluctant to move on from the desk, but that was a decision made by Establishments and not me. Charles was an ex-army man, and very polite and correct although he did make it clear to me that it was not his wish to move on. However he was very helpful and friendly in the handover and particularly over briefing on the staff I was to inherit. His approach was very much in army officer tradition and with a real concern for the welfare of his 'men'. He discussed members of staff in turn and how each responded to pressure, the quality of their work and even down to the form of address he perceived they felt comfortable with. I inherited two HEOs and Charles advised that the senior one like to be referred to as 'Mr' and the younger by his first name. Charles was in no way patronising or condescending but had a genuine concern for his staff and I much respected what I saw of him during a relatively short handover, which is the sort I like. I find handovers embarrassing for both parties, the shorter the better, and this is no reflection on the person I am handing over to or taking over from.

The learning curve was a steep one. Mike Treble, my new boss, suggested an early and extensive familiarisation tour of the patch, but first I needed to have some understanding of the history of each country, the pattern of respective trade, and current (and past) irritants to commercial and political relations. Charles Cammell passed on a number of pithy but useful generalisations and I still remember some of these. For example as a rough guide each country in the subcontinent particularly dislikes its immediate neighbour more than any other. This is a big generalisation but going clockwise around from Colombia it has some relevance and there were often local wars at some point in the not too distant past to illustrate the point. It is a fact, for example, that Brazilians are not over keen on Argentines and vice versa and neither worry too much about the Uruguayans. There is no love lost between the Argentine and Chile (and we capitalised on this in the Falkland conflict), and similarly with Chile and Peru and so on round the clock. I leave out the British, Dutch and French former territories on the north east shoulder, namely Guyana, Surinam and French Guiana which were dealt with in the office as part of the Central America and Caribbean desk. There were other rules of thumb like comparing the Argentines and Brazilians to the Greeks and Romans respectively. There is some truth in this in so far as the Argentines will spend ages arguing about the merits of proposal but never quite get around to the action whereas the Brazilians are the Romans. You want a straight road through hundreds of miles of virgin forest regardless of the challenges? Then the Brazilians will make the decision and do it, and usually very well. Argentina is always the country of great promise and a sleeping giant that continues to sleep. It has been said what God grows in the day the Argentines seem capable of destroying over night, and again there is a grain of truth as self-destruction is the reality rather than any exterior threat, be that economic or otherwise.

My staff had an excellent grasp of detail for their allocated countries and were enthusiastic and committed to seeing our trade increase. Although they were the front line for any inquiries from business people who wished an in-depth assessment of a market, none of the staff had ever visited the countries for which they were the responsible experts. For example the desk officer for Brazil would write briefs for Ministers visiting Brazil, brief businesses and including many well known household names, provide a view to the Export Credits Guarantee Department as to the risks involved in providing insurance cover for businesses operating in the market and much more, and all without having set foot in the country or having a knowledge of the language. The reason for this was partly cost but also, as I was to prove, a snobbishness about the ability of a mere Executive Officer or Higher Executive Officer being able to handle adequately an overseas familiarisation and briefing trip. There were shades here of the officer and other ranks split mirrored in the separate Administrative and Executive streams. After much huffing and puffing by my bosses I managed a small breakthrough and arranged for my HEO, Bob Mackay, to visit Brazil as a representative of the Department and as an escort officer to Princess Alexandra and her husband making a trade visit to Brazil at the time. The Princess was a great favourite with the Department and in contrast to some of my colleagues the Princess was most helpful and treated Bob Mackay with genuine warmth and included him where possible. I remember there was a scheduled overnight stop in Dakar, in Senegal, and an informal party was laid on for the royal entourage. Princess Alexandra insisted Bob join them. It was more than just a gracious gesture of the type that ensures the groom is fed and watered as my staff member was made welcome as a key member of the entourage. Subsequently I managed to secure one or two further overseas visits for staff.

I should explain that my staff were the country experts in the Department as far trade and commercial matters were concerned but also had to acquire a good overview of the politics within the market and how these impinged on business risks including physical risks, business and social conventions and under this heading we coyly included the conventions on bribery. As civil servants we were in a difficult position here as we could not be seen to condone any form of bribery, but nonetheless the practice was endemic in South America. We were aware many big contracts relied on 'facilitation' fees to various government officials and in some markets to the minister concerned. Some British firms claimed they would have nothing to do with such practices and I guess in certain cases this was true, but it was difficult to successfully cultivate many markets without succumbing to a degree of palm greasing. This would range from a small consideration for ensuring your customs paper work had been helpfully 'checked' and so easing release of your goods from a remote shed miles from anywhere, to serious sums of money to secure a contract. The official line was not to deny that bribery was often a fact of life but staff could not get involved in offering any advice to British businessmen as to who and how to bribe. We recommended contact with a number of British firms involved in 'consultancy' or facilitator operations that could provide this service. There was skill involved and not just in knowing whom to bribe but how to pitch the bribe. Offer the foreign official too small a 'fee' then he will be insulted and one is in a worse position than before. However offer too large an amount then one could frighten off the official to be bribed. Occasionally representatives of some of these bribery experts would drop into the office for a chat and some exchange of intelligence on a market. Many such operations were not much more than a man, a telephone and a list of contacts. This was an area where our access to more covert sources of information was, in practice, of little use to us. Sometimes such information confirmed only what we suspected, namely this official or that minister was on the take. In countries where such activity was endemic corroborating intelligence was hardly a revelation!

Our relationship with the Foreign Office was a complex one and in all my years involved in international trade it remained a cause of friction and frustration. The front line were the FCO staff employed overseas in nearly 200 embassies, consulates general, consulates and trade development offices. All our market information from official sources came from this large and expensive field force. It provided a raft of export intelligence material and also operated, on behalf of the British Overseas Trade Board, schemes to facilitate market penetration. Some services were tailor-made to the individual firm, who would profile their requirements and for a small fee would be sent a regular stream of export opportunities matching the products that the firm had on offer. This overseas operation also would provide us with product sector reports and some of these would be quite learned and comprehensive. Most 'posts' (our abbreviation for any FCO overseas operation, be that a full embassy or a satellite consulate) would provide, for example, a report on the market for agricultural machinery and this would list agents, main distributors and technical requirements of the particular market. Such sector reports would be updated on a rolling basis depending on priorities.

At the same time we received copies of ambassador and senior embassy staff reports covering the more political developments in the market. This type of reporting found its way into several government departments including the Exports Credit Guarantee Department (ECGD), Treasury, Bank of England, Overseas Development and of course to the FCO Headquarters where there were 'country desks' including a Latin American Department, which to some extent overlapped the role of my 'desk'. I found it amusing going to interdepartmental meetings to assess a particular market when we would all earnestly give our view, but most of us were drawing on the very same briefing material, supplied by the Foreign Office.

My first tour of my new patch involved a three week marathon journey starting in Buenos Aires and travelling north through Uruguay to Brazil calling at Consulates General in Rio and Sao Paulo and our Embassy in Brasilia, then on to La Paz and Santa Cruz in Bolivia and finally to Caracas in Venezuela. This was a gruelling exercise and added to by the convention that one was usually invited to stay in the homes of diplomatic staff, normally the Commercial Counsellor or the First Secretary in charge of commercial work. The Foreign Office, like the Armed Services, was very hierarchical and the invitation to stay came from an officer at roughly the equivalent level. As a Principal my equivalent would be First Secretary. This offer of hospitality was not entirely altruistic as diplomatic staff were provided with large houses with additional entertainment and bedroom space and these facilities were expected to be used. Statistics on usage were well crawled over by the Inspectors who descended on all overseas posts on a regular basis. These inspections have some parallel with HMI inspections of schools except they impinge much more on the individual than do HMI inspections. Inspectors recommend changes in local allowances and facilities, and much which directly affects the living standards as well as the status of the individual. So the generous living facilities have to be used and have to be seen to be so.

Some of my diplomatic service colleagues were delightful, friendly and genuinely welcoming. A significant minority went through the motions and the experience would not be much more welcoming than a superior 'bed and breakfast', or at least in terms of the surroundings. The size of house and furnishings, even down to the curtains, reflected grade, as most of the furniture and certainly the fixtures and fittings were provided by HMG. I remember arriving in Bolivia just after an Inspection and an ongoing dispute over the log allowance for evening fires, and these are a necessity in La Paz with altitudes up to 12,000 feet. The allowance was grade related, perhaps reflecting room sizes, but in practice it took as many logs to keep a lower grade diplomat and his family warm as a more senior rank. I found it amusing and slightly Gilbertian but not so my hosts.

Staying with colleagues, however charming and welcoming, means one can never completely relax after a long day of meetings and visits. Rarely, and understandably so, was one returning to a relaxing evening in a colleague's home but usually to a formal dinner arranged in your honour with up to a dozen guests that may be, if my host had worked hard at his guest list, interested in meeting me and sharing some mutual interest. After guests had disappeared, and happily in diplomatic circles guests are given and recognise the host's signal that it is time to leave, usually there was an informal debriefing session. This provided a useful checklist of the occasion including recall of bits and pieces of gossip that would be fed via a memo to colleagues the next morning. This time of the evening could be an opportunity to get to know your host's wife. I never encountered the reverse situation where my host was a women and meeting her husband. This may have reflected overseas posting policy and that South America was a very male dominated and 'macho' society. Occasionally these late night chats after guests had departed were very pleasant, even relaxing, and sometimes led to friendships which survived into the period of a posting back to London. On the other hand I can remember occasions where my stay in a colleague's house was a trying and unpleasant experience. On one occasion I was not well and had picked up a bug that caused me to take to my bed with the shivers and an obvious temperature. The wife of my host could not have cared less except it was an obvious concern to her that she was going to be burdened with a sick guest. There was a bit of a panic and antibiotics were purchased from the local pharmacist and by the next morning I was feeling better and able to move on. By some strange coincidence later I met a contact in Scotland who had a friend who had acted as a nanny to the couple in question. She was treated as badly.

During my stint in CRE2 I visited every market in my patch except Paraguay, where I could convince no one that the market justified the cost of my visit. Also I failed to secure a visit to Chile. I started my job on the Latin America desk about a month after the CIA-backed brutal overthrow on 11 September 1973 of the democratically elected Marxist government led by Salvador Allende. So, at that time, there was no question of my visiting Chile. A couple of years later all was in hand for me to visit Santiago. However, in 1975 a young British doctor, Sheila Cassidy, had been arrested and tortured by the Pinochet-led regime. There was outrage at home and as a result our Ambassador, Reggie Secondé, was recalled and my visit was cancelled. I was sorry to have missed the opportunity to visit this beautiful country and one with strong historical links with Britain, but I was so glad to see our Government, then a Labour-led one after Harold Wilson's election in October 1974, say enough was enough and take some action. I had access to the regular reports from our Embassy in Santiago which I saw as far from objective. Many 'expat' British in Chile took the view that the ends justified the means and that Chile's people had been mercifully freed from the yoke of Marxism. The way that three years of Marxist rule ended in Chile is said to haunt the imagination of the left and so it is for me. I had to wait for over twenty-five years and Pinochet's house arrest in England before I could ever consider our relations with Chile in anything like an objective manner. The help which Chile gave us during the Falkland Islands war just made matters worse as far as I was concerned. With friends like these... A DTI Minister at the time of the Cassidy affair was Michael Meacher, later also a Minister in the Blair administration. I had to see Meacher on a number of occasions and I remember him as one of the few Ministers that I dealt with who would ask questions and enter into debate with you on your briefing and advice. I remember him as polite and welcoming and I enjoyed my brief meetings in his office.

The Latin America job was the busiest I had in terms of the sheer volume of information to be read and assimilated. There was a daily stream of reports from 'posts'. Correspondence flowed not just from my opposite numbers in the commercial departments in posts but also included more political reports of one kind and another. Often these generated comment from home Whitehall departments including my own Department, the parent FCO but also ECGD, Bank of England, Treasury, British Council and Overseas Development. I would be the recipient of copy correspondence. Then there was the more routine commercial reporting ranging from notices on specific export opportunities to the steady stream of sector reports on the export potential for anything from power station equipment to cosmetics. Many of these detailed and knowledgeable market reports were usually, but not always, put together by those commercial staff in posts designated as 'locally engaged'. Such staff were recruited locally by the post and sometimes were resident British 'expats' but frequently were nationals of the country concerned. Many were excellent and in spite of their low status in the hierarchy put in a lot of work for a modest reward, with little or no career structure. However the commercial sections of large posts relied heavily on locally engaged staff and especially for the production of export opportunity notices, the basis of the Export Intelligence Service to which British businesses subscribed for a fee.

I got to know some of the locally engaged staff quite well. My wife and I have retained links over the years since with a delightful lady who worked in our embassy in Montevideo, Uruguay. I learnt much about this small but proud country from our friend. As I explained earlier, as a rule of thumb no Latin American country has much love for its immediate neighbour and Uruguayans are no exception, with a deep distrust of the Argentines who were seen as arrogant. However Uruguay, sandwiched between two large neighbours, Brazil and Argentina, has had to play a canny game. Both neighbours used Uruguay for recreation and for convenient placement of funds, ill-gotten or otherwise. Argentina and Uruguay share a small and continuing influential community of British descent, reflecting Britain's key earlier role in the development of the southern cone of the subcontinent, and this is particularly so in the Argentine, even down to an English public school clone, St George's, in Buenos Aires or 'BA' as it was known in the office. None of this is by way of personal criticism as I came to much admire both countries and their people. Like all associated with the region, I share the frustration that, and particularly with Argentina, they cannot 'get a grip' and realise the enormous potential which God has given them in terms of climate, land and raw materials. BA is by far the most sophisticated capital in Latin America, and more reminiscent of Paris and Europe. Indeed it is said that BA is a city with French architecture, with its people of Italian origin, speaking Spanish, but wishing to be British. Again, there is more than a grain of truth in this.

With my waking hours during visits to the patch monopolised by a programme set by my Diplomatic Service colleagues there was very little chance to get to know a country and its people other than seen through FCO eyes, FCO briefs and FCO choreographed cocktail and dinner parties arranged in my honour. The overseas reality and FCO reporting can sometimes diverge, for a number of reasons. Access to locally engaged staff was a useful check on the insight and objectivity of our own diplomatic team. It was for this reason I made a positive effort to get some time alone with the locally engaged staff when visiting overseas posts, as well as making time for them during their regular 'duty tours' or orientation visits to the UK. On many occasions we entertained local staff at our Surrey home, so giving them a break from the grind of a long UK tour with only a drab hotel room to return to each night. Our government was not generous with its UK subsistence rates, although overseas daily allowances were often more than adequate, no doubt reflecting that the rates overseas were influenced more by FCO Inspectors than the Treasury.

With the best will in the world there was bound to be friction in an arrangement where the home team was in one organisation, with a separate career structure and a different ethos, and its overseas sales force is in a completely different organisation. In essence the DTI, and its Board of Trade predecessor, supposedly took the lead on commercial and export policy and provided the main interface with its client, British business, whilst the Foreign Office were responsible for staffing and running the then 200 or so overseas posts with commercial responsibilities. However, it was even more complex than that since there were one or two exceptions to the home departmental links to industry, with old DHSS encouraging the export of medical supplies and equipment and the much maligned agricultural ministry, MAFF, responsible for some aspects of the food and drink trade and especially where there was a health or disease implication. MAFF for example had a veterinary officer stationed at the time in the Buenos Aires embassy. This was linked to earlier problems with corned and other beef imports from the Argentine and Uruguay.

Although the FCO Latin America desk focussed primarily on the broader political side of our relations, they nonetheless played an active role in setting commercial policy and were sometimes sufficiently proactive as to lead to tensions between us. The British Overseas Trade Board which included representation from both DTI and the FCO struggled to establish some market prioritisation, realising that we could not promote every market equally and some were a lot more important to our balance of payments than others. About 60% of our exports then went to the European Community with Germany sharing the top market place with the United States. At the time our total exports to South America accounted for 3% of total UK exports. I never disputed the potential of markets like Brazil but for many small British firms Europe was nearer and much easier.

The setting of market priorities was a cause for much game playing and could take up of lot of time and usually was, at best, unproductive and, at worst, detrimental to the UK export effort. Sometimes an agreement on market prioritisation would be undermined by a pushy Ambassador and his staff who, no doubt for career reasons, would promote their own market campaign. Market priorities were promoted to British business in the DTI magazine *Trade & Industry*, but this never stopped the regular flow of articles promoting the joys of exporting to minor markets in all corners of the globe. The result was that a firm's export director reading our literature and *Trade & Industry* was bombarded with a mishmash of 'opportunities' and no clear picture of the BOTB's main market thrust, or at least the thrust was diluted. I was guilty of this myself and I remember publishing a leaflet entitled 'And what about Bolivia?' I had just returned from a visit to the market and my Bolivia desk officer was keen to raise the flag for this forgotten market. However most initiatives for market promotions came from our diplomat colleagues in the market itself. Some thought that their market genuinely offered unrealised potential for British exporters and others, I suspect, saw their personal profile as needing a boost. Such campaigns could lead to a ministerial visit or, and even more prized, a visit to the market by a member of the royal family. Both were good for careers and in the case of a royal visit there was the lure of a personal decoration. Of these the easiest to capture was a visit by a UK Minister, and come the poorer weather at home I would expect at least one Ministerial visit to one of 'my' countries. Such overseas market visits entailed a lot of work for me in arranging and briefing but even more for colleagues in the country to be visited. I think FCO colleagues rather overestimated the value of such a visit in terms of brownie points for them, and rarely, in my view, did it help our export effort much. Occasionally, securing very large export orders can be influenced by visits from UK politicians and then only at Prime Minister or very senior Cabinet Minister level. The well-known examples are invariably controversial. On the whole Ministers enjoyed their visits and, cynically, we saw our primary role as ensuring they had a good time and were well looked after. We did not look for any new initiatives or expect them. Yes, Ministers came back enthusiastic but enthusiasm, like all holiday experiences, soon faded to be quickly replaced by the next visit to British Leyland or what other delights that the Minister's Private Office could cook up to keep their Minister constantly in motion.

Sometimes initiatives for such overseas visits were pursued without any consultation with my team. If we cautioned or queried a proposed export promotion strategy we would be rubbished by our Foreign Office colleagues, accusing us of knowing nothing of the market and that these decisions could only be taken by those on the ground, in the market. This was notwithstanding it was more likely that the home team had the better contact with exporters and a more realistic view of their capacity to cope with an ever widening focus of export effort and, more important, the management capacity of a business to cope with a new market.

Within the Latin American patch I tried valiantly to impose some sense of proportion and priority. This did not assist my popularity with some colleagues. Brazil was an important market and the posts there would press for constant exposure and position, risking the exclusion of other significant markets in the area. There was also rivalry between senior staff based respectively in Rio, San Paulo and Brasilia. Some pursued their place in the limelight by a bullying aggression, calling upon their London based colleagues or attempting to deal over my head within my own department. Neither approach worked and anyway my superiors had far more important problems to attend to than a bleat from a commercial counsellor in some far flung post. Other posts, and these were in the majority, thank God, used a mixture of charm and guile in raising the profile of their market, or more likely their personal profile.

The only foreign Head of State visit during my time on the desk was by President Ernesto Geisel of Brazil. This was a State Visit with all that entails including a full dress dinner at the Guildhall in May 1976, hosted by the Lord Mayor of London with Peter Shore, the Department of

Trade's Secretary of State and the Duke and Duchess of Kent present. The Duke was Vice-President of the British Overseas Trade Board with an office and staff in the 1, Victoria Street building that I worked in at the time. Fiona and I were invited to the Guildhall, as was my Assistant Secretary, Mike Treble and his wife, along with many other Whitehall officials and partners. A lot of work went into briefing and planning although the lion's share of the work was undertaken by my opposite number in the FCO Latin American Department, and for our efforts we both received medals from President Geisel. I did experience a slight frisson when my turn came to shake hands with a military dictator who is alleged to have said that 'democracy is far too delicate a flower to be entrusted to the people'. There have been times during a career in public service when I have felt sympathetic to this interpretation. My only other brush with dictatorial power was in Uruguay when a senior general running some aspect of government offered to show us his pay slip to demonstrate he was just an 'ordinary soldier doing a difficult job'. He might well have been but we declined his offer. It was an unpleasant period in that country's history.

The British Overseas Trade Board or 'BOTB' was a Board of the good and great of British business with, at the time, a token woman member who doubled up as the representative of small business. The Board was always chaired by a senior businessman although perhaps its most flamboyant Chair was more a political hybrid in the form of Lord Jellicoe to whom I will return later. The oddity was the appointment of the Duke of Kent as Vice-Chair. I suspect this was more a convenience job created for him. Indeed a similar role subsequently was taken on by Andrew, Duke of York. In fairness the Duke of Kent took his role seriously and worked hard at it although his personality, in my view, made it difficult for him to reach out to people. With officials he was formal to the extent of coldness, but correct and polite. In a later job in DTI as Director of Exports for the South East of England I used to accompany him on many visits to firms and events. He was never in any way difficult but there was never any small talk. On one occasion only did he ever offer me a lift in his official car. He was usually accompanied by a military serviceman as his aide who behaved in exactly the same manner as his master. I would meet the Duke at the visit location and would get into my own transport when we moved on to the next point on the itinerary. In the case of the BOTB Chairmen I served under I would always accompany them in their official car. This made good sense for them since we were able to deal with last minute briefing during the journey, and perhaps more important, the debriefing where I would be given a clear steer as to follow-up action.

Towards the end of my career at the Department I got a little bolder and would attempt to engage the Duke in discussion of trade and export policy or matters more immediate to the visit. It was hard work, but not because he was not knowledgeable, as all said he had a good grasp of international trade matters. I can only remember one exchange that might be described as a debate, and that concerned the then BOTB role at the Royal Agricultural Show at Stoneleigh where I had built up a significant presence over the years. The Ministry of Agriculture was belatedly getting its export promotion act together and the suggestion had been made that we should pass our promotional activity at the Royal over to Agriculture. The Duke said he was strongly against the BOTB opting out.

The Duke was assigned a relatively junior official who ran his office in 1,Victoria Street. I got to know one such Secretary quite well and was relieved to find out in the early days of my contact with the Duke that it was not just me who found the whole process such hard work. However unlike some other senior royals, the Duke of Kent was respected by staff.

Below the Board itself was another layer of business advisers based on geographic groupings. For example there was a European Trade Committee, a Latin America Advisory Group and so on, covering all markets, and each charged with advising the British Overseas Trade Board on trade opportunities, trade barriers, marketing, and market prioritisation in their patch. I was responsible for oversight of and agreeing the funding of the Area Advisory Group covering Latin America, which during my time was based in Canning House, in Belgrave Square. This was once the home of George Canning (1770-1827) who was British Foreign Secretary in 1823 and was particularly helpful in the move to independence by the former Spanish colonies in South America.

The advisory group was made up largely of businessmen with UK commercial interests in the Latin American markets. The service industries such as banking, shipping and insurance featured strongly with manufacturing in the minority, but included also those who were essentially traders representing a number of UK firms. The Whitehall family was well represented including the FCO, and ECGD. I remember well the FCO's Hugh Carless, who was the then Head of the Latin America Department. Hugh was the archetypal urbane and, usually, unruffled diplomat, although I was able to occasionally ruffle a feather, but this was barely perceptible to those who were not old hands at the games played. In spite of all the failures of British foreign policy over the years and some very silly diplomats, I envied the ease with which FCO colleagues were able to influence the views of my business colleagues on the advisory group. However transparent and political the line being peddled, FCO colleagues had the powerful retort if challenged by the likes of me (businessmen rarely challenged) that they had the expertise on the ground, and it was difficult to effectively counter this. It was unlikely that any of our businessmen gave their time to Canning House for purely altruistic reasons and access to inside knowledge was a key incentive to turn up and give of their time. It was usually imprudent for businessmen to upset the Foreign Office, as that intimate chat with the Ambassador or Commercial Counsellor over lunch or dinner when next in Quito, or wherever, would be lost to them, with a black mark besides their names and a label as 'difficult' or 'indiscreet'.

I respected Hugh and he was certainly no fool. He was Eric Newby's travel companion in Newby's book "A walk in the Hindu Kush". My immediate boss at DTI, Mike Treble, affected a similar laid-back stance but underneath was more prickly with, I suspect, a very different background to Carless. I was never quite sure of Mike's strategy but it seemed to me that I was always left with the sometimes unpopular task of opposing some aspect of the FCO's strategy. Mike was a master at delegation and particularly when it came to the annual exercise of auditing Canning House's accounts, and agreeing the next tranche of grant needed to run the Canning House institution with its library, staff, business and cultural events. Never did I get Mike's endorsement, or otherwise, for the policy line and government grant I recommended. However whatever I recommended was provided and Canning House's Chief Executive seemed grateful.

One of the roles of Canning House was to provide a forum for business to meet visiting Latin American dignitaries as well as FCO staff home on leave and making duty tours. These usually took the form of a reception and a presentation before an audience of businessmen and members of the Whitehall 'family'. There were often present strangers, to me anyway, badged as belonging to the FCO Latin American Department. I could not understand why I did not recognise their names as I did have a directory of the Department and thought I knew everyone pretty well. At one such reception I approached a particularly striking young lady and asked why I had not come across her during the course of my work with the FCO. She was evasive and it was not until some time afterwards, and with the help of a colleague to compare notes, that I realised she was a representative of 'our friends'. She must have thought me somewhat naive.

I worked with a number of Chairmen of the Advisory Committee and all, bar one, were helpful and delightful to work with. I recall particularly David Montgomery who inherited his father's title as Viscount Montgomery of Alamein. David was down to earth and approachable. His business interests in the Latin American markets included consumer goods. Another Chairman was from Barings, and one a journalist and Labour promoted peer, Lord Chalfont.

Canning House also gave me and my staff the opportunity to meet diplomats from the London-based embassies of the countries we were responsible for. The most active and professional were the Brazilians but equally persistent was little Ecuador and mainly in the form of the Ambassador himself. He was a frequent visitor to our office with his plea that we should import more Ecuadorian bananas. Ecuador is a large producer but not in the league of its Andean neighbour, Colombia. The international market in bananas is a complex one with large US fruit firms dominating the central and south America distribution and marketing chains. The United Kingdom and similarly the French have operated a commonwealth or colonial preference scheme giving the likes of the Windward Islands a chance to compete when, in practice, there is very little else they can grow and then with some difficulty because of soil and climate. The banana trade continues to create tension between the US and the European Community and the arguments have changed little since my time on the desk. Of all the countries I visited Ecuador was the most delightful with a climate in Quito that is eternal spring due to its position almost on the equator and its altitude. However down in Guayaquil on the coast it is hot and steamy. On one visit I took the option of travelling down from Quito to Guayaquil in the embassy's Range Rover. It was a hair-raising experience with an embassy driver who spoke no English and with brakes that eventually failed halfway through the 8,000 feet descent. The brake failure was seen by the driver as a huge joke as we hurtled through small villages scattering livestock and children alike. What was interesting, when I could tear my eyes from the road, was the change in vegetation and towards the lower end mile upon mile of banana plantations.

Rarely did my career in the Civil Service provide many social occasions that included Fiona but my time on the Latin America desk was an exception and we did attend quite a few receptions together as guests of embassies and business. The highlight for Fiona was the annual reception at Claridges as guest of Sir Raymond Smith. Sir Raymond was an arms dealer based in Caracas with close links to one of the ruling parties in

Venezuela at the time. His receptions were generous affairs with lots of champagne and a good time was had by all. I visited Sir Raymond at his office in Caracas with my boss. He spoke so quietly one had to lean forward across his desk to hear him. We were never sure whether this was a negotiating technique but, along with a strong smell of old fashioned cologne, his trade and his links with the military in Venezuela, combined to make a visit to Raymond Smith a slightly sinister occasion.

There were many other uncomfortable occasions experienced during my travels in the subcontinent. On my first visit to Bolivia the Ambassador and his wife took me out for a weekend drive in the embassy Land Rover. There were not too many places one could drive to from La Paz without a four-wheel drive vehicle and so this was the Ambassador's official car. I expected to join the Hope-Joneses with a locally employed driver but what I was not expecting was another passenger in the front seat carrying a sub-machine gun. I was told not to worry and it was highly unlikely anything would happen to us! The Hope-Joneses were unconventional diplomat material and slightly dotty, but in the most endearing way. Mrs Hope-Jones was a keen gardener and proudly showed me her new greenhouse but what she was more proud of was winning a battle of wits with the FCO Works Department in disguising the end use of this addition to Her Britannic Majesty's Embassy in La Paz. As I said earlier one's view of a visit to a post is very much coloured by how you were treated. I was lucky in La Paz because as well as the Hope-Joneses I was looked after by First Secretary Green and his wife. The Greens were a young couple and I suspect not long married. They were kind and helpful and I enjoyed their company. I was asked to join them on a skiing trip. I explained that I could not ski but they pressed me to come along for the ride. They had an elderly short wheel base Land Rover and with me in the back plus a lot of equipment and petrol for the ski tow we crawled from the 12,000 feet at the top end of La Paz to the 17,000 feet of the makeshift ski facility. I tottered out from the shack that acted as base and with the aid of a stout bamboo pole attempted to walk up the slope. The altitude was too much for me and I felt very sick. I was invalided down to the shack and plied with coca leaf tea which I was assured would sort my sickness. It worked a treat but I stayed inside and enjoyed the view from a chair. This was pioneering skiing and for the enthusiast. The scenery was, literally, breathtaking. I gather the Greens decided shortly after that diplomatic life was not for them. I remember them expressing an interest in aid work. One of those strange coincidences of life was that for a short while at Cranleigh I was taught maths by an old, tatty and very eccentric master also called Hope-Jones. This was the Ambassador's father.

I was to enjoy another ride with armed escort during one of my visits to Brazil. British banking and steel were involved in the building of the long bridge linking Rio de Janeiro to Niteroi on the other side of Rio's spectacular bay. I was in town for the official opening of the new bridge and was standing beside Leo Rothschild the banker awaiting allocation of a car in the cavalcade that would formally drive us across the bridge. I was expecting a place somewhere towards the back of the pecking order but that was not to be. I was separated from Leo Rothschild and ushered into the first car heading up the cavalcade. Inside was a policeman with a machine gun of sorts and a driver. The idea was that the first car would travel some way in front just in case there were 'problems'. It was clear, as far as HMG were concerned, I was dispensable.

Overall I enjoyed my three years or so dealing with Latin America and learnt so much about a part of the world that even now rarely features on British holiday itineraries. I had a superb staff and a very happy office. Ideally I could have expected a more supportive boss but, in comparison to experiences to come later in my career, Mike Treble was reasonable and approachable. I gained a good insight to life in an overseas post and left thinking I would try for a secondment to the FCO. There was a regular if smallish exchange of staff between DTI and the FCO and I made my wishes known to our Establishments people. However there were aspects of life overseas that at the time I had experienced but had tended to overlook. A constant niggle for me whenever I mixed in a social context with colleagues was the tendency for their politics to be further to the right than one would have expected in colleagues of similar backgrounds back in Victoria Street. Even worse were the wives who became more Conservative than any similar group one could find even in Surrey's leafy lanes. Maybe there are social pressures in a small and tight knit group holed up in a foreign country to conform to the officer group norms set by the Ambassador or Consul General, and particularly where there is no formal division between the officer class and other ranks.

My overseas colleagues, on the whole, lived well and in spite of frequent moans furniture and equipment provided by 'Works' was of good, if uniform, design and standard. Some of the posts in the patch were not 'hardship' postings although climate in the likes of Rio and the altitude in La Paz, Bogota and Quito could exacerbate any health weaknesses. There were also real dangers of kidnap or worse in such as Colombia and, during my time, Bolivia. Most colleagues at my level and above did have their own houses in the UK that they let to cover the mortgage payments during overseas postings. Families were required to move and establish a new set of friends every three to four years, with a home posting, apart from leave, every six or seven years. Some countries had good English schools, at least at primary school age, but most parents seemed to favour sending older children home to boarding schools. The FCO heavily subsidised the fees but for better public schools parents still had to find an appreciable shortfall. I guess a subsidised boarding school package in the UK provided some with access to an education package for their children that would otherwise not be available, and this coloured their behaviour and political outlook. During a Labour government I was shocked to hear the political hostility expressed by some of my FCO colleagues. There did not seem to be the degree of studied Civil Service neutrality and professionalism that we took for granted in Whitehall.

Few take on the FCO and win as Labour ministers have found. Foreign Office networking is legendary and impressive. Tessa Blackstone, now Baroness Blackstone, produced a report critical of the FCO overseas operation but its recommendations were efficiently rubbished by businessmen and many others who were wheeled out to support the status quo. The report was buried.

Chapter 10

Fraternal greetings

Amongst the pages of advice given by Establishments Division on joining Mintech was the official blessing and encouragement to join a Civil Service union which was couched in terms of making a contribution to the life and fabric of the Department. I was very quickly approached by the union appropriate to my grade and status, namely the First Division Association or the 'FDA'. This union catered for the top-level of Civil Servants from Assistant Principal through to Permanent Secretary, or in other words the then Administrative Class. I cannot think that a union in any other organisation would take the name the First Division Association which is not in the least coy nor disguises in any way the perception by its membership of their own importance. The FDA was in many ways very low key and almost apologetic about being a trade union at all, but come the challenge it can be surprisingly effective in protecting its members' interests. It will produce quite good papers, as one would expect from a body representing some of the best wordsmiths in the land. It would never be as crude to talk in terms of strikes or work to rule or any of the traditional vocabulary of the rest of the trade union movement, preferring to work behind the scenes and using the Whitehall networking that is the tool of trade of the FDA membership.

I remember, as we headed into the seventies and Civil Service pay rates were beginning to seriously lag, going to an FDA meeting, which was a rare event apart from the Christmas sherry party, when the Branch Secretary or Chairman lectured us on the 'public interest'. I thought to myself at the time this is not what I pay my union dues for and here began my search for a union that would unashamedly champion my interests and leave the 'public interest', whatever that was, to those on the 'Official Side' of the table. The 'Official Side' description of 'management' or employer derives from the elaborate consultation procedure set up under the system of joint employer and employee committees or Whitley Councils, which served the Civil Service well for many years and was robust enough to cope with most disputes. However the system was inadequate to deal with then growing unrest over pay where decisions lay essentially with Ministers and the politically dominated machine established within the Treasury or later the Civil Service Department and its successor bodies.

I was not alone in my increasing sense of frustration over how pay was being handled. In the early seventies mainstream Civil Service unions were quiescent and the more strident traditions of industrial unions were still foreign to the likes of the then Society of Civil and Public servants (SCPS), the union representing the bulk of the Executive Class. This included an overlap at Principal grade with the First Division Association, or at least as far as those Principals emerging from the Executive Class were concerned. At the time of the Fulton Report in 1970 about forty per cent of the Principal grade had their origins in the Executive Class, indicating that the barrier between the Administrative and Executive classes was more permeable than was often the impression. There was a growing clamour by middle management grades for a more militant approach to wage negotiation which was not being met by Civil Service trade unions. This was spotted by Clive Jenkins who was the charismatic General Secretary of ASTMS, the union representing scientific, technical and managerial staff in business and industry. ASTMS (Astims) was a fast growing white collar union reflecting the parallel growth of technology in industry. Clive Jenkins launched a campaign to recruit Civil Servants, notwithstanding the Bridlington Agreement which was the TUC-blessed agreement to prevent poaching of members of one union by another. I joined ASTMS but cancelled my membership when ASTMS failed to achieve negotiating rights within the Service. However the ASTMS initiative certainly contributed to alerting the likes of the Society of Civil and Public Servants to the needs of their members and very quickly we saw a new militancy in the two main Civil Service unions, namely the SCPS and the union representing the clerical grades, the CPSA. I joined the SCPS branch at 1, Victoria Street and stayed with this union until the end of my Civil Service career.

For most of the time I was on the Branch Committee, although this was never by election since the Branch Committee struggled to get enough volunteers let alone arranging a competition. Over the years I became Branch Vice-Chairman and for one year I stood for and was elected to the DTI National Committee. At branch committee level we had a dedicated and committed little group with a moderate and pleasant Chairman and a Branch Secretary who was more politically committed. I am not sure whether any of us were card-carrying members of the Labour Party, although I am pretty sure none of us were Tory. I doubt if any union branch committee is representative of its members. By nature most people are passive and look for a quiet life and although union membership was high in the Civil Service at that time (91% in 1979) the rank and file membership were not in any way militant or politically motivated. Indeed one would not expect otherwise in an organisation still with a strong public service ethos and a tradition of political neutrality, and especially at middle management grades and above. The cliché of Civil Servants as holders of the ring, searching for the balanced view and middle ground and preferring the *Guardian* to the *Telegraph* was, in my experience, nonetheless true. Civil Servants were conservative and wary of political extremes, be they right or left. However those that take on the work of running the union locally must be committed, almost by definition. Our Victoria Street Branch represented the DTI headquarters staff and the degree of apathy was likely to be more than in one of the many DTI regional sites including a significant membership in Scotland and South Wales. In Scotland there was a degree of militancy seen in more traditional blue collar unions and it was no coincidence that many senior office holders in the union had a Scottish connection.

Most work at Branch Committee level is routine and verging on the boring but in line with the 90% perspiration and 10% inspiration rule applying to most tasks. We dealt with health and safety matters and here I came into my own with my scientific background. I became the Chair of the office Health and Safety Committee provided for under the Health & Safety at Work etc Act, 1974. The Branch Committee also dealt with individual cases of grievance, disciplinary cases as well as looking at and commenting on papers coming from union headquarters and the local Whitley Council apparatus. Important work was preparing for the Annual Conference of the union.

Every year we tried hard to involve the membership in preparing for Conference. We called meetings for members, circulated Motions for comment as well as proposals as to the line we intended to take. Rarely did we attract more than a couple of dozen members apart from those on the Branch Committee. That we covered the DTI Headquarters and Ministers' offices should have produced a well briefed and participating membership, although one could argue the obverse and this was a contributory factor in membership apathy. We were mindful that the Branch Committee was probably unrepresentative but there was little more we could do to get the ordinary member to involve him or herself. Again most of the crawling through the wad of draft Motions circulated by the DTI National Committee was boring but necessary work. As a Branch we put forward our own Motions for Conference and even these failed to fire the rank and file members. It would be true that the mandate we gave to those attending Conference on behalf of the Branch would likely be more strident than the average member would wish, if he or she were to express their wishes, which they did not. I guess most of the rank and file saw us activists at best harmless and at worst a minor irritant, and that we might just nudge the Government to a better pay deal. The union's role in fighting for better conditions, as opposed to pay, was even more of a turn-off, as most of our members saw their work terms and conditions as quite good, and I suppose they were. Our members did not worry about old offices and furniture and some took a perverse joy in tatty and drab surroundings. This, again, linked to the strong public service ethos that then prevailed.

Annual Conference was the highlight of the year for those lucky enough to be chosen as Branch delegates. I attended four conferences of the SCPS at venues including Blackpool, Southport and Brighton. When I was on the DTI National Committee there was a DTI pre-Conference and then the main Conference. I enjoyed these get-togethers hugely. There was a lot of partying and for us the invitation most sought after was to the party held by the Scottish contingent. These were always convivial as one would expect with Scotland-west and Glasgow predominating. I remember particularly one such event when towards the end of the evening there was a collection for the *Morning Star*, the respected communist daily newspaper. A hat was passed around and I have never seen so much paper money accumulate in so short a time. I began to wonder about the politics of the inner circle of the union. On asking around it seemed accepted that many senior office holders, if not card carrying CP (Communist Party) members, were likely fellow travellers of some kind. I was advised that if I wished to go on to greater things in the union it would help if I were Scottish or acquired some 'broad left' connections or pedigree. At the time two of our senior full-time and paid officials were Scottish. My position was anyway made quite clear to me during my time on the DTI National Committee where I was expected to do as I was told during an apprenticeship or test period. I was not consulted on the subcommittee I was allocated to and in spite of protest I was ignored. In the circumstances I refused to serve on the allocated subcommittee and so was isolated. In retrospect I see I was a total outsider and probably not trusted. I did not feel bitter about this and chalked it all up to experience. Similarly, I was unconcerned if indeed the influential levels at the top of the union were highly politically motivated. I saw this to be in the wider interests of the membership at a time when militancy was needed, even if that was not going to be provided by the rank and file. Come the battle one has to choose some strange bed fellows, rather like the UK Government choosing President Pinochet of Chile during the Falkland war.

I am grateful to the union for providing me with the opportunity to attend Conference and visit towns which in the normal scheme of things I would have not got to know. I have in mind particularly Blackpool. Although one is tempted to compare Southend-on-Sea, where I was brought up, to Blackpool, the resorts have little in common. Southend as a holiday resort died in the fifties and perhaps never recovered from the war years and social changes. Blackpool, almost alone, survived as a thriving example of the traditional working class English seaside resort. During Conference I was assigned to a small B&B in one of the streets behind the Tower. I shared a small room with my Branch Secretary but apart from sleeping and breakfast we spent very little time in the 'hotel'. It had the Blackpool front room bar and the food was generous although very plain. I remember Blackpool as very professional and hospitable. Also I remember it as remarkable value for money, be that the 'hotel' or the pubs and restaurants. In spite of the attraction of cheap continental holidays Blackpool survives although it does seem that a change in the gaming laws governing casinos will be the key to its future.

Southport was altogether a different cup of tea with a veneer of old fashioned Northern respectability with a slight feeling of Harrogate and the splendid Betty's Tearooms.

I was on the Branch Committee during the first and second strike in the Civil Service. This was not pleasant and I have every sympathy with those that feel they must take such action as I know it is a last resort and a decision that is not taken lightly by members and activists alike. I took more than my share of picket duty since Branch Committee members are expected to offer some leadership and set an example. It was unpleasant physically but more so to see your colleagues walk past you at the door and especially so when you were the object of abuse. On one wet and windy day I was on picket duty at the front door of 1, Victoria Street and had a Minister purposely shake his wet umbrella over me. Some staff felt guilty that they were not supporting you and would slip in the door with eyes cast downwards mumbling some, usually feeble, excuse. Some bolder individuals would stop and chat, express sympathy, and march in with confidence. Most very senior staff in the Department were correct, although icily so, and polite. It was a thankless and miserable experience. The only bright spots were the occasional release from duty and adjournment to a coffee shop and the consistent support from the likes of

HAPF and sister Helen on holday in Switzerland 1947

State University of South Dakota, 1964: left to right – Ronnie Munro, Jennifer Adam, Dr L C Smith, Bob Stark, Penny Herford and HAPF

Lord Jellicoe (right), Chaiman of BOTB at Royal Show, Stoneleigh

Vincent, Howard and Andrew – three generations of Cranleighans, atCranleigh School 1990

Fiona and children 1978

Duke of Kent, Vice Chairman BOTB, at Royal Show (left – Daphne Wilmot of DTI)

HAPF at Alamo, San Antonio, Texas

Grampian Region Structure Plan Team 1992 – Allan Garvie, Assistant Director, on right of HAPF

Councillor Jim Davidson, Chair of Economic Development & Planning, GRC, March 1996

From left: Sir Bob Reid, Chancellor RGU; Principal Prof. Bill Stevely; former Principal Dr David Kennedy , and Chairman of Governors HAPF

Post Office van drivers and from some stationery supply firms in turning back at our picket line.

We learnt quickly that an all out strike was not effective either in terms of cost to union funds or in terms of member support, and subsequent and more effective action needed to be targeted. We targeted the Government's cash raising and cash disbursement operations, where pulling out a small number of staff could cause a disproportionate nuisance to the Government. Such areas would cover accounts operations for example. This sort of action better husbanded the union's funds but also allowed all members to participate via a modest levy but at the same time remaining at their desk. I am not sure how important the money raised through the levy was but the exercise did keep the issue before members. I think only slightly better than picket duty was going around offices and collecting the levy from each individual. Many were only too glad to be let off the strike hook and contribute a couple of quid a week but a significant minority used every trick and excuse in the book to avoid paying the levy. I respected better those who said outright 'I disagree with this and am not paying' than those who imposed conditions they hoped would never be met. Such colleagues would say, 'Yes, I will contribute when we stop the action and start to negotiate' and similar provisions. When their conditions were met, they would then move the goal posts to avoid paying. It was difficult to appear pleasant and not lose one's temper with their likes. It did change my attitude to the time I put into union work on behalf of colleagues like these, who were always ready to accept the improvement in pay that the action, in my view, undoubtedly achieved. My Branch Committee all found this a dispiriting exercise, but we saw it through.

There is no doubt that such activity damaged my career. At the time strikers were threatened with pension reprisals, loss of Honours eligibility and promotion rights. Some of the threats were blatant and some more subtle and vague. On the other hand there were some staff who held trade union office who were regularly promoted including those who had significant proportions of official time off for trade union duties, such as those who held union Branch Secretary posts. Some I would judge were promoted well beyond their capabilities. This always puzzled me and as time went on I became suspicious. One such colleague in particular never displayed a full hand and could be relied on to take a view that was sympathetic to the official side or, in industrial trade union terms, a 'management' view but at the same time presented a 'macho' facade to the membership at large. A number of us, quite independently, had reached the view that this colleague was a management 'plant'. After we had shared our views with each other we took precautions to discuss more sensitive aspects in private. During industrial action we rarely used the telephone and would hold discussions in corridors and lift vestibules just in case the union office or our own offices were bugged. Some may have thought at the time that this was a little paranoid but there was anecdotal evidence of interference with our telephones. In the light of my reading since of the activities of various government agencies during the coal miners strike in the Thatcher years, and the role of the Security Service and Stella Rimington, later to become Director of the Security Service, I do not think we were particularly paranoid. What I do know is that we observed filming of our protest marches and not by the BBC and ITN. Again we know now this is standard practice in order to spot, record and catalogue activists. I suspect that all our unions were well penetrated by, if not the more glamorous agencies, then by staff who were willing to curry favour with senior departmental managers.

Ministers in the Department tended to keep their distance from any approaches during a dispute, notwithstanding approaches to them at Branch Committee level. However one Minister was sympathetic and did agree to meet a deputation from the Branch Committee. The Minister was Labour's Les Huckfield. He was as helpful as he could be in circumstances where he had little clout. But he did take the time to receive us courteously and was able to offer some advice. He said that our picketing technique left something to be desired but conceded that it was appropriately low key and perhaps more suitable to Civil Service traditions. I have a lot to thank Les Huckfield for, apart from a little tea and sympathy during our strikes, and that is the role in 1977 he played in bullying the then GMWU General Secretary, David Basnett, into accepting me and another DTI colleague on to an industrial trade union course for the General and Municipal Workers own shop stewards and full time union officials (see Chapter 7).

By the time I had left the Civil Service in 1988 the tide had firmly turned against any pretence that trade union membership was to be encouraged by 'management' or Ministers. A perceived turning point in 1984 was the banning of trade union membership at the Government's main eavesdropping and code-breaking operation at GCHQ, based in Cheltenham. At the time many of us saw this as the thin end of the wedge and the next step would be to withdraw trade union membership rights from the mainstream areas of the Civil Service, perhaps starting with senior grades. That did not come about and the very spirited campaign in support of GCHQ staff may have blunted political enthusiasm. A few brave souls at GCHQ stuck it out for a number of years and finally union membership rights were restored. I still have the GCHQ coffee mug that I purchased at the time to raise money for those suspended because they would not give up their union membership.

Meanwhile the FDA soldiers on and indeed was very active in support of Clive Ponting, the Ministry of Defence official who was unsuccessfully prosecuted in 1985 under Section 2 of the Official Secrets Act for passing details surrounding the sinking of the Argentine warship, the *Belgrano*, to the Labour MP, Tam Dalyell. The other mainstream Civil Service unions have seen a succession of mergers with my own union merging with the Inland Revenue Staff Association. With the changes in the management of the current Civil Service, with grading and pay rates left more to individual departments and the growth of stand alone or 'next steps' agencies, the negotiating role of the unions has been reduced. It is much harder to 'organise', in trade union jargon, where the work units are small and there is little sense of belonging to a larger organisation with all the shared conditions, values and identity. Indeed it has been said that there has been so much change that the Civil Service as a distinct institution of public service identified through certain characteristics and qualities rather than through any strictly legal definition, no longer exists. Nonetheless if I were to return to Whitehall today the institution that I worked in for twenty years would not be beyond recognition. Of real concern is three out of five Civil Servants in 1995 agreed with the statement that 'speaking up can damage career prospects' (Mori poll, 1995). I began to personally experience that more or less from the beginning of Thatcher's term as Prime Minister in 1979.

To be fair I think that this reflected more personal circumstances and a difficult period beginning in my own career rather than the erosion of the 'willingness to speak truth to power' that undoubtedly was a casualty as the Thatcher years advanced. One of the many catchphrases of the period was 'Is he one of us?', which the lady is said to have asked before giving her blessing to senior Civil Service appointments. I think that points to the growing need of Ministers since, and no less New Labour, to have Civil Servants sympathetic to Government policies. I do not think I am naive enough to believe that was never the case but politicisation of the Civil Service by successive governments since Thatcher is much more blatant, and one could argue that the Blair Government's treatment of career Civil Servants has been cruder and more brutal than ever was the reality during the Thatcher years. I would single out the Blair Government's treatment of

Departmental Information Officers and their replacement, in practice, by an army of politically appointed 'advisers' as being the best example of a cynical assassination of the best traditions of British public service and the slow, but now certain, death of the public service ethos. I will return to this later but the curbs on the ability to speak truth to power were a factor in my decision to leave the Service in 1988.

Chapter 11

Disenchantment

The three years or so from December 1976 to March 1980 were for me the most depressing experience of my Civil Service career. I had during that period, as far as I was concerned, some of the less helpful line managers at both Assistant Secretary and Under Secretary level. At the same time it was a period of underemployment, with two posts where the work did not require somebody of my grade. In both cases the post was eliminated after my departure. The period coincided with demanding roles for many of my contemporaries in DTI covering, as it did, Callaghan's time as Prime Minister and the election of the Conservatives with Thatcher as Prime Minister in May 1979. The man behind the strategy that was to become 'Thatcherism' and all the changes the new philosophy of monetarism wrought was Sir Keith Joseph and he was appointed as Secretary of State for Industry, which was my Department at the time. DTI, in Ministerial terms, had been split into two Departments, the Department of Trade and the Department of Industry. As far as most officials were concerned this made little difference to careers and daily life as the staff were administered as if one Department by a common personnel division, which was very sensible since at a later date the two parts became one in a 'born again' DTI.

My old boss, Mike Treble, said to me that what a Civil Servant must pray for is war or pestilence and when prayers are answered not only is the work more stimulating but promotion opportunities are at their optimum. Well, winters of discontent and new and rampant Thatcherism were not far short of these career success criteria. Whatever one's talents, being in the right place at the right time is the essential bit of luck needed for a successful career. I sure was in the 'wrongest' place I could be with a posting to General Division (the very title says it all) and then to a backwater in Iron and Steel Division, even with my period in the latter coinciding with a major strike by the members of the Iron and Steel Trades Confederation led by Bill Sirs.

My discussions with Establishments towards the end of my time on the Latin America desk in 1976 were far from satisfactory. A look at the DTI functional directory was enough to see that the job offered as my next posting was, to put it mildly, unexciting. The preliminary interview with my prospective Assistant Secretary confirmed my view that this was a dead end. General Division was a rag bag of jobs and my responsibilities included negotiation of various tariff quotas with the European Community including newsprint quotas, as well as of suspensions of the Common Customs Tariff (CCT). I left my prospective boss in no doubt that G Division was about the last place I wished to work but he was a kindly man and always treated me with respect and, in fairness, deserved better. He tried to convince me that it could be a stepping stone to better things and indeed my predecessor in the job had been promoted. I had been a colleague of this lucky man in a previous posting, and how he achieved a promotion with the material at his disposal in G Division was a mystery that remains with me. I remonstrated with Establishments but to no avail. I felt strongly enough to make a formal complaint to Josh White, the Establishments' Assistant Secretary in charge of Principal grade career moves. I asked that should the job not work out that I would be moved in less than the usual stint of two to three years in post. I doubt if my request had much to do with my escape in just a year. However Josh White meant well and I give him the benefit of doubt.

It was the practice that, although at the end of the day the needs of the Service must take precedence over personal wishes, staff were consulted on their career postings. There was also folk law that said one could reasonably refuse a first job offer, but thereafter room to manoeuvre became tight and you were expected to take the third offer as a direction. However the posting of an individual to a new post was the outcome of a triangle of forces with the accepting officer, Establishments and the individual to be posted at each corner. If you were well thought of, either as the accepting officer (usually one grade your senior) or as the officer to be posted your wishes would likely prevail. Establishments would go the way of least resistance. You could influence your marketability by direct approach to a future boss and this could be used to cut Establishments out of the loop altogether, bar the formalities. It works in reverse where you can convince a prospective boss that you are not the man for him. Few will wish to take on a reluctant recruit which later may reflect on their own success. So this route is a relatively easy one but there is a cost to your standing and marketability. The perceived Whitehall high flyer can pick his own posting at these middle levels, or at least can agree a package of jobs to increase his or her experience or, to use a well-worn Civil Service phrase, to 'stretch' one's capability. In the case of G Division my boss to be had no clout and neither did I and it was one of the rarer examples where the triangle of forces is dominated by Establishments. I suspect my new boss felt he was lucky to get anyone and he certainly did not expect to be allocated a star or 'high flyer'.

Over my career Establishments, soon to adopt the more mainstream label 'Personnel', were as helpful as they could be and over time I realised that they had, in practice, considerably less influence over one's career than I initially imagined. They were essentially technicians and there to oil the wheels, keep records, and keep as many of their clients as happy as possible. A rotten job. We did have career reviews with Personnel where the idea was to take stock and try and map out future training needs and career moves. Personnel were always accessible on request and I gather there was a rush of colleagues to see Personnel after the summer holiday period. I was typical, and after those 'Where the hell am I going' thoughts on some far from DTI beach or mountain I would charge back to the office determined to say my piece. In the event most personnel officers I dealt with were kind and patient and any anger on my part was soon dissipated and I left a meeting feeling the better, for a while anyway. It was the practice then to appoint mainstream officers to Personnel and not to use professionally trained personnel officers. At the time I thought this perverse but having had experience of professional personnel folk since I feel now the Civil Service was rather wise. Placement of staff in Personnel who shared the same experiences of the job as their 'clients', with the same fresh posting every two to three years, was healthy, and a spell in Establishments or Personnel being merely part of the lottery of Civil Service job posting.

So just before Christmas in 1977 I turned up at Kingsgate House in Victoria Street to meet my new staff and to make the most of the posting to General Division. Of DTI's central London property portfolio Kingsgate House, in the middle of Victoria Street and a few doors from Westminster City Council headquarters, was one of its more depressing buildings. Kingsgate was rather dark and also oddly featureless. There was nothing wrong with the individual offices as such and I had been in worse, but somehow the colour scheme and the lighting combined to create an air of gloom. At a later date Kingsgate was refurbished but never did redeem itself in my eyes. My own office looked out to a less than stimulating scene behind the north side of Victoria Street and did nothing to lift the feeling of rejection on moving to Kingsgate from the hub of DTI at No.1, Victoria Street. My staff were welcoming but with the tinge of suspicion that usually greets a new boss. The small staff was headed up by Roger Philpot, a Senior Executive Officer. Roger was a cheerful and competent officer and was quite able to run the office with little input from me or any one else. It became clear in the first couple of weeks that I would have to create a role and this would be at Roger's expense. God only knows what my predecessor found to do that justified promotion. Supporting Roger were two lady Higher Executive Officers, who were archetypal female HEOs being middle-aged, single or not married, and devoted to the public service ethic. Both were very competent at their jobs but did test my abilities in staff management. One of these ladies could get very emotional and it was my first experience of handling staff tears. Most of the time I failed miserably. It was not that the lady used tears to get her way but they were more expressions of frustration over my meddling in her responsibilities, and where most of the time she was doing very nicely without my help. The other lady was more wily and it was not so much that I was better in dealing with her but more she was better in managing me than her colleague. There would be occasions during the early months of my time in G Division when I could not wish these two ladies far enough away, but as I matured into this non-job I began to better appreciate their knowledge and wisdom. They were the quality of staff that I would regret not having to hand in later years when working in local government. In contrast to these two ladies I had also a young female Executive Officer, Janice, who was equally bright but with none of the need for me to take care before entering her office to avoid a confrontation. Janice had a cheerful disposition and was the cement that kept the unit together and defused many a difficult situation between me and her female superiors. Roger as SEO was the line manager for his all female staff and by using a light touch and leaving what were competent staff to their own devices coped rather well, and certainly better than me.

On the first day I reported to my Assistant Secretary. I learned little more about my job or indeed his wider portfolio. He tried his best to convince me that here was a demanding and worthwhile job, but even at this stage I could not help but feel he was trying to convince himself rather than me. I was to find that much of the work was worthwhile and some quite important, but demanding it was not.

Any attempt by me to answer the question "What do you do?" at social gatherings was sure to lose a potential friend. At first I would try to explain the joys of negotiating suspensions of the CCT but very quickly had reduced this to explaining my role in settling the British baked bean quota. This always got a laugh and placed my credibility at least on hold. In reality some of the work was quite interesting and actually did include such exotics as baked beans and red cabbage. In simple terms all imports into the European Community have to cross a protective tariff or customs duty barrier with a duty to pay by the importer. The tariff rates are fixed by the Community but taking into account commitments agreed with various international trade groups such as the World Trade Commission (formerly GATT). The tariffs protect manufacturers within the Community so making competitor products from outside the Community likely more expensive. However there are products that the Community does not produce and so it is not in Community consumer interest for them to pay more than is necessary. In such circumstances the Community suspends the tariff and one of my roles was to negotiate such suspension of the duty or 'CCT' on behalf of importers. By this stage of a less than frivolous answer to the question "...and what do you do?", any potential friend at a social event would have long found a reason to attend to urgent business elsewhere!

The task is a little more complex than this, as often a Community member state will claim to make a 'similar' product and will object to the UK's case to suspend the Common Customs Tariff or CCT. Then there is the situation where a competitor state in the industrial sector concerned will have no interest in seeing a UK company obtain a competitive edge by gaining a cheaper, or lower tariff access to a better product, and will wish to block the UK application to a suspension of the CCT. Surely the UK would not stoop to such tactics? Of course we did, and I was involved in a never spoken of but nonetheless real alliance with my French colleagues to protect our mutual superiority in the aerospace industry. A significant part of the negotiations in Brussels on CCT were linked to consideration of various bits of aerospace hardware including quite complex aviation electronic equipment or 'avionics'. There had been a long post war history of co-operation with the French on aviation projects from Concorde and space programmes to collaboration on the commercially very successful Airbus, although on most of these it was French persistence that took projects through to successful conclusion whereas the British would have thrown in the towel and lost their nerve.

Working with my French colleagues on aviation matters was a model of Anglo-French collaboration. I experienced none of the apocryphal stories of French perfidy or arrogance but what I did experience was a straightforward and workman-like honesty. My first job with Eric Wood in Aviation Secretariat helped enormously with terminology as well as some idea of the aviation industry's structure. We would meet occasionally outwith the Brussels committee meetings and alternately in Paris and London. The highlight for me was an invitation to the Paris air show and meetings with senior French aerospace manufacturers including meeting one of the Dassault family. However on other industry sectors where our objectives did not coincide, the French could be less helpful although refusal was often couched in a civilised and even an amusing way. The same could not be said of German or Dutch colleagues.

Request for suspension of CCT applied to a wide range of goods and materials from agricultural produce to chemical intermediates. In the UK, a request came from an individual firm or more often via a trade association. The UK applicant was expected to provide all the necessary briefing to enable me to summit a case to the European Commission. Applications were circulated to all Member States to allow consultation with respective indigenous industries and their representative bodies. At the same time that my office was dealing with UK submissions we were consulting on submissions from other Community countries. Briefing could be as straightforward as simple acquiescence to CCT suspension, or more often entail the making of a technically complex case against a competitor achieving a CCT suspension. With multinationals, briefing often indicated as much about the country in which they saw their best interests represented than the case in hand, and I have in mind here chemical and pharmaceutical companies. Many requests were processed with little debate but a significant proportion were fought over for weeks on end, and here the applicant firms were very much in the hands of me and my Member State counterparts. As Scottish fishermen have found to their cost bargaining in Brussels sometimes is less about the facts of the case, but more a balancing act where you may need to make concessions in return for concessions, and often any concessions gained relate to a later and unconnected request.

When I took up the reins of the Brussels negotiations I tried to tackle each request on its merits and avoid being dragged into what could be a complex and chess-like bargaining process. I found that this soon created tension and put me on a collision course with the German chair of the CCT group. My Community colleagues probably saw me as unsophisticated and naive, and I now feel they were probably correct. However, the German colleague apart, my Community counterparts were good-natured and patient. I remember one of my applications was from a UK based multinational manufacturer of a well-known brand-name toothpaste, and the request was for the suspension of CCT on the plastic squeeze tubes we all now take for granted. At that time the norm was the metallic malleable tube that often fractured before the toothpaste was all dispensed. There was total opposition all round on the grounds that there were perfectly usable alternatives produced in the Community whereas, at the time, I think the applicant's new technology tubes were being imported from the United States. It was up to my judgement whether to drop a case or pursue it over a number of meetings. In this case it was not that I felt the application was so critical to the UK economy or that the applicant had produced a particularly good case but more about my own frustration with the bendy metal tubes and this did seem a useful advance. Just before I left General Division my colleagues in Brussels relented and agreed that duty on the 'new and improved' tube should be suspended. I doubt whether this had anything to do with my powers of persuasion or pity for my plight but likely more to do with the multinational concerned getting its pan European briefing together and channelling the request in parallel through other Member States.

One of the most complex areas was dealing with suspensions of CCT for the pharmaceutical industry. Although I trained as a chemist and biochemist my knowledge was not up to the accuracy needed in naming chemical compounds accurately and by their full chemical name and not their trade name. Many of the compounds we dealt with were pharmaceutical intermediates and did not have trade names. So critical was chemical nomenclature that we used to take at least two members of the Laboratory of the Government Chemist (LGC) with us and the UK acted as the experts on nomenclature on behalf of all the Member States.

This 'gift' of expertise from the UK gave us a little status with our European colleagues but for me provided a very congenial bunch of colleagues to share off-duty time in Brussels, and with visits in some peak activity periods being on a fortnightly basis this was important. Being a chemist by training helped and I was soon an accepted member of the LGC group which taught me a few of the wrinkles of making one's subsistence rates go as far as possible. We were given a fixed rate of subsistence by the Department to cover all expenses and how this sum was apportioned between accommodation and meals etc. was up to the individual. It was a system I tried to introduce to my local authority some years later as it was less open to 'fiddling'. My experience as a manager of staff is that a system of claims rigourously vetted against individual expenditure and receipts encourages deceit. One of the commonest dodges, and facilitated by taxi drivers everywhere, is to over-claim on taxi fares against bogus receipts. However the Civil Service system provided you with a lump sum that was just the underside of generous, at least for overseas trips, and left the rest to the individual. Taxi fares could be claimed but most felt no need to abuse the system and anyway the

Brussels public transport was very efficient and cheap. Brussels is, although unsung, a gastronomic capital and so the aim of my LGC colleagues was to spend on good eating what we saved on accommodation. We enjoyed wine but looked for value for money rather than expensive estates. Besides good eating the subsistence package was stretched to cover a modest box of Belgian chocolates for "her indoors" and the duty free allowance of then one bottle of spirits. To take home spare cash was, in a perhaps odd way, seen as somewhat immoral by the group. All the LGC team were members of the Stevenage-based 'Wine Society' and I remain grateful to my time in G Division, if for nothing else, than my introduction to this admirable institution, founded at the time of the 1874 International Exhibition. I have fond memories of the many happy evenings spent in good company exploring the delights of Brussels' excellent restaurants.

By the autumn of 1977 I think I had convinced my Assistant Secretary that I was surplus to requirements and that Roger Philpot could do the job more than adequately. I suspect also that Roger was doing his own lobbying as since my arrival he had to take a bit of a back seat in the negotiations in Brussels, although Roger was never anything but helpful and pleasant. Thanks to links through my trade union work with Les Huckfield, a junior Minister at the time in the Department, I was selected to join a four week training course run by the General and Municipal Workers Union (now GMB) at their residential college in Woodstock near Surbiton, Surrey (Chapter 7 refers). This reduced my time in G Division to a bare eleven months and at the time I was not sorry to leave, but had I known what was around the corner I would have fought to stay in General Division.

My posting to Iron and Steel Division was not against my will as I welcomed a spell in an 'industry sponsor' Division. The concept of 'sponsorship' was a long established one in DTI and its predecessor departments. The term implied an oversight of industry and watching role for the Department and its Ministers. There were assumptions implied of 'being there' when things went wrong , in the same way a mother and father are an ever present safety net even when their children are adults. The analogy continues as sponsorship often meant baling out firms that hit difficult times or what became known as the DTI 'lame duck' facility. The sponsorship concept spanned private industry as well as nationalised industries, although for nationalised industries oversight was more tightly exercised. Troublesome industries tended to get whole DTI Divisions to themselves like the motor industry (Vehicles Division), but others were corralled in a rag bag collection. In the later years of my time at DTI such obvious industry sponsorship labelling was diluted but the DTI sponsor function lived on with Sir Keith Joseph and through the Thatcher years.

On paper, Iron & Steel Division seemed to me a good bet, with its sponsorship responsibilities for a key nationalised industry in British Steel but also a significant private sector in both the steel and foundry sectors. Unfortunately I knew nobody to make that essential off-the-record inquiry or to give me any 'SP'. I was assigned to IS2 Branch and to John Morris as my Assistant Secretary. My responsibilities included BSC's overseas investment policy, and scrap metal export control. I had responsibilities also for some overseas aspects of the iron and steel industry, including membership of one of the international organisations which allowed me to visit the still unlikely tourist destination of Algeria.

Again, it quickly became apparent that the job was not enough to fully occupy my time and, unlike G Division, I came into conflict with my Under Secretary, Solly Gross. One of my roles was to brief the Under Secretary for his meetings with BSC on their extensive overseas operations. BSC's interests included a large commitment to the development of iron ore mines overseas with the aim, I always assumed, of better securing raw material supplies. I am not sure I fully understood the justification for these ventures as iron ore was never a mineral that was other than well distributed in friendly countries around the world. I got on quite well with my BSC opposite numbers or at least they tolerated me as well as any other DTI official. I cannot say the organisation was obstructive when asking for details of investments and other information behind balance sheet conclusions. I was sent on a Civil Service course to provide me with some better ability to unravel business accounts. I found it useful but not as much as my Assistant Secretary expected. I think he thought that mere reading of a balance sheet and published accounts would reveal so much more about, not only BSC's profitability in overseas operations, but the reasons behind decisions and any BSC hidden agenda.

The period coincided with BSC's seemingly boundless optimism in its production forecasts. The feeling in the office was that these were wildly unrealistic and so there was always a suspicion that what we were told was only part of the story. Solly Gross never shared with me any of his views or strategy with regards to the part of BSC that I dealt with and so it was difficult to brief him intelligently. Likewise I never got any debriefing after his visit to BSC's head offices in Grosvenor Place. I did not find Gross easy to deal with. I think other colleagues found him more amenable but always we seemed to clash. At the time I was heavily involved in trade union work and he did not appreciate this commitment and similarly his assumption as to my politics likely grated. If my job had been more demanding, and that was within Gross's gift, I would not have had so much time on my hands to spend on the union Branch Committee. Neither he nor John Morris made any sustained effort to make the job more rewarding. I pressed my case constantly and only on one occasion did I get an opportunity to get my teeth into a substantial piece of work, and that was when I was asked to research the setting up of a stockpile of strategic minerals.

This was towards the end of my spell with IS2 but I grabbed the opportunity with relish. At the time there were a number of minerals required by the steel industry, and especially for manufacture of specialised steels, that were sourced from a small spread of countries and where supply was seen as vulnerable for political reasons. These minerals were the source of chrome, vanadium, molybdenum, nickel and manganese. Southern Africa together with the former Soviet Union were key sources for a number of these minerals including chrome. So it was easy to envisage a scenario where we could quite suddenly see our supplies of these key minerals cut off. The Americans already had a strategic minerals stockpile run by a government agency. We had no such experience to my knowledge although I was aware the Ministry of Agriculture maintained strategic stockpiles around the country for the likes of fats and sugar etc. This was public knowledge but to get MAFF to share their experience was difficult, although I very much needed their advice in terms of how one handles the mechanics, for example of turnover of stock, the use of private sector agents, and how to avoid undue effect on the market price when setting up a stockpile and turning it over. The whole exercise required extensive consultation but in a relatively short time I was able to draft a paper with clear recommendations on the minerals that we should stockpile, and how we should go about it. My Assistant Secretary did acknowledge it was a good piece of work.

I never knew whether the Government went ahead with such a stockpile or whether it encouraged both BSC and the substantial steel private sector to make provision themselves. Since then the world geopolitical map has changed and the UK also has a smaller steel industry, and much of this is in foreign ownership. I have no idea to what extent the current Government takes the long view and one that might include the possibility at some point, due to war or some other major catastrophe, our country will be thrown back on its own resources and the need now to keep options open. Coal is the most cited resource that we may be neglecting at our peril. We sit on massive coal reserves that will surely be needed at some point in the future. Should we not maintain some research and capacity to generate energy from not only coal directly but also petroleum from coal as was done by South Africa during the times of apartheid linked blockades?

During my time in Iron and Steel Division the problems facing BSC were not those of increasing production and therefore any desperate need for more raw materials, but more one of mounting losses and a succession of plant closures. The main union was the ISTC (Iron & Steel Trades Confederation) with Bill Sirs as General Secretary. Sirs was a moderate trade union leader from whatever stand point in the political spectrum. Even this man was forced to draw a line after closures at Shotton, Corby and Consett, and in November 1979 the threat of a further 10,000 jobs losses was the last straw. I was still in IS2 when a national steel strike was called for 2 January 1980. The strike lasted until the beginning of April that year.

It was a period of intense activity in IS Division but, unfortunately, not for me. There were odd moments of light relief such as the occasion when trade union members in the office sent a donation to the ISTC strike fund. We also had on loan from the Post Office a very pleasant and sociable Assistant Secretary who advised us that old-fashioned mail was least likely to be intercepted by the security services since it meant a 'Mr Plod' type or, worse still, 'management' leaning over a Post Office sorter and saying "Have you any letters for Brown" or whoever. Post Office sorting staff did not take kindly to this and, anyway, it was time-consuming and difficult to extract a letter from a 'sellotape' sealed envelope. Even in the late seventies and with the old mechanical exchanges phone-tapping was easy. It is so much easier now.

Another moment of light relief was the occasion when the Secretary of State's Private Office consulted me on the choice of a present for a delegation of senior officials from China who BSC were trying to inveigle into some deal or other. We looked around and decided on something made from stainless steel. The Private Office was set on a canteen of cutlery. We advised that perhaps this was not such a good idea as the Chinese do not use table knives and forks, as well as the small problem that at this stage in time it was difficult to guarantee the provenance of 'British' stainless steel cutlery. A lot of cutlery was imported from the Far East. A more suitable gift was chosen and the Chinese seemed pleased enough.

The administration of ferrous scrap export licensing was one of my responsibilities. Scrap was an important raw material for the steel industry and it was important to the economy, and not least that British generated scrap was available to the UK steel industry at a reasonable price. Export controls ensured that scrap merchants were forced to seek internal markets for scrap before selling to overseas markets. My role was to monitor the market and in consultation with the steel industry and scrap merchants maintain a market that was not too distorted in favour of one group or the other. I was lobbied intensely by both sides of the trade but most enjoyable was the opportunity to get to know a section of British industry that rarely got good press. The 'Steptoe' image of the small scrap trader was certainly still alive at one end of the business but less so at the end I came into contact with. I tended to deal with the trade association but interestingly also directly with some of the bigger firms in the business. These firms had very large yards and multimillion pound businesses, but in spite of that the obviously wealthy individuals that ran these businesses were not too far removed from Harold Steptoe. Like Harold they were self-made, grafters and entrepreneurs par excellence. However hard a firm tries a scrapyard is a messy and unsightly operation. The job is usually dirty, noisy and dangerous, with the use of heavy machinery for metal separation and shredding. I visited one firm in the Midlands and was met in the owner's Jaguar and taken to his very comfortable house. However, the effect was somewhat spoilt in that his grand house was just by his yard and works. He was still capable of taking off his jacket and getting his hands dirty. Also I met his son working on the sorting line, covered in rust, dust and oil. The industry I remember was tough and with tough men at the top. At first I was a little afraid of some of the characters in the scrap business but as I got to know one or two individuals I enjoyed their banter and leg pulling. I was in a vulnerable position since I alone set the export quotas. Occasionally my Assistant Secretary would have an attack of nerves when he was lobbied by BSC, and BISPA, the independent steel producers association. I was warned on taking up the job that I would be vulnerable and should be careful not to compromise myself. I was never offered a bribe beyond a good meal, and indeed it is one of my slight regrets that during the whole of my career as a public servant I was never offered a bribe. I guess it was not so much that I presented an image of total incorruptibility, but more likely that I never had an important enough position that might have attracted such an approach.

Arising out of my attendance at the GMWU college at Surbiton I had arranged a reciprocal exchange with then ISTC Divisional Officer Roy Evans, who was to become Bill Sirs' successor as General Secretary. All I managed to negotiate with the Department was for Roy to spend a week in the office in April 1978. This was the only follow-up action I managed to achieve after my GMWU course. The arrival of Thatcher ensured that the initiative was dead even if my bosses were enthusiastic, which they were not. Roy was a very pleasant and friendly man and Fiona and I invited him down to Wonersh for a meal and an overnight during his week with DTI. I do remember a very boozy night out at a pub deep in the Surrey countryside. It was me as the driver that was the worse for wear, but these were the days before any of us worried too much about drink and driving.

The office had a well-qualified technical staff who knew all about the making of steel and were content to restrict their input to this professional view. On one occasion I was asked to produce figures on BSC coke oven capacity, and closure plans for these. Armed with this information I was sent as the junior to accompany one of the technical staff to a meeting between our Minister, Eric Varley and Tony Benn, then at the separate Energy Ministry. The technical official was a lot senior to me in the parallel hierarchy of the scientific grades and was the 'lead' official. The meeting between Varley and Benn, in the latter's office in Thames House South, was a somewhat frosty affair. Benn asked questions as to the true extent of coke oven closures and Varley looked to his own team to answer, insofar as he gave no reply to Benn, leaving a pregnant silence. My colleague said nothing. I felt it was my duty to support my Minister and gave the information that I had prepared to Benn. Benn challenged a point or two and again a silence from Varley and my technical colleague. Once more I pitched in. Varley seemed uneasy and the meeting wound up shortly after. I never saw the Minutes that would have been made by the respective Private Offices. All I remember was volunteering to return home to the office the same way as I had come, on foot. This seemed to cause a ripple with Varley's staff. If they had wanted me to join them for a short debriefing then this was not mentioned. Clearly, I did not do as was expected by Varley, but no one ever explained before or after what was expected and I, to this day, feel my performance resulted in a black mark on my record. The frustration of Civil Service life is that often nobody will explain the situation so you can correct mistakes. The training of potential high flyers is non-specific and more a process of osmosis where one absorbs the atmosphere and becomes instinctively to know whether an action or behaviour is right or wrong.

Just before I left IS2 in March 1980 I produced the piece of work I was most proud of and that was a health and safety report into the chemicals used in the Department's offset litho printing operation. My report resulted in a change of chemicals through out the Civil Service. I was pleased that something good came of my two years plus of underemployment in Iron and Steel Division.

I left IS2 depressed and demoralised. I had been in the Civil Service for about thirteen years and it was from this moment I began to wonder whether I could stay much longer. I had no one I could talk to with confidence in Establishments. I did go and see the line Deputy Secretary but his advice was not to worry, "the sun is still shining outside", and in essence to go away and not bother him. The conversation was conducted in a typically urbane and light-hearted way but also very skilfully as I did go away thinking I had no case. A couple of days after, my views had changed to anger and to a feeling of being abused and cheated.

Chapter 12

The Home Front

With two children our flat in Rochford was becoming a bit crowded and after nearly four years there we moved in 1971 from Essex to Surrey, and to Wonersh, a delightful village three miles south of Guildford. Fiona was never very happy in Rochford although she liked this small town which, even now, still retains most of its historic centre. We were perhaps a little too handy for my mother and father who lived some four to five miles away in Leigh-on-Sea, although we did consider the option of remaining in the Southend area. We looked at the house my father had built for my grandfather in Kings Road, in Westcliff-on-Sea. This was a large and quality built house in a sought after part of town, within easy walking distance of Chalkwell station and the Fenchurch Street line to the City. My grandfather died in 1941 and so the house had seen at least one other owner since then. I was tempted by the house, its position overlooking the sea, and the provenance. It would have been fitting for a Fisher to have returned to this house but Fiona was very much against and her judgement proved wise. We decided to move to Surrey because we wanted to live in the countryside, although many would debate whether Surrey, with its exquisitely manicured villages and lanes, was truly rural. We also had a vague idea that we would educate the children privately and my son would be the third generation Fisher at Cranleigh School. The only way we were going to be able to afford this was to live nearby facilitating attendance as a day pupil.

I focussed our house search on the villages between Guildford and Cranleigh, namely Shalford, Shamley, Bramley, Chilworth and Wonersh. I undertook the initial search, making the tiresome three hour road journey from south-east Essex to the Guildford area and leaving Fiona, expecting our second child, at home in Rochford. It did not take me long to discover what we could afford, and remembering the estate agents' maxim of 'location, location, location' focussed on the little village of Wonersh. The village is fairly typical of Surrey with a cricket green at the centre and a setting of well-wooded hills. Two hills dominate the village. On one is perched a grand house built for the Cook family, of Thos. Cook travel fame, and on the opposite hill is Chinthurst Hill House, a Lutyens house in the Surrey vernacular. Wonersh has its middle class ghetto, a prewar executive housing estate built in the grounds of a former deer park, Wonersh Park, but also has a stock of modest but pleasant post-war housing that blends acceptably with the mellow ancient village. Ours was to be one of the latter; a semi-detached and brick house backing onto a small cul-de-sac of similar houses, with a view to Chinthurst Hill in the winter but hidden from view in the summer by a belt of mature oaks and hawthorn.

We fell in love with Wonersh at first sight and we still refer to this as home, even though we left for Aberdeenshire in the summer of 1989. Moving to Surrey and particularly Wonersh was the best decision we ever made. I never tired of my daily walks through the village as part of my commuting to and from London. I rarely missed a conscious prayer of gratitude for the opportunity to live in this most pleasant corner of the Home Counties.

Fiona settled immediately, and quickly we made a number of friends which have remained so to this day. Some were neighbours, and some Fiona met through the children and schools, where I got to know the partners in due course. One couple followed us from the Southend area, settled in the next village and became good friends. Like most commuters I had a separate collection of friends at the office and although we tried to integrate the two sets via dinner parties etc., it rarely worked. Commuting can result in colleagues' homes being up to a hundred miles apart, with London in between. Also we had no room to accommodate visitors for an over night and this did not assist 'get togethers' with office colleagues. We could better accommodate relations as they would accept makeshift sleeping arrangements.

The children's education dominated so much of our nineteen years in Wonersh. We were at the very margin of being able to afford the schools we had chosen. Both children followed the Prep and then public school route and without some real sacrifices by the whole family this would not have been possible. Fancy summer holidays to the likes of Tuscany and the Dordogne were out, relying instead on a holiday chalet in Ayrshire, near Turnberry, belonging to my mother-in-law. Out also were status symbol cars. We bought a new Series 3 short-wheel base Land Rover in 1972 and this lasted us until we left for Scotland some 16 years later. With some regret and a few tears Fiona sold the old 'Landy' to an enthusiast for more than we paid for it, and so it owed us nothing. When the children were very young I made small bunks in the back and the old girl saw countless trips to Scotland. I remain a 'Landy' enthusiast, notwithstanding the poor build quality, and this remained the case until very recently, with the Solihull works seemingly immune to efforts of the firm's various owners.

We bought our house in Wonersh for £7,750 and so the mortgage repayments were modest, although it never seemed so at the time I was making repayments. Domestic economies were not enough and Fiona decided to return to work. Like all working mothers the challenge was to find a job that allowed for school hours. Without use of expensive child minders, which we could not afford, the only solution was night work. Although not a nurse by training, Fiona worked for seven years at a private residential clinic in the nearby area. I do not know how she managed two nights a week and at the same time coping with the family. I was no help, leaving home at seven in the morning and arriving back at just after seven in the evening.

By 1983 both children were relatively independent, allowing Fiona to take up a full time job as Assistant Matron at Cranleigh Prep School where Andrew was in his Common Entrance year. Cranleigh contributed so much more to our lives than the excellent education of our son. Fiona went on to become Matron and Domestic Bursar and these years at Cranleigh Prep with Alan Wyatt (a former Treasury Civil Servant) as headmaster were to become some of the happiest and most fulfilling times of her life. We have still a number of close and valued friends from that period from both Prep and the senior schools. Fiona remained at the Prep school until just before we left Surrey, coinciding with Andrew, our son, leaving the sixth form to follow in the footsteps of his art master, the successful landscape painter, Alistair McMorrine, to the prestigious Glasgow School of Art. We did manage to board Andrew for his last two years at Cranleigh, and although financially a considerable additional burden, it was well worth it. A few years earlier Fiona's mother had made over to her a small sum of money. For all the children's school years it was a challenge to find the fees for Cranleigh and Farlington but I always consoled my self that should there be an emergency then there was always 'Fiona's money'. I found out some years after the children had left school that this sum had long been spent in topping up the school fees. Fiona managed all our accounts and in this role made out the cheques for the school Bursar and, although I fretted alongside, she hid some of the knife edge economics, whilst assuring me all was well and 'not to worry'. I felt so guilty when she told me that her small private funds had gone. People sometimes misjudge Fiona and fail to realise that under that mild and always polite exterior is a strong woman. My father also set up a modest fund for the children which I was able to draw on for educational purposes once the children were at senior school. This was a great help representing as it did over 10% of the total fees to be found.

We sometimes envied the parents of our children's friends, with their big houses, and exotic holidays. Some of the parents looked down upon our family because we lived in a small house in the unfashionable end of the village. Such silly and vacuous people were in the minority and indeed many parents were in the same position and similarly struggled to educate their children at both Cranleigh or Farlington. Both our children now are grateful for the sacrifice that we made and I guess Fiona and I would do it all again.

After a couple of years in Wonersh I and a friend, Bill Loader, took on an allotment just up the road in the neighbouring small village of Blackheath. This Blackheath is some forty miles from the one in south-east London, but that did not deter the occasional motorist winding down his window and asking us, going about our business on the allotment, directions for the centre of Blackheath, and clearly meaning the other one. We would direct the car up to the cross roads and "The Volunteer", our 'local'. Bill and his wife Elaine became, and still are, very good friends and although our time in Wonersh overlapped for only five years, these were the early years when both our respective families were young. We did a lot together as a foursome and got on very well. Elaine was from Edinburgh and so shared a Scottish link with Fiona. Bill was a country lad from Hampshire. To be honest both the 'girls' were long-suffering since Bill and I spent a lot of time on the allotment and *aprés* -allotment in the 'Volly' pub at Blackheath. Bill had an ancient tandem bicycle complete with oil lamps. We were always a talking point arriving at the pub on this machine. However leaving the pub on dark evenings was more of a spectacle with the lighting of the oil lamps and me trying to negotiate the fixed wheel drive mechanism. On one occasion we had a mishap with the lamps and a minor fire resulted, which was impressive to onlookers.

Bill also introduced me to the Wonersh Working Men's Club and the joys of the local darts team. We lived in the heart of what the press referred to as the Surrey 'stockbroker belt', or more unkindly then as the 'gin and Jag' belt, and so it seemed odd that every village around us boasted a working men's club or sometimes masquerading under the banner of the British Legion. Perhaps it was for this very reason that such clubs thrived in that they provided a refuge for ordinary working men in an area of conspicuous consumption and wealth. Anyway, the beer was a lot cheaper. For a small fee to the Clubs and Institutes Union (CIU) you could visit all 'affiliated' institutions. However my membership of the Wonersh Club darts team provided me with a good knowledge of all the clubs in the Tillingbourne Valley darts league. I was a lousy darts player but in Bill's reflected glory, and he was a up to reasonable pub standard, I managed to secure a place in the first team. We had some tremendous nights although it was difficult to get too worse the wear on the then Watneys 'Starlight' keg beer. Fiona and Elaine were often horrified at our 'club' activities and to my knowledge neither set foot in the Wonersh club. However one night we were all out together in a pub just outside Cranleigh and the two of them were inveigled into a game of darts against the resident 'ladies' team. I use the description 'ladies' with some hesitation as both were big girls and not the sort one would wish to meet on a dark night. The ladies were, by local reputation, 'mustard at the arrows'. Our wives had beginners' luck and came close to beating this home team. I think Bill and I were rather glad that they did not win.

Bill's father was a great character, a very knowledgeable countryman and a bee keeper. Bill knew his way around bees also and so we brought a couple of hives of bees up from his dad's Hampshire home in the back of my Land Rover. Moving bees around in the same cabin space as yourself is always a little nerve racking. Over the years we did quite well and managed to keep three or four hives in production with harvests of up to 200 pounds of honey. We produced our own label and sold some but most was given away or used to 'spread a little bread on the waters'.

Towards the end of our time in Wonersh I started exhibiting produce from my allotment at the village horticultural show and I did rather well, always winning a prize or two. As a newcomer to the local horticultural society I think I surprised a few. Luckily I ran a very large allotment and when sorting out a show sample, of potatoes for example, I had a lot of crop to select from. Finding five perfect and matching potatoes from a small sample is quite difficult, but not so difficult if one is lifting a couple of hundredweight at one time. Showing was all good fun but I grew primarily to eat and any crop up to show standard was a bonus. We were self-sufficient in vegetables for most of the year except for a late spring gap when the stored harvest is finished and spring crops such as early cabbage have yet to come on. In the growing season I spent a significant part of the weekend hoeing and cultivating the plot as well as putting on a good display in our garden. It was all very relaxing after difficult times at work. I set out in life to be a farmer and this was the nearest I could get to the outdoor life and fulfilling that dream. I remain a keen gardener and countryman to this day. I still work an allotment. I get very restless, even in retirement, if I cannot get outdoors for a time during the day, if only to potter and poke at a border or tidy up a wind-damaged tree.

Holidays are always a bit of a problem for the keen gardener and particularly at the time of life when families and schools dictate a holiday in high summer. There was a frantic race to harvest the broad beans just before our annual trip to Scotland at the beginning of August. If we had left the harvest until our return I would have lost the crop except for use as seed. During the week preceding our holiday I would bring down sacks of broad beans from the allotment to be podded, blanched and frozen. It was all hands to the pump and the children remember well being sat down with a pile of beans and a big bowl for the podded beans. I was doing the same and Fiona was operating a near production line in the kitchen blanching, chilling in cold water and bagging for our freezer. The kids moaned but pulled their weight and we never failed to complete this, regardless of season, although sometimes the beans were a little young, but this is the favoured stage of picking for the commercial crop

Packing up the Land Rover was a bit like packing for a safari, with little room for luggage inside it all had to go on the roof. I hate roof racks although ours was pretty robust. Not for us the rows of neat and matching luggage but more a collection of old boxes, school trunks and a plastic 'Mothers Pride' bread delivery crate, probably tossed overboard from a Clyde ferry boat and harvested by the children from the Ayrshire shore. I am a belt and braces man when it comes to roping a load, but I have never managed to relax with a full roof rack, whatever the vehicle. Taking the best part of twelve hours in the Land Rover, it was a slow old journey from Guildford to Ayrshire. Apart from short comfort stops we did the journey in one leg. We did have a radio but the old Series 3 Land Rover was so noisy that it was difficult to listen to above the engine and tyre noise. Sometimes we drove through the night, putting the children to bed in the back. This would not be considered safe practice these days but it avoided trying to entertain youngsters on a journey that we all found tiring. We made one trip to Scotland for Christmas when our daughter, Kathleen, was not much more than six weeks old. There was snow in Cumbria and I remember, or rather Fiona remembers, stopping in the snow on a side road and breast feeding the new baby. My grown up daughter would not have even contemplated such a journey when her children were young. I am not sure whether we were foolish or brave.

We had many low budget but very happy holidays in my mother-in-law's holiday cabin overlooking the Firth of Clyde to the Isle of Arran and of course that odd bun shaped island, Ailsa Craig, famous for curling stones. We walked a lot and were lucky to have nearby Culzean Castle, built by one of the Adam family for the Kennedys. Occasionally we would treat ourselves to a week in the Lakes or Dales and then go on to finish our holiday in Ayrshire.

My parents were regular visitors to Wonersh and would eventually follow us to a new home beside us in Aberdeenshire. My father lived to a ripe old age of 95, with all his faculties to the end including driving a new Honda car. At least every other weekend Mother and Father would motor the eighty miles or so from their home in Leigh-on-Sea to spend two or three hours with us. I do not know where my father got the energy from as at the time we came to Surrey he was already in his seventies, and by the time we left he was in his late eighties. With Cranleigh School so near my father would join with me at all the Old Cranleighan events. Towards the end he was one of the oldest to turn up to his old school. I did manage to get a photograph in the school quadrangle of the three generations of Fishers that attended Cranleigh. I think my father, in his typically understated and low key way, was very proud of this moment.

Without this full and happy home life, and our friends in Surrey, as well as one good friend I met at my very first Civil Service training course, Roy Cunningham, I do not think I would have lasted as long as I did in the Service. Roy and I used to meet, and often on a weekly basis, throughout the nineteen years I was London based. We would swap experiences, rail against the injustices of this and that government policy and generally put the world to rights. I doubt if Roy ever shared much of my political philosophy but that in no way hindered our friendship. I know that if in a tight spot he would move mountains to help. Both of us over the years have had to call upon that friendship. Our meetings were usually in the less than salubrious bars within five minutes jogging time from platform 11, where the Network South East 'Intercity' for Guildford and Portsmouth Harbour departed. Roy worked for DHSS at the Elephant and Castle for a number of years and so a train from Waterloo East was not too much out of his way. The 'Hole in the Wall', under the arches opposite the main ramp up to the station, was a favoured retreat, mainly because it was nearest to the platform, but we did wander into the Waterloo Road on occasions to enjoy a fish supper at the 'Fishcoteque' restaurant. Many are the telephone calls Fiona received from Roy to announce I was on the 21.50 apologising for keeping me. At that hour it meant she had to leave the children and make the journey to Guildford to pick me up, but somehow Roy's charm lowered the temperature. I was rarely seriously the worse for wear and on most occasions I escaped with a mild and patient rebuke.

I will return to my decision to leave the Civil Service later. I had very mixed feelings on leaving the Service but having to leave Wonersh was a wrench that took many years to recover from. I doubt if we would have ever wandered far from the Surrey and West Sussex borders if I had finished my working life as a Civil Servant.

Chapter 13

'Sunshine'

In March 1980 I was posted to what was shortly to become the new Exports to Europe Branch (EEB). I felt a great weight had been lifted from me as I returned to the bosom of DTI and the British Overseas Trade Board at the No 1, Victoria Street headquarters. I was to remain under the BOTB marketing banner until leaving the Civil Service in the winter of 1988.

Negotiations leading to my posting to EEB were surprisingly painless, but this might have reflected more that the Branch was in the process of being reorganised and the sitting tenant Assistant Secretary was having his own problems. He announced shortly after I arrived that he was going to leave the Civil Service. The office gossip was that he had suffered some career discrimination and he was going to seek success elsewhere. Anyway, I saw little of him although what I saw I liked, and felt I could have got along with. His replacement, David Wiseman, was an ex-naval officer. I had worked previously with a number of ex-servicemen and David was in that tradition. He had excellent people skills, was polite, engaging, even charismatic, and cared about his staff. He was ever cheerful and welcoming, whatever the problems. Intellectually David was up to the job, although no intellectual. It was his first job on promotion to Assistant Secretary and so he was enthusiastic and anxious to make his mark. His enthusiasm showed and was obvious to all, although in strict Civil Service tradition this was not an attribute always welcomed in those marked out for greater things.

So from the beginning the new job was looking good, but I was also happy to be back on the trade side of the Department and under the 'BOTB' banner. The Department, at the time, spent a lot of money on branding and presenting its export and trade relations efforts under this banner. I am far from clear how much that was aimed at staff as well as the business users of the array of services to assist the export effort. The BOTB was not a separate sister department like the Export Credits Guarantee Department (ECGD), which is the export insurance arm of Government, paralleling the Exim Bank in the United States and similar institutions in Europe such as Hermes in Germany. There was a distinct

BOTB ethos at grass roots level which was apart from any hangover from the 'free trading' tendency, with its roots in the old Board of Trade, and which traditionally eschewed the likes of quotas, barriers and import controls. I think the free trading stance was more an affectation of some senior staff than one of real substance. I suspect the reality was the propaganda aimed at exporters rubbed off on our staff and they began to see themselves as BOTB rather than DTI staff. My theory is supported by the often derogatory remarks made by one BOTB chief executive about the Board, its Chair and Vice Chair. Later treatment of DTI regional office staff dedicated to provision of export services reinforced my view that the front line staff's allegiance to the BOTB was an embarrassment to senior managers who welcomed the reorganisational opportunities to dilute this. The attitude of non-BOTB based senior managers was also coloured by the split-reporting of the regional Directors of Export.

The creation of Exports to Europe Branch was in recognition of the fact that we were not taking sufficient advantage of access to this huge market, covering not only European Community countries but also the EFTA (European Free Trade Area) markets, many of which are now within the Community, or now more correctly the European Union. The combined Community and EFTA market accounted for something like 80% of our exports, and so dwarfing our exports to any other market including the United States, which accounted for about the same percentage share as the then Federal Republic of Germany. So, what was the problem? It was not so much that the focus of our export effort was wrong but more that our share of each of these markets, with the exception of the anomaly of the Republic of Ireland, was smaller than their reciprocal share of the UK market. In other words our Community and EFTA competitors were doing much better in our market than we were in their markets. The publicity we put out focussed on the easy access to this huge market of about 350 million on our doorstep, and one which should be our 'natural' market and the market of first choice. Implied was that these near continental neighbours were an easier export market than North America or Commonwealth alternatives. Exports to Europe Branch set out to change perceptions and misconceptions about selling to Europe.

We used the whole public relations and advertising armoury of newspaper advertisements, videocassettes, talks by staff to export clubs and chambers of commerce, leaflets and high powered, expensive and stage managed conferences to get the message across. A favoured format was to use a well known media face, such as BBC's then front man, Brian

Redhead, to act as host and master of ceremonies with an invited audience. We would arrange for businessmen to tell of their export efforts, 'warts and all'. Then the same businessmen would be quizzed by Redhead to make the points we required. Through commissioned market research we were well aware of the obstacles, real or perceived, to firms exporting. These included fear of foreign languages, foreign currency trading, customs documentation, freight complications and, seemingly obvious, giving the European customer what he wants. We laboured this last point and the need for firms to undertake professional market research. We knew that markets within Europe differed, for example, in the acceptability of some colours, and not only in the case of textiles but even for DIY products. Of course there was a BOTB scheme offering subsidised help for market research, as well as help for just about every other aspect of exporting.

Brian Redhead's delivery was unique and I can still recall the parting line in the video with which we opened each conference. Filmed on the dockside at Dover and pointing over the Channel to France, he reminded the audience, "if you cannot export to those over there, then the likelihood is that your firm will fail in the home market here, because the competition is increasingly the same". This is even truer now twenty years on. A visit to any shopping centre in the Community will demonstrate that many of the brand names of goods on sale are the same, and this goes also for a stroll around any mall in North America. It is brought home in a practical way when on a trip to Europe one looks for something to take home to a friend or partner that is distinctive to the market and that is not easily purchased at home. It is quite a challenge.

David Wiseman allocated work to his four Principals in the new branch on the basis of a market and product matrix. I was allocated specific responsibilities for Italy, Greece, Spain and Portugal, affectionately referred to as the 'dago desk'. I was also assigned a number of industry sector responsibilities which included the DIY sector, agricultural machinery and produce, including breeding livestock and food. These sector responsibilities were 'horizontal' in that they were across all markets and not just my southern European clutch. It sounds a bit messy and we all thought so initially, but with a bit of good will and David Wiseman's 'can do' enthusiasm it worked quite well. The sector priorities reflected inputs from the European Trade Committee, one of the geographical area advisory committees spawned by the BOTB Board. The European Trade Committee was serviced by the Exports to Europe Branch and was ably chaired by Sir Derek Ezra, then Chair of the

National Coal Board. The Committee, like the BOTB Board, had senior representation from most of manufacturing industry, and I worked very closely with a number of them including the Hon. Michael Sieff of Marks and Spencer, Eddie Rayne of shoe fame and Barry Reed of the store group Austin Reed. Priorities also reflected advice from the commercial staff in our European embassies and consulates, as well as our own collective wisdom in EEB. At least we had clear priorities, unlike my Latin America desk experience where we were often left to the whim of career opportunists in the FCO. We wasted far less time in EEB on turf wars with the FCO thanks to a number of strong individuals on the European Trade Committee who were universally respected, and their judgement was rarely challenged by an eager Consul Commercial in one of our overseas posts. However there were exceptions. For me, my burden was the staff in Milan, from where the FCO directed their commercial operations in Italy. My colleague covering France had similar difficulties with Paris who always thought they knew best.

A number of our businessmen advisers were a joy to work with. I would single out Michael Sieff for particular praise. Alas, Michael is no longer with us. He was the brother of Lord Marcus Sieff and, with his brother, a Director of Marks and Spencer. He was a delightful man, with a good sense of humour, unfailingly polite and considerate. My staff loved him, as did the canteen staff at No 1, Victoria Street, where he always made a point of going behind the scenes to thank them for a lunch or buffet. I and members of my staff were frequent visitors to M&S headquarters in Baker Street for meetings with Michael. Often we would be invited to lunch. This was beautifully served with good but not over the top fare. Michael would proudly boast what parts of the meal were from the 'shop'. I had the privilege of accompanying Michael on a market research trip to Italy to look at the potential for UK produced building and DIY goods in that market. Through his contacts we met the founder of the Texas Homecare chain of DIY shops, another successful Jewish businessman, Manny Cohen. I got to know Michael reasonably well or at least well enough to visit him in hospital after a heart condition scare and to be invited to his house at Wentworth.

Wally Johnstone was an ICI Plant Protection man and was our adviser on the export potential for agricultural hardware, pesticides, chemicals and other farm inputs. Wally hailed from the West of Scotland and his name was actually William or Willy, but in Scotland this is often pronounced Wullie and in translation to Haslemere, where he was based, this became Wally. One could not imagine two more different people than Wally Johnstone and Michael Sieff. Wally was endearingly pompous, and insisted his status as a senior executive was reflected in choice of travel means and quality of hotel. However I soon got used to his little foibles and came to appreciate the very kindly man underneath that blustering exterior. Like me he appreciated a tincture or two, but I never saw him the worse for wear, which is more than I can say for some businessmen I have had the misfortune to be closeted with on overseas trips. When the chips were down Wally was a pleasant enough travelling companion. This was well tested when we took an exploratory visit through northern Greece from Salonica towards the Turkish border looking at Greek agriculture, with a view to better trade in both directions. The hotels were not up to Wally's standard and neither was the food but, in spite of a gruelling schedule and his age, he coped well. I managed to ensure when we returned to Athens he had a good hotel and excellent food. He quickly forgot all the 'hardship' when seated in plush surroundings with a firm grip on a gin and tonic. I respected Wally but I cannot say that I learnt much from him, but quoting such a senior businessman was useful to impose my own judgement of market potentials.

Sometimes we got our choice of businessmen horribly wrong! It had become the fashion for Ministers, and no less the Chairman of the BOTB, to take a bevy of business people on an overseas mission. For Ministers it helped deflect some of the criticisms of overseas 'jollies' at the public expense, but for the BOTB it was an opportunity to capture press publicity for the export effort and services of the BOTB. The occasion I have in mind occurred during a trip to Italy with our then BOTB Chairman, Lord George Jellicoe. I thought we should try and find a recently self-made businessman from the engineering sector, who still remembered what it was like to have dirty hands. With Jellicoe's blessing to the idea and help of colleagues in our West Midlands office, I came up with what I thought was the ideal candidate. He was self-made and successful, and complete with a strong Black Country accent he would send the right message to numerous small engineering firms in the hoped-for home press coverage of the mission. I got an inkling during the car journey from the airport in Rome that all might not go to plan when Jellicoe, to break the ice, spotted my man's regimental tie and asked him which regiment he had been with. He said he did not know but he had a whole collection of regimental ties. For a second or two Jellicoe was, unusually, lost for words. He then burst into laughter and we all joined in. I am not sure whether my man saw it as that funny. All went well that evening with only a report he had enjoyed a drink or two, but he did not appear for breakfast the next morning and neither took part in the schedule of visits arranged for that day. Eventually I caught up with him and he said he found it all too much for him and he was going home. I think he felt he was out of his depth and was a bit in awe of Jellicoe. A pity because Jellicoe was not a snob and neither were the rest of the business team with us in any way stuffy. This 'failure' came as a complete surprise as I had met him and had a long conversation in the preceding weeks and he seemed robust, normal (whatever normal is) and affable. There was another trip with businessmen where one gentleman spent most of the time under the influence and I wish he had gone home early, but I was really disappointed my engineer from the West Midlands did not stay the course.

I regret that I never managed to accompany a Minister on an overseas trip, which was odd since I spent over seven years on country 'desks'. In the case of my Latin America stint, Ministers all took their Private Secretary and sometimes a Press Officer. This left little reason to add yet another official. In the case of European Community countries, it was hard for Ministers to justify a trade mission and so Ministerial visits tended to be short and for very specific purpose. If it was to discuss vehicle emissions, or steel for example then they took the relevant specialist from the 'sponsor ' branch. In many ways for me to accompany the Chairman of the BOTB was a better bet. There was less pressure and I am sure, especially with Jellicoe, a lot more fun.

Make no mistake Jellicoe could be demanding. He was pernickety about his speeches but eventually I acquired a style he was happy with. Sometimes he would depart from the script I had prepared and on one occasion put the draft aside altogether. I got quite a kick from hearing my words spoken at an important reception. He was demanding in the bringing together of a visit programme, whether that was at home or overseas. He wanted a programme that was intrinsically interesting and entertaining. He would do the bread and butter stuff as long as a there was also something that grabbed his personal interest. On occasions he would get quite irate. On one visit we were being regaled by the Milton Keynes Development Corporation, including their chairman on the joys of life in this new town. Jellicoe was getting visibly agitated and suddenly asked the assembled company of some twenty Milton Keynes senior officials and dignitaries "Which of you buggers actually live in Milton Keynes?" There was some embarrassed mumbling with the upshot that not one of the company present lived in this Shangri La. Jellicoe said something about resting his case.

After over three years of underemployment it was a joy to be back in a busy job. I had a staff of fifteen which is quite large by Principal standards, but reflected that we were largely engaged in delivery of a service rather than policy work. Most of the policy input was confined to myself and a couple of HEOs. The rest of the staff had their country desk responsibilities which were to collate all the trade and export related information from the FCO and other sources, and tailor this to the face-to-face dealings with individual exporters as well as Chambers of Commerce and exports clubs across the country. These staff would also be the interface on all matters concerning their country responsibility with our regional offices. Desk officers would be expected to be knowledgeable on a whole range of industry and business sectors as well as have grasp of the mechanics of exporting, from customs documentation to freight and insurance. All this and never having exported a bean between the lot of us!

Training for the job was provided by the Department but I never rated the quality very highly. Some very motivated staff studied for the Institute of Export qualification which was first class, but these staff were in the minority. One of the disincentives was the little career reward or advancement offered by the Department. We ran a scheme also to second young staff to FCO posts overseas for six months. This was popular and staff with this experience had a better understanding of the overseas export intelligence gathering operation, as well as the opportunity to see how some of the many BOTB schemes to assist exporters operated in practice. In spite of the inadequacies of formal training, my staff took great pride in the quality of the service offered to the exporter, and became very proficient in what they did. I would receive many compliments from business people about my staff, but I was far from sure how much their dedication and work was appreciated by those very senior managers in both the BOTB and DTI at large. Subsequent events were to confirm my doubts.

Even at the time of the formal launch of the Exports to Europe there was significant distrust by export services staff of management's intentions for the core of the BOTB services. I was at the time on the Branch Committee of the union and was aware of the reports from other Branches. One of the biggest concentrations of BOTB staff was at Export House by Ludgate Hill. Here was the hub of the numerous services provided by the BOTB to exporters, including the Export Intelligence Service which for a highly subsidised fee provide businesses with specific export opportunities, categorised both by industry sector and by market.

This information was gathered by the Foreign Office's then 200 overseas embassies and consulates. The Export Intelligence Service edited, catalogued and dispatched the information to individual businesses against the profile of interest specified by the firm. Export House was also responsible for a whole raft of other services to exporters. It was not a 'policy' operation but a large and complex service job. As such the work was seen as low grade by senior managers and of an 'executive' nature, at least in terms of the pre-Fulton Report Administrative/Executive split of staff. Even when distinctions have been formally swept away we British are curiously resourceful and have means of hanging on to such class divisions and, although never referred to as such, there is a wealth of complex and coded undertone that ensure continuance of subtle discrimination. So it was for Export House, with constant snipes and snide remarks by senior staff across town at No.1, Victoria Street, notwithstanding that a lot of the Victoria Street-based country desk staff had worked in Export House at one time or another.

By chance, at the time of the preparations for EEB's public launch, one of the Export House staff had come across a piece of paper with outline plans to dismember large parts of the Export House operation. Although not directly involved I was aware of this leak, and what was at stake for the continuing quality of service to exporters if DTI was to go ahead with the cuts in service suggested in the leaked document. On the day of the press launch of EEB, the leaked document had found its way to the papers and grabbed the headlines. David Wiseman was furious of course and although most of us sympathised with whoever passed the internal document to the press, we felt really sorry for David. There was a lot of backtracking by senior staff and although the authenticity of the proposals concerning Export House was acknowledged, the official explanation was that the document was nothing more than the thoughts of one person and was not policy. Export House survived for the time being and to my knowledge, as was usually the case in the then very leaky DTI, the culprit was never discovered or acknowledged. I do remember one occasion in DTI, after a series of leaks in the Thatcher years, the Permanent Secretary sent round a confidential memo aimed at stemming the growing leak problem. The next day the memo was featured in the press. It is a bit like the freedom fighter/ guerrilla conundrum, it depends where you stand as to whether the unauthorised release of information is a leak or is whistle-blowing.

One senior member of staff got most of the blame for growing morale problems amongst export services staff in BOTB and that was our

Deputy Secretary, John Caines. The growing staff discontent was dubbed the Caine Mutiny. At the time there was a relatively new in-house newspaper called *Ti-Line* ('Ti' from Trade & Industry), and was like any other in-house newspaper, a tool of management, but none the worse for that. A small group of export services staff took the title and produced an alternative and underground news sheet called *Sigh Line*. This was crudely produced on an office photocopier. All senior staff and particularly Caines and my Under Secretary, Stephen Burbridge, were lampooned in the style of the satirical weekly *Private Eye*. There was even a titillating serial story of sex in the office featuring various and supposedly fictitious senior staff members, as well as the adventures of a man-hungry personal secretary with lesbian tendencies. It was not too hard to identify the lady or any of the lead characters. Good fun and required reading by all, and not least by my Under Secretary at the time. After twenty-five or so editions it had served its purpose and faded away. I still have a much passed around and so rather ragged copy of *Sigh-Line*. I have no clue who wrote for *Sigh-Line* although there was plenty of gossip at the time.

As had been my experience through most of my Civil Service career I was again blessed with excellent staff who were a joy to work with. I would single out Daphne Wilmot. Daphne was one of that breed of loyal and remarkable lady HEOs of a 'certain age'. She was a keen gardener and I delegated to her the responsibility for contact with the horticultural equipment manufacturers. England had, and still has, a worldwide reputation as a nation of gardeners and a growing number of firms were reaching a stage where exporting was a viable option for them. Daphne took up the challenge and soon had us committed to a stand at the annual horticultural trades 'British Growers Look Ahead' exhibition in Harrogate. From this small beginning we became major exhibitors at the Stoneleigh 'Royal Show'. Our first appearance at Stoneleigh was an amateurish affair with not much bigger than a scout tent, but we built up over the years to a sophisticated and professionally designed pavilion that attracted many VIPs including our Vice-Chairman, the Duke of Kent. We learnt quickly the importance of being in the driving seat with stand designers and having one's own clear vision of the theme and layout. Daphne enjoyed negotiating with designers and exhibitors, and was very successful in obtaining sponsorship for hospitality. I remember particularly a very good deal on quality English wine.

Manning a stand at a big exhibition is one of the most physically demanding and mentally exhausting tasks. The Royal is very much an open-air occasion and we were lucky in that most of our appearances at the

Royal coincided with warm weather, but working on a stand twelve hours a day in a warm pavilion is draining. However Daphne was one for her creature comforts and she started early in the year in finding us a suitable hotel, which was not easy in the Coventry and Warwickshire area at the time of the Royal. High on her list of priorities was good food to return to. The bar was not so much of a problem since Daphne was always well prepared and ensured we had a good bottle of single malt to accompany our review of the day's events on returning to the hotel in the evening.

By the time I had left the Exports to Europe Branch we were running a big operation at the Royal Show with at least four staff and additional staff who would come up for the day as well as those from the DTI West Midlands office in Birmingham. Was it all cost effective? I have never known a trade show or overseas mission where any of the organisers and paymasters have been anything less that 'very satisfied' and usually in even more upbeat terms. So it was for me, although oddly no one asked me to to justify the cost in terms of number of trade inquiries, new exporter customers or even the ratio of leaflets handed out to free drinks given at our daily five o'clock reception on the stand. If the Chairman or the Vice Chairman of the BOTB went away impressed and one or two VIPs said nice things about the stand, then Daphne and I were happy. The cost of the stand was not met from my immediate budget but was paid for by the generously budgeted Fairs and Promotions Branch who were responsible for putting on British trade fairs around the world. These people were real professionals and however difficult the country or locality of a trade fair, it was always 'all right on the night'. I learnt a lot about staging fairs and this was to stand me in good stead in a future job in Scotland, although there I was to attempt to take firmer control of costs and try and relate them, in some small way, to effectiveness.

I look back on my involvement with the agricultural and horticultural industry as one of the most satisfying aspects of my work in EEB. I had my difficulties, and perhaps surprisingly, with the Ministry of Agriculture. The Royal was a big event in MAFF's calendar, with involvement of many of their Ministers and the good and the great of the industry, but they did not see it as their responsibility to get too closely involved with the export promotion side of the business, at least as far as the inputs to agriculture, such as farm machinery for example, were concerned. At the same time, although I really tried to build bridges, the response I got was dismissive and even arrogant. In later years I observed with interest MAFF's handling of BSE and the Foot and Mouth outbreak and I saw again that arrogance, but an arrogance that accompanied an incompetence. In the case of BSE I would judge their handling of control measures as bordering on criminal incompetence. During my years at the Royal I would ask my MAFF colleagues to receptions on the BOTB stand and for the most part they would accept. However, never was I asked to attend one MAFF reception, notwithstanding I had a good friend in their Press Office at the time. My work for agricultural machinery firms and other manufacturing allied to the agricultural industry was publicly rubbished on one occasion, with the suggestion that I knew little about farming. Unlike most of my Administrative colleagues in MAFF I did have an agricultural degree and as part of that had worked on a farm. Eventually, and after my period of involvement, MAFF took on our export services role at the Royal. MAFF aside, I made some good friends in the industry and I suppose this work, although but a small proportion of my portfolio, enabled me to live little bits of a life that might have been if I had stuck to my dream of being a farmer.

Rarely was Fiona able to join me on a trip away from the office. The Civil Service is just not like that, but in my pursuance of increased exports of breeding livestock she accompanied me on a research trip to the West Country to look at the South Devon and 'red ruby' Devon breed societies, in Newton Abbot and Wiveliscombe respectively. The Devons are a beef breed with the dark coat of a red setter dog. The breed society had been working with Peter Scott-King of the British Consulate in Florence to introduce the breed to the sparse hillsides of northern Italy. Unlike the huge and necessarily pampered continental beef breeds, the Devons are hardy low maintenance beasts, and will graze happily on the parched hill pastures of an Italian summer as well as suffer the cold of the winters. A breakthrough was made in establishing a two hundred cow herd with a communist led co-operative at Monghidoro, near Bologna, and at the time was proving successful. So Fiona and I were received with open arms by the society's Secretary, Mr Tony Pascoe, and were taken to a number of farms in the Exmoor area. I got some flak from my colleagues in the South West office in Bristol, saying that my visit was a waste of time. I had the chance later to visit the herd in Italy where the young communist mayor of the small farming commune greeted us as minor royalty. I am not aware we exported any more Red Devons to Italy but this herd did wonders for the profile of British beef in Italy. I have wasted time and resources on many occasions in wild goose chases but I feel I was just on the right side of the line here. I am the proud wearer of a Devon breed society tie and so am still doing my bit to justify a very pleasant three days in the West Country and, incidentally, the land of my fathers. Even now when visiting county shows I head straight for the cattle lines and the 'red rubies'.

Unfortunately David Wiseman decided to leave the Civil Service and for the last part of my time with EEB I had a change of boss. David's successor was more of a time server and had none of David's style and chutzpah. Although I did not always see eye to eye with David, I enjoyed his style and above all his fresh enthusiasm. I think my fellow Principal colleagues were also very sorry to see him go. I have retained contact with David's personal assistant, Jean. Jean shared an office with Carole, the PA to the Under Secretary. In some respects these two ladies ran the office. Carole was so much larger than life, was well spoken, tall, good looking and was said to be from a relatively comfortable background. One of her admirers was a BT engineer assigned to servicing DTI's telephones, and affectionately known to all as 'Busby' after a cartoon bird used in a BT television advertisement of the time. He became almost a member of staff as he was around so much. When I first arrived in EEB I was a little wary of visiting Carol and Jean's office. They were merciless to any slightly naive male but once you had survived the baptism, both were colleagues you could rely on. Both were excellent at their jobs, but Jean was more measured and, if it was possible, a steadying influence in the office. Jean was also an excellent personal assistant and I know she was much valued by her boss. How much the Under Secretary valued Carole is difficult for me to judge. She sent him up, like the rest of us did, but I am not sure how far he was aware of this. In my personal dealings with him, I found little sense of humour and indeed he rarely impinged on my life in the office. I do know he did not like my outspokenness and I was to suffer for this. Principals did not have personal secretaries or personal assistants and I used to wonder how I would cope with a larger than life Carole-equivalent sitting guard over me and my office. In a few months time I was promoted and was allocated a secretary. She was nothing like Carole.

I served nearly five years in EEB which was by far my longest posting. As my fortieth birthday passed I was becoming impatient over lack of promotion. This posting had enabled me to recover my reputation somewhat from the dark days of Iron and Steel and General Divisions. I was getting markings in my last three annual reports in EEB as 'fit for promotion' to Assistant Secretary, but promotion was not happening. I became very frustrated and from about 1984 started to look for opportunities outside the Civil Service, although I looked also at a transfer to the Northern Ireland Civil Service and the Scottish Office, believing the grass might be greener. I had made regular business visits to

Ulster and liked what I saw. Amongst the avenues investigated over the next five years were the Royal Agriculture Society of Ulster, British Agrochemicals Association, Royal College of Surgeons, Chief Executive of the Falkland Islands Government, Chief Executive of the Slough Chamber of Commerce, economic development officer for the Shetland Islands Council and a similar role in a Fylde coast development body. I looked also into a twelve months exchange with the Australian government in Canberra, but pulled out of negotiations since I realised I would have faced the same problems on returning to our Civil Service. Although I did not secure an interview, the Falkland application almost caused a major rift with my wife. We came to an amicable compromise and should I have got the job I would have left Fiona at home for part of the year. Although all friends thought I was quite mad, I would have loved the challenge and was disappointed not to get even an interview. In one of those odd coincidences of life my predecessor but one at the job I was to take up in Grampian in 1988 was a Falkland Islands Chief Executive. Also a long retired Chief Executive lived in Wonersh, although I never met him.

As in most offices, the convention was to hold a 'going away party' for the benefit of the staff. The convention was also used by the ambitious to invite a sprinkling of senior and possibly influential colleagues, presumably all in the name of networking. However I saw my leaving party as simply a way of thanking those who had worked for me. EEB had been a happy as well as very sociable period in my Civil Service career. I can recall the many agreeable evenings, or 'soirees' as they were dubbed, spent with staff in various hostelries between Victoria Street and the City. Favourites were the Cheshire Cheese in Fleet Street and the Buckingham Arms in Petty France behind Victoria Street. It followed that my leaving 'do' had to be in a pub and not the office. The venue was the bar then on the platform of the District and Circle line at Sloane Square. Bars on Underground stations were rare, and indeed the only other such bar I can recall was on Liverpool Street's Circle Line platform. Kew had a pub which joined the Underground station, although the line is over ground here. The Sloane Square station bar was tiny and opened directly onto the platform. We managed to fill the bar nicely. Again according to convention I was taken for a farewell lunch by my then Assistant Secretary, but I do not recall more than a rather stiff and formal occasion. I was really sorry to leave EEB and my staff, but I was going on promotion.

Chapter 14

Zero

The South East Regional Office of the Department of Trade & Industry was located in Ebury Bridge House, a low-key block of offices on the corner of Ebury Bridge Road and Pimlico Road, and a couple of hundred yards beyond Victoria coach station. The coach station is an island of down-at-heel seediness on the very edge of Belgravia and within easy walking distance of Sloane Square. Ebury Bridge House straddled that no man's land. Beside it were council flats but a hundred yards towards Sloane Square were all the smart restaurants and art shops that were the haunt of the legendary Sloane Rangers and their ilk. Ebury Bridge House was a collectors item 1930s style building and, until a recent 'renovation', would have seen little change since the day it was built, complete with metal window frames. This was to be my office for the next couple of years and, apart from a brief sojourn up the road to Bridge Place, a building overlooking the platforms of Victoria station, was to be my last Civil Service office.

The DTI South East Regional Office was a large bureaucracy with responsibilities for putting the region's economic case to Ministers and for the services to business and exporters in the South East. The area was vast, covering fifteen counties as well as London, the City and its boroughs, stretching from Oxfordshire, and Hampshire in the west and south, and from Norfolk to Kent. The Isle of Wight, with which I was to have quite a lot of contact, is included as a county, long having split from its mainland neighbour, Hampshire. The region was dominated by the Capital and little of the patch could be considered as having its own and independent character distinct from London, with the exception of Norwich which, with Aberdeen, is probably the best UK example of a city region. By this I mean a large area that is dominated both culturally and economically by a single city, with no nearby competition to dilute the influence of the city on its surrounding countryside. One of the biggest centres of population outside the M25 orbital road is to be found in the 'twin' conurbation of Portsmouth and Southampton. These two, sometimes referred to collectively as Solent City, are hardly a Minneapolis/St Paul and indeed they hated to be bracketed together. In spite of considerable respective local pride, the office did not see a local identity and culture here that was that separate from that of London. It is hard to escape the gravitational pull of London.

This gravitational pull was responsible for many of the problems that faced the South East Regional Office. In the Thatcher boom years there was an unwillingness to accept that the South East was anything else other than prosperous and the power house of the UK economy. It was and still is of course, but within the region and within the Capital itself there were pockets of unemployment and appalling deprivation. Some of these black spots were well known and only too obvious, for example the problems that faced inner London boroughs such as Tower Hamlets and Brent. Because of the battles of some of these boroughs with the Government, their problems were high profile, notwithstanding the attempts of the Government to body swerve real problems by blaming ' loony left' councils for inefficiency in their use of public funds. At the same time there were pockets of similar economic hardship outside London that were given no publicity and Ministers were quite content that should remain so. Part of the Regional Office's role was to draw Ministers' attention to the problems and try to secure some redress via the various regional development aid packages or similar intervention. One such area was East Kent and another the Isle of Wight. The island exhibited most of the problems of island communities wherever they may be found in the UK, be it the Hebrides or the Scilly Isles, and these were reliance on seasonal tourism, high freight costs and so high raw materials costs and a resulting lack of investment over the years. Most of the south coast resort towns had chronic unemployment during the out-of-season months and this was exacerbated on an island. Isle of Wight people are fiercely proud and not content with securing county status separate from Hampshire across the Solent it was said that there was even a small independence movement.

Popular belief has it that all the heavy and dirty manufacturing industry is to be found other than in south-east England. Nothing could be further from the truth. In the eighties the region accounted for a third of manufacturing industry and a half of potential UK exporters. One associates the vehicle industry with the Midlands although a substantial part of UK manufacture was in the south-east, with Ford at Dagenham, Leyland at Cowley and Vauxhall at Luton. The south-east even now remains a focus of specialist car manufacture with Aston Martin Lagonda near Milton Keynes, the new BMW owned Rolls Royce and Caterham cars and a number of world famous racing car builders scattered around the home counties.

The DTI regional office was headed up by an Assistant Secretary working with four Senior Principals, or equivalent, and something over 130 staff. Export services staff accounted for 54 of the office staff total. Gerry Bradshaw was the Assistant Secretary and it was to Gerry that I reported on 5 February 1985.

The 'normal' route to promotion from Principal was in fact far from normal and straightforward. For all grades below this, with the exception of the fast stream graduate entry, promotion was by appearance before a Promotion Board. Boards were held periodically throughout the year, depending on the Department's need to fill vacancies. Access to a Board depended on Annual Confidential Report recommendations and Personnel would trawl all such reports, bringing forward all those with 'fitted' or 'well fitted' for promotion markings. All things being equal this was fairly automatic and routine and, importantly, individuals got to make their mark before a board. Often I acted as an 'external' member of such boards and they were a model of fairness and objectivity. However for promotion from Principal there was then no board procedure, except in the case of a few specialist jobs. Personnel would do similar sifts of Annual Reports and there would be some panel of senior staff to determine who should be promoted, but the individual never got to make his or her case before a board in the full light of day. Decisions were made behind closed doors and rarely did one find out why promotion was slow or absent. However the ten DTI Regional 'Directors/Export' posts were subject to a board appearance and one could indicate an interest in any such vacancy. The job was advertised amongst BOTB staff and I applied, was interviewed and got the job. I was a bit surprised, even though I was very well qualified for the role, because I was by now convinced that there was a black mark against my name and any promotion was blocked. It was because of this assumption I had been searching for a job outside the Service. All I did find out from my new boss, and as a result of private discussion by the board members after my appearance, was that views amongst senior management were split equally between those who could not stand me and those who thought I was 'brilliant' and a breath of fresh air. I was ultimately to fall foul of the former, ably assisted by reports from my last boss in the Civil Service.

Directors/Exports were somewhat a law unto themselves and had a profile and wielded influence beyond that normally associated with Senior Principal (later Grade 6) seniority. In colloquial terms, they punched above their weight and the position was somewhat analogous to a trusted sergeant major. Part of the reason for this was that most of them were time-served BOTB export specialists. Many were 'characters' and were the object of many and likely apocryphal tales, as indeed was our Assistant Secretary, Gerry Bradshaw. Also, by nature of the job, they were well known in every UK embassy and consulate the world over, and similarly with the 1, Victoria Street 'country desks', including Exports to Europe Branch where I had just spent five years. All had direct and easy access to the BOTB, and to individual members of the Board, including the Chief Executive, who held the grade of Deputy Secretary. Most would have been on close terms with the Chairman of the Board and on first name terms with most of the key industrialists in their region.

I was delighted to get the job and assume the title of Director/Export (South East), but like so much in this region all was not what it seemed. The post had been unoccupied for a number of months and the staff were demoralised and lacked leadership. The South-East export staff had a poor reputation at home and overseas and so much so that the office was widely referred to internally by a corruption of its initials, SERO (South East Regional Office), as 'ZERO'. I was aware of this reputation from my previous work in EEB where my staff constantly complained of the negative response they received to inquiries of SERO. I was not daunted by this and rather relished the opportunity of turning 'ZERO' into the premier regional export team that the businesses in the south-east deserved.

Gerry Bradshaw was very welcoming and supportive, although he was happy to leave sorting out the export staff to me. His forte was the office's link with industry and the associated structural problems in the south-east, where he was assisted by a very knowledgeable and skilled staff. That is not to say that Gerry was not interested in my branch of his large portfolio, and indeed would often set aside the time for a chat. We were amidst the Thatcher years and it was important that the philosophy of the office reflected the values set by our political masters. Gerry never found this particularly difficult and my guess was that his own politics were right of centre, although modestly so, as one would expect in a seasoned Civil Servant. At the same time he was fiercely supportive of those areas and industries that were suffering in a new and 'bracing' economic environment. This was a difficult balancing act for him and his staff in dealing with the fallout of the government's policy, but at the same time ensuring the DTI South East office was as supportive to business as possible in the circumstances. A lot of the pressure the office could exert had to be behind the scenes via briefings to Ministers in the hope of changing their minds on some issues. Gerry was very good at dealing with individual businessmen, helped by his extrovert character. He never appeared too cerebral which also, oddly and typically British, helped in relations with business, who tended to be suspicious of Whitehall intellectuals. He was popular in the office and this was helped by Gerry's willingness to give staff their head.

Gerry was also anxious that my links with business should be developed as well as my understanding of the business psyche. To that end he put in considerable effort to find me a non-executive appointment with one of the firms in our patch. This was not easy, partly for the reasons I refer to above and firms' suspicion of Whitehall officials. Eventually I was fixed up with a firm making large-scale industrial equipment. At the time there were only three to four large manufacturers of such equipment and a number of smaller firms. I was not able to secure a full non-executive board appointment but was invited to attend all board meetings of the firm and see all the papers. I was also provided with good access to the firm's directors, including the finance director. I would attend meetings about once a month and this arrangement lasted for just over two years. During that period the firm's financial position deteriorated. In my view the firm had long outgrown the Chairman's skills. The financial director was young and inexperienced and during my period he was to part company with the firm. The fact that the finance director was allowed to retain his position as long he did was surprising to me, but obviously not to Chairman and the other senior directors. Accounting practices and systems were at best nebulous and questions on cash flow remained unanswered. It was an eye-opener as to how business works and how amateurish management can be. In the end I think the Chairman became concerned about my DTI links and that I might break the pledge of confidentiality I agreed to when I began to attend board meetings. Finally I was asked not to attend meetings "until they had got things sorted out", and in spite of attempts to make further contact, all my subsequent communications were ignored. My position as an informal board member made it difficult to make much of a contribution to the firm. I think I did achieve an improvement in the standard of financial reporting to the board, as well as making some practical suggestions on product development, new technology appraisal and board appointments.

Throughout the slide in the fortunes of the company, the directors' cars got no smaller and the Chairman's life style never seemed threatened. I was unlucky in Gerry's choice of firm in one way, but in another it was a revelation to see the workings of the business world. I never again accepted the assumption that somehow a private sector operation is superior and more efficiently run than its public sector equivalent. The sectors are different, and each has different requirements in the effective running of their respective operations, but neither is intrinsically any more or less efficient or 'better'. The constant criticism by Ministers of public sector enterprises, together with their staff, was a factor in my growing disillusionment with the Civil Service during the eighties. Unfortunately the prejudice against public sector capability to run enterprises efficiently is still with us, in spite of the disaster of our railways privatisation, and the catastrophic failure of the likes of Marconi, Enron and the many household names in the UK financial services industry. It is difficult to suppress the satisfying sense of *schadenfreude* when another trumpeted icon of private enterprise bites the dust, as in the case of the effective return in 2002 of Railtrack to the public sector.

With Gerry Bradshaw's blessing I set about raising the morale of my new office. The region was split between the staff on a geographical basis. Each HEO and his staff had two or three counties apiece with special arrangements for London with, for example, the person in charge of delivering BOTB export services in Surrey would also cover south-west London boroughs such as Richmond and Kingston. I started by accompanying my HEOs on a typical day on the road visiting clients. Most calls were on request but the staff also did some 'cold' calling. It was not long before the bean counters had allocated targets for the office including the need to call on a specified number of firms each week. As an experienced bureaucrat I now know that anyone with half a brain can always beat such crude work measurement systems, and without any increase in real efficiency. Early attempts by staff to beat the system were also crude with one staff member bumping up his number of calls on 'engineering' firms by a quick call on garages in his area. The tighter the screws were applied the more sophisticated the staff came in beating the system. In a later job I was myself subjected to crude quantitative targets. With the SERO experience under my belt rarely did such targets or norms cause me a problem. First of all they are rarely imposed arbitrarily, as the person setting them lacks the knowledge and therefore the confidence to ask you to meet a target that you have not agreed to. So such mutually agreed targets are set at a level you know you can meet and reflect the speed of the slowest ship. One also holds a fair margin in hand to demonstrate 'improvements' in the months ahead. My problem was to raise the morale of staff and not to see them distracted by office number games that had little bearing on the quality of the service that the staff could give to British exporters.

Like all good managers I spent a lot of time talking to staff and seeing what their problems were. This alone was almost enough to turn matters around, but I was anxious to overcome the 'Zero' tag. Even if we improved our response to internal customers it would take years to eradicate the perception of a negative office. We had to have a quick fix makeover that clearly said 'under new management'. I had a Senior Executive Officer (SEO), Peter Morris, who had worked for a private sector firm specialising in 'event management', which entailed arranging seminars and exhibitions for clients. I do not know why Peter came back to the Civil Service as he had a real flair for this work. I guess the Service offered a more stable and secure life. Peter was extremely bright and talented but I fear the Department's treatment of him was shabby. He was very much the intellectual and as such he was seen by some as reaching above his station. I got on very well with Peter and together we rebranded the office with a new logo, new stationery and ensured all staff had visiting cards, which was not the case before we started. We did not seek specific permission for these changes on the basis of the old adage that if you put senior management on the spot by asking permission, then for safety they will say 'no'. Peter commissioned graphic designers and produced a smart and snappy 'BOTB Southeast' logo instead of the bland DTI Southeast Regional Office masthead, although I must admit we were influenced by the British Rail branding of their 'Network Southeast' operation. I am sure these changes helped boost internal morale as much as it did to improve our image to both internal and external customers alike. After all was in place we got the odd gasp of astonishment from the heavens in DTI including from the then BOTB Chief Executive who muttered to me under his breath "You can't do that". However that was as far as it went and we carried on promoting our new image. Eventually the whole of the South East office adopted the snappier 'DTI Southeast' title, but minus our pastel coloured lettering that was fashionable at the time.

This was just the start of the task of raising our profile. By that time, in the mid eighties, numerous local radio stations were springing up in the south-east. The BBC had stations in most counties in the patch, for example BBC Radio Kent and BBC Radio Surrey. There were often overlapping independent radio stations and one we worked with closely was Radio 210 (now 2Ten FM) in Reading. London was more of a problem since stations there were 'national' in character rather than local and no station served the immediate locality as did the stations outside the capital. I encouraged staff to get alongside local stations in their respective patches and try and access, if possible on a regular basis, the news and business programmes. In the case of some staff you could see the fear in their faces when I made the suggestion that they should get involved with radio. A few took to broadcasting like ducks to water but some, in spite of professional media training arranged by Peter Morris, never overcame their fears, although all were capable of addressing public gatherings of exporters at local chambers of commerce and export clubs. In the early stages Peter and I blazed the trail negotiating regular broadcasting slots on business news and discussion programmes around the area. With the odd exception we found out that only the BBC stations were worth pursuing as only they had a schedule that included a business orientated programme. The one exception was the Reading independent station which took their business listeners seriously enough to dedicate a weekly programme to them. These would often take the form of a live studio discussion with questions 'phoned in by listeners. This was a first for me and all good experience. I took advantage of a first class media training course paid for by the Department and this has stood me in good stead over the years since.

We had great fun and got to know one or two radio station managers quite well. In the case of BBC Radio Kent we instituted a Kent 'Exporter of the Year' award. This was successful, and with separate programmes interviewing finalists as well as broadcasting the final awards ceremony it created more publicity than we could have ever bought by advertisement placements in the local press. Radio Kent were pleased too since they had a strong community commitment to their listeners beyond just entertainment. Also we wrote a regular script for a London radio station featuring export news stories, and where possible relating these to London based industry. We would also run regular features on specific markets, but we were not involved in these broadcasts as such. After a short settling down period our scripts were used unedited. We tried to farm out the script writing around the office, but try as we did only a couple of colleagues had the aptitude. So, much of the burden of meeting a regular script deadline fell to Peter and me. I learnt quickly how a deadline can focus the mind and where just getting something down on paper was the priority. How different from the hours of careful consultation and research required in drafting the answer to a Parliamentary Question. Again I learnt a lot from Peter about writing for broadcasting and writing copy for publicity brochures.

We produced our own promotional video, using a film company but writing the script, providing the direction and the front of camera talent. We tried to break from the style of actor John Cleese in Monty Python's 'government spokesman' and make the commentary chatty and friendly. It worked at the time but is slightly quaint when viewed nearly twenty years later. All this was done from BOTB promotional budgets without a murmur from the purse string holders. It had not been done before by a regional office, and no one had written the rule book. A quirk of large bureaucracies is asking for something quite small, like the proverbial roll of sticky tape, is sure to produce some little Hitler in charge of a stationery cupboard who will say 'no', but ask for something really large and expensive then the machine fails, and individuals in charge are reluctant to shoulder the responsibility of refusal. It was so with our promotional budgets, I suspect.

We initiated a regular series of export seminars using the elegant Royal Society of Arts building as a venue. These were run by a contractor on a commercial basis and proved very popular with exporters. At the same time we started to talk to local authorities about what they could do to help firms in the area. Some, like Surrey, took the line that this was not their responsibility but others, and usually those counties that had unemployment problems, took quite a different line. Both Essex and Kent were active and anxious to encourage their industry to look to their neighbours across the North Sea and Channel for business. These counties were only too aware that continental firms had their eyes firmly fixed on our markets here. Kent was particularly assiduous in building bridges with the French local authorities in the Pas de Calais region. Both Essex and Kent welcomed our approaches and a number of joint events aimed at exporters and potential exporters followed quickly. Our involvement in Essex was helped by a very go-ahead young assistant to the County Council's Chief Executive. Our assessment of David Henshaw proved to be correct as he in later years went on to become the Chief Executive of Liverpool City Council. Also helpful was the Manager of the 'Essex Export Centre', Roy McClarty, who coincidentally was the brother of my wife's close friend from Strathaven in Lanarkshire. We all worked well together, including the local chamber of commerce and my office's excellent 'man in Essex', George Burns. The end result was the establishment of a one-stop shop for business involving central government, via the secondment of one of my young export staff, with local authority and chamber of commerce inputs. The Essex initiative went on for a number of years under the guidance of Wilma Garvin who I was jointly responsible for appointing. We have heard a lot about 'one-stop shops' over the years since but I believe I was the first to set up one involving a government department.

From that small beginning in the Essex Export Centre in Chelmsford I negotiated similar joint offices in Chatham, Norwich with the Norfolk and Norwich Chamber, and Portsmouth with its Chamber. The rest of the Regional Office was to follow the BOTB Southeast initiative, setting up local offices in Reading, Reigate and Cambridge, although these were DTI outposts and not one-stop shops as such. My BOTB one-stop shop venture with partners continued alongside the subsequent partial dispersal of the regional office from central London.

One of the bonuses of this job was the opportunity to visit and become familiar with parts of the south-east I had never visited, but more important likely would not have visited in a private capacity. Into this latter category I would place Slough, Watford and Luton. Because of the success and importance of the chamber of commerce in Slough, I was a frequent visitor there. Indeed the Chief Executive's post became vacant during my time in SERO and I applied, unsuccessfully, for the job. The Isle of Wight falls into the former category as it was somewhere I was always curious about but, although relatively near to home in Guildford, somehow the opportunity to visit never arose in a family context. I was to make several visits to the island during my time at SERO. I referred earlier to the similarities of the economy of this island with most other UK islands but also similar is the experience of getting on a boat and the feeling of leaving some of the cares of mainland life behind. In the case of leaving from Oban this feeling is very real, but it was still a factor for me in travelling to the Isle of Wight, even though towns on the island were little different from parts of Portsmouth, that is somewhat run down and depressed. The Wight countryside on the other hand was glorious. I had a good relationship with the small Isle of Wight Chamber and because Lord Jellicoe had spent some part of his childhood on the island, I had no trouble in getting him to make a visit to island firms. My visits were always rewarding as the people I met were so pleased to see a government official pay them any attention.

All this activity restored SERO's image and impressed senior staff including the Chairman, Lord Jellicoe, who made a special visit to meet my staff at Ebury Bridge House. The staff were surprised and very pleased, and this visit alone did so much to boost staff morale. I have much to thank George Jellicoe for. He was very supportive and stood by me and the office when things got a little difficult.

Unexpectedly the South East office provided opportunity for travel to destinations a tad more exotic than even the Isle of Wight. As the largest of the regional operations my office had very close relations with the commercial departments of our embassies and consulates in all overseas markets. Markets such as the United States and Germany had large FCO operations with many locally engaged commercial staff besides career diplomats. Running these operations was a major logistical exercise, with many problems similar to running my own office at home. To better plan deployment of staff the British Trade Development Office (BTDO) in New York would hold an annual 'commercial conference'. Colleagues from the BOTB operation at home would be invited to attend and usually asked to address the conference. Directors/Exports meeting together would decide who should represent them and I was usually chosen to attend the New York conference, along with my colleague who ran the Export House operation. These were very much family affairs as no outsiders were involved and most of us knew each other well.

The New York office co-ordinated the whole of the UK export effort across the United States through commercial offices in most of the large centres of population. I was lucky that my visits coincided with Jimmy Mellon's period as Head of the British Trade Development Office. I had met Jimmy many years earlier when he was a lecturer on a course run by the short-lived branch of the Civil Service College in Edinburgh. Jimmy had been involved in early Common Market entry negotiations and was lecturing to the course on European Community institutions. He was a no nonsense Scot and was an able chair at such internal conferences, where discussion could become quite heated. He allowed real debate and discussion, and took criticism where it was warranted, and regardless of the seniority of the source. He had none of the pretence and snobbery that I had learned to associate with many of my FCO colleagues. His refreshing approach was admired by businessmen also. He said it as he saw it, without the flannel. I remember a visit I made a year or two later with a delegation of politicians and businessmen from Grampian in Scotland when he opened a briefing session for the assembled group with the advice that 'although we and the Americans may share a language and some aspects of culture, it is important to remember that they are as foreign as say the French or the Germans'. This surprised my new colleagues in Scotland but it was sound advice and for me borne out by experience. In other words do not be misled by the initial easy access in the United States to corporate bosses, and the friendly and glad-handing approach. One should expect no quarter to be given to common ancestry when it comes to closing a deal. I am in no way implying criticism of Americans here. I have found them generally some of the most hospitable and sociable people one could wish to meet, but business is different and there all sentimentality ends, and one should forget about vaguely shared conventions and values. They are foreigners.

For a number of years I had been working closely with the trade associations covering the agricultural inputs industry. One of these, the British Agricultural Exports Council (BAEC), had co-operated with me on a number of initiatives to encourage exports by the industry. BAEC also ran overseas trade missions and exhibitions, and usually with our financial support. Whilst in the South East office I was asked by the then Chief Executive of BAEC, John Thorneloe, to join him and the collection of firms he was taking to China. I had never had a lot of contact with China but my office did deal with the FCO's commercial staff in Beijing and also Hong Kong. I was also an occasional banquet guest at the Chinese embassy's commercial operation in Blackheath. I thought my chances of getting my bosses to agree were somewhat slim but on the basis of the theory that the bigger the request the more likely it is to granted, I sought permission to join the trade mission in China. The theory held and permission was granted without a murmur of concern about relevancy or value for money. I spent one pretty uncomfortable week in Beijing but a very rewarding week in Hong Kong, where I stayed in a friend's flat in Happy Valley.

I have mentioned embassies before and embassy colleagues. This trip was without doubt my worst experience in the hands of the Foreign Office. Beijing in those days only had three to four hotels of western quality and with China beginning to open wide it was extremely difficult to obtain a hotel room. I arrived to find that the embassy had not found a room for me and, more distressing, cared less. Eventually I was found a room in a Chinese local 'hotel' not far from the airport. The room was so awful that I could have cried. The curtains were made from what looked like a dirty piece of cheese cloth and the walls were stained and had not seen paint for many a year. I inspected the bed for life but it seemed clean enough, and there was a cracked basin that had cold running water. I did not undress to go to bed that night as I was also worried about my security. I saw no other Europeans at the hotel. Next morning and after some heated words with the our embassy I was found a room in the Great Wall Hotel. This was one of the new breed of western managed hotels and was excellent. My Ministry of Agriculture colleague was similarly poorly treated but did escape the Chinese 'hotel' treatment, although towards the end of the week he was forced to camp in my room at the Great Wall. The embassy were petty in so many other ways and excluded me from any of the functions they had laid on to welcome the British agricultural firms exhibiting at the agricultural trade fair in Beijing. I did eventually complain to the Ambassador. His response was to complain about me to my boss! It is difficult to beat the FCO and particularly when you are at their mercy, in what was then a difficult country. However the Chinese treated me well enough and I was included with all the UK business people in receptions and the odd banquet.

The second leg of my Far East trip was spent in Hong Kong where my colleagues in the British High Commission, in total contrast to those in the Beijing embassy, could not have been more helpful. They laid on a full programme for the week and escorted me on visits to Sino-British operations, including a visit to the Hong Kong Shanghai bank and their marvellous headquarters building. Also I met with departments of the government administration in Hong Kong. The High Commission were anxious to put me up in a good hotel, but I decided to stay with Martin, my engineer friend from Guildford, who was spending a year in Hong Kong working for his company on the infrastructure for the new airport. The deal with Martin was that I would pay for all meals during my stay. Over the week we dined well and each night in a different restaurant sampling Chinese regional cuisine from Mongolia to Shanghai and I began to see Hong Kong in a different light. I had been prepared for a frenetic city that was void of any redeeming features except the making of money. I was pleasantly surprised, and found a city that could delight as well as assault the senses. One could find peace and quiet and even rural idyll. Martin and I spent a pleasant day walking amongst the small family farms and fishing villages on Lantau island where the bustle of the big city seemed miles away.

A tram ride brought me close to a serious mishap during my stay in Hong Kong. It was rush hour and I was on my way back to the flat in Happy Valley. The tram was crowded and I was standing at the front on the top deck. The tram lurched and I reached quickly over the heads of the seated passengers and put my hand out to the window pane to steady myself. This would have been fine except there was no window pane. The windows were all wound down because of the humid temperature. I ended sprawled across two none too pleased Chinese ladies. It was a near thing and I could have gone through the window. After recovering, and still fresh in mind my treatment in Beijing, I contemplated what might have been headlines in the *Surrey Advertiser*: 'British civil servant falls from tram. Was he pushed?' I loved Hong Kong but hated Beijing. China is a fascinating country but I have no wish to return. The T-shirt is sufficient.

Although I had been thinking for some time about leaving the Service,

I was enjoying my regional office posting and my contributions were beginning to be acknowledged. I had an excellent Under Secretary, Alan Titchener, on the BOTB side of the split in the command chain and Gerry Bradshaw was very supportive as my immediate boss. I never saw the Under Secretary in charge of the regional network, although this person countersigned my annual performance report. I was getting good reports and was recommended for promotion. All looked rosy in my garden and I was beginning to wonder whether there just might be a future for me in the Department. This was all to change with Gerry moving on to the part of the Department dealing with home and overseas trade fairs, a dream job for him incidentally, with a ticket to roam the world at HMG's expense.

The new man was much more hands on and it quickly became my view that he wanted a part of my role as Director/Exports. Obviously I was a source of particular irritation to him. I tried hard to understand the psychology of the relationship and to this end took soundings amongst my colleagues elsewhere in the office. I was none the wiser and remain confused to this day. I can cope with most situations and relationships if I can understand why individuals behave in a certain way and what motivates them. With this man I drew a blank.

It all came to a head following a Christmas party for my staff that got a little bit out of control. I looked in on this party but did not stay long as there were a number of my more senior and mature staff present. The upshot was damage to a small dictation tape recorder, some erasure fluid spill on a desk and, more seriously, some burning paper thrown out of a window. My new boss wanted a name to blame. He asked me to find the ringleaders but I was not optimistic of the chances of 'fingering' individuals but nonetheless I interviewed all staff at the party. As I expected no one was willing to name a colleague as responsible for any of the damage. The man became angry when I reported this deadend to my inquiries and instructed me to go away and try again. I made a few more inquiries but with the same result. He pressed me again and asked me to let him have a list of those I suspected. I remonstrated and said this was unfair as I had no proof or any indication of the likely culprits. Mere suspicion was not sufficient basis to blame. I held my ground and was advised that this would damage my career. The next performance report was the nail in my Civil Service career coffin. Sources indicated that I was on the cusp of breaking through the barrier that I seemed to have come up against over the years, and this report ensured that my last chance of promotion was dead.

With some regret I left the Civil Service after 21 years of service in December 1988 for a new career in local government in Grampian.

Chapter 15

Rationalisation

If my career in the Civil Service had gone to plan then, in spite of many misgivings over the changes that were taking place, I would not have left. At the same time it is doubtful even if all things had been equal whether I would have gone through to the normal retirement age of sixty. From about the time I left in 1988 the Service was offering generous retirement packages to senior staff and many took this option. From the mid-nineties there were cuts of up to twenty-five per cent in departmental staff. The Treasury picked up the tab over an eighteen months window of opportunity, with pension enhancements up to a maximum of six and two thirds years. This would mean if one opted to retire at, say, age fifty, the minimum eligible age for this Treasury financed package, then one would retire on a pension as if aged fifty-six and two thirds years. All this was voluntary retirement and such staff were not sacked or coerced in any crude way. The Civil Service has more subtle ways of making it clear at senior levels that there is little further on offer in terms of career advancement, and many when faced with that option and still wishing to retain an element of self-respect will go quietly, and did in large numbers. A number of my friends found themselves in this position and, although they severed the cord with some regret, went on to find fulfilment elsewhere, and few admitting to any long term withdrawal symptoms. One friend now successfully sells his services back to Whitehall and has no doubts that the Service lost staff that it later was to regret. The change of heart was reflected in the less attractive retirement terms now on offer and where the tab has to be met from a department's own resources. There remain early retirement packages, as has always been the case, for individuals with health problems and where the individual is seen to be 'burnt out', for whatever reasons and is retired in the interests of the 'efficiency' of the department.

I was only forty-seven when I left DTI and so there was no case to be made for a retirement package. As I moved to a job within the Civil Service pension 'club', my pension was easily transferable to a local authority. This would not have been the case, for example, had I moved to a commercial company, rather than a public sector body. As the normal retirement age in local government is sixty-five, I did very well in the package I was eventually offered when leaving Grampian Regional Council some seven years later in 1996, with a final pension enhancement of over nine years when I retired at fifty five. With many years at university I would have been short of full pension rights if I had stayed in the Civil Service but my final settlement more than compensated for this.

However it was not pension that had prompted me to leave the Service. Although there were many aspects of my twenty-one years in the Service that were rewarding and satisfying I remain hurt at the way I was treated by the Department. I guess that less than a dozen people were involved in decisions that not only wasted many middle years but also that I was not to be trusted with more responsible jobs. Although I prodded and sought guidance as to what the problems were, I got no clear answers. One of my later Under Secretaries gave a clue in his letter to me on leaving where he hoped that my new job in Grampian would allow scope for my initiative and imagination "which I know was too often stifled in a larger bureaucracy". This gentleman went on to say that he greatly valued the innovative and occasionally offbeat solutions that I offered to the problems that confronted the office at the time. I think telling was his comment that the monthly meetings of Directors of Exports would have been dull without me! My last Under Secretary in the Exports to Europe Branch said that he found me stimulating to work with and "it is Whitehall's loss that it cannot give more scope and more advancement to someone whom it may not have found comfortable". I guess this links to comments I made about my earlier life and that I have always been one of life's observers rather than 'joiners'. My years in the Civil Service were those of the observer looking in and never a team member on the inside participating in the mutual exchange of warmth and security that is so essential to team work. The need is analogous to climbers being lost on the hill and having to huddle together to share each other's body warmth to survive. I have always feared such brigading and I suppose it might reflect a fear of being hurt but I leave this to the psychologists. The bottom line is that many of my superiors mistrusted me because I was not willing to submit to all the prerequisites that make the good team player, but almost as many welcomed the different and fresh contribution that I could make. I have always had an innovative mind and am, I suppose, what organisations would call an 'ideas man'. However I remember reading an article in a management magazine which said that all organisations needed ideas men, but acknowledged that they tended to be disruptive and rarely made the top positions.

There were many brighter people than me in the Service but I never felt that intellectual shortcomings were any way a barrier to my advancement. I was often too outspoken for my own good. Instead of keeping a low profile when I saw poor decisions made by my superiors I would often give my view. However anybody who knows me will not see me as one of nature's extroverts and so it is not that I am the loud 'in your face' type. Eye to eye meetings take a lot out of me and I, even now, have to screw up courage to make an intervention or join a group at a reception. Nonetheless I have learned to live with this and get on with what has to be done. Prime Minister Blair is not alone in his capacity to soak a shirt in sweat within a few minutes. Like many basically shy people I have no problem in addressing a large audience as this is not an 'eyeball to eyeball' situation. Similarly some find it hard to believe that many stage actors are shy people. It is the small meetings across the desk that are the challenge and not a theatre of people to address.

There were other aspects of the Service that I was beginning to find uncomfortable. The Thatcher years saw a slow but perceptible change in Civil Service life. There was at the time a lot of talk of politicisation of the Civil Service. The press reported the question "Is he one of us?" asked by Thatcher on the appointment of senior Civil Servants. I suppose the question implied that appointees were expected to share the beliefs of her government. When I joined the Service in the late sixties it was not so much that one shared the politics of one's Minister but rather you were capable of loyalty to him, and when the Minister was replaced by one of another political persuasion then you would have no hesitation in transferring your loyalty. I used to share with my colleagues a professional pride that whether it was Karl Marx or Margaret Thatcher I could provide exactly the same loyalty and professional service to my Minister. That pride remained core to my sense of professionalism throughout my public service. I have never been persuaded that personal belief in a policy is in any way a prerequisite of the job, and indeed it could be argued that objectivity might be at risk in too close a personal identity with a policy line. I cannot deny life is a lot easier if the policy that you are directed to pursue is to one's personal liking.

At the time of writing the Blair government, rather than reverse the politicisation of Civil Service, has consolidated what was begun by Thatcher. We see more and more use of politically appointed 'advisers' and even to the point in the case of Government Information Officers where the professional Civil Servants have had to take the back seat. The implications of this trend were well demonstrated by the row over Jo

Moore, the politically appointed adviser to the then Transport Secretary, Byers. There was a newspaper article some while after where four former Whitehall mandarins debated Labour's 'war on Whitehall'. I find it sad but not surprising that Sir Peter Kemp, the former Permanent Secretary at the Cabinet Office, was reported as saying "Ministers always tell lies and they always have done, from Lloyd George onwards". He went on to say that " Neither is it important if he [Byers] shafted civil servants. What matters is this: is he a competent Minister?" I am glad that I no longer am associated with such ethics. The turning point for me was Lord Armstrong's, then Head of the Civil Service, comment suggesting it was all right to be 'economical with the truth'. How can one continue to have confidence in a boss and especially one that heads up an organisation that has always prided itself as being truthful and incorruptible after such a statement?

There is something increasingly vulgar about modern politics and this has rubbed off on the Civil Service. The casualty has been the public service ethos. The fact that applications via the Civil Service Selection Board, the fast stream entry to government service, hold up well does not give me any comfort or invalidate my concern over some loss of that commitment to public service. The Service I joined seemed to place more emphasis on integrity and objectivity than the current obsession with presentation.

Chapter 16

Northlight

Like most people from the South of England, and indeed also from the South of Scotland, I knew little about Aberdeen. I was aware of the folklore about the meanness of Aberdonians and that it was a long way from anywhere, was cold, and was the focus of the UK offshore oil industry. Indeed I had only been to Aberdeen once and that was to talk to the Chamber of Commerce about exporting to Europe. As is often the case on such business visits I remembered very little of Aberdeen, with a car to meet and return me to the city's airport at Dyce. I had met a number of refugees from Aberdeen over the years including one that worked for me in the DTI. Most of our friends were concerned when they learned that I had applied for a job there and could not see how that was an improvement on life in Surrey. I was to later better understand the nature of the concern of our friends when I found out that one of the questions asked in a Grampian Television commissioned survey of London based advertising executives was whether there was 'cocktail society in Aberdeen'. Although looking for an escape from DTI, Aberdeen was just about the last place I would have chosen, all other things being equal, and that is mainly because I knew so little about the north-east of Scotland or Aberdeen. However, a year or two earlier I had applied and been accepted for a post with the Shetland Islands Council but because the Council there were not able to guarantee me a longer term future I did not take up their offer. By 1987 I was getting pretty desperate and anxious to escape from DTI. The timing was just right with the family leaving the nest. Our son was due to leave Cranleigh at the end of the 1989 summer term and was expecting to secure a place at the Glasgow School of Art and our daughter was studying for her nursing qualifications at St Mary's, Paddington.

None of us wanted to leave Wonersh and sever links with Surrey. Our house was very small and that was a bone of contention. If we had stayed I dare say that without the burden of school fees we would have moved within the locality to a detached house. Fiona was also enjoying her job at Cranleigh 'prep' school and leaving her friends and colleagues was going to be difficult. We had addressed the dilemma many times but such was my state of mind and disenchantment with the Civil Service we approached any reasonable job opportunity at the time with few preconditions. The advertisement for the post of Head of Economic Development at Grampian Regional Council in Aberdeen indicated a reasonable salary and offered a real chance of a new life in what was an attractive part of Scotland and, by Scottish standards, with a better climate than most areas. I did not think in a too analytical way about it and sent off the application. Even on securing an interview I was still unprepared for the possibility of landing the job and consequently journeyed up to Aberdeen with few nerves.

As on my only previous visit I flew to Dyce and arranged a hotel near to Woodhill House, the Regional Council's headquarters on the busy A96 trunk road that connects Aberdeen to Inverness. The interview process was a gruelling one in so far as there was a lot of nerve-racking waiting around with people who were my competitors, and in the circumstances polite chit-chat dries up after an hour or so. One of the candidates was internal and the rest were largely from local authority backgrounds. Another candidate did provide a bit of amusement as on the day of the interviews he was also in charge of a golfing competition somewhere along the Dee valley. Unfortunately for him he was last in interview order and was pressing up against his deadline. At last he was called and appeared to be away a short time. I asked had it gone well and he said that he had rather rushed the affair and disappeared in a great hurry to his car and his golf rendezvous. Here was a man that seemed to have his job in perspective. Later I was to get to know him quite well and discovered that he indeed was a civilised and sensible individual with his feet firmly on the ground.

Candidates were interviewed in turn before the whole Council, which numbered at full strength fifty-seven councillors. We were handed a sheet with three questions with ten minutes to consider and prepare a short presentation to the Council, and then there was the usual question and answer session. I cannot remember the questions asked but they were relevant to the job description and were in no way unexpected. I enjoyed this part of the interview as I was in control. I do not remember being particularly nervous and even at this stage I was not expecting to get the job. When the offer was made I was so surprised and shocked that I said little and even to the extent that the Council's Chief Executive asked me if I was pleased. I am not sure what messages my face was sending but I suspect it was shock. I was unprepared to move to the north of Scotland and my face must have said this. I rang Fiona from the Chief Executive's office with the news and told her to dust off the copy of the 'Northern Lights of Aberdeen' , incidentally not as old a song as one tends to think.

There was one small hiccup and that was the starting salary. I had been reading just before the journey to Aberdeen that one should not change job at my stage in career (I was forty-eight) with less than a ten thousand pounds increase in salary. The jump in salary was to be a lot less than that and I said I could not afford a move of that magnitude without some additional increments on the scale. This caused quite a panic but I was eventually assured that my salary on appointment would shortly rise as it was under review at the time. I accepted this and that was the case and within a short while there was a significant salary increase.

Even on arriving back in Wonersh my mind remained in a turmoil as to the implications of the move to such different both work and living environments. It was late summer in 1988 and I was due to take up the appointment at Grampian Regional Council in the December of that year. Fiona was magnificent, and calmly addressed the timing of putting the house on the market as well as leaving her job at the school. We were anxious that life should go on as calmly as possible in the interim. Our son still had a year to go at Cranleigh and although he was at this stage boarding he needed the support of home during the all important lead up to his A level examinations. So the house sale had to be timed to coincide with our plans to leave Wonersh at sometime the following summer. There was no alternative for me other than going on ahead and starting my job in December as well as beginning the search for a home in Grampian. We were blessed with a Guildford estate agent that was a model of what the profession could be and the services of our friend Graham Oliver as an equally sensible and first class solicitor. The house went on the market in the early spring of 1989 leaving Fiona with the responsibility of dealing with the professionals and prospective buyers. Like all house sales it had its hairy moments but nonetheless we managed to time the sale to coincide with our needs. I would travel every other weekend from Aberdeen to add support and keep the garden planted and looking good, as much for our own pleasure than any prospective buyer.

Working out my notice at DTI was not enjoyable and particularly in the circumstances that had finally tipped the balance of the likelihood of a continuing and fulfilling career in the Civil Service. I did take advantage of the notice period to research most of the local authorities in my patch and see what they were doing about economic development strategies. For example I undertook with Peter Morris, one of my senior staff, the task of visiting all the London Borough Chief Executives or their economic development directors. This was a most rewarding operation for both me and the office. Some of the most talented individuals were to be found toiling in Government-maligned boroughs such as Brent and Tower Hamlets. With an interest in architecture, a bonus for me was the opportunity to see a range of magnificent town halls. I remember particularly Waltham Forest's town hall and its decorations in tribute to the early socialist thinker and designer William Morris, who was born in Walthamstow. Kent County Council also provided a model which I was to draw on, and similarly so for Essex. At an early stage in the new job I was to take a small party of Grampian councillors to visit these two counties.

Grampian provided some modest finance for Fiona and me to make a familiarisation trip before taking up my new post. Like most first time visitors entering the region from the south by road, we were not prepared for a landscape so dedicated to arable farming. From Dundee northwards to Peterhead and all along the Moray Firth coastal strip, and to the hills in the far west of the region, Grampian is intensively farmed with barley, rape and potatoes as the predominant crops with grass and beef production making it Scotland's prime food producing area. To find 'calendar' Scotland one has to move to the Grampian foothills in the west and into Moray and Banffshire. That is not to say that Grampian is flat. Parts of Buchan can be bleak but the majority of the farmed landscape is gently rolling and broken with the occasional landmark hills. The house we were to purchase looks towards a modest mountain called Bennachie which, at 1,733 feet, is one of these prominent landmarks. A tourism survey described Grampian's scenery as "nice but not spectacular". I think that is fair although as one moves west the scenery does develop a grandeur as indeed the Regional boundaries encompass Ben Macdui at 4,296 feet and other 'Munros', the collective noun given to mountains over 3,000 feet. The other striking feature to the first time visitor to the greater Aberdeen area is the almost monotone nature of the built environment. Most older properties are built of grey granite, with a small minority of pink granite. On a grey day in winter the effect can be quite depressing although on a sunny day the mica chips in the stone can sparkle and hence one of Aberdeen's marketing names as 'the Silver City'. With the trees in full leaf and some summer sun the city approaches the description of beautiful. Unfortunately the planners with responsibilities covering the countryside towns and villages around Aberdeen have taken the granite theme to ridiculous lengths by insisting that 'new builds' are rendered (locally 'harled') in a stone dash of ground granite, usually 'Kemnay grey' or use a reconstituted granite block. The result is a greyness and uniformity that has none of the attributes of the original material and the net effect is a Stalinist or East European quality to some new housing estates, and not too different from the efforts of industrial Lanarkshire. As I was soon to learn it is difficult to offer any constructive criticism.

During our short familiarisation visit the priority was to arrange my accommodation during the first few months by myself in Aberdeen. With the help of the Convener, who chairs the Council, and his staff I managed to fix myself up with a National Trust cottage at Drum Castle, a few miles along the Dee valley from Aberdeen. Drum sounded grand and so it was but my cottage was as bland as they come and without any central heating. At the time I was grateful to have a place to live for a month or two. We had no time to get a feel for the city but at least Fiona had seen where I was to work and live.

What was left of the summer and autumn in Wonersh raced by and we took the opportunity to relish every last moment of it. I was still working a big allotment up the lane in Blackheath but what I did not need to bother about now was digging the plot over for the year ahead. On the other hand we did need to take a decision on our old 'Series III' Land Rover. The repair costs were beginning to mount with the cross members of the steel ladder frame coming up for replacement. In retrospect I wished I had nursed it up to Scotland but we decided to sell and Fiona sold it to a young Land Rover enthusiast for more than we paid for it some sixteen years earlier. We replaced it with a small Seat Ibiza hatchback from our local garage and this budget car served us well for many years and subsequently our daughter. I used it for commuting to my new job and also as beast of burden for many a sack of cement and even paving stones during the renovation of the property we bought in Grampian.

As the end of year approached I began to think more and more about the new job. Grampian had suffered badly during the oil price crash in 1986 when a low of $8.5 a barrel was reached. With as many as one in five employed in Aberdeen directly involved in oil the effect was disastrous. There are stories of houses abandoned as oil workers and their families went elsewhere to find work but unable to sell their homes. One friend who had a graphic design business recalled that quite suddenly his telephones stopped ringing and business for many came to a similar abrupt halt. It was a shock to authorities responsible for the economic well-being of the Region. One of these, Grampian Regional Council, vowed it must never happen again. In 1987 it started to take stock of its economic spend and there was cross-party agreement that the Council's development resources could be better co-ordinated. It was deemed there should be more effort directed to developing non-oil industries to ensure Grampian was less reliant on oil employment in the future and was better prepared for the day when North Sea reserves would run out. To that end the Council agreed to create a new post at Chief Officer level who would have overall direction of the Council's twenty million pounds economic spend and develop a corporate economic development strategy for the Region. The post-holder would also have responsibility for marketing and promoting the Region, which was Scotland's third largest, both in terms of land area and population. This new position was the one I was to take up in December 1988.

My appointment was not welcomed by all, and least of all by a number of senior staff with a role in economic development including Planning and the Council's existing economic development agency, the North East of Scotland Development Agency or NESDA. The political thrust behind the reorganisation of responsibilities was a young Liberal councillor, Nicol Stephen. I was to learn, and quite quickly, that he was one of the brightest of my new political masters. A lawyer by training, specialising in corporate law, he was articulate and easy to get along with. However like most politicians he rarely disclosed his full hand and one or two times I was to be left holding the baby with little support, and in those early years I had few friends amongst my colleagues. The Chief Executive, Douglas Macnaughton, had been in the job for most of the Regional Council's life and I think he felt that the changes driven by the Liberals were an attempt to destabilise his position. He was a popular Chief Executive with staff but that may be because he left most of them well alone. However before I arrived he did involve himself, and in considerable detail, in economic development matters and this was to continue well after my arrival. He found it very hard to let go and was hostile to the changes I was to recommend.

On setting off from Wonersh for Aberdeen in December 1988 I had little idea of what lay before me. The change from central to local government was to be more of a culture shock than I ever expected, quite apart from the differences in the character of people in the north-east of Scotland compared not only with the south-east of England but also with those in the west of Scotland, or indeed any other part of Scotland for that matter. Grampian and its people are unique, in many ways. I was also unprepared for how hard I was going to have to work in terms of hours. Working away from home in rented accommodation for the first seven months meant I had few family responsibilities. So I was able to work for just about all the waking hours and to the extent I sometimes felt quite ill. I had never believed that mental exertion, for me anyway, could cause problems other than tiredness, but I did get to the stage that I had to take some recreation and at Drum Castle fine woodlands and gardens were to hand.

A difficult decision on arrival was how much time I should spend in touring a region about which I knew very little but at the same time was expected, within six months, to produce a blueprint for the Region's future. One idea was to take two weeks out of the office and spend it visiting all the main settlements and familiarising myself with the geography. The area is a large one with Inverness a hundred miles to the north-west of Aberdeen and Dundee seventy miles south. Braemar is some sixty miles west of Aberdeen, towards the Cairngorm mountain range. In the event I decided against this strategy but did take the opportunity to travel whenever I could. I made early trips to the headquarters of the five District authorities that made up the second tier of local government in Grampian at the time, namely Kincardine & Deeside, Gordon, Banff & Buchan and Moray based, respectively, in Stonehaven, Inverurie, Banff, and Elgin. Aberdeen itself was the fifth District authority. Other significant towns are Peterhead and Fraserburgh and I made a pilgrimage to these two important fishing ports within my first few weeks. What I lacked at the time was any guidance as to the realities of my responsibilities and unfortunately these emerged too slowly over the next three years. This certainly inhibited my input and ability to produce the results which I thought were expected. The Chief Executive was no help and, oddly I thought, I got little political guidance. Nonetheless the first few months were nothing but exhilarating. I remain proud of what I achieved in spite of hostile forces at work. The first two years at Grampian Region were to be the most satisfying of my whole professional career.

Chapter 17

"Together to the Future"

My experience of moving jobs within the Civil Service was that very little happened in the first week or two, with few telephone calls and few written communications. It took a while for your name to be known and to be added to copy communications and for one to be included in the constant round of meetings. Arriving at the Regional Council's headquarters at Woodhill House in December 1988 was nothing like that. Already agreed by the Council was for a large mission of businessmen, councillors and officials to go to New York at the end of March, and in early May a similar mission to the annual 'OTC' oil exhibition in Houston, Texas. In those early days I had few staff apart from a new personal secretary, Margaret Erasmuson and a senior administrative officer, Moira Catto, as well as oversight of some clerical staff and two senior seconded staff to the promotional arm of the Council, the Grampian Initiative. Margaret and Moira were with me for the whole of my period with the Council and I cannot finds words adequate to express my gratitude to them. There were times of tears and times of elation but whatever the circumstances these two ladies never faltered. They coped with an amazing flow of paper, and fielded much of the day-to-day distraction of office life. My staff knew whatever Margaret and Moira said carried my authority, and in addition Margaret had a natural air of authority that was rarely challenged by staff, regardless of grade. Having said that I should not give the impression that she was some ogre. Far from it and indeed Margaret had a great sense of humour and was supportive of colleagues with problems. Moira was a very different character with a background of local authority committee clerking but with a wish to move into policy work. To that end she took an Open University degree, graduating just before I arrived. Her potential was spotted and she was seconded to the recently established Grampian Initiative unit. Shortly after I arrived she was appointed on promotion to be my assistant. Moira, like me, was an enthusiast and thrived on adrenaline, and was at her best when under pressure. These ladies were the equal of anyone I was privileged to work with in the Civil Service.

The first few weeks were filled with meetings both internally and, importantly, externally. My appointment had created a lot of local press interest and particularly from the *Press and Journal*, the lead daily newspaper for the North East and the Highlands of Scotland. The *Evening Express* is from the same stable but with an essentially Aberdeen city readership. It would be a serious mistake to assume that talking to just the one would suffice and that the editorial teams worked hand in hand. In fact their respective editors were, and are, serious rivals and care had to be taken therefore in handling the Council's news releases. We were helped considerably by having Bill Neish, a former 'P&J' journalist, as the Council's Press Officer. Bill was very helpful and I would often consult him on Press Releases and how to handle local journalists, but at the same time he encouraged me to build my own relations with individual journalists. In the first weeks I got many requests for interviews from the P&J, the *Evening Express*, numerous local weeklies as well as from the Grampian based TV and radio stations. At that time the BBC had an active regional operation based at Beechgrove Terrace in the City's west end. I got to know many of the locally based journalists quite well including some, such as Jane Franchi, who found their way to the BBC headquarters at Glasgow's Queen Margaret Drive studios. One radio reporter at Beechgrove, Douglas Ness, became a good friend and was to join us on a number of Grampian overseas missions. Taking a journalist on overseas visits was a ploy I had used to good effect in DTI. There had to be a mutual trust as the journalist expected, and from me got, unfettered editorial freedom as well as access to all formal and informal discussions amongst the mission members. As was to be expected Councillors, who had not always enjoyed the best of local press, were extremely suspicious and took a lot of convincing. I had some hard times with my employers at Grampian but through the good and bad times I can say without exception that I was never let down or compromised by the local media.

So good was the publicity during my first couple of years at Grampian that it caused some problems with my political masters, and although this amounted to little more than gentle leg pulling there was a clear warning that I needed to dilute my own profile or at least share it. One of the bylines that stuck was the description of me as the Region's 'economic supremo'. It was flattering and landed me in the odd embarrassing situation when I was interviewed or asked to speak as an 'economist'. Later I was also to become the Region's Director of Planning but again I am not a professional planner. It helped my conscience to call upon the old Civil Service mantra about having 'experts on tap but never on top'.

For sure I had plenty of experts on tap, although the Council had few who could describe themselves as economists, and so I was never challenged internally on this point. It became a bit more embarrassing when I met real economists from the likes of banks, including the Bank of England.

DTI had given me a lot of public speaking experience but I still was worried about my ability to live up to my press image when asked to address the Aberdeen Chamber of Commerce at one of their regular lunchtime events. These are large events held in the city's biggest function suites and I was the guest speaker following in the footsteps of household name politicians, captains of industry and most from the Scottish 'good and the great' list. It was the occasion where I could bury my reputation or establish myself as an official to be reckoned with and a break with the locally perceived image of a council employee.

I took 'quality' and 'partnership' as the themes for my address to the Chamber and these qualities were to be at the core of the economic development strategy I was to produce by the June in 1989. After a robust overview of the threats that faced the Region I built an upbeat vision of what Grampian could be, if we all worked together. I highlighted one of the Region's greatest assets and that was our environment. Grampian was blessed with a clean rivers and clean air with no smokestack industries to speak of. We had a land that stretched from the fine seascapes of the east and north through a rich and rolling countryside, with broad valleys to the grandeur of the western massif. The City of Aberdeen and our towns were attractive and clean but we needed to be ever vigilant to keep the countryside and the built environment this way. I pointed to the decisions that were around the corner if we wished to stay so and singled out the commitment to the use of the sea for sewage disposal. Little did I know at the time that the European directives on effluent disposal would bite sooner than later, and we would in just seven years on begin to pay dearly for the lack of local authority investment in water supply and waste water disposal. I went on to apply the quality goal to Grampian's industry saying that with our geography and relatively small population we had to produce at the top end of the market and compete on quality and technology input. The audience were well aware of the importance to the locality of brand names like Baxters and Walkers in the food industry and Johnstons in cashmere textiles, and it was not hard to sell the idea that we should extend the standards set by these and similar companies to all we do. Lunchtime speeches need to be short and punchy and I was anxious that the press should pick up the message for a wider audience. To that end I finished with a parody of Martin Luther King's 'I have a dream' speech to the civil rights marchers on Washington in 1963. In essence my dream was to see the people of Grampian as the most envied dwellers in the land. The "Ich bin ein Grampian" commitment was the final flourish which ensured good coverage in the P&J and *Evening Express*. I think it went down well and I left the hotel venue none-the-worse for the occasion.

A distraction, in some senses, in the early weeks of getting to grips with the job was the two trips to America agreed before my arrival. The first of these, scheduled for the end of March, was a large mission of business people, councillors and officials to New York. This had arisen through the good offices of the Forbes family and their eponymous magazine. Grandfather Bertie Forbes had come from Pitsligo in Grampian and had gone to America to seek his fortune and founded the *Forbes Magazine*. Bertie Forbes' ashes were returned to his native Grampian and the family continued to value their links with Scotland. The Forbes family offered to facilitate a business mission to New York and use of their prestigious headquarters and museum on Fifth Avenue. Within three weeks of the New York mission was the annual visit to the oil exhibition in Houston and again with a retinue of councillors and officials. I was no stranger to such missions but at the same time I had been urged by my Committee Chairman to produce the Region's first economic development strategy within six months of arrival and so with a target of June that year.

Moira Catto was a first class lieutenant in bringing together the arrangements, dealing with Forbes and travel agents as well as meeting my requirements for briefing the group travelling to NewYork. I was able to impose Civil Service standards of briefing and I assured elected Members that their briefing would be to Ministerial standards. Although the existing briefing standards were pitiful, Members had become used to them and some even resented the quantum leap in quality. I think this resentment had more to do with the reluctance of some to play their part and they realised that a full brief meant more was expected of them than coasting through the visit and drifting from one reception to another without making an input, apart from consuming the refreshments provided. However the main players such as the Convener of the Council and key committee chairpersons were grateful for the better information, and steering briefs that enabled them to be more credible and play a fuller role. I maintained that standard throughout my period at the Council although I suspected many briefs were never opened much beyond the pages dealing with the daily itinerary.

The New York mission was not popular with my former colleagues in the British Trade Development Office (BTDO) there and they advised strongly against it. They maintained that little business would result and they were right. Like Oscar Wilde, the last thing I needed at the time was 'good advice'. My role was to deliver the Council's wishes and to work with BTDO to make the best of the situation. When New York colleagues saw we were determined they pulled out all the stops. Our colleagues in the Scottish Development Agency and the Locate-in-Scotland agency were less than generous with their support. To add some value I got agreement from my new masters to extend the mission to Toronto. Every businessman rushes to New York but few realise that the easier market is Canada and colleagues in Toronto were pleased to see us.

The event went off well enough in terms of the mechanics. The team of business people we fielded was quite impressive with many of the Region's business 'movers and shakers' involved. Amongst those participating were Alan Shiach, then Chairman of The Macallan whisky and well known screenwriter, Mike Steven, the Managing Director and co-founder of the Grampian Country food group, the largest poultry operation in Scotland, Richard Cole-Hamilton as Chief Executive of the Clydesdale Bank, Professor Phil Love, Vice-Principal of Aberdeen University (who later went on to become Principal of Liverpool University), the Sales Director of soup manufacturers Baxter's of Speyside, and John Moorhouse, Shell Expro's Director of Public Affairs. The mission, totalling twenty-seven of us, was headed up by the Regional Council Convener, Dr Geoff Hadley. The Forbes family did us proud with an impressive array of first division New York business people.

However, and in retrospect, our business people made less of the opportunities than I expected, and notwithstanding the prognosis of failure from BTDO colleagues. The match of our firms to those in New York invited by Forbes to participate was often not perfect but my investigation of follow-up by the Grampian team indicated a disappointing application of effort. Some of our councillors were angry at being let down, as they rightly judged the situation. I was harried to provide follow up services but all I could do was try and exhort or shame the business representatives on the mission into some action. To this day I am unaware of any business deal or co-operative venture as a result of the Regional Council's initiative and the considerable effort and expense put in by the Forbes family. Thereafter our links with Forbes waned. I had no pressure to pursue the relationship further and would have found it somewhat embarrassing to do so. Some thirteen years later the University of Aberdeen, through their Principal, Professor Duncan Rice, did use the

Forbes family link although Professor Rice had his own contacts with the family from the time he held a lead position at a New York university. For me it was enjoyable and also gave me the opportunity to demonstrate that I knew my way around international trade and, perhaps most important, it was an opportunity to get to know at an early stage a number of important Grampian-based business people that I would later need to work with in one way and another. Perhaps most important was the time spent with my Committee Chairman, Nicol Stephen, and to assess him in a social context as well as a politician. A 'collectors' item meeting whilst in New York was with Forbes' Publisher, the former US Defence Secretary, Caspar Weinberger.

The visit three weeks later to the 'Offshore Technology Conference and Exhibition', or better known as 'OTC', in Houston was a somewhat complementary experience. The annual Houston exhibition and conference was the most important gathering of oil expertise in the world. All firms with any pretence of being taken seriously in the oil business were at 'OTC' and Scotland, with its maturing offshore industry, had one of the largest international delegations in Houston for the event, as well as one of the largest collection of exhibits. Grampian Regional Council, with a number of partners, had its own large and prestigious stand, under the 'Grampian' banner, which was a slight problem since few Americans could place Grampian, and many struggled to even place Scotland on the map. Coincidentally, I had visited Dallas and Houston just before I left DTI but I knew little or nothing of the oil industry and the part played by Houston based firms in oil operations across the globe. Although by choice I would have never taken the time out so early in my new job, the visit to Houston was timely. Over ten days I was able to get an excellent feel for the scope of the industry and some of the technology, as well as begin to understand the importance of Grampian in the UK's oil bonanza. I was also, even at that stage, beginning to get concerned about the return our region was getting for its input to the wealth of the nation. Clearly it was too little.

Never far from my thoughts during these trips in the Spring of 1989 was the end of June deadline to produce an economic development plan for the Region. On returning from Houston I had only two months to deliver the strategy to my new political masters. By that time I realised that one of the major obstacles was my Chief Executive, Douglas Macnaughton, ably assisted by one or two key officials. My approach to producing a strategy should have been one whereby my colleagues were included and contributed to the strategy, with the end result being a truly corporate document with large measure of agreement before it was forwarded for consideration to our politicians. All my training and experience in the Civil Service pointed to this as the prudent approach. Indeed Dr Hadley our Convener had urged me along those lines, although I guess he well understood the pressures from those who had no interest in seeing a new and radical strategy. Against his and my own better judgement I decided to keep my thoughts to myself until I had clear proposals set down in the form of an overarching and integrated strategy. I knew if proposals were shared with colleagues in a sequential manner that each would be systematically destroyed or, at best, neutered. During the build-up of the strategy I kept my Committee Chairman, Councillor Nicol Stephen, fully informed and although he was well aware of my decision to work in some secrecy he never counselled against this strategy and was supportive. He was well aware of the hostility of the Chief Executive and I was also aware of quite a few sharp exchanges between the two where my operation was the tinder. There is no doubt that I lost a lot of the goodwill of fellow Chief Officers because of my reluctance to share my thoughts, and regrettably also amongst those were some who were open-minded and saw change was needed. It took me some years to recover their respect. There were some colleagues that never gave up the battle but in all honesty I worry little about these as most were lacking in stature and what they resented most was the disturbance of their all too cosy professional lifestyle.

During this period the only direct staff responsibility I had, apart from my 'private office' staff, was for the half a dozen or so who worked in the 'Grampian Initiative' office with the task of raising internal and external awareness of the region's assets and opportunities. These staff were on secondments from other departments although over the months following my arrival most were transferred formally to my charge. The Grampian Initiative had its origins in the oil price crash a couple of years earlier in 1986 when the vow by both Grampian's business and the public sectors was 'that this should never happen again'. There was a car bumper (fender) sticker to be seen in Houston in the late eighties that summed up the mood on both sides of the Atlantic and it said "Please God give us another chance, we promise not to piss it all away again". The Grampian Initiative predated by about a year the decision that led to my appointment as the economic 'supremo', but both decisions were a response to the realisation that without oil the future prospects for the region were grim. Indeed as early as 1969 a report by Professor Maxwell Gaskin of Aberdeen University indicated few real opportunities to haul up the north-east economy notwithstanding that North Sea oil discovery, as opposed to earlier gas discoveries in the south, was already involving Aberdeen. Six years later in 1975 the Queen turned on the tap that initiated the flow from the vast Forties field and the Gaskin report was a distant joke for Aberdonians. However the Gaskin report did prompt the beginnings of necessary economic co-operation between the various public authorities by the establishment of the North East of Scotland Development Agency (or NESDA), which recognised the importance of oil to the Region's future. NESDA was later to become part of a new Department that I was to head up from April 1990.

Most of the Grampian Initiative staff had loyalties to their parent departments and were of limited help to me during the first six months. However the Initiative also employed the services of a graphic design firm called 'Format'. This small firm had been set up by Greg Rae and a colleague. I am not sure whether it was part of his contract, but in practice Greg had become a part-time member of the Grampian Initiative team, in that he was a frequent visitor to the Initiative office in Woodhill House. So much so I was confused in those early days in the job as to exactly what his status was. Greg turned out to be tower of strength and dwarfed most of my own staff in his enthusiasm and vision.

I came to rely on Greg not only for his professional input but as a confidant and somebody I could bounce ideas off and share some of the frustrations of life as a Council employee. Greg had initially studied architecture but I guess that his salesman skills would have been somewhat lost in a career in architecture. However, at the same time, I never saw him as an archetypal entrepreneur. We relied on his firm for much of the promotional material for the Initiative including the distinctive north-east pointing arrow that the Grampian Initiative had adopted as a logo. The decline of the influence of the Initiative after the 1990 local authority elections can be laid firmly at the door of Grampian's politicians and not through any shortcomings in the marketing tools that Format continued to provide.

At the time of considering the printed form of the economic development strategy Greg had just acquired the latest word-processing package which enabled not only attractive presentation but also encouraged tidy and logical assembly of the strategy document. There were many stimulating meetings in Format's office where we brainstormed a whole series of policy options. We both thrived on the adrenaline-derived buzz from these sessions and I recall that adrenaline was the only stimulant involved as neither of us liked mixing alcohol and business, although there were many social occasions where there were no such inhibitions. I retain an enthusiasm for the potential of the Grampian area but this is now tempered by experience and the gut feeling that its true potential will never be realised. However in those early months of 1989 the seeds of cynicism had yet to germinate and the experience of working with Greg, together with Moira and Margaret in my office, was an intoxicating one.

It would be wrong to say that all I met in the Council was hostility and resistance, although there was a lot of this, some overt but mainly covert. Being a new boy has its benefits in that you can get away with more but one of the disadvantages is that you know little of colleagues' track record and what motivates them. My assistant, Moira Catto, had been with the Council for many years and was able to brief me on most of the senior staff. She had worked as a Committee Clerk before being seconded to the Grampian Initiative team and so knew most people, and importantly was also well known by officials and politicians alike. I like to know what motivates staff to take one course rather than another and here I was lucky to be able to use the services of the Operational Research and Development Unit. The Unit produced a number of confidential reports which demonstrated a clarity of thought that was all too rare in the Council. An analysis of senior staff attitudes was extremely helpful.

I was, more or less, able to start with a clean sheet of paper when deciding what to include in a strategy document. There had been one or two attempts by the planning department to tidy the mess that masqueraded as an economic plan but there was neither the political nor executive will to see this pursued. My predecessor as Director of Planning, Trevor Sprott, did a magnificent job in preparing the Region for the oil boom years and I suspect that this task consumed most of his energies leaving little surplus for a battle with numerous vested interests intent on maintaining the status quo, and not least Douglas Macnaughton as the Chief Executive. I researched the archives as far as I could within the limitations of the authority's chaotic filing system, excepting the formal records of committee papers and committee minutes which were well maintained. In my future work I was to miss the ability to pursue an 'audit trail' of decisions within the department as one could in my old Whitehall job. In some senses I was rather glad to be free from policy precedents. However what was clear was that the authority took every opportunity to build its industrial property portfolio. This often came about when considering an application for financial help from a firm within the region and more often than not the firm had exhausted more conventional sources of fund-raising, such as commercial overdraft facilities. A loophole in the central government control of local authority capital expenditure allowed the Council to buy the business premises from a firm and then lease them back to the same firm. This provided the firm with fresh funds to meet its commitments or to invest in upgrading facilities. In many cases the ploy worked well but in a significant minority of cases we were clearly pursuing a lame duck policy and propping up industries and firms where the sell-by date had long passed. The buy and lease back policy was pursued with misplaced vigour by Councillor Bob Middleton when he was Convener of the Council for the four years from May 1990. Against my advice, public money was poured into a number of projects that invariably lacked viability. Bob Middleton believed it was his mission to save the remnants of Grampian's textile industry. In one case we 'rescued' a modest textile factory in one of our smaller towns three times within Bob's tenure as Regional Convener (Chairman). A turning point in my relations with Bob Middleton was at the time of the receipt of the news that the prestigious textile firm of Crombie was to withdraw from Aberdeen, and my subsequent advice that we would never see textile manufacture on the old Crombie site again. In spite of all the ingenious efforts of a compliant colleague on the property side of the Council it is now an upmarket housing estate, just as I predicted.

In my early weeks I asked the Chief Executive what was the point of the build up of our large industrial property portfolio when often much of it could be unloaded onto the private sector. I could see the role of the Council as a last resort channel of support to a firm in difficulties but there was no point in building and retaining a property empire merely as a status symbol of the Council's manhood. My challenges were met with aggression by Douglas Macnaughton. I suspect he enjoyed the power of being able to quickly sort out a problem, although a very short term fix in many cases. In the last months of the Council's life in 1996 most of the industrial and commercial property was sold off and the spoils distributed amongst the three successor councils.

My only other policy challenge to the Chief Executive in those early months was over water and sewerage charges. At the time these services were run by the Regional level authorities in Scotland and waste charges were a matter for the councils concerned. In listening to the debate on the setting of charges for the year ahead I became increasingly concerned about the Council's policy of keeping industrial effluent charges to a minimum. At the same time European Community instigated restrictions were already on the horizon and the Community line was governed by the 'polluter pays principle', which I had a hand in drafting some years earlier when at DTI. I could see that we were doing our local firms no favours by artificially protecting them from the effluent standards and charges they would soon have to meet. Again, instead of a reasoned debate I met with hostility and even accusations of disloyalty to my colleagues in the water department. At a personal level I had no problems with water department colleagues and indeed quite the reverse. The chickens were, some years later, to come home to roost when on 'nationalisation' of Scotland's water industry in 1996 we were made aware of the huge under-investment in the water industry whilst under local authority control. This was plain to me a few weeks into my time with Grampian Region and I guess, and indeed hope, that it was so to my water colleague professionals, some of which went on to serve in senior positions in what is now Scottish Water. However none shared any such thoughts with me when together we served the Regional Council. I was later to serve on the consumer watchdog body set up to monitor the North of Scotland Water Authority in a new centralised operation.

A new economic development strategy would have to address how we dealt with maintaining our existing industrial base but also address the need to encourage new industries that might replace oil employment in years to come when employment in the North Sea declines. It would need to commit the Council to some prioritisation of development expenditure. Our revenue expenditure in 1988 devoted to economic development activity was just over twenty million pounds (gross), although the largest share of that was taken up by the Region's responsibility for four further education colleges. What was left included some £5 million on the more traditional economic development activities such as grants to firms, industrial estates and £4.7million on urban aid related issues including training services to the long term unemployed. By the time I took up post in the December of 1988 we were spending some £700,000 a year on promotion of the Region via the Grampian Initiative, the only budget for which I was directly responsible at that stage. It seemed to me at the time that the main reason why I had been recruited was to make some sense of this quite significant overall expenditure, which roughly equated to the expenditure of the Aberdeen outpost of the Scottish Development Agency. This body was shortly to become a Local Enterprise Company under the chairmanship of Ian Wood of the fast-growing John Wood engineering and oil services group. I put great emphasis in the strategy on providing the foundations for a council that was much more corporate in its approach to all its activities and not just economic development. The key to this was to drag together into some coherent whole the departments core to economic development policy formulation and delivery. The draft strategy was to make radical recommendations about departmental structure and organisation. I suppose I was pressing the limits of my remit and so bringing me into quite acrimonious confrontation with Douglas Macnaughton, but I was supported in this line by my Chairman, Councillor Nicol Stephen. At this stage I thought I had nothing to lose, although I was to find out within the first year that I stood to lose my job as a result of the acceptance of some of my recommendations.

Already a central theme to the Grampian Initiative's work and also that of the various local business advisers to the Initiative was 'quality'. The view was, and quite rightly, that if the Region was not only to survive but prosper, and bearing in mind its geographical as well a perceived isolation from the main markets, it would have to produce goods and services at the top end of the market, although quality is also about fitness for purpose and not necessarily implying 'luxury'. Therefore I adopted 'quality' as the 'keystone' to the future of the Region. I saw this as linked to every aspect of the council's work from quality of townscapes, our environment, the goods and services we produced to the way the council dealt with its staff and customers. To underline this I recommended that the council should adopt Total Quality Management (TQM) techniques to achieve our internal quality goals. This was one of many fuses the strategy lit and in this case the Grampian Region went on to win an award for excellence in 1995 for progress in developing services driven by Total Quality principles.

The introduction of the quality theme allowed me to address our corporate style and change to a customer-driven approach with an emphasis on client care. Part of this was addressed by using Total Quality Management techniques but I was also able to influence how the council presented itself through signage and stationery. I got Greg Rae to photograph a number of boards outside council property including schools and offices and it was quite a shock to councillors to realise that we had no consistent corporate style. The Grampian Initiative was very good at this, thanks to the professional services of Greg Rae's company Format, with clear rules for all publications, down to the correct green to be used, identified by a 'Pantone' number. On the coat tails of the Grampian Initiative I devised a sympathetic housestyle for my new department's stationery and publications which were to be adopted for all the council's operations, once we had a change of Chief Executive.

Although I had little delegated responsibility I drew on my DTI experience in the South East Regional Office and ignored the rules and just got on with changes.

Although Douglas Macnaughton enjoyed playing the saviour and matchmaking on the industrial development side, he tended to see many departments (and there were a lot) as almost as self-governing overseas territories and, apart from the annual budget round, rarely interfered. He was most happy when dealing with small issues and seemed oblivious to the larger picture. One is tempted to classify him as the old-fashioned town clerk, but he lacked the gravitas, steel and discipline that these relics of the Victorian zenith of local government displayed. At the same time he was certainly not in the new mould of chief executive-cum-city manager, with the emphasis on management backed up by good information systems. I suppose one could say, in modern management speak, he 'empowered' his chief officials, but there is a distinction between staff empowerment and delegation, and a laissez-faire approach to management. Grampian Regional Council was in fact a loose federation of semi-autonomous departments. This played into the hands of the politicians and the committee system with more or less one committee and a councillor chair and vice-chair for each department. Chairs and their vice-chairs had no interest in seeing a more corporate approach and certainly not fewer departments as this would likely mean less committees, and less corresponding positions of power with their associated responsibility pay supplements. In contrast it was in the interest of the Council's Convener to see a more corporate approach and, besides, this strengthened the power base of the Convener. Such 'power' considerations did nor worry my first Convener, Dr Geoff Hadley, but they were manna to Bob Middleton, his successor. Bob saw the Convener's role as more one of control and direction, and where the Council's constitution frustrated his desires to make changes and enhance his role he achieved his objectives by bullying staff and colleagues. I was unaware of the character of the man at the time but it does explain why he showed so much interest whilst in opposition in the development of my economic strategy and the proposed changes in organisation and operation of the Council. Behind closed doors he was very supportive of my chairman in the early stages of discussion on my proposals. He knew that Labour stood a good chance of taking over the Administration after the 1990 elections and as leader of the Labour Group he expected, reasonably, to be the next Convener.

My final draft strategy proposed the merger of a number of

departments with a corresponding reduction in chief officers, as well as giving a real role to the deputy to the Chief Executive. Central to the proposals was the formation of a new Environment Department incorporating the functions of the existing Water, Roads and Estates (property services) departments, and a Development Department taking in the existing Planning, Urban Aid, North East of Scotland Development Agency (NESDA), the Grampian Initiative, and the Economic Development Unit which was essentially me and my office staff. Macnaughton was just short of incandescent when I shared these ideas with him. He said the proposals were outwith my remit, which in all honesty they probably were but I was not going to concede this point. As far as I remember Nicol Stephen was well aware of what I had in mind and was encouraging. At this stage these proposals were only known to a few people and certainly not to those with departments disappearing in my proposed reorganisation. It was always a mystery to me why this was not leaked to my colleagues. One reason may have been that Douglas Macnaughton himself felt challenged and he did not wish to add further to rumours already rife about my arrival and what politicians had in mind, and here I guess I mean the Liberal councillors led along a road signposted 'change' by Nicol Stephen, their brightest star.

My relations with Douglas Macnaughton were already difficult and if I had any hope of getting the core proposals through Council then I would have to offer some concessions. Later and during the committee discussion stage I had to acquiesce to restricting organisational streamlining to bringing together the main economic developments functions under one director, and drop the parallel brigading of a number of other departments into one environment department.

By early June in 1989 I had completed my draft strategy, and now with the title 'Together to the Future', was eager to present it to the full Council. Up until that point only the Chief Executive, my Chair, and my inner office had any idea what the strategy was to contain. I was anxious that the denouement should be a special occasion and not part of a longer committee agenda. I thought that it would help focus if I could get councillors away from our HQ in Woodhill House. I was looking for their endorsement of change and my presentation was to make the point that little had changed since the new Regional Council had moved into Woodhill House in the mid-seventies. Greg Rae and I carefully considered a number of venues that would avoid the wrong messages. We looked at a lecture theatre in the Scott Sutherland School of Architecture at what is now The Robert Gordon University. We thought this was sufficiently neutral but at the same time a gracious venue and pleasantly situated in parkland by the River Dee, and also it had the advantage that we would have been charged little for its use.

Council business schedules are always crowded and so we thought, perhaps naively, that we would go for a Saturday morning. I cleared all this with my Chair and finally with the Convener, before seeking the blessing of the the opposition leaders, namely Bob Middleton and the ever-sensible Leader of the Conservatives, John Porter. On 9 June a memo was sent from the Convener's office to all Members inviting them to attend a presentation on 24 June but with the proviso that this was ratified by the Council's Policy and Resources Committee (P&R) on 22 June. Prior to this I was to receive an unhelpful note from the Director of Legal Services, Allen Campbell. Allen was in charge of the committee procedure amongst other duties and was later to become the Regional Council's Chief Executive.

Long before the P&R Committee meeting on 22 June it was plain that there would be no presentation to the Council before the summer recess. However I somehow believed it would be 'all right on the night' and so it was quite a shock to witness so many objecting to the presentation. The *Press and Journal* reported "Top official at centre of amazing row" and so it was, with the opposition parties split but when put to the vote the motion that the presentation should go ahead was carried 14 to 7. I thought it was all over and we were home and dry! Far from it when on a procedural point concerning the Council's Standing Orders the vote result was considered void. The 'P&J' reported a "solemn-faced Dr Fisher immediately stood up from his seat ...and strode from the committee room". I was furious as I had been urged to produce this strategy by June and to meet this deadline had worked to the point of exhaustion. There is no doubt that I did walk out of the meeting with no pretence that I was seeking a 'comfort break'. I do not think it did me any harm, but probably not much good. My image in the community at large, I guess, would have had a fillip.

It was not until the other side of the summer recess before I got my masters' attention again and I realised I would then have some fence mending to do. I needed to get politicians to better understand where I was coming from but perhaps more important to try and get them to consider the future of the Region in a wider context. Finally I needed to build a bit of goodwill and so in September I suggested a look at a number of authorities in the south-east of England and see how they were tackling problems very similar in nature to Grampian. This idea went down rather well and with three days at our disposal I arranged in

October 1989 a very full schedule of visits to councils from Norfolk through Essex to Kent.

Six of us flew south to Stansted and in a self-drive minibus undertook an exhausting schedule with meetings, working lunches, and dinners peppered with key guests with good knowledge of the local economy. Many of the guests I had met in my previous role at DTI. I made sure our evenings were as relaxed as possible and in surroundings that showed off the best that these counties could offer. With good local contacts I managed, within budget, to surprise my masters with an even more interesting hotel each successive evening. Starting modestly in Norwich we progressed to the ancient Swan Hotel in Lavenham, which must be every Scotsman's romantic idea of England, and then for our final night to the Chilston Park Hotel in Lenham, Kent, to be met by staff in full 'downstairs' uniform of yesteryear and extending to dinner in an elegant private dining room lit only by candles. The visit was long remembered, but perhaps more for the evening venues than the content of three very busy days. However there is no doubt it did open eyes and I hope it contributed to a less insular outlook by those who accompanied us and the message was passed on to their colleagues. It certainly did wonders for my reputation as a fixer.

I got to make my presentation to the full Council on the draft economic development strategy in mid-August, on a weekday and in Woodhill House. However, I still had one or two novelties up my sleeve. With the help of Format Communications we put together an introductory two minute multi-projector slide presentation. Also, as the audience were assembling, we broadcast a low and continuous electronically generated sound. At first it was just a hum that was almost indistinguishable from the white noise of the air conditioning system, but over about ten minutes we increased the volume of this hum to quite annoying levels. The idea was to create a certain audience unease and anticipation. As soon as all were seated the hum was stopped and all that appeared on the large screen was a picture of Woodhill House in the snow against a silent sound track. We held this picture and the silence for a good few seconds and then launched into the the audio-visual presentation, which featured a rapid presentation of icons of advance and change since the Regional Council had been set up in the mid-seventies. The music chosen was rock, and loud. At the end of the A/V sequence all went silent and Woodhill House appeared on the screen and the image was left to linger with no sound track. The audience by this stage also was silent and clearly had no idea of what was coming next. In the silence and darkened room I took my place at a podium to make the presentation, and started by referring to the screen and saying that little had changed in Woodhill House over the fifteen years covered by the A/V slide show. The point was made, and I had their attention for the next forty minutes as I went through the strategy with the aid of slides, and a teleprompter. I had used one of these before. If done well it never amazes me how many people are fooled into thinking you did it all without reference to notes, and so it was with a number of my councillor audience. I had rehearsed the occasion several times with Format's staff and so it all went off reasonably well. I even got an ovation at the end.

Little did I realise it at the time, my troubles had only just started. The document that I had presented in mid-August had to be discussed and agreed by the Council and had to be given wider circulation within both public and private sectors to obtain comment on a strategy which made much of a partnership approach. We went public with a press release on 14 September 1989 and started a more formal consultation with Aberdeen City and the four other District Councils that made up Grampian Region, as well as numerous other representative bodies of government and business.

The local authorities were cautious and suspicious. There was little love lost between the District Councils and the Region, and particularly between Aberdeen City and the Region. However the turf wars were generally fought at the political level, whereas officials in the respective authorities got on quite well in spite of attempts by some of the Region's councillors to provoke conflict. In fact I got on very well with my opposite numbers and indeed most of the Chief Executives and District Council Chairmen, or Lord Provost in the case of the City of Aberdeen. Silly games were played by both sides but the Region's politicians, in my view, were often the more childish. The Region was the senior partner in that it held the best hand in terms of resources, and so its behaviour was the more bizarre. In the circumstances I was not expecting to be heaped with praise. One comment I treasure was that reported from a Gordon District councillor (P&J, 11/10/89) where he described the 'Together to the Future' strategy as having "Thatcherite tendencies". Indeed there were many councillors in my own organisation who saw me as right wing and to the end of my time with them few had any idea of my true political leanings, and indeed this is how it should be. I addressed a meeting of each District Council in turn, explaining the details of the strategy and answering questions. I was received by all politely, although with a healthy degree of scepticism.

In contrast the government-supported agencies or 'quangos' were positively hostile. For example the Scottish Development Agency was just so. It was often known to its employees as ' the Agency' (and invariably with a Glaswegian intonation), leaving one with the impression it might be some sort of tartan CIA out of Langley rather than a big gravy train out of Glasgow Central. The 'SDA' operated a large office in Aberdeen under the direction of Bob Downes. I had experienced scarcely veiled hostility from the SDA and its satellite organisations from more or less the day of my arrival in Aberdeen. I suppose I was seen as a rival to their power base in economic development and my arrival was a sign that Grampian Regional Council was determined to take the lead in better positioning the region's economy for the years ahead and ones that could not rely on oil to the extent we had done so up to the oil price crash in 1986. My arrival coincided also with the Scottish Office's decision to revamp the SDA leviathan with the establishment of the lookalike 'Scottish Enterprise' and its supporting network of 'Local Enterprise Companies'. I will return later to the fascinating politics resulting from the establishment of our local incarnation of this change in the form of Grampian Enterprise Limited, which became known to us in local authorities as 'Gel'. Although the names changed the officials remained largely the same and the hostility I experienced from SDA continued without interruption into Scottish Enterprise and Gel. Some was overt and plainly abusive, but most was covert and corrosive. One senior individual in SDA in Glasgow at the time has the distinction of being the rudest public official I have ever met. His outburst was prompted by sight of my draft strategy and was completely unprovoked by me as I had never met the man before or even corresponded with him. The strategy was critical of the policy and the mechanism that locates inward investment to Scotland and indicated that Grampian region had not done well out of SDA-directed inward investment through their 'Locate in Scotland' subsidiary. That was a fact then and remains so some fifteen years on.

Such outright and personal rudeness was generally the exception and the majority of consultees were to comment on the strategy in more constructive terms or to ignore it altogether! Most individual business people welcomed the fact that their local authority was, at last, getting to grips with the problem of the post oil economy and I received many 'go for it' type messages. Stewart Macphie of Macphies of Glenbervie, one of the area's foremost food processing companies, was particularly perceptive with the observation that the obstacles I would face were within my own organisation and I would have to be very single minded to succeed.

Each department within the council prepared comments on the strategy for its dedicated Committee, that is Roads Department for the Transportation and Roads Committee, Education Department for the Education Committee and so on through most of the Council's many departments. On the whole these were pretty objective although many departmental directors saw their own operations at risk in the sweeping reorganisational changes recommended. At the same time officials were uncertain as to the likely response of their political masters and so their initial reaction was probably tempered with caution linked to self-interest. All internal comments, both political from committees and official were channelled to a series of special meetings of the Economic Development and Planning Committee (EDP) chaired by Councillor Nicol Stephen. His strategy was crucial in seeing through the recommendations contained in the 'Together to the Future' document. I expected that this committee would take the document and recommendations line by line. In practice this is what did happen but importantly Nicol moved at the first meeting that the committee approve the whole document in principle. This caused an outcry but Nicol kept his nerve and with some covert Labour support (the Council elections were only six months away in May 1990) the Liberal/Scottish National Party/ Independent led administration won the day. It was a shrewd move by Nicol as from then on the debate on individual parts of the strategy was less of a matter of 'if', and more of a matter of 'how'. Nonetheless the debates were often bitter and stormy and it was not until the fifth of January 1990 that the details of the strategy were agreed by the politicians and a final draft was produced. This differed little from the original draft that I presented to politicians apart from the omission of some of the recommendations covering the streamlining of the council's numerous Director level led departments.

The Council did accept my recommendations to bring physical planning, the economic development agency (NESDA), urban aid and the Grampian Initiative promotional arm of the council into one development department, eventually to become the Department of Economic Development and Planning. The proposed Environment Department bringing together Roads, Water and Property Services was too rich for many but I suspect the hand on the hatchet was the Chief Executive's. The directors of the constituent departments that were to make up the new economic development department were not happy, as I was soon to find out,. I was never sure of how far Nicol Stephen was behind my proposals on Council departmental reorganisation. He rarely shared his political strategy with me. In retrospect I feel I was 'used' by the then political Administration leading the Council and particularly by the Liberal partners in that Administration. Although I have spent my career in public service it was only on arrival in Grampian was I exposed to 'red in tooth and claw' politics and recognised what a protected life I had led in Whitehall where, at my level, politicians tended to treat officials with respect and officials were left out of the political loop.

The first four months of 1990 were particularly stressful as I battled to establish the terms of reference of my new department. The future of two directors was at stake. These were the directors of planning and of the development agency, NESDA. Understandably both were feeling pretty sore with the prospect of working as a number two to me or taking an early retirement package. The council was not insisting on compulsory redundancy and in theory both could have stayed if they had wished. I did all I could to make the situation as comfortable for them as I could and we were able to talk through most of the obstacles in a civilised manner, helped by a break together in Braemar. As a result of this I organised new notepaper which featured all our names as Directors and offered a partnership approach to running the new combined department. The Planning Director was an absolute gentleman and much respected in his profession, as I was to discover. I would have been glad to see him stay with us. The Development Director was more of a challenge. His staff in NESDA were very loyal and supportive and he had done much to raise the council's economic development profile. However I think we would have found it difficult to work together, and I suspect he shared this view. By late summer of 1990 the two finally decided to take a voluntary severance package and leave. It was an uncomfortable time for all of us but I feel both men were treated fairly.

This left me with an even more difficult situation as the Director of Personnel advised that under council rules the post that I was to take over was new and sufficiently different that it should be advertised. So I would have to compete again for what was really my own job. The only concession was that application was restricted to internal candidates, although this restriction also heightened the tensions within the new organisation that I was struggling to bring together. The main contender was the deputy who had run the planning department during his director's long absence due to illness. My appearance on the scene had likely thrown into disarray the reasonable prospects that he would succeed his boss to become the planning director. He was shortlisted for the Head of Economic Development post that I was appointed to on arrival in Grampian and here again he was to face me in a competition where the prize was the new combined economic development and physical planning department. The only difference between me and the other candidates was that if I was not selected I was out of a job with all the implications for my family having moved only eighteen months before from the other end of the country. I was offered no 'comfort' zone by the council and any severance package would have been the minimum I suspect. It was a wretched time for me and my wife and we began to regret our move to Grampian.

The interview procedure was much as the one I had experienced and it was clear that the competition was essentially between me and the deputy planning director. With so much political heat having been generated by the debate over the economic development strategy I was far from sure who my political supporters would be. All I do know is that I saw some Tory councillors leaving the committee room where the interviews took place in advance of notification of the outcome to the candidates. I remember recalling at the time a letter of warm support I had received from the leader of the Conservative group, Councillor John Porter. In this letter, dated 11 January and just some three months earlier, he said how much he held me in high esteem and valued the experience I had brought to the council.

I gather the contest was a close run thing and politics intervened. Again the local council elections, just one month away, were sharpening councillors' minds and some politicians were taking stock of which officials they would prefer to be working with, and here was an opportunity to influence events. Bob Middleton, as Leader of the Labour Group, had worked quietly with myself and my Chairman in pushing through my strategy. But as we moved towards the elections he saw his chances of being the next Convener of the Council improving, and some suspect he and a number of others were looking for somebody more compliant than myself.

I did get the job but to this day I am left with a sour taste, as is Fiona. The contest left me uncertain of my position and my relationship with my Committee Chairman Nicol Stephen. However a month later on eighteenth May 1990 council elections saw the Labour group under Bob Middleton's convenership take control of the Council but in coalition with the Liberals. Nicol Stephen continued as my Chairman, with a Labour Vice-Chair, until the Spring of 1991 when Nicol contested and won the Kincardine and Deeside Westminster seat that had become vacant on the unexpected death of the much admired local Tory MP, Alick Buchanan-Smith. At the general election a year later on ninth of

April 1992 the seat was won back by George Kynoch for the Conservatives. Nicol was eventually to secure a seat in the first Scottish parliament and became a Scottish Minister and then, as leader of the Scottish Liberal Democrats, became Deputy First Minister.

Nicol Stephen's period as Chair of the Economic Development and Planning Committee under the Labour led coalition at Grampian was a useful shoulder year for me and provided some element of continuity and a buffer between me and the new Convener Middleton. However I have to say that subsequent chairs of EDP Committee were always kind, helpful and usually protective in most circumstances. Nicol's successor as Chairman was Rob Hunter who was every bit Nicol's intellectual equal and more, but as Rob would be the first to admit he was no politician. Of all my Chairs and Vice-Chairs I suppose I respected Rob the most as a man. He was a quiet and cultured man and with his law training had worked as a lecturer at Aberdeen University and had established quite a reputation in the field of arbitration. He was always the gentleman and bent over backwards to help colleagues less able and less articulate make their point. So much so that on occasions he would assist an opposition colleague frame a motion or an amendment to a motion, and sometimes to the detriment of his own party's interests. There was one marvellous occasion where Rob had turned up at committee armed with a large pile of learned looking reference books with a view to making some point rooted in Scottish history. I do not remember what the point was but he was challenged by Middleton who quoted Nigel Tranter, a popular historical novelist, as his source. I had never, up to this point and indeed since, seen Rob visibly angry, but at the point of Bob Middleton quoting Tranter, he lost it. He was quite beside himself with anger and I think because Middleton had, in Rob's view, so trivialised the point he was making. To the rest of us it was a huge joke but not to Rob. It was not that this thoroughly decent man did not have a sense of humour but rather Middleton's couthie and, in this instance, ignorant approach had devalued the research and effort Rob Hunter had put in on the point.

Over the next two years I put all my effort into implementing the actions agreed by Council in the economic development strategy. It was an uphill effort, working with some staff who, if not plain obstructive, were difficult and devious. Often I longed for the quality of staff and the discipline of the Civil Service. The Convener, Bob Middleton, contrived to make my life as difficult as possible, although most of the ruling Administration and opposition councillors were supportive and constructive. I was helped within the Labour group by the fact that many were often on the receiving end of exactly the type of treatment I was receiving from the Convener. Neither Douglas Macnaughton nor the chief executives that were to follow were particularly supportive. In all fairness to them they had their own difficulties in meeting Middleton's demands.

As we moved through the four years of the Labour-led Administration it became harder for me to initiate fresh and new ideas. Happily the 'Together to the Future' strategy had plenty to keep me busy, although progress was more in spite of the Administration than because of it. I spent a lot of unproductive time fire-fighting, and looking behind me. Some major fallout from the development strategy maintained my interest but it was an unhappy period. The marketing arm of the council, the Grampian Initiative, also entered a period of decline which proved to be terminal. The marketing campaign lost momentum and credibility, both inside and outside the Grampian area. It became little more than a convenient publicity platform for politicians, raising the profile of individuals and losing sight of the goal of raising the Region's profile. Also we lost the support of the very best of the private sector. Over the last five years of the Regional Council's life we threw away a resource that was much admired and even copied by other authorities in the UK. We were never to be as successful in changing our image as the wonderful 'Glasgow's Miles Better' campaign of Dr Michael Kelly, but we were changing negative perceptions of the area, and starting to address the all important self-image. If a city or region does not believe in itself then it has little hope of convincing others. Civic self-belief is much more than a willingness to defend your culture, come what may, and more about a quiet confidence that your area and peoples can compete and cope with all comers, and all this without the need to resort to the parish pump jingoism that the North East of Scotland is so good at. With confident self-belief the whole business of attracting inward investment to an area, new people with new ideas, and the investment to match becomes so much easier.

In recent years the City of Dundee has been a good example of what can be achieved to turn a city's image around in a relatively short period. For many in Aberdeen it will be a new and useful lesson to look at their near and oft maligned neighbour down the coast and see it as a serious rival for innovative ideas and the resources to put these ideas into practice.

Chapter 18

Grampian Ambassador

......'But westward, look, the land is bright'

I mentioned that on arriving in Grampian there was already a commitment to accompany a delegation of our councillors to the oil exhibition and conference, known as 'OTC', in Houston, Texas. This was for some councillors and officials a sort of annual holiday at the beginning of May or thereabouts. To be fair other Scottish councils involved in the oil industry in some way also sent representatives including the Shetland Islands, Orkney and Tayside. Most delegates from Scotland availed themselves of the package put together every year by an Aberdeen travel agent together with the sponsorship of the *Press and Journal*. In this case the relationship between the travel firm and the P&J was an almost symbiotic one, but the link worked to the advantage of the delegates. The arrangements and logistics were well honed over the years and the result was a very club-like experience with most of the delegates from all over Scotland, as well as a sprinkling from the north of England, accommodated in the same Houston hotel. This hotel, the Post Oak Double Tree, went to considerable effort to make us welcome, including generous free use of the hotel minibuses and other facilities.

The experience of staying at the Double Tree for up to ten days was very much like attending a political or trade union conference where one knew most of the guests, if not by name then certainly by sight. Even the P&J arrived daily on the afternoon flight from the UK as did reciprocal reports of goings on in Houston appear for home consumption. However, many were glad that the P&J stopped short of reporting gossip about the Scottish delegates in Houston. Most of our business people worked hard but almost as many played quite hard as well! All indiscretions during play time were strictly off-the-record. There was one occasion this was put in jeopardy when a delegate got himself shot. Apparently he got lost on a circuitous return from an evening at the local country and western dance hall and so knocked on a Houston resident's front door for directions. In this part of the world 'good ol' boys' tend to shoot first and ask questions afterwards and so it appeared to be the case in this instance. It was rare for delegates to get themselves into too much bother. All were warned of the dangers of walking alone, even though the Double Tree was situated only five minutes' walk from the prestigious Galleria shopping complex. There was also a good sense of collective responsibility and all would check that the last person was out of a bar, restaurant or night club before the group left to return to the Double Tree and to bed, or at least the safety of the hotel bar.

I attended the OTC exhibition every year but one during my time at Grampian. As the senior official I had responsibility for just about everything including ensuring that the large Grampian exhibition stand was set up and functioned efficiently, dealing with exhibitor problems on the stand, overseeing stand staff including some locally engaged staff, arranging, writing and sometimes making speeches at major delegate and guest receptions, arranging the separate programme for our councillors, and accompanying them on visits. Often I acted as their banker as well as being there to sign their bar bills. Although councillors received the same daily allowance in Houston as myself, they rarely bought drinks unless they were sure the Regional Council, or an official was going to pick up the tab. Bar and other entertainment bills were, in fact, small beer besides the overall costs of Grampian's stand and presence at OTC.

Most councillors turned out to be pleasant and undemanding travel companions. I would go further and say many were excellent company, as was so often the case when they were away from home and the Woodhill House headquarters. There were two or three exceptions with sullen and demanding behaviour and always looking for an opportunity to complain. At the other extreme there was one councillor who hardly ever appeared from his room except when required on parade for a group visit. He rarely appeared for meals unless they were paid for as part of offered hospitality. However, he had found a nearby supermarket and was said to exist on a diet of biscuits consumed in his room. We officials assumed the object of the exercise was to save in order to take home as much of his daily subsistence allowance as possible. The arrangement we used at the time was that the money for daily subsistence was a 'right', and how one spent or apportioned it was up to the individual. Our Director of Finance was uneasy about this but in my experience it was the cleanest method of financing councillors and staff, and provided less temptation to fiddle expenses claims via taxi receipts and the like. If one is away for ten days I think it is right that the daily subsistence rate should cover the purchase of the odd refreshment as well as meals. I set out my interpretation of the rules to the Finance Department and my line was never challenged. If individuals decided to live on a diet of biscuits in their rooms then this was within the rules and I was content, provided they appeared when needed and did the job. The individual concerned on this occasion was no problem and there was never any question of over-indulgence the night before nor chasing him to the morning parade ground, unlike a number of his colleagues, and one or two officials.

By my third visit to OTC in 1991 I began to see that the annual pilgrimage brought little measurable returns. The event that year was costing some £40,000 including the cost to the council of the subsidy to firms taking booths on the Grampian stand, a very large reception together with an expensive audio/visual presentation at the Double Tree hotel, and much else. In spite of a lot of staff time spent in chasing firms to exhibit with us and a subsidy in 1990 of £1600 per firm we attracted few manufacturing companies from our area, leaving the rest of the stand to be filled with a motley selection of service firms including accountancy, staff recruitment, publishing, a hotel group and our local fire brigade. In my view most of these firms would have attended OTC without our subsidy and stand facilities. The option was always present for these firms to join the adjacent UK stand also sponsored, in one way or another, from public funds. Before the decision was taken to attend the 1992 OTC exhibition I put my misgivings in a paper to the Economic Development and Planning Committee (EDP Committee). I reported we had no evidence whatsoever of a commercial contract gained or product sold in return for our over £40,000 annual investment at OTC, over and above that which would have happened anyway without our involvement. It was difficult to counter the argument that as a major oil producing region 'Grampian had to be at OTC', both in terms of our profile and the possible positive effect of our presence in Houston on inward investment to Grampian. Councillor Middleton, when he was Convener, trotted out the phrase 'no one owes us a living and we have to go out and fight for it' in justification of every overseas venture. It is the same with all non-specific marketing and similarly in our case with expenditure on marketing the 'Grampian' brand, and that is it is very difficult to quantify the returns. There is a tired old marketing mantra which says half of marketing spend is wasted but the trick is to spot which half. We faced the same dilemma in the Grampian Initiative where we spent a small fortune on marketing over five years from 1988. In 1990/1991 alone the spend was over £200,000. Even the results of marketing spend at home were difficult to quantify, especially outwith Scotland. If it was a struggle in Houston, and it was, to get Americans to understand the geographical and political relationship of Scotland to the rest of the United Kingdom, what hope had we of selling a place called Grampian, which they had never heard of. However it has to be admitted we had almost as much trouble explaining the whereabouts of Grampian to colleagues from England and especially those from the 'Deep South'.

My paper to the Committee suggesting we think again about a stand at OTC went down like a lead balloon. It was not a message that any politician wished to hear. Attendance at OTC was seen as very much a Council virility symbol, quite apart from the views of those senior councillors who valued their chances of a none too strenuous seven to ten days break in a warm and sunny Texas in May. I was made to feel disloyal at worst, and misguided at best. The Committee finally agreed unanimously in August 1991 that the Council would again be represented at OTC, notwithstanding my report that the £41,000 spend produced few returns. In the light of my report I expected my presence in Houston would not be requested in 1992 and that was the case.

However I was to return to Houston for OTC in 1993 with Councillor Ironside, the Labour Chair of the Grampian Initiative, together with about the same number of businesses on our stand as in previous years. A potentially tricky situation for me was inclusion of political representation from the City of Aberdeen. Happily, neither the City's Councillor Cooney, nor Councillor Ironside had any interest in picking over the old turf wars so much enjoyed by many of their colleagues back in their respective council chambers. The City fielded also two excellent officials and one, Andrew Stephen, I got to know quite well.

It was good to be back in Houston and with another chance to try again to reap some better return for the Region than had been the case to date. With Councillor Len Ironside leading the team we at least stood a chance. Len's strengths were his ability to deliver a speech and to present a policy or 'line' at a meeting or press occasion, and I needed to ensure his talents were put to good use. He had the ability to speak well and clearly but at the same time not losing his local accent. He had also a gift for projecting sincerity, an essential attribute for any successful politician. At the same time we needed a platform that was fresh and to that end we, for the second year, had retained the services of Phil Taggart, a Houston based PR expert. We had to overcome the handicap of Grampian being relatively unknown in Houston, although it was the UK's and probably Europe's 'oil capital' at the time. The previous year Phil Taggart had achieved a colour photograph of the Grampian stand on the business page of the *Houston Chronicle*, as well as other local newspaper and television interviews. This year we were better prepared in briefing Taggart and as a result we reaped rewards far beyond our expectations. We were helped by the coincidence of a government announcement earlier in the Spring of 1993 of changes in the fiscal policy dealing with the taxation of oil companies operating on the UK continental shelf.

These Treasury-announced changes were unexpected, and seemingly also so by DTI Ministers as much as the oil related industry in Grampian. The effects of the changes were complex, difficult to assess and did not affect companies or sectors evenly. Some of the big players with large mature fields were to do very well as a result of proposed changes in the Petroleum Revenue Tax (PRT). Analysts at the time estimated that BP Exploration would benefit by as much as £400 million over the three years to 1996. At the same time other equally well known companies stood to lose many millions and Amerada Hess was one of the more outspoken casualties of the tax changes. Many household names in the oil business were understandably coy about joining their smaller brethren in the outcry against these changes in the oil tax regime. One aspect of the Treasury announcement that was of particular concern in Grampian was the abolition of exploration and appraisal tax relief for commitments incurred after 16 March 1993. Chevron claimed the withdrawal of tax relief would increase fourfold the cost of finding new oil on the UK continental shelf. It was more the deleterious effect on exploration that was of particular concern to the local community in Grampian. As a result there was a frenzy of lobbying activity with numerous papers and input from all concerned including the intellectually redoubtable Professor Alex Kemp of Aberdeen University. Professor Kemp regularly provided my department, and others, with advice on the economics of the oil industry and was much respected by government and industry alike. He had the advantage of looking like a boffin from central casting and had a very academic delivery when on a platform. I felt intimidated in his presence although he was always very humble and a delightful person to meet. Armed with Alex Kemp and data from Alan Campbell, a senior expert in my own department, councillors from the Region and the City put up a spirited opposition to the 'PRT' changes. Alan was to come to my and the council's rescue on many occasions.

However Councillor Len Ironside's finest hour was to come in Houston in the May of 1993 when we were able to raise the PRT issue in front of the international press present for the oil exhibition. We had briefed our retained publicity expert on the tax issue and left him to secure interviews as well as place articles in the local press. What we did not expect was his proposal that we hold a major press conference in the the very same room that our Energy Minister, Tim Eggar, was to meet the press later that day. Len and I must have looked a bit shocked when offered this opportunity by Phil Taggart as he asked whether we were up to the challenge. I feared we had bitten off more than we could cope with. One thing for sure was that we could expect no support from our colleagues in the Grampian delegation and we would be on our own. I give all credit to Len for unhesitatingly grasping the opportunity when many of his colleagues would have retreated. So we assured Phil Taggart that we 'were on' and he went away to book the conference room at the press centre. In the hour or so before the press conference I prepared a statement with Len, and we rehearsed the questions that might be asked and also how we should divide the questions between us.

At the appointed time the two of us took the platform before a decent showing of journalists including a very nervous lady who looked after press relations at our Consulate General in Houston. Len spoke to the release we had agreed with Phil Taggart and I then went on to field most of the questions from reporters. It seemed to go well and we managed to direct a number of questions to the press to ask the Minister later. I left the platform totally exhausted after the rush of adrenaline in the lead up to and through the ordeal, and returned with Len to our stand in the main exhibition hall for a fix of black coffee. The news had already reached our colleagues on the stand and almost to a man they were already putting a respectable political distance between themselves and the outcome of the press conference. All were nervous of taking the lobby against PRT changes to Houston and so putting our Minister on the spot. The lady from the Consulate General was busy briefing officials at Scottish Enterprise as well as the Offshore Supplies Office, a quango which had been set up by our government, initially to make sure that as much as possible of the business from the North Sea came to British firms. The Minister would have been similarly briefed. The charge was not that our line was wrong but rather we had breached a convention that domestic quarrels are left at home and that when overseas it was in all our interests to present a united front. A sort of extended cabinet responsibility I suppose.

Officials were furious and the Minister later snubbed Len Ironside on his duty tour of exhibitors on our stand. However neither of us had any regrets then, and certainly not with hindsight. The press coverage was good locally, but perhaps more important it was good at home. Len's profile was considerably enhanced and the whole episode did him a lot of good. That many of my colleagues, both in the council but also in the wider business community represented in the Grampian delegation to

Houston, left the kitchen when the heat was on was of little surprise, as I had long got their measure in the four years I had been working for the Regional Council. Len met Eggar on home ground sometime later and the Minister was professional and indicated no personal ill feelings towards Len or the Region as a result of the Houston episode. On return to Scotland Len wrote me a note to thank me for all my support, advice and the work I had done for the Region in Houston.

With the benefit of hindsight, were the PRT changes announced in 1993 as economically devastating as we saw them at the time? The answer in all honesty is that they were not and business, as does the individual, quickly learns to compensate and cope with change. The worst fear of the oil industry is a fiscal policy that is constantly and unpredictably changing as the industry needs to plan many years in advance. One might almost go as far as saying it does not matter what the tax regime is as long as it is a stable one. It did not help that the PRT changes were totally unexpected although I guess some of the larger players would have been sounded out. The Treasury and the government provided Grampian with a timely common enemy, and a threat to our continuing and oil led prosperity that was perceived as significant and real. What was good for us locally was the pressure to work closely together and bury, for a while, rivalries and differences.

The rest of OTC was somewhat tame after the confrontation with our Energy Minister, Tim Eggar. However as part of the councillors' programme of activities I had scheduled a visit to San Antonio. This visit was a precursor to the most fraught and disastrous overseas visit that I was involved in during my time at Grampian Regional Council. A few weeks before, Bob Middleton had indicated his wish to lead a trade delegation to Mexico City. I advised him that we were already very stretched on the international front with a number of courtships with other centres from Calgary to Murmansk. I advised also that Mexico was a likely difficult market for the sort of local firms that might benefit from local authority support. But all my advice was to no avail even though I understood that many of his colleagues shared my doubts. We needed a lightning conductor to channel his ambitions to a destination with at least the likelihood of some return for the rate payers' money. At the time, and again against my advice, we had taken on the services of Lennap, a small export services company set up in Houston under the auspices of the accountancy firm, Pannell Kerr Forster, and at a cost to the council of £60,000. Lennap ('Pannel' spelt backwards) used the services of a former British Consulate General and locally engaged Houston staff member,

Craig deStiguer. I knew Craig from my old DTI days and so I felt able to share with him my dilemma. He came up with the idea that we should look at San Antonio as a base from which to tackle the Mexican market. It was not only the focus for much trade with Mexico, being near the border, but it was also a much friendlier place from which to access the Mexican market. The argument made a lot of sense but I was far from sure that even via the US it was a market where our smaller firms could be successful and I remained convinced that the council's resources were over-stretched and lacked market focus. I therefore made space in Len Ironside's programme for an exploratory day trip to San Antonio where we met various bodies dealing with cross-border trade including the San Antonio city authorities. This all went well and we were quite enthusiastically received. On the basis of this, and the assurance from Craig deStiguer he would flesh out the details (the Region was already paying for his services anyway), we sold Bob Middleton the idea that San Antonio was a better bet for him than Mexico City.

By the October of that year (1993) at Bob Middleton's request we had assembled a mission of three councillors, six businessmen, myself, and one other official. The band of businessmen was more by way of rent-a-crowd to bolster Middleton's confidence and to add respectability to the occasion, with the added inducement of a council subsidy of £750 each. I had little evidence at this stage of our incipient courtship with San Antonio that there were any immediate business prospects, at least that justified taking this retinue of Grampian businessmen. To be fair to Middleton the advice from our Lennap executive, Craig deStiguer, was enticing. Unfortunately the cracks in the facade began to appear only a few days before the Grampian ensemble was due to leave for Texas. Craig had been in touch with officials in San Antonio about the programme for our visit. It was clear that San Antonio had reappraised its priorities and had downgraded the importance of the mission from Grampian. This was a bombshell for me and especially at that late stage. I decided there was little point in telling Bob Middleton as I would give myself two crises to deal with and it was better to focus my energies on trying to recover the situation as best as I could. The first task was to stiffen the resolve of my colleague Craig and convince him that he had a duty to pull out all the stops, and calling in the resources of Consul General if necessary. I asked him to relay to San Antonio at the highest level that the course they were embarking on would have diplomatic repercussions as well a bad press for the city, and that I would ensure that was the case.

Craig did the best job he could in recovering the situation with only five days to go before our arrival. San Antonio, very reluctantly, acknowledged some significance to our visit but, as we were to find out on arrival, our presence was to coincide with visits by delegations from Indonesia, Holland and Japan. Clearly we were at the bottom of the list, or that was the impression given both by the gentleman in charge of San Antonio's international links and the reality of the programme for our first day of business. It was the view of a number of us, and certainly of Craig deStiguer and me, that part of our problem was the untimely death of the CEO of the World Trade Center for South Texas, who had shown Craig, myself and Councillor Ironside so much enthusiasm when we saw him earlier that year.

Before our entourage left the safety of the Double Tree Hotel in Houston for San Antonio I had to tell Middleton of the problems we had been experiencing with our less than enthusiastic hosts. He was incandescent with rage. It was reasonable for him to ask why I had not warned him earlier of problems, but I think any bystander on that occasion would have understood why I chose not to. In retrospect I realise I should have warned him before leaving home but I remain of the view he could have done little more than me to pull the mission back on track after San Antonio's very late second thoughts about us. Bullies rarely get the best out of their staff and here was a case in point.

After a long and boring presentation and an even more boring video on the second day, it was plainly obvious to us all that our time in San Antonio was being filled with little enthusiasm by our hosts and we were wasting our time. At this point Bob Middleton's patience was exhausted and he demanded to see the mayor. After a little delay the mayor was brought out and this man realised quickly that he had a crisis on his hands. From then on the stops were pulled out and by the end of our discussions with Mayor Wolff and the councillor with European interest responsibilities, Ruth McClendon, our credibility had visibly grown.

Most businessmen in the Grampian delegation were understanding and made the most of the situation with the changing programme and shifts in our status as potential and credible trading partners. There was one exception where the individual did not receive the local acclaim we and he had initially expected and spent the rest of his time with us in Texas sulking.

The visit had lighter moments, or perhaps surreal and bizarre are the more apt adjectives. One such occasion was a pilgrimage to the mission chapel marking the spot of the battle of the Alamo. For me the Alamo is difficult to distinguish from John Wayne and all my fantasies nurtured by a flickering nine inch early television and the regular afternoon adventures with Tex Ritter and Hopalong Cassidy shared with my friends. Whereas the Alamo is, in fact, the site of a real and heroic battle with the status in Texas of a revered national shrine. This was only too obvious as a visitor to the mission where the exhibits and relics were viewed in hushed tones. So it was with some delight when I was instructed by our Convener to arrange a visit and a wreath laying ceremony in honour of those Scots who had given their lives in a battle in 1836 with a 5,000 strong Mexican army under the leadership of General Antonio Lopez Santa Anna. Middleton's knowledge of history was obviously much better than mine as on discussion with the guides at the mission the Scottish contribution was confirmed. I got Lennap's Craig deStiguer to make all the arrangements and a very large wreath on a sort of easel arrived on cue. Our party from Grampian was assembled outside the mission entrance and, if I remember rightly, Bob Middleton said a few appropriate words followed by a suitable silence for private prayer and contemplation. Photographs were taken and we all returned to meetings at the San Antonio World Trade Centre. Before leaving I could not resist having my picture taken at the mission alongside the Grampian wreath. I think we were taken seriously by the folk at the Alamo but I must admit my misgivings over the whole episode.

The other event that will remain with me is a dinner on the water. San Antonio has made the best of its position in some rather bleak countryside to become a major convention and tourist destination. The city's charms are mainly modern in origin. It is easy for us British to sneer at US attempts at sophisticated lifestyle in the land of the hard sell and the quick buck. San Antonio is well supplied with hotels and restaurants but the city has also made efforts to create atmosphere, and especially after dark. A small river running through the centre of town has been accomodated to create a waterway walk, the Paseo Del Rio. This is bordered by many restaurants and bars and with the climate in south Texas, many visitors eat and drink out of doors. I suppose it has a fiesta feel being only a hundred miles from the Mexican border. It certainly beats a night in many UK cities and my own experiences here would include Coventry, Watford and Carlisle.

We were to sample all these delights first hand. Such had been the pressure exerted by first me and Craig deStiguer and then Middleton to gives us the respect we thought we deserved San Antonio City dined us on two small motor boats on the small central waterway. I had assumed we would be entertained at the moorings but the whole meal, which was excellent, was consumed on the move. At first, as we passed diners and revellers on the banks, we got many cheery waves and shouted inquiries as to where we were from but after many circuits of the system our party lost its celebrity status, and a few calls became derisory. Our hosts were very generous and a good time was had by all. Even Bob Middleton and the group sulk hit dry land in a very mellow mood.

Much of the programme that had been arranged by Craig turned out to be very useful and a lot of contacts were made. Of potential value were the meetings with the various 'casas' or trade offices, each representing one of the states within Mexico. All these were keen to pursue trade opportunities and learn more about what we had to offer. Investment in their respective states was a high priority for them but not to the exclusion of imports. It was obvious to me that very few Grampian firms at home were up to this degree of commitment, even if the trade was channelled through San Antonio or Laredo rather than the additional hassle of dealing directly with Mexico. It was a hard enough task getting our indigenous oil and services related firms to trade with Texas, and here we did have a critical mass of significant companies with experience in exporting, let alone the sectors represented by the businessmen on this delegation.

More elusive was our objective to convince the City of San Antonio to commit themselves to a more formal trade link with Grampian. For years we had tried to move our 'sister city' (city twinning) links with Houston beyond the annual exchanges under the banner of the Grampian Houston Association and its round of receptions and repeated vows of undying friendship. There is nothing wrong in this apart from the pretence that it assisted business. I have no evidence during my association with this delightful and hospital bunch of people that it was any more than an opportunity for fellowship. So, apart from San Antonio being a diversionary tactic to steer Middleton from Mexico, there was just a hope that this city just might be the US-based trade link we were looking for. If it had all worked out, then our rationalisation was already drafted.

There is an old saying amongst civil servants in the overseas trade business and that is there is no such thing as a failed mission. The main reason is that the participants have a vested interest in justifying their time away from the office, especially if there is little concrete by way of orders to take home, and officials, ministers and councillors have to justify the considerable public expenditure involved. In this particular case the business people were no doubt mindful of the degree of public subsidy they received and nobody likes to bite the hand that might provide further such handouts. It was a pretty miserable mission for me and there were weaknesses and mistakes, but true to form the verdict at a review lunch a short while after our return to Aberdeen was that overall the mission was a success.

Needless to say the services of Lennap were quietly dispensed with and I was never again to meet Craig deStiguer, which was a pity as, in spite of all the problems, I enjoyed working with him. I am grateful to him also for introducing me to the oil-well fire-fighter 'Red' Adair. Red was truly a legend in his own lifetime, and an old friend of Craig's father. Contrary to my expectations he was a shy and modest man. This misunderstanding of the man was to embarrass the Aberdeen Chamber of Commerce when they invited Red Adair to address one of their regular all-member lunchtime meetings in Aberdeen. A flamboyant oil man was expected with a string of colourful anecdotes of daring well fire fights from around the world. What we got (and I was present) was an apparently very shy man who stood up and said little more than a word or two of thanks and sat down after what seemed to be less than five minutes. The Chief Executive of the Chamber was as surprised as the rest of the large assembly of Aberdeen's finest.

In spite of repeated attempts, invitations to visit Grampian, access to our services in Brussels and more, San Antonio never made it to the altar with us. I think it must have been a relief when on the change of Administration in Grampian to one led by the Liberals and Nationalists I managed to get the new Convener to write a letter to his opposite number quietly indicating we had no wish to continue the negotiations. We never heard from San Antonio during the rest of my period in the Regional Council. I suspect San Antonio were as relieved as I was to draw a line under this excursion.

However arising out of my frustration with Grampian's one-sided love affair with Houston was something far more rewarding than the brief flirtation with San Antonio. Since the early days of the establishment of the Grampian Initiative after the 1986 oil price crash Greg Rae, our PR contractor and adviser, had been searching the literature for the experiences of similar city regions to Grampian in planning their long term futures. When I joined the council I too was anxious to find comfort and ideas from areas with similar problems. In 1990 I came across a reference to a recent report entitled 'Calgary...Into the 21st Century' and obtained a copy from Calgary's economic development department. From a quick scan of the summary alone I knew I had hit upon gold. Calgary, in Canada's cowboy west, is the centre of the country's oil industry. It was Alberta's gas rather than oil deposits that initiated its rise to become Canada's answer to Houston. The report was prompted by concern of both the business community and the city fathers over the need to plan for a time when the oil and gas boom begins to fade. The report closely parallels Grampian's concerns about the future that had led to my appointment in 1988. Just prior to this a partnership was established by Grampian Regional Council with business and academia to plan for a future after oil, and to ensure the local economy was less vulnerable in any future drop in the price of oil, as had been experienced in the 1986 price crash. Although Calgary at over three quarters of a million population was much larger than Aberdeen and indeed the whole of Grampian Region, it was unlikely to be as arrogantly dismissive of our part of Scotland as Houston was.

After reading Calgary's vision document I made contact with David Crowe, the senior executive in the Calgary Economic Development Authority in charge of international links. 'CEDA', as it was usually known, promoted the near fiction, as did the Grampian Initiative, that it was a private-public sector partnership. The reality, as similarly for the Grampian Initiative, was that CEDA was overwhelmingly financed and staffed by the City of Calgary and it was the City that was the driving force. There was an instant rapport between me and David Crowe, helped initially by his West of Scotland and Motherwell origins. It became apparent very quickly that it would not have mattered where David came from as he was naturally charming and helpful but also with a sense of humour and an element of cynicism, which chimed well with my own character and approach to our respective responsibilities. Over the six years we worked together David and his wife, Donna, became my good friends and this friendship has continued into our retirements. Our friendship took us through some difficult periods, where respective authorities did not always see eye to eye, and enabled us to head off or smooth out many a problem.

The timing of the 1990 'OTC' exhibition coincided with our local authority elections and with our politicians busy fighting to retain their seats at home I was free of the usual responsibility of providing them support in Houston. The way was clear to journey on to Calgary from Houston after OTC. I asked Greg Rae, who was out in Houston on our behalf dealing with our presentational needs, to accompany me. He was very keen and I could not have wished for a colleague better suited to the task in hand. We needed to create a good impression and demonstrate we were not there as time-wasting business tourists.

David had made all the arrangements with a full programme of meetings, receptions and visits. Arriving in Calgary after Houston is so refreshing. Whilst a substantial-sized city, the centre is quite compact and walking and public transport are practical, and indeed widely practised and used. At the same time Calgary is safe and in no sense does one feel threatened in walking back to the hotel after dark. Calgary is also a very friendly city, where courtesy prevails and goes beyond the automatic 'Have a nice day' of Houston. There are superficial similarities between the two and not least Calgary's continuing love affair with the cowboy culture of its heyday as a centre of the cattle industry. This culture reaches a zenith at the time of the world famous Calgary Stampede and its chuck wagon racing and associated western fare. During Stampede week city employees are urged to dress in western style and most do. There are no shortages of emporiums selling western gear and even outside the Stampede festival the occasional Stetson is to be seen in bars and restaurants. Calgary shares that odd convention that it is OK for men to wear western headgear indoors. There is some rivalry between Texan and Calgary cowboys with references to the other as being just saloon cowboys. At the same time Calgary is fiercely proud of a uniquely Canadian past. The original settlement that became the current city was named after a small bay on the north west coast of the Isle of Mull by a frontier officer returning from leave on the island. I visited the original Calgary when on holiday and it is no more than a dozen scattered houses on a wide and remote bay. It is attractive but Mull has far more spectacular spots to jostle for a place in the memory and then carry all the way back to the Canadian West and use it to name a small military outpost.

One of the meetings that David had arranged for us was a breakfast meeting with the City's Chamber of Commerce. These somewhat unnatural events are now the norm in Grampian, but at the time it was my DTI overseas experience that already had made me a seasoned player in scrums around the breakfast buffet. The trick was to get in before the last minute arrivals and assemble something that approximates to a full English breakfast from the usually sparse pickings at the buffet counter. If the torture of being talked at for about an hour at 7.30 in the morning is inevitable it might as well be done in style with a full breakfast, which was not normally on offer in the Fisher household, for one good reason or another. From what I remember the sustenance offered at North American business breakfasts was somewhat sparser than that enjoyed at similar events in Blighty, where our obsession with cholesterol had yet to reach US and Canadian proportions. There is a limit to how much healthy orange juice and decaffeinated coffee, and especially if the latter is served in a polystyrene cup with 'whitener', that one can imbibe to give the impression of bushy tailed alertness.

The Calgary Chamber meeting was a bit slow and at some stage later in the proceedings the guest visitor from Scotland was asked what he expected to obtain from his visit to Calgary. I had not prepared too well for such a question as our visit was very much an exploratory or 'fishing' expedition. To this day I cannot understand how what I was to subsequently say came out. Something seemed to trip in my mind and there I was in uninhibited full stream and overdrive. What I proposed to the Chamber was a new form of strategic alliance linking the western world's three oil capitals, namely Calgary, Houston and Grampian/Aberdeen. I proposed that we should work more closely together where our interests overlapped, and not only closer co-operation between our city regions but co-operation together in third markets. I was at great pains to avoid any idea of yet another round of 'sister city' or twinning arrangements, and by implication such as Grampian had with Houston. The mood of the Chamber members visibly changed up a gear. I had clearly captured their attention and they wanted to hear more. I left with the undertaking to work up the idea into a detailed proposal.

My travelling companion and Grampian Initiative colleague, Greg Rae, was flabbergasted at my proposal, but only in so far it was unexpected and I had not hinted earlier at or discussed such an idea in any form. His comments shortly after were that I was 'magnificent'! Praise indeed. Although I was confident of my ability to think on my feet I thought that this attribute was modest enough and well under control, so to speak. This was as near as a 'eureka' event I have experienced.

The rest of our programme in Calgary was almost subsidiary in our minds after the denouement of the idea of a strategic alliance and its encouraging reception by our hosts including David Crowe. However David can be a canny and quite a political bureaucrat and was careful to keep some of his powder dry at this stage. Greg and I retired that night on a high, still discussing the potential of the alliance idea. As it happened there had been a bit of confusion over the booking of our rooms and as a stop gap measure the hotel had asked if we minded sharing a suite. We were well past the period of life where we were happy to share but on inspecting the suite it was acceptable, with an odd split of sleeping arrangements with one bed on a sort of raised gallery or mezzanine balcony within the suite. We continued conversation after retiring to our respective areas of the suite and it was then when Greg came up with his inspired name for the proposed strategic alliance. His suggestion was we name it 'E3' or preferably e^3, with the small case 'e' linking the concept of 'e' for energy, e^3 representing the three city regions and also Einstein's $e=mc^2$ the equation linking mass and energy. Greg, with a gift for graphic design, saw e^3 as a very usable logo that would assist in selling the idea. Sleep for me did not come easy that night with my mind in a whirl as to how we would take this forward.

Before leaving we promised to get back to colleagues in Calgary with a detailed proposal using David Crowe as our contact. This was the beginning of a long and fruitful collaboration with David, although with a few blind alleys and wrong turns along the way. On return to Aberdeen I got together one or two business people including the universities to assist in putting some clothes on the idea of a strategic alliance with Calgary and Houston. This group drew up a list of the areas of co-operation of likely mutual interest. We were determined that we should avoid all the old clichés that accompany the traditional city twinning arrangements and that e^3 should be so much more than civic exchanges and fine phrases. The emphasis would be on practical collaboration across a whole number of sectors from distance learning and work-place training, environmental protection, land use and disaster planning, rural diversification, international trade co-operation, to the more commercial areas of co-operation in manufacturing, energy-related industry and much else. I packaged this into a short proposal with clear and succinct objectives, highlighting the opportunities to share experiences, with the joint development of strategies and programmes to tackle the many challenges that bound the three cities together.

I included the mutual development of new trade opportunities, and not only between us but together in third markets. Here I saw all three cities had much to gain as each had a particular sphere of influence that could be exploited by the other. Canada was respected internationally amongst non-aligned nations and sometimes had easier market access where the US did not. I suppose our strength as part of the UK was our link with the European Union and, to a declining extent, with the Commonwealth. Since the two wars with Iraq much has changed in world politics and in terms of influences and access the UK will be perceived as more closely aligned with the USA. My guess is that Canada retains a degree of innocence and a credibility in trading in the more politically sensitive markets. All this may be a little idealistic but was acknowledged at the time by some Calgary colleagues. Houston, typically, never acknowledged it had any need of help or co-operation from anywhere.

The e^3 proposal document was circulated to Calgary and Houston in June 1990 with clear recommendations on follow up. In Calgary the contact with the City was through the CEDA development agency, which was in essence an arm of the City Council with direct political links to the mayor, Al Duerr. In Houston the links were more nebulous. Formally we were dealing with the Greater Houston Partnership which included the Houston Chamber of Commerce. The Greater Houston Partnership was run, as far as I could ever detect, by the private sector with the blessing and some funding from the city. Unlike Calgary, there was never any sense of a direct line to the city's politicians and most attempts to access the Mayor were frustrated, unless it was in the margins of some ceremonial occasion that suited the local political needs of the moment. I was unaware of any Grampian Regional Council-led discussion with the Mayor of Houston or any senior political figures to discuss details of co-operation with the city, bearing in mind our much vaunted (largely by the Houston Grampian Association) 'sister city' status with Houston. Sure, we were warmly received whenever, at the time of the OTC oil exhibition, I took my councillors along to meet Greater Houston Partnership officials. But come the tabling of e^3 my attempts to move beyond the backslapping and the 'Good to see yawl' met with a wall of bland assurances that the mechanisms we had through the sister city links were adequate.

In January of 1991, some six months after I had produced the formal proposal document, I arranged to meet my Calgary colleagues in Houston in a joint effort to sell to the Greater Houston Partnership the benefits of the e^3 proposals. Calgary brought a strong team down including a lawyer, Francis Saville QC, of Calgary law firm Milner and Fennerty (who had links with a Houston law firm), Bruce McDonald the CEO of the Calgary Economic Development Authority (CEDA), and of course CEDA anchor man, David Crowe. My team was rather low key in comparison, with just Greg Rae and another member of the Grampian business community. Calgary at that juncture had still to be entirely convinced of the merits of the e^3 proposals but were willing to journey to Houston to explore the potential and were anxious to secure any inside track with Houston that e^3 might offer. Like us, they knew Houston well through the many Calgary based firms with parent companies in Houston, but had few political or civic links with the city. The Calgary representatives were a more co-ordinated and organised team than we were. I became aware that my objectives differed markedly from those of my Grampian private sector colleagues, who soon demonstrated quite a different game plan to the one I envisaged when we set out. This led to considerable friction between myself and one colleague. I knew my political masters would wish to be at the forefront of any agreement and its implementation, but my private sector colleagues appeared to have other ideas. It led to some pretty unpleasant scenes but I stuck to my brief. My concern was not so much the quality or bitterness of the debate within the Grampian group, but more that this should not slop over to the negotiations with Houston and Calgary and prejudice any accord. Happily I had now a close relationship with David Crowe and was able to share my concerns with him.

The discussions with Houston were difficult. The Greater Houston Partnership team wanted to keep the discussions low key and leave all options open. Calgary seemed frustrated at this but were not prepared to press the point. If there is any mileage in the old 'nice cop, nasty cop' routine in interrogation and negotiation then I took on the nasty cop role as I was prepared to push Houston for substantive answers instead of platitudes. Calgary appeared happy enough for me to take on this role, but colleagues in my own team were most unhappy and demonstrated this by clearly distancing themselves, even physically, from me and my approach. I felt isolated and very hurt at the time but in retrospect I am certain my approach was right as we were able to get Houston's true measure. One or two of the key Greater Houston Partnership officials we met were clearly more committed to links with Central and South America, no doubt also reflecting Texas' business and ethnic ties to Mexico and the Spanish speaking countries to the south. In my subsequent discussions with Calgary the word 'arrogant' was to crop up regularly in descriptions of our treatment by Houston then and in later confrontations.

During the long flight back to Aberdeen I had much to think about including the possibility that I might have lost Calgary's support, but on the contrary, and somewhat unexpectedly, they further warmed to the concept of a strategic alliance with Grampian. I think they felt more comfortable with us alone than with a *ménage à trois* adventure that included Houston, where we were both unsure of that city's game plan.

On returning home I set about drafting an agreement linking us and Calgary in a strategic alliance. I had never drafted such a document before but had seen plenty in my DTI days. I rooted out my copy of the Treaty of Accession and associated European Union agreements, as well as an international environmental agreement from my time dealing with pollution, for guidance on style, and particularly the often lengthy preamble paragraphs. As the agreement with Calgary, by mutual consent, was to have no legal status it was accepted that the document should be called a Memorandum of Understanding (MOU). My draft was shunted backward and forwards a few times, but was still recognisable as my draft even after Calgary's legal department's amendments.

The MOU was not formally signed until a visit to Grampian by Calgary's mayor at the time of Aberdeen's biennial 'Offshore Europe' oil exhibition in the September of 1991. The mayoral visit was preceded by another visit by us to Calgary following the Houston oil exhibition in the May of that same year, only this time I was accompanied by my Committee Chairman, Councillor Nicol Stephen and the Grampian Initiative Chair, Councillor Len Ironside. This was a very successful visit thanks to the preparation in Calgary by David Crowe and also, and importantly after my trip to Houston in January, we all sang from the same hymn sheet. A bonus was that my two politicians, although from different parties, got on rather well together. The meeting with Al Duerr, the young and charismatic Mayor of Calgary was a great success, with our councillors establishing an instant rapport. Duerr, a planner by training, was highly intelligent, with a pleasant manner, and a low key and sincere approach. I saw Nicol Stephen as having many attributes in common with Duerr although I judged Duerr to have the edge as far as people skills were concerned. I was glad to witness Duerr make clear, in unambiguous terms, that he wished to conclude an agreement with Grampian, regardless of what Houston might, or might not, do. We quickly moved to confirm Duerr's visit to Grampian that autumn when the Memorandum of Understanding would be signed linking Calgary and Grampian in a strategic alliance, with the emphasis on economic co-operation. Also we agreed to get ahead with exchanges of staff, leaving me to make the arrangements. I had continued to keep my old FCO colleagues informed of progress via the British Consulate General in Edmonton. Our efforts coincided with a British Overseas Trade Board campaign, 'North America Now', aimed at increasing the UK's share of this lucrative market. This coincidence made FCO support easier but we would have got that help from the respective Consulates General anyway.

Besides a very full official programme in Calgary, David Crowe found time to take the three of us to his cabin up in the Rockies, on the British Columbia side of the divide. The scenery was grand and alpine compared with Scotland's gentler and rounded landscape. The butt of many jokes was the room and bunk accommodation the three of us shared at David's cabin. It was a welcome break from the pressure of a very crowded programme in Calgary. That trip to Calgary and British Columbia was one I look back on with some nostalgia, in contrast to the trip to Houston at the beginning of that year.

A year on from the breakfast meeting at the Calgary Chamber of Commerce in 1990 the e^3 concept was 'looking good', even if it was just e^2 at that stage. The MOU we were to sign with Calgary at the Offshore Europe exhibition was to set the pattern for a series of further strategic alliances concluded by Grampian Regional Council, some sensible and some ill conceived and naive in approach. Over the next three years there were two Grampian return missions to Calgary. Bob Middleton, who had yet to commit himself fully to the alliance concept, led a visit in June 1992. The mob-handed approach that Middleton so favoured was adopted and we travelled with a team that included five councillors, three officials, three journalists, a university Principal and five business people. The numbers were way over the top but maybe it was a case of 'never mind the quality, feel the width'. The mission was justified insofar as it was at Mayor Duerr's invitation and an opportunity to return the hospitality he had received in Grampian. All went well although I doubt, with one exception, was much business done by private sector colleagues.

In a sophisticated market like Canada it is difficult to make the case that the presence of politicians somehow facilitates business deals. It may be so in less developed countries. What politicians can do through the likes of the strategic alliance we had signed with Calgary is raise awareness in each other's markets, ensure our respective firms have access to the best market intelligence and provide them with a degree of insider status during the early stages of familiarisation with the market. To try and capitalise on all the advantages of the alliance coincidental with a 'state visit' of politicians and their entourage will rarely bring returns, even if the firms are offered sweeteners to travel with the political entourage. The time of the host agencies, such as CEDA in this case, are often otherwise involved and the circus is rarely in town long enough for serious business discussion. UK Ministers probably set the trend in taking a bevy of businessmen with them on overseas visits, although the device was usually restricted to really difficult markets with state-controlled purchasing agencies in centrally managed economies. My masters in local government used the business mission device but often for the wrong reasons. These varied from the crude need to politically desensitise what might be seen at home as an overseas 'jolly', to the need to bolster the ego or flagging profile of an elected councillor. In my experience at Grampian it was often a combination of all of these. On a number of occasions I would question the need for such large accompanying teams but to no avail.

One of the best 'jollies' I was associated with was a trip in July 1993 to Calgary at the time of the Calgary Stampede. As part of the strategic alliance links our award winning Grampian Police Pipe Band were invited to take part in the Stampede parade and associated pipe band competition together with nineteen bands from across Canada, the United States and with representation from Germany. The total cost for the band to attend was £25,000. In addition to myself there were three councillors, one representing the Convener, the Chairman of Public Protection which covers police and fire services, and the chair of the Economic Development and Planning Committee. Before going I wrote a memo to the Chief Executive expressing concern about the number of people and money involved in this visit. I mentioned my concern should the Internal Audit subsequently pick on this mission for detailed investigation. I got no formal reply although I had raised my concern informally before writing to him.

Duty done I set out to relive boyhood dreams and enjoy a few days in full western dress at the council taxpayers' expense. I had already been made an honorary Calgary cowboy and had been presented with a splendid white felt cowboy hat and had carefully nursed this on the 'plane journey across Canada. I had bought the required high heel boots from Houston, together with boot leg jeans, and I purchased a western style shirt in a shop behind our hotel in Calgary. Were it not for the fact that most of the city was in western dress then there is no doubt that I would have looked an idiot. I felt a bit self-conscious when I first went on parade but that soon faded when I joined David Crowe and the Mayor similarly attired at the formal unveiling of a pink granite plaque in the Town Hall, recording the city's alliance with Grampian.

Against the background of Stampede we did manage to conduct some serious business including a review of e^3 and the alliance. The police band did rather well, winning second place overall with the band's Drum Major winning first prize. The band had a great time (as did I) and certainly created a lot of publicity for us. The Chair of Public Protection, Councillor Thomaneck, undertook his role with dignity and charm. He was accompanied, at his own expense, by his wife and daughter. The Thomaneck family were a positive asset to the delegation as well as being good company. Needless to say we were all well looked after by our hosts, sometimes together with the band and sometimes with a separate programme. One memorable occasion was a visit to Big Rock Brewery, where the marketing director had Scottish links. I had visited this brewery with David Crowe on a previous occasion and had met the founder, a former rancher, Ed McNally. Big Rock was a small brewery specialising in unpasteurised high quality darker beers. The brewery had a good export market to California, taking advantage of returning temperature-controlled trucks bringing fruit and vegetables from California. However the visit had little to do with the intricacies of the international beer market and more to do with having a good time, which the band certainly did. Mr McNally was very generous, dispensing not only copious quantities of his flavoursome brews but also a good supply of food. It was not long before whistles were adequately whetted to allow the lads to pump up their pipes and let rip. All this was within a smallish hospitality room at the brewery. The great Scottish pipes are very loud instruments, even in the open air, but in a small room they rival any disco noise level but without assisted amplification. I am not a pipes aficionado but with the help of a Big Rock pint or two I could be converted. Many onlookers, including the brewery's expatriate marketing manager, were overcome by the more emotional laments played, with tears rolling down cheeks, although certainly short of 'tired and emotional' in the tabloid sense.

There were to be many more contacts with Calgary over the years and David Crowe was a frequent visitor. It was the Regional Council's first such alliance and I would judge its most dynamic. Like all marriages both partners have to work very hard for success. For a strategic alliance to deliver benefits each partner, in my view, needs a dedicated individual with a personal commitment and responsibility to make the alliance work. It is an ongoing task requiring day-to-day communication between partners, frequent visits in both directions, and regular meetings of partners at a senior level via some form of 'joint commission' which should review progress and sets targets. There is need for a dedicated budget to handle associated publicity, since if business and academic links are unaware of the new mechanisms and opportunities then the idea of a strategic alliance is nothing more than a piece of paper with one or two enthusiastic officials and politicians glad handing. In other words, nothing more than the traditional city twinning agreement, and that is just what I was trying to avoid. Unfortunately we were sidetracked at home by handing the follow-through arrangements over to private sector leadership. This was disastrous as the individuals neither had the time, resources and, much more importantly, the skills to take this forward. The skills necessary are a combination of diplomacy, networking with both business, local authority and government agencies and the good old-fashioned administrative skills of the experienced public servant. Our businessmen involved were not the good all rounders that were needed although they were good at running their own specialised businesses. As I have found so often over my career many business people, however successful they are at running their own business, are rarely flexible and effective in applying those skills in a different context. This was certainly true of the private sector handling of the alliance and my colleague in Calgary reported a similar experience. Why was this allowed to occur in Grampian? It was largely through the perverseness of Bob Middleton and also the somewhat misguided view of a small number of politicians that the private sector might be able to deliver the benefits more effectively and more cheaply, and so saving on council staff involvement.

At the same time as our links with Calgary were drifting without direction, others had spotted the potential of the e^3 idea of linking the oil capitals, including Newfoundland and Nova Scotia, both with growing oil interests. But more importantly our Norwegian neighbour Stavanger, who was as well established as ourselves in the North Sea, was knocking at the e^3 door. During Middleton's time as Convener, Stavanger had informally approached us to join e^3 but this was rejected out of hand by Middleton. I am not quite sure why he took this stance, apart from Stavanger's links with the City of Aberdeen and, as I have previously explained, many of Grampian's councillors had a paranoid mistrust of their colleagues in the City. By 1994, and only a short while to go before the Region was due to hand over control to the successor authorities, Stavanger and Aberdeen were already taking the initiative to broaden the oil capitals forum to form a new organisation that would be known as the World Energy Cities (WEC). Grampian never did get Houston to formally sign up to e^3, but Houston did join WEC, as did Perth in Western Australia, a city in Vietnam, and others including Calgary. Interestingly Houston, after being so elusive in those early stages of e^3, provided a permanent secretariat to WEC. There were some very odd characters from Houston who attended the early WEC negotiations. I often wonder if the Houston strategy was to join WEC more to keep an eye on the competition than for any reasons of what positive co-operation with other oil cities might bring to Houston. The conspiracy theorists might have even seen the shadowy hand of a US intelligence gathering agency such as the CIA?

Our other main market focus outside North America was Russia and here I stayed well clear of the Region's adventures. These were very much driven by Bob Middleton with the close assistance of my Planning

Manager. It started with a request from Murmansk for help, ending finally with a representative office of our own in Tyumen in western Siberia. We had a Russian lady, Svetlana Kossoukhina, installed in Tyumen and a very bright Russian-speaking executive in my office in Aberdeen. A lot of money was spent but, as far as I was aware, there was little return. Very few of our firms in Grampian had the resources, products or stamina to attack this market successfully, and those that did from the energy business would be more than capable of succeeding without our help. I advised against all the Russian initiatives, but again to no avail. For my staff involved it was glamorous, in a way, and some perceived that the close and direct links with councillors would be good for their careers. It certainly made my task of establishing priorities, achieving value for money, and finally imposing some discipline within the Department difficult. Such a situation with respect to staff control could not have occurred in the Civil Service. On the winding up of the Regional Council we tried to 'sell' the Siberian office to Scottish Enterprise and Scottish Trade International (part of the Scottish Office) but in the end the Siberian office was abandoned. Aberdeen City, as a successor authority from 1996 onwards, had to address its overseas links and priorities sensibly and in doing so ditched the Russian links set up by the Region. Aberdeenshire, the neighbouring successor authority to the Regional Council, neither had the skills nor appetite to take on the Russian market links that Aberdeen did not want.

I remember well as a Director of Exports in DTI discussing with colleagues whether it would make any difference to the UK's export figures if all the then British Overseas Trade Board staff and services were withdrawn. None of us were convinced that we made all that difference at the end of the day. I wonder similarly about the Regional Council's overseas work in support of exports and inward investment. Many of my Council colleagues would argue that we did make a difference, but I suspect those Grampian based firms that used our services regularly and accessed the subsidised overseas visits, and subsidised stands at exhibitions would have survived just as well if that support had not been available.

Chapter 19

'When I was at home, I was in a better place'

At about eleven or twelve years old I can remember being fascinated by maps and particularly the excellent Ordnance Survey series. I had a map of the part of Essex where I lived and would spend hours scouring it for landmarks I knew. I would then go out on my bike to find other features marked, such as a square tower church or post office. I became so absorbed in maps that I produced a map of an imaginary small town, which I called Tintonville. Why this name? I have no idea, and especially as towns or villages ending in 'ville' are rare in England. Bourneville and Waterlooville come to mind but I think a more likely influence on my choice of name was a nearby street in Leigh-on-Sea called Leighville Grove. Although I had no childhood dreams of becoming a town planner I regularly reviewed my town plan and added features such as new housing and factories to my map, drawn to a scale of something like six inches to the mile. I am sure my father's occupation was an influence, but I got little encouragement as he found the whole venture quite amusing and constantly reminded me so. In parallel I also ran my own air force with a neat inventory of planes from trainers, through fighters to bombers and all based on an early 'Observer's Book of Aircraft'. Somewhere in my genes must have been the script for a planner of sorts although it was to be nearly forty years before I could indulge in a bit of town and country planning for real.

When I first arrived in Grampian I had no idea that within less than two years I would become the Region's Director of Planning. As I indicated earlier this was to be a fraught progression. At the time I was the only Director of Planning in Scotland who was not a planner through professional training, although there were already local authority chief officers in England who were not qualified planners but included planning in their portfolio of responsibilities. Before my appointment, one or two of my soon to be planning colleagues within the council tried to suggest that it was a statutory requirement that the planning director was a professionally qualified planner, as it was a requirement for a Director of Social Work to be professionally qualified as such. I knew that precedent had been set south of the border but one could never be sure the same applied under Scottish law and conventions. I bought and studied Young and Robinson's book 'Scottish Planning Law and Procedure' to see whether a planning qualification was a statutory requirement. There was clearly none. I put all this in a paper to the Chief Executive who was the conduit for the misgivings of some of my new planning colleagues. Although no planning colleague actually challenged my fitness for the job to my face, as that was not their style, one made it quite plain that he was not happy working to me. This view became less obliquely expressed as soon as I began to challenge some of the work practices in the planning section. Not so long after I had taken up post as Director two planners left on terms less than gracious.

I asked a lot of questions in those early weeks including how planners discerned their role. One old hand and senior member of the planning team saw his role as similar to that of a policeman, keeping a check on society's excesses with an eye to the general overall good. There is some justification for this interpretation of the physical planning role but also it goes to the heart of much of what is wrong with local authority planning services. There is a hint of arrogance and the 'we know what is best for you' approach in the statement. More importantly it illustrates the problem that town and country planning is perceived as negative in approach, and more about what you cannot do rather than positively encouraging good design and good development. The enlightened amongst my colleagues did not see their role in these terms and were anxious to present themselves as part of a 'can do' agency of local government, and one where professional staff welcomed working with the public to achieve the best possible outcome in any application for planning permission. In other words, to say more about what can be done within the planning regulations than what cannot. One would like to believe the negative attitude is long gone but as a previous Planning Director at Banff and Buchan District Council complained during my period at Grampian, there were still planning officers who saw it as their professional duty to find a problem in any application before them. However, never did I witness anything like this approach amongst my own staff.

Before taking on the physical planning role I had envisaged that professional planners would be a stimulating bunch with lots of talk about design, the building of a local Shangri La and I would be entering an imaginative and a creative social environment. It was nothing like this. I am not saying my new colleagues were boring and dull as they were not, but what was missing for me was much sense of mission or vision, or indeed an urgency. There were exceptions and one was Allan Garvie, the Assistant Director in charge of producing the first single structure plan to cover the whole region. Allan was not only a very hard worker, and no mean opponent at a public hearing or consultation, but also had the ability to see beyond research-derived projections of what is likely, to a vision of what could be. Allan was a very precise professional who set himself exacting standards but one would not guess the calibre of the man by his office environment. Allan had two large desks and each was piled high with paper with not a square inch of the desk top visible. It looked chaotic but I never saw Allan lose a paper or file. Our dread was he might be taken suddenly sick and we would have to try and retrieve papers from his idiosyncratic filing system.

I would not like to give the impression that the great majority of my planning staff were anything other than delightful to work with, although I would have wished for a bit of fire now and again. They taught me a lot and I hope I was able to add something to the deficit in vision and the broad view. In that sense it was an advantage that I was not a planner by training as I could throw in the apparently daft suggestion without fear of putting my professional reputation at stake.

Occasionally I would offer myself as a stalking horse or, what is known locally as 'playing the daft laddie'. On one occasion a politician asked me to take on this role in trying to break the development log jam in Inverurie, the prosperous small town that was at the centre of the former Gordon District Council. For political reasons, and others imposed by the Region, Inverurie's development had been shoe-horned into a corridor bounded by a relief trunk road and a railway. Part of the political impasse was due to rivalry between a local land owner who was also a former Tory convener of the Regional Council, and Councillor Middleton, the then Labour Regional Council convener. These two did not see eye to eye, and Middleton once famously said 'that over my dead body would that man make any money out of selling his (strategically placed) farmland for development'. But more relevant was the much delayed delivery of a new structure plan, and I will come to this later. To try and get around this I brought together planners from both my department at Regional level and our opposite numbers in the Gordon District, the second tier authority. The aim was to try and remove the development blockage and allow Inverurie to expand sensibly. I thought I was doing quite well in brokering a deal until the councillor that had set me up got cold feet and pulled the rug from under me. My last public words on the subject were it was not 'if' but rather 'when' we would break out of the planning imposed straightjacket that was constricting the growth of this booming community. That proved to be the case and the deadlock has since been broken allowing Inverurie and its hinterland to achieve one of the fastest growth rates in Scotland.

With the production of the first draft of the 'Together to the Future' strategy I had lit the fuse to a time bomb that would explode in the later stages of the structure plan debate. In drafting the strategy I looked for that spark or ingredient that can provide a city or region with a fresh focus and so an edge over its competitors. I called this ingredient 'Factor X' , where 'X' can range from a new metro system like Newcastle, an event that will kick start local pride such as a garden festival (like Stoke), or a public relations campaign that captures imagination, and here 'Glasgow's miles better' campaign has been the most successful over recent years. Other initiatives and international accolades such as European City of Culture or Architecture, or a World Heritage Site listing can similarly focus attention and attract resources. Some cities and regions have managed to capitalise on being the location for a successful TV series and examples abound ranging from Jersey and 'Bergerac', the Yorkshire Dales and the 'All creatures great and small' stories of a country veterinary practice, and more recently the Lochaber area of the Highlands and the successful 'Monarch of the Glen' series. I spent hours over the years at Grampian brainstorming what might be Aberdeen's 'X' factor. The problem with Aberdeen is most of the associations conjured up by the name are not negative enough to give a notoriety, like Liverpool for example, but are just sufficiently negative to create barriers to positive external perception. Oil has been our great success story but oil does not do for Grampian what is does for perceptions of Dallas and Houston. True, Dallas was helped by the eponymous TV series, but this does not apply to Houston. What does Houston have that Aberdeen does not? In terms of size and wealth we are minnows, and Houston also trades on the Texan character which all Texans play up to, and its history. The Texan character is larger than life whereas the Grampian indigenous character is low key and sparing of hyperbole in both speech and lifestyle. It all adds up to a PR man's nightmare as it is almost better to have a notorious and bad image than a bland low key image as the raw material for a PR campaign. That was, in essence, the dilemma that Dr Michael Kelly faced, the man behind the 'Glasgow's miles better ' campaign, when I asked him what he could do for Aberdeen and Grampian. He admitted it 'was a difficult one'.

I never did find the Grampian 'X' factor but I did include two possibilities in the strategic plan. One was what I described as a 'new science village'. The idea had a number of origins. In an odd way part of the inspiration was 'Stepford Wives', which was a science fiction film about a community where the men get together to replace their women folk with humanoid machines embracing all the attributes they would ascribe to the ideal wife. The setting of this cult film is a small town dominated by a high technology firm, in attractive countryside with associated and equally attractive executive style homes. Perhaps this was my science village? My reading had also turned up developments in the United States which were very similar where clean high technology factories and research facilities are located in sylvan settings alongside housing, but without the robots in Laura Ashley-style dresses. For Grampian my idea was to establish a focus of all that was best in living and work, at the frontiers of science and technology. A sort of Cambridge science park with adjacent housing and a setting that would not disgrace Sunningdale or Wentworth in terms of gracious living.

Aberdeen already had a unique concentration in Scotland of life scientists working in the city's two universities as well as a number of world-class government laboratories, of which perhaps the Rowett Institute dealing with human and animal nutrition is the best known. Somehow we were missing out and were failing to capitalise on this asset. The science village idea was also aimed at building upon this resource. Using such an existing critical mass was later to be rebranded by government agencies in Scotland as the 'cluster' theory, whereby similar industries locating together would create a 'synergy' leading to 'spin off' and 'cross fertilisation' of ideas and 'new firm growth'. Unfortunately many of my contacts in the Scottish Enterprise organisation and its Scottish Development Agency predecessor spoke in these terms during normal conversation, with phraseology lifted straight from the paperbacks on management. Much worse, they actually believed every word. My Calgary City Council colleague told me of a game sometimes played in his office dubbed 'Bullshit Bingo' ...divide a piece of paper into 25 equal squares and in each square write a management jargon word or phrase such as 'synergy' and 'think out side the box', 'leverage' etc., take it to your next office meeting, seminar or conference and cross off the word or phrase as it comes up during the meeting. Any straight horizontal, vertical or diagonal line completed is a bingo score and should be called. Players are said to have markedly improved their attention span at meetings by playing this game.

However my goal was much more than might be offered by any

'cluster' theory. We took much inspiration from the new town of Woodlands, some thirty miles north of Houston. I visited Woodlands first in 1990 with Greg Rae and then with my Chairman, Nicol Stephen, in 1991 at the time of the Houston oil exhibition. Woodlands, as the name indicates, is situated on 25,000 acres of woods or forest. Unlike so much development in America the town, then with a 30,000 population, was planned in considerable detail with controls on layout and design at all levels. This has been possible since the initiative was the brainchild and vision of one man, George P. Mitchell, the owner of one of the largest privately owned energy corporations in the United States. Housing, community buildings and state of the art research facilities, all linked by pedestrian paths and cycleways, nestle amongst the trees and so preserving as much as possible of the natural environment. Housing is grouped in small hamlets within the overall plan, with their associated shopping centres and extensive recreational and cultural facilities. The overall result is one of the most attractive living environments I have witnessed, and just as their seductive advertising material says it has the feel of 'A real home town'. The marketing is also some of the best I have seen, including a video which is a collector's item in the genre of the folksy travelogue. The recurrent phrase is "Come home to Woodlands – a real home town". They use also a quotation from Shakespeare's 'As you like it' in their brochure which again emphasizes the family based security of Woodlands –"When I was at home, I was in a better place".

My Chairman was also impressed by the Woodlands example and particularly the the links to high technology employment. Woodlands is the home of the Houston Advanced Research Centre (HARC) which is the joint initiative of a number of Houston based universities. HARC relies to a large extent on government research contracts and has done much work on the human genome. This flagship institution has attracted many other biosciences related firms to Woodlands. I and my Chairman adopted Woodlands as the template for the science village trailed in Grampian Region's economic development strategy. Perhaps, unfortunately, we were a little unguarded in our statements to the press at the time when we boasted that the approach to Grampian's new town or 'village' should be unashamedly elitist. It was an unfortunate turn of phrase in political terms and was taken by the Labour leadership to imply some element of social exclusion. In fact all we were trying to convey was that any such new town should be of the highest quality in terms of design and planning so that the settlement would attract people and investment from all over the United Kingdom. Even before we had returned from Houston the local press and some politicians had put the best of the Region's long standing traditions of parochialism and isolationism to good effect. Editorials were dismissive of 'dreams of planners' and of course 'it has been tried before and it did not work'. Even now I remain of the view that Aberdeen and its hinterland have a sort of pupation wish and I am reminded of one of the many descriptions of Argentina's failure, a country of unfulfilled promise.

The Grampian new town saga was to run for the next four years. In September, just before the publication of the draft structure plan in October 1992, Allan Garvie and I took an all-party group of councillors, as a softening up exercise, down to Essex to see another successful and also attractive new town. South Woodham Ferrers is situated between Chelmsford and Southend-on-Sea overlooking the River Crouch. This new town is no Basildon, Harlow or even a Milton Keynes, but more a large village with an intimate and traditional feel. Essex County Council owned the land and strictly vetted the developers employed and at the same time rigourously enforced a set of design guidelines. These covered such design aspects as roof pitch, window shape, finishes, materials and, in the case of commercial and industrial premises, design that hid from sight outdoor storage areas which blight so many commercial centres. The town centre reflects many of the traditional design features of buildings from an earlier Essex such as overhanging first floors, and the use of black external cladding which was common on Essex coastal and marshland buildings, although historically would have been black pitch or tar painted board. Another feature of Essex (and Suffolk) historic buildings used at South Woodham Ferrers is 'pargetting', which is the decoration of external plaster work with patterns and ornaments either in relief or engraved on the plaster. The overall effect of use of these vernacular traits is an intimacy and warmth which is usually absent in most UK new towns. This intimacy is further assisted by use of small culs-de-sac, or vennels as we would describe them in Scotland, and the avoidance of straight rows of housing. All who visited South Woodham Ferrers with me were impressed and agreed we had much to learn from Essex. We went as far as asking whether we could retain the Essex County Council planner concerned to advise us further. Essex Council had one major advantage which under the capital expenditure restraints imposed by central government on local authorities we could not hope to copy, and that was the council's ownership of the land at South Woodham Ferrers. This gave Essex, a bit like Mr Mitchell at Houston's Woodlands, firm control over design.

We went ahead and incorporated a proposal for a new town of some 3,300 houses in our draft structure plan. A report by consultants commissioned by my department indicated that a new town would only be viable within ten miles of the Aberdeen city centre. We recommended it should be sited just south-west of the Aberdeen, within an area known as Banchory-Devenick. The site chosen provided easy access to and from the city via the A90 trunk road which links Aberdeen to Dundee, Perth and the south. Others factors taken into consideration included the availability of secondary schooling, water supply and waste water treatment capacity, and any sensitivity with respect to the site itself. Someone said at the time that we could not have found a more boring and featureless tract of land if we had tried. The site was not in the Green Belt and had few houses but included a moss area which was of limited conservation importance. We were reasonably sure we were not going to be alerted at the last moment that the site was of some archaeological, biological or landscape significance. Like all developers we dreaded the unexpected discovery of the habitat of a rare toad, bog plant or similar. No, it was quite boring in all respects, that is until we announced the site or, more strictly speaking, the target area, on the publication of the draft structure plan. Then we had the establishment of a new lobby group consisting of members of the public who mostly did not live in the target area but were fearful that their amenities would be prejudiced none the less. The proposed new town site was not too far from a corridor of land bounded to the north by the River Dee and favoured by commuters. During the consultation procedure I was to be accused of all sorts, not only from the lobby group but also by one of my own councillors. At one public hearing I attended on the structure plan a local laird waved a sword at the platform party, although all in good humour!

Two of the accusations made against me at the time were bordering on what might have been actionable in law. How my bosses dealt with the attack on the professional integrity of a senior staff member of the council is interesting. The initial response from the Chief Executive was to the effect it was up to me to seek redress, and at my own cost. Although my Chief Executive said he supported planning officials "absolutely against the scurrilous accusations", he explained it was the view of the council's Director of Legal Services "that the Council had not been defamed and that the procedure would require an action raised by those defamed individuals". I remonstrated with the Chief Executive and also with the Convener explaining that a slur on a council officer carrying out the instructions of the council was a slur on the council, and I had no intention of spending my own resources on defending my position. Happily this was not put to the test as the accusers backed down when challenged by the council's legal officers, but it was a warning for the future as to how much I could rely on my employers if the going got difficult.

In parallel with the publication of the draft structure plan for public consultation we sought advice on how we could best ensure that the proposed new town was of the quality we wished. To this end we drew up a design brief for developers indicating what was expected of them. We had two serious contenders including the Aberdeen-based Stewart Milne Group. The other contender was Alfred McAlpine. Both spent a lot of money, and Stewart Milne up to one million pounds, and time in putting forward excellent development plans for the new town. Of course these exercises are a trade-off between what the local authority would like to see the developer include by way of community facilities and infrastructure and the profit for the developer. At the same time it is not in the community's interest to see the development fail because of an unreasonable burden placed upon the developer in the name of 'planning gain'. In the case of the proposed Banchory-Devenick new town the Stewart Milne Group were on track to agree planning gain in the order of £55 million. Often I felt uneasy about the leverage used by planning authorities to extract as much they could in terms of infrastructure and amenity costs from the developer. Sometimes it becomes almost a blackmail operation, although the developer can decide the site is not for him and walk away from the negotiations. Like all deals the best outcome is where both sides consider they have secured a good deal. In the case of our proposed new town attractive proposals were put forward by both contenders although we never reached the stage of having to make a choice. On balance I favoured the proposals from the Stewart Milne Group but that was a personal view.

Around the November of 1993 the council rejected the proposal for a new settlement south-west of the city and charged me and my department to come up with location alternatives. At no stage in the long drawn out saga did the majority of the council reject the idea of a new settlement *per se*. The obstacles were political. The rejection of the south-west of the city location was all about territorial political control, both current at the time and, in the light of possible boundary changes, at some future date. My analysis, and agreed by many, was that the Labour group supported a new town south-west of the centre as this was an area, should the new town become a success, that was ripe for a boundary change that would include the new town within the city's boundaries. At that time the Labour Party saw political control of Aberdeen, as for the other three large Scottish cities, as part of its birthright and inconceivable it could be anything else than Labour controlled. The Liberal group's power base in the Regional Council lay to the north-west of the city and so saw little in it for them to support a new town to the south-west, even though the Liberal group were not opposed to the new town proposal. The other main power base within the Regional Council, the Scottish National Party (SNP) had no interest in a new town in the Aberdeen area, and since it was a non-starter elsewhere, they opposed it 'on principle'. The SNP were also fed some, and what I believe were spurious, arguments that gave credence to the SNP stance that any new town in the Aberdeen area would pull resources from the rural hinterland and in particular from the two northern districts of Moray, and Banff and Buchan, the then heartland of Nationalist Party support.

At the end of 1993 the Council directed my department to prepare a list of alternative new town locations. This seemed to cause my planning staff some professional difficulty. In advising that south-west of the city was the best location they had given the only sensible option, based on all the evidence that the planning team had been assembling over nearly four years. After some squirming and going through not much more than the motions of a further review of possible sites, we presented to the council our second choice, and that was an area north-west of the city, just south of the small town of Kintore which straddles the A96 trunk road. In saying we went through the motions, I do not mean to imply we did not do a professional job but rather the data was already available and it was just a matter of picking a second best. It was being on record as professionally recommending second best that upset my colleagues. As an old Civil Servant I had no qualms in subjugating my professional reputation to the right and proper, in this case, requirements of my political masters.

All our hand-wringing was in vain. Kintore was in Gordon District and a stronghold of the Liberal Party and so they pounced upon the proposed new siting south of Kintore and became supportive of a new town in that location. At the same time the Labour group saw nothing in this for them and agreement risked handing the Liberals a considerable prize and a potential boost to their power base in Gordon District, and in turn on the Regional Council. So, we had a stalemate, with both the Liberals and Labour wanting a new settlement but not in the other's back garden. A combined Liberal and Labour vote for a new town would easily have carried the proposal. Neither was willing to compromise, and with the SNP having no interest in a new town anywhere sensible the idea fell.

So far we had had two public consultations on new housing allocation;

one in October 1992 in the context of the original structure plan draft with its proposal for a new settlement south-west of the city, and in March 1994 another on the proposal for the same north-west of the city. The rejection, in essence by default, of a new town meant then we had to go back to the beginning and reallocate the tranche of housing assigned to the new town across the Aberdeen housing market area. We entered our third round of public consultation in the August of 1994 with proposals for distributing the 3,300 houses, originally assigned to the new town, amongst existing settlements. This meant that some towns and villages, like Stonehaven and Portlethen for example, would get an extra housing allocation that the residents were not to welcome. I must admit to having enjoyed a certain *schadenfreude* at the time as my planning team I and had taken so much stick for pursuing a new town solution to our housing requirements as opposed to a policy of wider dispersal. Part of our justification for a new town was to give many existing settlements a well earned rest after the oil-led rapid growth of house building in earlier years and allow them a quieter spell of consolidation. The oil-led growth in the small towns around Aberdeen resulted in 'bolt-ons' that tended to swamp local character by both the size and pace of growth during the boom years. Such carbuncles are still obvious in small commuter towns like Ellon.

The debate about housing allocation was often distorted by those with an axe to grind. A common cry from those who feared the consequences of growth for one reason or another was a claim that oil production had reached its peak in the North Sea, and anyway because of technology changes there would be less employed both on and off shore in the energy industry. There was some truth in these arguments but, even with a static economy and zero population growth, demographic trends indicated Grampian was going to need more rather than fewer new houses . We published updated forecasts during the drawn-out structure plan process which added even further to our requirement for new housing. This dumbfounded many critics, who thought we were massaging the statistics. The facts are that families are getting smaller insofar as there are now fewer inhabitants per house, more split families, more single people and more youngsters leaving to set up their own homes, all adding to the region's housing requirements, even with a static population. Grampian, in fact, had a growing population at the time. Some critics felt that Grampian had more than enough people and any further growth in population would 'spoil it' for those already here. The reality is a region with a relatively small population and outside the Greater Aberdeen area was, and remains, sparsely populated. I have always said, and on many occasions in public, that what the region needs is a lot more people and not less, and indeed Scotland's overall low birth rate remains a cause for concern. In many sectors we lacked the necessary critical mass of population to adequately support facilities, and here I would include cultural and leisure facilities and, in the rural hinterland, social services and state of the art communications. In spite of the self-styled title 'Offshore Oil Capital of Europe' Aberdeen has no direct air link with North America or a roll-on roll-off ferry link with Europe. A sore point is that the electrification of the main east coast railway line from London stops at Edinburgh. This is not likely to change in the foreseeable future and mainly because Grampian's population base is too small to provide the return on the investment needed. In that sense Aberdeen was and remains peripheral.

By February 1995 we finally submitted the structure plan to the Secretary of State for approval. Scottish Ministers and their officials then took nearly two and a half years to make modifications and clear the plan for final publication in December 1997. I am not sure of the reasons for the delay in Edinburgh but politics and the 1997 General Election in May would be a reasonable bet.

I should be in a better position to explain the delay at the Grampian end, and why it took us from March 1991 to February 1995, nearly four years, to produce a final draft structure plan. In retrospect it may be fair to apportion the blame equally between officials and our politicians in Woodhill House. By the time of the publication of the first draft in October 1992 we were almost a year behind the schedule set in March 1989 by my Director of Planning predecessor, Trevor Sprott. There is no doubt that the uncertainty created by my appointment will have had its effect on senior planning managers. During the subsequent and later stages of preparation of the plan my control of the department was undermined by the then Convener, Bob Middleton, to a degree where it was difficult to effectively direct my most senior staff. This was more an annoyance than a real obstacle to progress as Allan Garvie took on most of the responsibility for the structure plan. I hinted earlier that some staff in my department lacked a sense of urgency. It was not that any individual was lazy, but when five o'clock came they were out of the door, whatever the urgency of the work before them. There were notable exceptions but as we dropped further and further behind there was no corresponding acceleration of the machine to compensate. Allan Garvie set himself exacting standards and drove himself to the limits, but he was somewhat gentler with his staff. However the quality of work of my planning staff was of the highest calibre and maybe my impatience was misplaced, and more haste might have sacrificed the quality of the end result.

At the same time I must lay at elected members' door responsibility for most of the delays incurred between about June 1993 and the submission of the plan to the Secretary of State in February 1995. I had thought that the political process at its best was about deals and compromises reached in smoke-filled rooms with some genuflection to the outcome being to the public good. The debates over the housing allocation in the Aberdeen housing market area and what role, if any, a new town might play in the allocation were more like trench warfare than politics. I was not in a position to know whether private discussions took place between the political parties during this period. If discussions did take place then the stand-off positions taken up by the Labour and Liberal groups in the council chamber gave no clue whatsoever. I would not have expected the SNP to act as honest broker, as clearly their policy from early stages in the debate were to stop any move to establish a new town in the Aberdeen area. It seemed a logical move for the Labour and Liberal groups in the council to do a deal as both welcomed the new town idea in principle. I suspect part of the obstacle to a deal was the personal antipathy between the respective lead personalities, as well as an eye to any future gains (although very speculative) the parties might make as the result of the establishment of a successful new town near Aberdeen.

There is no doubt that the delays in producing a new structure plan caused many problems for the five district authorities within Grampian Region, and in turn this generated quite a lot of tension and ill feeling between the two tiers of local government in Grampian. At the time some district councils were trying to finalise their local plans and the absence of an up-to-date structure plan frustrated this. The absence of a new structure plan also caused problems for the developers and builders and made it difficult for them to plan ahead with any confidence.

I would see the failure to establish a new town and all that might have meant in raising the profile of the region in terms of quality investment in new industries, and attracting much needed new entrepreneurs and new ideas, as the biggest disappointment of my time at Grampian Regional Council. It was an opportunity missed. I am convinced it could have been the elusive Factor 'X' that I had referred to in the 'Together to the Future' economic development strategy

By way of a postscript the Stewart Milne Group did not give up on their attempts to secure planning permission for a new town on the Banchory-

Devenick site to the south west of Aberdeen. The idea of a new town was still supported by Aberdeen District Council and their Director of Planning, the much respected Bert Allen, was reported in the *Press and Journal* of 3 April 1995 as saying " ...the City Council remains of the view that the balance of advantage lies in the inclusion of a new settlement as part of Grampian's development strategy". The 'P&J' also reported Gordon Cochrane, executive director of the Stewart Milne Group, as saying "GRC had rejected the settlement option for no sound financial or planning reasons". That in my view is a fair statement. After the Regional Council had turned down an application for outline planning permission, the firm appealed in April 1995 to the Secretary of State. There followed a Scottish Office public inquiry in early 1996 and this was expected to find in accordance with the structure plan finally submitted by the region in 1995.

However that was not the end of the story. The public inquiry into the Stewart Milne application was reopened by Donald Dewar, as Secretary of State, in August 1997, in the wake of the adoption of the Grampian structure plan. The arrival of a Labour Secretary of State had encouraged hopes of a favourable outcome for the Stewart Milne Group. In spite of some encouraging rumours, this was not to be the case, and perhaps it was no surprise that the Minister with planning responsibilities, Sarah Boyack MSP, finally rejected the new town proposal in July 1999 as a breach of council policy.

By the time of Sarah Boyack's decision I had been away from local authority work for over three years, and there had been radical changes in the organisation of Scottish local government with the old Region and the five District councils being replaced by three single tier authorities covering the former Grampian Region. Both the successor authorities covering the Aberdeen housing market area, namely Aberdeenshire Council and Aberdeen City Council opposed the idea of a new town at the reopened inquiry. A lot of water had flowed under many bridges since Stewart Milne's initial outline application in 1993 and the likelihood of any co-operation or understanding between the two successor authorities to the former Regional Council was even less than before local government reorganisation in 1996.

There was also a developer-led attempt to create a new village in the grounds of the former Roman Catholic seminary at Blairs on south Deeside, but as this was firmly in the green belt it was a non-starter. However there is still a need at the time of writing to find a role for this attractive site and its still-functioning and recently restored chapel. Some of the buildings are worthy of preservation and represent an important reminder of the history of the church in the north east of Scotland. There has been a succession of ideas from the developer working with the church authorities but all fall foul of green belt restrictions. Ideas have ranged from a university campus together with domestic housing (if the application had been for educational use alone there would have been few planning objections), through various leisure based complexes as vehicles for housing development. Here again I feel planning 'rules' are hampering sensible development of an important site.

Besides my disappointment in failing to secure a new town and all that might have meant for the future economy of the region, I regret also failing to successfully seed a debate amongst planners, architects, developers and builders that might have led to an improvement in design standards of the built environment in the region. There is no doubt that the townscapes of the north-east of Scotland are some of the greyest and bleakest of any in the UK. A regular comment of first time visitors from England is the greyness of the built environment. In defence I will rehearse the publicity 'copy' I used to write, about the sparkle of sunshine on mica in our granite, and the 'silver city' that is Aberdeen, but rarely are my guests impressed. I can point to the stone-built villages of the Yorkshire Dales and even the Lakes (although here sometimes helped by the green hues in slate) which are essentially grey in nature and on wet day can be quite as depressing an experience. I have to admit that it is not just the greyness of many of Scotland's north east villages and towns that jars but the absence, maybe, of a degree of quaintness found on the other side of the border. The small towns and villages of Cumbria and North Yorkshire can certainly be described as grey but they attract tourists in their thousands. By contrast the Grampian-built environment is often quite severe, austere and overwhelmingly practical. Maybe the fact that our local picture calendars rarely feature small town and village scenes is telling. With such magnificent countryside do we need to focus on the man-made?

It is not so much the inherited townscapes I am concerned about but rather the impact of developers and planners in more recent years. A game often played in my office was to try and point to the buildings that the oil boom years had provided us and that were of architectural merit. It was a short game. Although a bit tongue-in-cheek we would nominate the Safeway supermarket in Aberdeen's downtown Kings Street. In terms of the stock of commercial and corporate building since oil was brought ashore there is very little of outstanding merit. Some might cite Shell Exploration's almost pyramidal palace at Altens, the functional ASDA store at Bridge of Dee, and the new Norman Foster building at The Robert Gordon University's Deeside campus. This failure is the more noticeable in a city that is so richly endowed with fine public and domestic buildings from an earlier age

In an attempt to stimulate debate that might lead to change, in March 1992 I invited a number of key individuals to my house for supper and the chance to debate the whole question of building design in Grampian. Those attending that evening event included one of Scotland's most successful builders and manufacturers of systems built houses, Stewart Milne, together with another and local quality house builder, Malcolm Allan, as well as James Campbell and Douglas Forrest representing the architectural profession, a prominent local surveyor, the Director of the Aberdeen Art Gallery and distinguished modern water colourist, Ian Mackenzie-Smith, and Peter Suttie, Banff and Buchan District's Director of Planning. This group, later joined by Robert Gordon University's head of architecture, Professor Robin Webster, first addressed the definition of design and particularly 'good' design. One succinct definition proposed was that design was 'intellect made manifest'. More difficult was to determine the influences on architectural design and especially in domestic housing. We concluded it was unlikely that the customer as purchaser of a property was very influential in its design, although for the small number of individuals appointing their own architects the purchaser influence was, potentially, significant. In the majority of cases the responsibility for the design of new housing was shared between financiers, developers, builders, architects, and local authorities through planning controls, not forgetting the house purchaser entirely. The input or influence by each group would vary. Some local authorities, like Essex at South Woodham Ferrers, had drawn up clear design guidelines whereas in others the role appeared minimal. In our own patch some of the district planning officers had tried their best to raise design standards and at least acknowledged the local vernacular. However at the time of writing (2003) there are distressing signs that Aberdeenshire's attempts to impose a sense of the vernacular are in fact stifling good design and risk a townscape that is bereft of any high points. The result will be mediocrity at best and bland, grey and boring at worst.

One outcome from the discussions was at least an acknowledgement by both planners and architects, but surprisingly also by the builders that the standard of domestic housing design in the north-east of Scotland left much to be desired. I am not able to claim any improvement in processes or the quality of design in new domestic housing as a result of my initiative. Unfortunately one of the liveliest of the district planning directors and a supporter of my initiative, Peter Suttie, died unexpectedly a short while after my retirement. The post-1996 local government reorganisation in Scotland also removed or diluted the roles of a number of the more far-sighted former district council directors and any momentum for change that might have been generated was dissipated. The arrival of the new single tier councils saw the usual dip in the output curve that most organisations experience for at least two years after a reorganisation while they find their feet. During this tunnel period the emphasis is on burying everything from the former 'colonial' days and where, often ill-considered, 'macho' stances are de rigueur. One archetypal manifestation of this in the new Aberdeenshire authority was the push for a new headquarters building to replace an existing splendid and centrally sited building, although in Aberdeen and not Aberdeenshire. There is a precedent for a local authority having its HQ in the area of a neighbouring authority, and the best known is Surrey which has its HQ in the nearby London borough of Kingston. Happily we got through the macho phase and Aberdeenshire councillors saw sense and remained in Woodhill House, the former Grampian Regional Council headquarters building. By coincidence the same Woodhill House was originally built for another authority which also disappeared in an earlier local government reorganisation.

An encounter to discuss design matters with one planning official in Aberdeenshire some years later was a depressing experience when the attitude was defensive, prickly and parochial. On the brighter side and at the same time there were other officials in the Aberdeenshire planning team that could see the impact of the unimaginative nature of the current policy and moves were afoot to set up a small group to look at building design afresh, and indeed as I had tried to do some twelve years earlier. My own attempts were hampered by lack of support amongst the local authorities themselves. Detailed aspects of planning such as housing design were then the prerogative of the second tier district authorities. The Regional Council did have 'call in' powers over individual planning applications where structure plan requirements were likely to be infringed, but in general were restricted to intervention in more strategic issues rather than the detail of day-to-day planning and building control matters.

Occasions where the individual's choice and freedom of action is decided by a group of councillors are rare and when this happens considerable power is put into the hands of politicians. Planning remains one of these such areas where local government politicians have a real influence on our lives and can take decisions that are case-related to the individual, as well as decisions on generic policy that relates to all the local population or at least a large section of it. Membership of a planning committee therefore provides the opportunity to exercise real power and influence but also exposes councillors to temptation and corruption more than most other committee roles. On the other hand in areas such as education and social work it is unusual for the politician to make a formal council decision on a specific case dealing with an individual. In social work most such decisions will be taken by the professional staff and in education, with the arrival of school boards, councillor links with individual parents or students are even rarer. So membership of the planning committee, which included economic development, was prized by councillors in Grampian. The text books may say that whilst decisions on significant planning matters, both policy and case work, are taken by lay politicians in the planning committee or by referral to full council in some cases, in practice the politicians are acting as proxy for their planning officials and their professional recommendations. For the majority of planning recommendations I dealt with that may have appeared to have been the case, but for a significant minority professional advice was not followed.

In my experience very few decisions went through committee 'on the nod'. There was no political whip applied in the planning committee but many decisions did follow a party line, and not just in major planning applications where there was obviously a political dimension. Major decisions on land use are certainly political in nature, but sometimes also political are decisions whether the individual should build a house in a location that could establish a precedent. On occasions that much used and abused phrase of the political right 'the politics of envy' was apt. On other occasions one could detect the reverse with an obsequious reverence by those councillors of leftish leanings (and here one must include elements within the SNP) to an applicant at the top of the social pile. On the whole my experience was a good one in so far as most planning applications got a good hearing and the decision was a fair one for the applicant, although at Regional level, as I explained above, we only dealt with the cases that we judged ran counter to the structure plan policies. At the same time I have no evidence from my time at Grampian that planning colleagues and their respective political masters in the five district councils (including Aberdeen), were not dealing with planning applications in an equally effective way.

Apart from the offer of a hospitality day at a golf tournament at Gleneagles (which I turned down) in my seven years as a local government official at Grampian Regional Council I was never propositioned or offered a bribe of any sort by a developer or a planning applicant. I would include here offers of embarrassingly valuable Christmas 'boxes', lavish entertainment or travel. In the business world that sort of hospitality would not be considered bribery but I believe the public sector must enforce a stricter code. I never had to admonish or warn my planning staff of the pitfalls as their self-discipline on such matters was beyond reproach. I felt comfortable also with our elected members and similarly I was unaware of any member of the planning committee that was dishonest or open to bribery. At the same time one must understand that unfavourable planning decisions can lose votes and this can influence decisions at committee. The current system we have in local government, with relatively small wards or constituencies together with a voter turn out that is often pathetically low, is such that a very small change in voting pattern can win or lose a seat. I think we were all mature enough in Grampian to recognise this and the 'local member', that is the councillor covering the location of the particular planning application under consideration, was always allowed to make his case. This was listened to with respect although on occasions the stance taken by the councillor clearly reflected his (or her) assessment of the vote count at the next election. The rest of his colleagues would normally make 'allowance' for the stance of the 'local member'. On the other hand there were many occasions were the local member would be in a position to give an insight to the application that was not obvious from the papers prepared by officials, and where this enlightenment would properly influence the debate and outcome.

There always seems to be some ongoing review of the planning system to make it either fairer, quicker, or more democratic (which usually means slower), and I am sure improvements can be made. I came fresh to the whole process without any baggage and left with the firm impression that it was as fair as any system can be. Councillors do wield considerable power in the process but surely that is what local democracy is about? Planning parallels the lower courts process with lay justices working to well-established guidelines, with the advice of a body of full-time professionals (court clerks), but within the guidelines and professional advice room to exercise their own judgement, with still the opportunity for personal bias and weakness, and uncertainty of outcome. Most councillors, like most JPs (Justices of the Peace), are ordinary, honest and trying to do their best. I doubt if there is scope for much real improvement beyond tinkering and genuflection to fashion and political whim. There are one or two gaps in the planning system that should be plugged such as greater control over agricultural buildings as is the case in some national parks, and the erection of mobile telephone masts, although some steps have been taken in the case of masts at the time of writing. More controversial is the planning process as it relates to large scale assaults on the countryside such as new airports or additional runways to existing airports and motorway extensions. Some would say the procedure is too drawn out. Any curtailment of the procedure in such circumstances will likely be at the expense of the rights of individuals with a relevant interest, and at some expense to the democratic procedure. Some cynics would go as far to argue the benign dictatorship case in such planning hearings. I would not, although a benign dictatorship, I have to admit, would be a lot more efficient and would more than likely arrive at the same end point. We officials often bemoaned the lack of political 'leadership' in Grampian but I sometimes wonder if this was an expression of a deep-seated wish of all officials to work within a more totalitarian regime? There is no doubt that strong government can make official life easier.

By way of 'closure', in the spring of 2004, I went to see Stewart Milne at his Elrick headquarters to the west of Aberdeen. Since the new town saga his firm has gone from strength to strength, with then fifty per cent of his business outside the region, and a new factory producing timber-framed buildings at Witney in Oxfordshire. Stewart was philosophical about the seven years his company had spent in pursuing a new town in Grampian, but did feel the region had lost an important opportunity to plan for the long term. He expects that his business in north-east Scotland will become the minor part of the group's operations and soon the firm will need to take a view on where their interests lie. Key will be the assessment of whether Grampian is really 'Going Places'. He is clear that individual house purchasers will increasingly expect information on the long-term development of the area into which they are buying. As part of this he would expect local councils to have strategy plans that look 20 to 25 years ahead. This requires local leadership and I suspect that this very successful Grampian-born entrepreneur will find this wanting when his firm come to weigh their local assets against opportunities further south.

Chapter 20

Partnership

Belief in one's own publicity is the trap facing any propagandist but a certain amount of belief in the product one is selling is essential for the best results. For me an element of crusading idealism is important if I am to give of my best. On arriving in Grampian and quickly getting to know the area it was not difficult for me to believe in the product. There are elements of the countryside and its history that are just magical. Few areas of the UK could equal the experience provided by the Grampian countryside on a crisp winter's night, with snow on the ground, air that is keen, clean and sharp, and stars that are crystal clear. Daylight hours can be as seductive as the evenings. Many film makers and photographers comment on the unique clarity of our light. Autumn light can be flattering anywhere but mix in Grampian's scenery with the luminosity of our north light and one can be transported to a better life. I never tired of the day's end drive from Aberdeen to my home in the countryside. Not far from home one emerges from a left-hand bend to see the landscape setting of our village with its backdrop of Bennachie, associated smaller hills and a prospect of more distant peaks that seem to promise a glimpse of the mighty Cairngorm massif that provides a natural border to the western edge of the Region.

The only staff reporting to me on my arrival in Aberdeen at the end of 1988 were those responsible for telling the world of these and other aspects of this still little known part of the UK. This staff represented my responsibility for the 'Grampian Initiative', a partnership of six local authorities, academia and local business brought together by the Regional Council in 1987. The origins of the initiative are interesting in that the initial idea came from outside the council and the name Greg Rae crops up again. Greg at that time was running a small graphic design company from premises in Cotton Street not far from Aberdeen's sea front. He tells the story of how early during the oil price crash of 1986 his office telephones ceased ringing when the oil companies' spending in the local community abruptly stopped, and Greg's business faced disaster. However, for some time he had been tracking from a marketing perspective how a number of cities and city regions had coped with economic recovery. One of these was the State of California. With few alternative sources of business on offer, Greg and a partner from his firm scraped together enough funds and made the trip to California to see what they could learn from the experience there. By some foot-in-the-door cheek they got to see the Governor and his staff. What they found was an impressive partnership approach to job creation and marketing the State. On return they made a presentation of their findings to the Region's then development arm, 'NESDA' (soon to become part of my new department). Through some quirk of fate Greg had a link to one of the youngest and brightest of Grampian's councillors, Nicol Stephen, and the same presentation was made to him. Greg explained what the Californians had achieved and how he believed their approach was just what was required in Grampian to counter the economic crisis precipitated by the oil price crash.

What emerged from the Regional Council in a markedly short time was an initiative based very much on that Californian experience researched by Greg and his colleague, and similarly involving the private sector. The council spent less than a year working up the concept and all was revealed to the wider public in launches of a Grampian 'initiative' in the spring of 1988, including a £48,000 launch at the Queen Elizabeth II conference centre in London's Westminster. By some coincidence I received an invitation to the Westminster launch in my DTI capacity and before I had considered a job in Grampian. At the time £48,000 was a large amount of money to spend on a publicity launch but it was a measure of how seriously the council were taking the need to get a better grip on the local economy. Greg's firm, Format Communications, bid for and was appointed to handle the marketing of what was to become known formally as the 'Grampian Initiative'. Format created the arrow style logo (representing the outline of the coast of north east Scotland) and the first strap line, 'Grampian's Going Places', together with the typeset, font and soon ubiquitous Grampian Initiative green house colour (Pantone 361). Format also devised the later strap line 'Grampian. Scots for Quality' which we tended to use more in product-related promotions and particularly for the food industry.

Staff were seconded to a new Grampian Initiative office from existing council departments including close support from Format Communication's Greg Rae. Some of the staff may have been less than ideal, but such was the pace of events in those early days together with cross-party political support and support from other senior staff from the chief executive and his deputy downwards that the small unit of enthusiastic seconded staff 'got by'. I arrived on the scene some six months later and by this stage the staff in the Grampian Initiative were struggling. The staff also were responsible for servicing the four task forces that had been established to examine and draw up action plans in fulfilment of the mission to 'stimulate the economy of Grampian Region through partnership transcending political and commercial self-interest'.

Priority targets were chosen at an early stage and task forces were set up to examine the needs of the Grampian £1.14 billion turnover food industry, the energy sector and more specifically sub-sea technology, and tourism. The fourth task force was a rag bag of interests grouped together under the banner of Grampian research, education and training (the 'GREAT' Task Force) with a view to benefitting from the extensive 'learning' industry in the region via its two universities, a number of prestigious government research laboratories and a similar number of further education facilities including a teacher training college. Each task force was made up of experts from the private sector and academia as well as representatives and experts from local councils and occasionally government agencies such as the then Scottish Development Agency (SDA) via its Grampian office. The task forces were chaired by individuals from relevant private sector firms, but in the case of tourism the chair of that task force was provided by the chief executive of Aberdeen's tourism promotion operation.

The make-up of the task forces mirrored, to a large degree, the Grampian Initiative Working Party, the partnership's overseeing body. In the early days of the Initiative, before the Labour group had irretrievably politicised it after the May 1990 local elections, the Working Party was as non-political as the circumstances allowed, bearing in mind that the Regional Council provided the great majority of the funding and the piper called the tune. However debate within the Working Party was not dominated by politicians and allowed one or two from business and academia to make their mark. I suppose the dynamics of the Grampian Initiative Working Party were similar to many other committees with a minority making the running, measured in terms of noise anyway, with the majority led by the few. The input by politicians in those early days was constructive, rarely party politically influenced and absent also was the dogmatic approach that we were to increasingly see in later days. It would be fair to say it worked pretty well in terms of a partnership, notwithstanding its unequal nature in terms of funding. All decisions that implicated the Regional Council had to be ratified by a committee of the council, as under local authority rules unelected members of committees had no voting rights. The Grampian

Initiative Working Party was, in practice, an advisory committee to the council's Economic and Development and Planning Committee (EDP) and all Grampian Initiative Working Party minutes and recommendations had to be cleared by EDP.

Initially the prime focus of the Initiative was external decision makers, but a close second order priority was addressing the self-perception of Grampian's own citizens. Externally we were promoting the region's diversity, its record of innovation, a wish to be seen as internationalist and, finally, Grampian's quality of life. The aim was to sell Grampian as the ideal place in which to do business and a place to invest. A bit of poaching of firms to relocate within the UK seemed within the Scottish Office rules, but the overseas role was zealously protected by the then 'Locate in Scotland' arm of the the jumbo sized SDA quango (later Scottish Enterprise), in conjunction with the Scottish Office. However, if overseas activity was presented as 'export promotion' local authorities could get around the rules and, as covered in a previous chapter, we were pretty active overseas with inducement of inward investment to Grampian very much in mind. We were often assisted by sympathetic FCO colleagues who seemed either unaware or ignored the Scottish Office imposed restrictions on local authorities. The occasional disgruntled Locate in Scotland overseas placement officer was not unhelpful to us and in practice we were limited rather by our own efficiency and ingenuity than any Scottish Office imposed shackles.

The main concern for me in those early days was to try and change internal perspectives and overcome the north-east of Scotland's chronic parochialism and inability to think in terms of any dimension much beyond its borders. We had to take every opportunity to press home the need for a more international outlook and at the same time to instil pride in the capability of the local economy to produce world class products. There was a local pride but it was that prickly and resentful variety that so often restricts success. We concentrated on bringing home to the people of Grampian how important the area was not only in terms of oil, but also as a major source of the nation's food and particularly so as far as beef, fish, pork and chicken were concerned, and of course there was whisky where Grampian produced some 60% of the the finest, that is single malt whisky. Always at the heart of our message was the key word 'quality'.

We tried to promulgate the idea amongst manufacturers and service industries alike that Grampian should aim at the top end of the range. As a vehicle for our press campaign we invented a fictional character called Hugo Ramsay, who was an informed, sophisticated world traveller and a bon viveur who instinctively knew quality when he saw it, and was not prepared to accept second best. In one piece of copy by Format Communications where we sell the quality message Hugo Ramsay is quoted as saying "I am the diner in the restaurant: the queuer in the bank, the shop or supermarket; the cost-conscious consumer; the end user; the buyer. I am the customer. *Everyman.* ...And our quest is for Quality". We ran a series of slightly quirky newspaper advertisements featuring Hugo Ramsay in his search for quality in various locations across the region. Early intentions were to publicly acknowledge instances of outstanding service and quality reported to us. We got as far as acknowledging a public lavatory in Forres but all this was a bit too much for our partnership colleagues and the Hugo Ramsay based campaign was axed as being "too clever by half" and a "self-indulgent advertising person's campaign". The campaign never had a long enough run to enable us to make any objective assessment and its demise was premature. Interestingly Shetland instigated something similar that they called the 'Shetland Standard' whereby the Council, setting the example, urged that anything the Shetland Isles did or produced should be to a high standard. At least the Hugo Ramsay campaign left a legacy for me and my staff and that was a determination that any brochure produced, event or hospitality handled under the Grampian Initiative banner would be done to the highest standards, or not at all. There were many occasions where we declined to participate when resources prevented a production to a standard worthy of the Grampian Initiative label. Although this was never written as such into any of our guidelines, the key politicians involved in the Initiative never argued other than the 'quality first' approach. This was later enshrined in the 'Together to the Future' economic development strategy where 'quality' was described as the 'keystone' to all we do.

Another Grampian Initiative innovation was the creation of ambassadors. Over the eight years' life of the Initiative less than forty were created and on being appointed a Grampian Ambassador one joined an illustrious and select company that included the likes of the former US Defence Secretary, Caspar Weinberger, Stephen Forbes of the eponymous magazine, percussionist Evelyn Glennie, and senior businessmen such as Sir Ian Wood and Gordon Baxter (Baxters of Fochabers) and many others that were considered to have made an outstanding contribution to the Region. Although I was influential in the choice of ambassador appointment, the decision rested with the councillor who chaired the Grampian Initiative. There was only one nominee that I objected to and managed to block successfully on the grounds that the appointment was pressed on purely mischievous grounds by another councillor. Most recipients were genuinely flattered to receive the title of 'Grampian Ambassador' and a rather grand mounted and framed citation on parchment. The awards were presented at a formal dinner in Woodhill House where the Region were good hosts and these events always enjoyable. Few ambassadors took their subsequent role seriously enough but at the same time we failed to keep our ambassadors adequately briefed and so ensure their effective use in representing Grampian. One ambassador, John Moorhouse, who was with Shell at the time, took the role very seriously and requested a supply of headed paper complete with the 'Grampian Ambassador' title. The ambassador idea was of great interest to many of our competitors at home and overseas including Great Yarmouth, the service centre for the southern North Sea gas fields.

I was to be made a Grampian Ambassador in the closing weeks of the Regional Council in February 1996. Some might have expected a rather cynical response from me, but although the award was not unexpected I was flattered to receive it. I followed John Moorhouse's example and had visiting cards printed with the 'Grampian Ambassador' designation and my home address. I used these long after I left the Regional Council and to very good effect. Presentation of such a card always got a response and gave an opportunity to sing the praises of the region, as well as gaining a little extra respect.

A sort of precursor to the ambassador concept was the briefing of the city's taxi drivers in the early stages of the Initiative on what the city and its hinterland had to offer. At the same time we introduced 'bumper' stickers with the 'Grampian's Going Places' strap line. Even now, some fifteen years later, a Grampian sticker is still to be seen on old cars but I suspect for reasons of inertia on the part of the owners rather than any long held fervour and wish to promote the region.

The work of sector task forces brought me headaches as well as satisfaction. Some of the most successful were also some of the most troublesome. The food task force was a case in point. It was fairly representative of the larger food producers in the region. One of our objectives was to encourage the adding of value to the vast farm output of the region. We tended to avoid the farm end of a spectrum of supply that stretched from field to supermarket shelf. Anyway the farming industry had (and still does) enormous support via the Scottish Office agricultural department, intervention boards and the rest of the European Union support system through the Common Agricultural Policy. Not that this stopped farmers complaining, but does anything? Our food task force firms ranged from fish processing, shortbread, soup manufacture, whisky, supply of mixes and additives for the baking industry, chilled and frozen oven ready meals to beef portions for supermarkets, pork and chicken. Many of the bosses of these firms were often self-made businessmen (and occasionally women), and larger than life 'characters'. Some were endearing but a minority were tough, uncompromising and manipulative. This presented me with particular problems as I tried to get the task force to address the structural problems of the industry and move on from the situation where the Grampian Initiative was merely subsidising the attendance of the member firms at overseas exhibitions and other aspects of marketing. The food task force began to resemble a closed club where the members decided how they would carve up the budget provided by the Grampian Initiative. Like in Ministry of Agriculture, some of my staff became too closely identified with the industry they were serving.

I once remember a senior Ministry of Agriculture official telling me that it would likely be more efficient to hand the Ministry's various grants over to the National Farmers Union en bloc and cut out the middleman. We were approaching a similar position with our food task force when members saw access to council funds as their 'right' and objected to any questioning of costs and relating these to benefits or outcome. A report by consultants Conran Roche eventually gave me the ammunition to reposition the food task force and amalgamate it with a smaller and less effective consultative food group run by the local enterprise company, Grampian Enterprise. This turned out to be more of a fight than I expected. Since Grampian Enterprise had been set up in 1990 it had peddled a stream of propaganda to local authorities about the need to co-operate and better focus resources. On making our offer to combine respective food industry advisory groups, Grampian Enterprise and its chairman gave me a difficult time and came up with all sorts of minor obstacles to merger. Eventually, with most of the food firms onside, we had to get tough and threaten to ignore Grampian Enterprise altogether unless the quango co-operated. It did, less than graciously, and the Grampian Food Forum (my designation) was formed in 1993, and at the time of writing continues to operate successfully. Part of my agenda in pressing the establishment of the Grampian Food Forum was to provide sufficient resources to recruit the quality of staff necessary to do the job effectively. For a number of reasons I knew I could not achieve this within the context of the Grampian Initiative and my own staff. We recruited an excellent lady for the Food Forum who went on to achieve a senior position within Scottish Enterprise.

The Conran Roche report further provided me with leverage to set up two new sector-specific task forces, and without the encumbrance of the Grampian Initiative political obstacles. The report also gave me the opportunity to select the most suitable staff from the wider planning and economic development department to take proposals forward. In January 1995 I set up an Environmental Equipment and Services Task Force to champion the growing band of local firms involved in environmental clean-up, analysis, research, and engineering. This proved to be very successful and in a slightly different form continues to provide a focus for firms in this sector. Success so much depends on the individuals involved and particularly the choice of chairman. In the case of environmental equipment we got this right but in the case of the Technology in Grampian Task Force, established in November 1994, I was less successful, at least as far as achieving my objectives.

I saw the creation of the technology task force as particularly important as the need to diversify Grampian's industry away from oil and the more traditional agricultural and fishing linked industries was a pressing priority. Indeed it was this concern that was one of the main reasons behind the council's decision to appoint an economic development 'supremo'. By this stage I had suffered six frustrating years trying to get my political masters to see the bigger picture and commit themselves wholeheartedly to a plan for an economy 'after oil'. We started well with the 'Together to the Future' strategy but parochial politics and the more personal publicity requirements of some key politicians killed much of the early cross party momentum for change. By 1995 the Regional Council was in its dying stages with a hand over to the new single tier authorities the following year. So for me and the council it was a last throw of the dice. I was encouraged at the time by the government's 'Foresight' initiative which had established a number of sector-specific panels of experts under the aegis of initially the Cabinet Office and later DTI to predict future trends in technology. I spoke to the Cabinet Office link man and had suggested that my new technology task force might take on the role of a local Foresight link group. The Cabinet Office were encouraging. So I got together a reasonable cross-section of individuals with direct interest in technological development in Grampian to form the 'Tiger' or Technology in Grampian Task Force. The task force included representatives from the technology development units of both universities, the offshore energy operators trade association (UKOOA), Amec Engineering, the French-owned Hoskyns data handling company, and the head of Scottish Enterprise's oil and gas division, Kourosh Bassiti.

I acted as secretary with the Robert Gordon University then head of offshore engineering, Professor Danny Gorman, as vice-chair and a former oil company executive as the chairman. The task force also included David Capitanchik, then working at Aberdeen's further education college, a visionary and one of the liveliest minds in Aberdeen at the time. David, a specialist on Arab politics, was one of those individuals who could make a worthwhile contribution to any debate.

All the skills necessary were assembled to ably brainstorm Grampian's technological strengths and weaknesses, and come forward with clear recommendations as to opportunities to be pursued. Indeed the team did more or less that during the course of some lively sessions. I saw my role as producing a report based on these discussions, and one that would prompt a reaction from the wider community, generate essential further debate and research, and would lead in time to specific action programmes. So, as secretary I produced a draft report in a suitably challenging style and submitted this to task force colleagues. Unfortunately the chairman had quite a different and more political agenda. The result was a bland and 'motherhood' report designed, as the chairman's introduction says, to avoid treading on the toes of others. My initiative in setting up the task force was bitterly opposed by the Grampian Enterprise quango, and in my view largely because the Regional Council was in its dying days but also in part due to the 'not invented here' syndrome that had dogged so much of the council's relationship with this body. Others may say this interpretation says more about me than the task force and its chair and I am being unfair, but I did see a link between the emasculation of my draft and the antagonism of the quango body.

The task force's statement of purpose was to "raise the awareness and encourage the better deployment of technology and technological advancement in Grampian's industry and commerce" and vision "that Grampian be regarded as a world wide focus of technology". The resulting report attracted the minimum of press comment or indeed any other comment. The only good thing to come from the exercise as far as I was concerned was an excellent photograph of me and my task force chairman, taken on a staircase at the Aberdeen International Drilling and Downhole Technology Centre with a wholly inappropriate 'we can see the future' pose. Here was a variation on the music world's 'great video, rotten record'. Needless to add there was no follow up action and the link with the DTI 'Foresight' initiative was lost.

In many ways the Grampian Initiative provided some of the highest and most interesting points in my time with the Regional Council, but it has to be said that it also provided some of my lowest moments. The early days of the Initiative offered so much promise. We were generously funded. In the first five years we spent over £2.5 million and almost all of this provided by the Region. In the early years I judge we got value for money but in the last four to five years of the Grampian Initiative a lot of money was wasted, and especially as I lost control to politicians over my own staff and the direction of the campaign. I made several proposals for, in effect, a relaunch of the Initiative but all to no avail and the Initiative was to die with the demise of the Regional Council in the Spring of 1996. In March of the previous year we commissioned consultants 'Scotinform' to undertake a final market awareness survey. This survey found that the awareness of the 'Grampian' name outside the region was "relatively strong" but that the images (positive ones I assume) remained weak. The irony is that the successor authorities to Grampian Regional Council did all they could to bury the Grampian name, although it lives on in the name of many firms and the Grampian mountains.

One of the outcomes of my visit with councillors to Toronto in April 1989 was the commitment in my then draft economic development strategy to set up a body that would bring together in a partnership all the players in the local economy from the voluntary to business sectors, including the local authorities, academia and trade unions. Toronto is a vast metropolitan area made up of a number of separate authorities including the City of Toronto itself. To facilitate effective planning for the whole Metro Toronto area the authorities there had constituted an umbrella group bringing together all the economy's stakeholders. Although the Grampian scale was so much smaller the challenges were similar to Metro Toronto, with our one large city dominating the region's economy and a number of smaller satellite commuter towns within a thirty mile radius, and a still largely city-dependent hinterland beyond. It seemed to me to make good sense to establish a similar umbrella group to that in Toronto that would likewise bring together as many of the stakeholders in the region's economy as practicable. I never did find a snappy name to describe the body that we established and it remained as the Grampian Economic Development Advisory Council and shortened to an ugly 'GEDAC' – a bit like an Australian greeting.

GEDAC had a short life with a first preparatory meeting in April 1991, two further meetings and its last meeting in March less than a year later. The timing of the launch was not auspicious with the new Scottish Enterprise local agent, Grampian Enterprise (GEL), setting up its stall in the spring of 1990 and at the same time the local elections returning a Labour-led administration in the May of the same year. Both events produced leaders that wished to clearly establish their authority. The two gentlemen concerned were the Regional Council's Convener Bob Middleton and GEL's chairman, successful local businessman Sir Ian Wood of the John Wood Group. Middleton said at the time that he was anxious to build the role of the Regional Council convener as the undisputed senior local authority politician in the area and here the competition was the City of Aberdeen's Lord Provost, and I saw Ian Wood as anxious to see off any rivals to the newly established GEL. I will return to GEL later but inevitably the relationship between the Regional Council and GEL was going to be difficult and confrontational in many areas. However, in the case of GEDAC I saw unhelpful common cause in their respective approaches. Middleton did not wish to share the development of the region with any partnership body be it GEDAC or GEL, and he made that quite plain to me as well as through his unnecessary insistence that GEDAC should have no executive role and should be advisory only. At the same time GEL had been established in a political climate where the national government had been long hostile to the public sector and local government, and any initiative by Grampian Regional Council to establish an over-arching strategy development body would likely be resisted. I can think of no reason, bearing in mind the politics of the time, why GEL would wish success to the GEDAC initiative. If GEL had played an entirely passive role in the short life of GEDAC, the way would have been clear for Middleton to let GEDAC wither on the vine. This was exactly the outcome.

From the beginning I tried hard to get Councillor Len Ironside on side in his capacity as the chair of the Grampian Initiative and to convince him that GEDAC, in many ways, could become the new Grampian Initiative partnership, with a more credible and broader-based membership, and a role at the heart of the region's development. I advised him a combined Grampian Initiative and GEDAC presented the best opportunity the Regional Council would ever have to influence the future direction of the region. There had always been talk from Liberal councillors of spinning off the Grampian Initiative organisation from the Regional Council, if not financially (an unrealistic option) then presentationally and so invigorating the concept of partnership. I fear Middleton's bullying approach made it difficult for any of his own party to stand up to him, let alone the Liberal Democrats, his partners in the first administration that followed the May 1990 local elections. Even the

Liberals' brightest spark, Nicol Stephen, seemed powerless to attenuate the personal agenda of Convener Middleton.

I did get as far as appointing a 'Secretary General' to the new GEDAC that was not from the Regional Council. Aberdeen University's Principal offered Ron Taylor, who was at the time working for the university's technology marketing company. The job clearly needed much more time than the university could allow Ron but he did his best. With an unenthusiastic Middleton as the first and only GEDAC chair, even if we had had a full-time Secretary General, the task was doomed to failure. The full GEDAC Council was made up of some thirty members covering business, local authorities, academia, trade unions, the churches, and the voluntary sector. Such a rainbow membership provided plenty of opportunity for 'agenda management' and Middleton ensured that most of the items for debate were largely inconsequential or at least of a low priority. Perhaps it was not surprising, in the circumstances, that GEDAC members were not supplied with good and challenging papers, along with the necessary recommendations that just might lead to some executive action by the constituent organisations. On reflection GEDAC was dead before it was launched.

After what I have referred to as the 'emergent nation phase' that followed 1996 local authority organisation, the successor councils and GEL in 1998 saw the need for a similar broad partnership-based forum to GEDAC. They and others including the chamber of commerce established, in turn, the North East of Scotland Development & Economic Forum, and the North East Scotland Economic Forum with a mission to work "towards the development of a long term ambitious vision for the region's economy". I do not take much comfort from this decision as some six years were lost in the meantime. The experience of trying to establish GEDAC is a major reason for my pessimism as to whether north-east Scotland will ever overcome its crippling tribal parochialism.

I refer often to Grampian Enterprise Limited (later to be rebadged as SEG – Scottish Enterprise Grampian) not for reasons that the organisation was, or indeed has been since, central or significant in securing any quantum leap in the region's fortunes, but more that it contributed to so many of the obstacles to co-operation. I had hoped in the early stages that 'GEL' would have provided us with an element so missing in Grampian, that is leadership. The then Tory government set up Scottish Enterprise and its constituent local enterprise companies, of which GEL was but one, with an inbuilt private sector majority on their governing boards. I had hoped this might bring forward the quality of leadership that the region so desperately lacked. It did not, and that remains the case today. Another of my colleagues' parlour games was to name one indisputable Grampian leader or potential leader, from either the public or private sectors. During my years in the north-east of Scotland we have not produced a political leader that would measure up to the likes of London's Ken Livingstone, Glasgow's Pat Lally or Dr Michael Kelly, or going back a few years, even Newcastle's first city manager, T. Dan Smith. In the business world we have a number of individuals who have been successful in their chosen career, and a number of these have built impressive industrial empires from a Grampian base. But take them away from their firms and place them in a community context, then none have emerged as true community leaders with the ability to inspire, calm and settle turf wars and, incidentally, few who have put much back into their community.

Most senior business people linked with GEL seem to run out of steam very quickly, become the prisoners of their quasi civil servant staff, and similarly succumb to the numbers game that is worked to justify how successful GEL has been in achieving targets that seem irrelevant to the longer term challenges faced by the region. Ten years on from the 'Together to the Future' strategy the *Press and Journal* (6/5/1999, Offshore Journal supplement) quotes the then Chief Executive of GEL, former paper manufacturing executive Ed Gillespie, as saying "To have a vibrant, successful renaissance economy you need visionary leadership... and that's something we need to talk about in the North-east..." For me a sad sense of déjà vu. In the same newspaper (6/9/1995) I wrote of the "need for more charismatic leaders in both public and private sectors that can set examples, offer leadership and encourage by example rather than lecture".

From day one our relationship with the enterprise body was uneasy. As far as many of the Council's politicians were concerned GEL was imposed by the Thatcher government, which even the Regional Council's Tories found uncomfortable at best, and at worst, embarrassing. In many respects the new GEL was very little different from the local Aberdeen office of the old Scottish Development Authority, in so far as many of the staff were the same. However there was one important difference and that was the new Scottish Enterprise had been set up with local management boards, and GEL or Grampian Enterprise Limited was our local board. These local boards were self-appointed in so far as the government blessed what they saw as the most acceptable group 'bidding' (not in any financial sense) to run the new local incarnation of Scottish Enterprise. Although there was a rival group bidding for the role it stood no chance against the

Ian Wood-led group of businessmen. Wood was thought to have had the ear of the then Conservative government and, in the view of me and my colleagues at the time, there was no serious contest. The constitution of the new local enterprise companies was set by the government at a time of considerable antagonism to local authorities, and so public sector places were restricted to three out of the maximum allowed of twelve directors. Some enterprise companies (including GEL) got around this limit by co-opting 'advisers', and these co-opted individuals were, for all intents and purposes, full board members. Our local enterprise company was probably less local authority friendly than the average. These local management boards were not in any way democratically appointed but it was revealed some years later by Sir Ian Wood (in an after dinner speech on 24th August, 2005 at Aberdeen's Marcliffe Hotel, the occasion being the retirement of the Principal of the Robert Gordon University) that he was approached by Councillor Nicol Stephen to lead an initiative to establish a Grampian based local enterprise company. Nicol was to become one of the founder members of Sir Ian's subsequent and successful bid to lead a new enterprise body. The first GEL board was unelected and unrepresentative, yet it was alocated a budget of some £24 million of tax payers' money to disburse. Although this was only some five per cent of the Regional Council spend it was the lack of democratic accountability that irritated our elected councillors.

Much of what was unattractive in GEL's constitution we could have lived with, if the new team had gone out of its way to establish trust and a good working relationship. The first GEL chief executive inherited a staff from the old SDA Aberdeen office who were often, and continued under the new regime to be dismissive of the public sector operation as it impinged on GEL's operations, namely in the areas of training and economic development. There appeared to be no attempt to rein in some of the worst excesses of the staff, and at the working level our trust in GEL intentions and their staff remained at the low level it was with the predecessor SDA office.

The turf war continued until the winding up of the Regional Council in 1996, in spite of my many attempts to get alongside senior GEL staff and their chief executive. I initiated regular breakfast meetings with Derek Marnoch, the chamber of commerce's then chief executive, and one or two others and at an early stage asked GEL's then chief executive, Hance Fullerton, to join us. My idea was to give advance warnings of our respective plans and thoughts and in that way to ensure there were no surprises and so build an atmosphere of trust.

The local enterprise companies were required by the central Scottish Enterprise operation in Glasgow to manage their staff by liberal use of incentives and by setting targets and bonus trigger points. Therefore the motivation of my staff and those of GEL was quite different. The result was a more personally competitive culture at GEL and one in which ownership of a project was important in achieving their bonus-related targets. This led, perhaps understandably, to tension between respective staff in joint venture projects. Such collaborative projects were common because although GEL had a large disposable budget, it was rarely large enough to carry through any significant project without some local authority input. One might have thought this would have led to a situation where GEL would have needed to court and seduce local authorities to the table and keep them sweet.

A bit like the breed of beggars in London that ask for your support but curse you at the same time, GEL would seek your support and just when you thought relationships were going well they would stick in a pin or even the knife. A petty irritation was GEL's predilection for self-advertisement. As soon as some project was started, up went a hoarding or an advertisement was placed in the press proclaiming another first for GEL. Often there would be an 'oversight' and no mention of the partner contribution. I was far from being alone in my frustration in dealing with Scottish Enterprise and its satellite organisations. *Scotland on Sunday* (2/11/03) quotes Sun Microsystems' chief, Hugh Aitken, on resigning from Scottish Enterprise's manufacturing steering group in December 2002 as saying "I can't handle any more of these sessions. My head screams for a sense of urgency, a sense of change, a sense of innovation, a sense of what is best for Scotland and not how things fit into personal agendas". As TV lawyer Perry Mason would have said, "I rest my case".

In any civil war there are faults on both sides and it becomes difficult to spot the blameless. On one occasion the enterprise quango seemed convinced that it was my bloody-mindedness behind the Regional Council's antagonism and eventual withdrawal from a scheme to centralise local provision of information to business. I was accused of having my 'own agenda'. Whilst it was true I was always against the council's involvement in this collaboration, as long as my political masters thought it was the right course to collaborate in provision of these services, then I would carry out the council's wishes to the best of my endeavours. However when the council's political colour changed then I advised the new administration, as I had similarly done the outgoing, that we and the taxpayer were not getting value for money in supporting a joint provision of information services to business. My new set of political masters accepted my advice and we withdrew from this particular collaboration. I felt the pressure on GEL to 'rationalise' business advisory services was emanating from the centre at Scottish Enterprise and had little local relevance. I had no personal agenda other than to provide my bosses with the best possible advice. Scottish Enterprise eventually got their way although I suspect the local authority support for various business 'gateway' services is more lip service than a reality.

It would be false modesty to say that I did not know more than any of my public sector colleagues in Grampian about the organisation and provision of services to exporters. This experience was gained over many years in DTI and especially during my last post as Director/Exports for the south east of England. This experience was recognised by the then Scottish Office Industry Department, and resulted in my membership from 1992 to 1995 of the Scottish Exports Forum which was chaired by the current Industry Minister. Because of my background I was able to make a major contribution to streamlining local delivery of exports services in Scotland. I had already established in Grampian the concept of a 'local export partnership' that more closely linked the export documentation services provided by the chamber of commerce with those of the Regional Council and GEL. This approach was later adopted by Scottish Enterprise as the model for all locally provided export services. I had done this a number of years earlier in Essex, Kent and Norfolk.

My assessment of the chamber of commerce in Aberdeen was similar to that of most chambers in England, and that was the service it provided was lacklustre. To improve the chamber's service to exporters I arranged for the Regional Council to provide a subsidy of £10,000 per year towards the appointment of an export development executive. I am not sure the taxpayer got value for money. Co-operation with the Aberdeen chamber of commerce over the years was decidedly one way. That is the Regional Council helped the chamber, but the chamber rarely helped the Regional Council. There were occasions when I really needed the chamber's support for one of my own initiatives. One such occasion was the proposal to co-locate my department with the chamber of commerce and so provide a one-stop shop for the business community, but the chamber support was sparingly given. The chamber was very good at extracting the maximum from the public purse and was able to play one agency off against the other to extract the best deal. The shared office saga, where the chamber ended up getting into bed with GEL, was a good case in point. One might say 'fair enough' but it made personal relations difficult and it did sour my relations with the chamber's then chief executive. Events, as so often is the case, travelled the full circle and by 2003, the chamber saw fit to leave the GEL/Scottish Enterprise Grampian nest and return to its own set of offices and reassert a separate identity and role in provision of advisory services to business.

GEL's ambition was always to pull off a spectacular coup though, in my view, one that would put GEL, rather than Grampian, on the map. I suppose the parallel was the 'Factor 'X' in my 'Together to the Future' strategy. They tried a number of times but never did manage to get any of their large projects off the ground. Amongst their attempts was the project to establish a £15million 'oil experience centre' which would involve mooring an oil drilling rig in Aberdeen – the harbour is very accessible to the city centre. The objective was to create a flagship visitor attraction that would feature aspects of the oil industry and life offshore in a way as to both entertain and educate a predominately family based audience. The initiative was started in the days of Scottish Development Agency's short-lived rival to the Grampian Initiative, 'Aberdeen Beyond 2000' and continued under GEL. Initially the oil producers, led by Ian Henderson, Shell Expro operations director, pledged £2million towards the cost of the proposed oil experience centre and the Regional Council made pledges of a similar order of magnitude. It was an exciting idea and would have used the latest technology and included the use of a IMAX cinema, but it never happened.

The death of the oil experience centre was a slow and lingering one, and I never did see a death certificate as such. I am not sure why the idea foundered as the oil industry was to continue to prosper many years after the inception of the idea in the late eighties. Unfortunately the project lost Shell's Ian Henderson through retirement, and one of the most public-spirited of local oil bosses, although the field was not a crowded one when measured in terms of corporate generosity. There were many who had doubts as to the financial viability of such a project, even though the initial capital costs were to be written off. Few of my colleagues in the council seemed enthusiastic. To carry such a partnership project to successful completion needed community leadership and this was absent then, and remains a rare commodity today. Interestingly Houston had a similar idea and this also foundered.

The other large GEL project, and one where I was also involved, was the plan to roof over, or more accurately 'deck' over, a substantial part of a valley below Union Terrace, which links Aberdeen's shopping thoroughfare, Union Street, with Rosemount Viaduct. The proposed decking would have covered a main road, the rail link to the north and some formal gardens. The idea that the decked area would create a central piazza and focus to the city seems rather bizarre. A climate and location less suited to outdoor and pavement cafés than Aberdeen is difficult to imagine, but that was at the heart of the project, as were the thousands of square feet of new retail and office space to be created.

The politics of the supporters of the project were interesting. GEL were the lead agency and they picked up all the substantial costs of architects and property consultants. The Regional Council's convener, Bob Middleton was totally sold on the idea, but he lacked credibility and more than likely discouraged rather than rallied support. I was not aware he had much political support from his fellow councillors, but at the same time I was never able to put my finger on where the support came from amongst the GEL board members. There was the usual joint working party which, somewhat unexpectedly, was chaired by our chief executive, Alan Campbell, and I acted as unofficial secretary to, in so far as I took the minutes of the many meetings. From intelligence gathered in this role I was under no illusions as to the game play. It was to go along with an overt 'firm commitment' from the Regional Council, but at the same time confident in our private prediction that the project would die without any need for assassination by the Regional Council. Quite apart from any other consideration we were aware the Regional Council would long be gone by the time this project got off the ground. I suspect that a large part of the reason for failure was the absence of a credible champion. In my view the vision of a large city centre piazza development was flawed from the start. There was some concern about the ability of the market to take up the large amount of office space generated, apart from climate considerations. I must admit to many examples of cities with harsher climates than Aberdeen that have large piazzas or public squares, but the culture and history of the countries concerned is so different as to make such comparisons unhelpful. Red Square in Moscow and Tiananmen Square in Beijing come to mind. However, unlike Aberdeen both have warm summers!

It would be wrong to give the impression that all partnership collaborations with GEL were unsuccessful. Many were successful in outcome although the process was often tiresome. Collaboration with other partners was less fraught and some were a joy in that not only was the outcome successful but the experience was pleasurable. One such collaborative venture was the reinstatement of Duff House in Banff. This grand house was designed by William Adam and built between 1735 and

1740 as the seat of the Earls of Fife. However the Earl never did live in the house as he fell out with his architect over costs and fees and it was said that he could not even bear to look at it, closing the blinds of his carriage as he was driven past the site. The history of the house since has been a chequered one as a hotel, sanatorium and even housing for prisoners of war. The building eventually found itself in the hands of Historic Scotland on a care and maintenance basis, and latterly some restoration work had been initiated.

Through one of the coincidences of life I happened to know Graeme Munro who had not long been appointed as the Director of Historic Scotland. Graeme was a friend since their St Andrew's university days of Roy Cunningham, in turn my friend met shortly after we both joined the Civil Service in 1967. There had been some political attempts by both Regional and Banff and Buchan councils to find a use for Duff House, but attempts got bogged down in local politics and rivalries and no significant progress was made. I learned of the Duff House saga about a year after arriving in Grampian. I contacted Graeme in June 1990 and arranged that on one of his visits to Duff House he stay overnight with us as we are only 25 miles from Banff. I remember his visit well as it coincided with an impromptu celebration of my fiftieth birthday with Greg Rae and his wife Sandra. It was one of those beautiful Grampian summer evenings but also a rare warm and balmy one, and we were celebrating in the garden. By the time Graeme had arrived a fair amount of fizzy wine had flowed and all were in a good mood. There are a few social occasions that remain distinct in the memory many years after and often these are not the big 'set' events but occasions that are memorable because they were just happy. That July summer evening with just the five of us was one such happy occasion that I can recapture as clearly as yesterday. Following that meeting Graeme arranged that I join him and Timothy Clifford, the flamboyant and likeable then Director of the National Galleries for Scotland, to take forward a project that would complete the restoration of Duff House and turn it into a country gallery outpost of the National Gallery in Edinburgh. We managed to set up a team that successfully minimised the day-to-day interference of both my own politicians at the Region as well as their counterparts in Banff and Buchan Council.

It all worked so well, and Prince Charles opened the exquisitely renovated Duff House and gallery on 28 June 1995. It was a beautiful day and guests were treated to some rather fine food and refreshments on the lawns that surround the house while waiting for the helicopter bringing

Charles to the front of the house. I am reminded here of Leni Riefenstahl's Nazi propaganda masterpiece, 'The Triumph of the Will'. It was only the second time I had met him, and the previous time at a garden party just the day before at Falkland Palace. In spite of often negative publicity he does his job well and I felt at ease in the brief chat I had with him in the VIP line-up. Fiona and I joined a small party following the royal guest around the house. Timothy Clifford had not only done a splendid job with the paintings and their hanging, as one would expect, but had used all his ingenuity and contacts to provide sufficient furniture to turn what might have been a gallery setting into a country house setting. He had secured some of the original furnishings and also a magnificent chandelier he had spotted in an antique shop in a nearby small coastal community. The chandelier was in pieces and in poor shape but it was a measure of Timothy to spot what others would miss and he was some years later to use this skill to discover an old master in America.

Although Graeme and Timothy were chalk and cheese in terms of character, they were both a delight to work with. I used to look forward to our Duff House progress review meetings, and I cannot say that for too many meetings during my time working for local government. Graeme was the archetypal civil servant and I say this in the most respectful sense. There were times when his diplomatic skills were tested when I, and certainly Timothy, were on the verge of losing our cool when dealing with some of the obstacles placed in our way by the Banff and Buchan District Council as we struggled through the final stages to get the gallery up and running, and as the public opening date neared. The problem was often one of style; Timothy Clifford had it and some representatives from Banff and Buchan plainly did not. Also, problems arose because later the local authorities objected to meeting their share of the running costs, which excluded the capital costs of the upkeep of the building itself which continued to be met by Historic Scotland. There was an unrealistic local authority expectation that such a facility should attract sufficient visitors and income to cover costs. For almost every publicly financed visitor attraction that was established in the region there was to be a running costs deficit. If such projects were to be profitable it is unlikely that the public sector would need to be involved in the first place. We were fortunate indeed to capture this world-class collection of paintings and, in essence, an extension of the National Gallery of Scotland in Grampian. I see the local authority support as a long term investment that will bring returns in not only tourism but also in the enrichment that such a facility brings to the life of Grampian's citizens. I managed to ensure the Regional

Council played its part in the financial package and I achieved this with only the odd whimper from politicians.

In my experience most of the public sector partnership ventures the Regional Council entered into commenced from a position of weakness because we had neither the resources nor the political confidence to proceed alone. Often we were bullied into co-operation out of fear of not appearing *communautaire,* where some senior council leaders feared being criticised, ostracised and left out of the fold by the big business that dominated the local quango boards. We feared also if we were 'unco-operative' that government and Scottish Office representation of Grampian's interests in Brussels may be less than helpful in such areas as fishing quotas and EU designated special support zones. Being within an area designated by the EU as 'remote' or in some way 'disadvantaged' opened the gates to significant new monies, and having the government and its agencies on your side to achieve a favourable designation was important. At the same time Grampian felt it was being unfairly further penalised for its perceived wealth by Scottish Enterprise in Glasgow, and its sister body 'Locate in Scotland', in terms of critical inward investment direction to Grampian. Finally many of our councillors and, perversely, more so Labour politicians, were in awe of big business and particularly of successful and powerful local individuals. It was a shared joke amongst officials that one well-known businessman had a technique of invading one's personal space and gently grabbing an elbow to indicate he wanted your support. This businessman did not like being thwarted by mere local councillors. I had been on the receiving end of this elbow steer.

I wonder if the council had 'walked tall' in dealings with GEL and various other 'partners' we would have been any worse off? I suspect not, but life would have certainly been a lot less stressful and the turf wars shorter and more quickly resolved.

Chapter 21

Grampian Going Places

From my first day at Grampian Regional Council in late 1988 I was aware of proposals for another reorganisation of Scotland's local authorities, and only some thirteen years after the Wheatley Report which created the two tier delivery system I was to become part of for the next seven years. However I was not aware of this small cloud when I applied for the Grampian job, and anyway I do not think it would have changed my mind as in 1988 it all seemed a long way off and the outcome uncertain. For the first three or so years in Aberdeen the fact that the Regional Council's life was limited rarely crossed my mind as I was far too absorbed with the task in hand. The full implications of change only came into focus for me on the publication of the consultative document in October 1992 and then the publication of the 'Local Government etc. (Scotland) Act 1994' which decreed from 1 April 1996 the two tier set up of regional and district councils would be replaced by single tier authorities.

The Conservative government's public justification for this upheaval, after a relatively short period since the Wheatley changes, was that a single tier system would create greater efficiency in the delivery of services and therefore a saving of money. The government claimed the changes would remove a lot of wasteful overlap in the provision of services to the community and make the system more democratic and accountable. The cynical amongst us saw the changes as yet another Tory attack on local government where its antagonism had been a distinct signature of the Thatcher years. It was also a widely held view that the boundaries of the new authorities were being manipulated to increase the number of authorities under Conservative control, and especially in the west of Scotland. There were even parallels to that government's paranoid attitude to the Greater London Council in England and now a Tory wish to see the end of the large and powerful Labour-led Strathclyde Regional Council, with Glasgow at its heart. In fact Strathclyde was never a 'lefty' council and certainly generated no such thorns in the Tory side as the Greater London Council had in London. If there was such a rogue council in Scotland then Edinburgh on the other side of the country better fitted the bill. In truth Strathclyde was a remarkably successful council, delivering a more than acceptable level of service to over a third of Scotland's population throughout a vast and diverse area that included a number of the inner western isles such as Islay and Jura, the remotest regions of Argyll as well as Scotland's largest conurbation.

The presence of Glasgow as the 'junior' partner in Strathclyde Regional Council inevitably lead to tensions, as indeed was the case and similar tensions between Aberdeen and Grampian Regional Council. It was a rich comment to swallow when Strathclyde councillors would remind fractious Glasgow district council members that they were from but one of nineteen districts within the region. That same sort of pinpricking went on in Grampian and many scores nourished over 21 years were settled on the demise of Grampian Regional Council in 1996. Such irritations were not one-sided. A constant source of resentment at regional headquarters in both these cities was the fact that after the 1975 reorganisation the Lord Lieutenancy remained with the respective city Lord Provosts, notwithstanding the regional council 'Conveners' saw themselves as the senior partners. This rankled Bob Middleton, Grampian's convener between 1990 and 1994, and his oft expressed intent was to 'build the role of the regional council convener'. Of course he meant build his own personal profile. Having to stand in line behind the City of Aberdeen's Lord Provost during visits of royalty was bad enough but that experience also led to Middleton's silly squabbles over his status relative to our chief constable. In the process Middleton would try and see how far he could press the delicate and sensitive boundaries between regional council and Scottish Office control of police chiefs. Happily these games were never joined by the chief constable himself, thus better allowing the rest of us to relax and enjoy this spectator sport at Council meetings.

I never understood why councillors in Grampian allowed the silly rivalries between district and region to irritate them as the size, income, headquarters, staff quality (the region paid senior staff more reflecting their supposedly greater responsibilities) comfortably surpassed that of any of the five district councils (including Aberdeen) that made up the second tier authorities. I could understand some justifiable irritation from the district councils but not the other way around. Many, normally quite reasonable, regional councillors would often become irrational and childlike if one of their officials were seen even talking to a district councillor, and to quote one at committee was a sure recipe for a dressing down. Dealings with Aberdeen city councillors were particularly suspect.

I remember being quizzed after I was seen having a long discussion at an evening reception at Aberdeen's 'Town House' headquarters with Lord Provost Robert Robertson. At the time Robertson was being shunned by his own Labour members and I felt rather sorry for him standing alone at his own reception with no one to talk to. However I got on quite well with him and would have spoken to him in any normal course of events. Although nothing to do with Robertson's internal problems at the time, those most suspicious of my 'liaison' were regional councillors of the same broad political church as the Lord Provost.

The divisions between regional and district councillors lived on long after reorganisation in 1996, just as did the divisions between county, city and the new regional council after the 1975 reorganisation. Few councillors from Grampian Region did well on transfer to the the new Aberdeen or Aberdeenshire Councils. For example it was expected that Bob Middleton, or perhaps more correctly he expected, to move seamlessly across to Aberdeen and become Lord Provost. It was not to be, although after a period of 'good behaviour' he was allowed to become chair of the finance committee and from reports did rather well in this. The only regional councillor to do really well on crossover was Len Ironside, the former Grampian Initiative chairman. He went on to become the Leader of Aberdeen council, although not Lord Provost. It could be argued, as he did, that Leader was the more powerful position.

The lot of senior regional officials on reorganisation also had a tendency to mirror that of elected members but to a lesser extent. There were one or two officials that were unfairly penalised by the new authorities because their profile had been high in pursuing the former region's policies, and particularly in the closing years. If I can legitimately accuse the regional council in Grampian of sometimes being parochial and small-minded then the new district councils that were to replace it were even more so. One senior official of Grampian Regional Council was to suffer from a tendency of the new councillors to recruit senior officials that more closely reflected their own social background. For some, with the right accent and roots in the north-east, this was to work in their favour.

Whereas senior staff could compete for positions advertised anywhere in Scotland, for the large majority of rank and file staff it was a matter of being allocated to one of the successor councils within the area of the outgoing regional council, and in Grampian that meant allocation to either the new Aberdeen, Aberdeenshire or Morayshire councils. Staff were given a chance to indicate a preference and where possible this was accommodated. In Grampian the carve up of staff was left to individual heads of service. I did my best to meet the wishes of my Economic Development & Planning staff but at the same time ensure a fair distribution of both skills and talent to the successor councils. One problem was that few staff wished to join the Morayshire authority, based in the small town of Elgin. The main reason for Moray's unpopularity was the need to relocate (Elgin is over 60 miles from Aberdeen) and all the dislocation that would mean for staff and their families. At the same time, it has to be said, the people of Moray had a poor reputation, in my department anyway, as being unwelcoming to strangers and even more inward looking than other rural areas of the Grampian region. There was an appeal board of regional councillors but at the end of the day there was still some rough justice meted out.

There was already employment legislation enacted ensuring the transfer of certain undertakings when a firm or organisation is taken over or merges with another. This protected, to some extent, conditions of service and salary on transfer to the new employer. Some staff were transferred but with no clear post to go to and under the legislation their salary level was protected. All three new councils in Grampian ended up wary of taking on such staff whereas most councils started out concerned that they might not get their fair share of staff. New councils had to take more or less whoever was allocated to them by the likes of me, and that included the dross as well as the odd star. I had some half-hearted lobbying by the new councils but this was considered somewhat improper and was ignored. Such attempts were more to head off allocation of staff they did not want than vice versa. In the initial transfer none of my staff was made redundant as such, or left without a job in a no man's land. I suppose it all worked out better than I imagined it would when we started the process, and very few of my own staff seemed unhappy at the end of the day.

At senior levels all posts in the thirty-two new councils across Scotland were up for grabs. So there was a mighty and sometimes unattractive scramble for the best appointments. Certain rules were imposed by a joint staff commission set up by the government, although somewhat late in the day in my view. There was competition between new councils to get the best people as well as competition to get the best positions in these councils by individuals. There was an element of a race and councils that left recruitment interviews late tended to get the leftovers. There were some surprises as a result. There were the occasions where the 'chancer', that is the person who applied for a job well above his or her station or realistic expectation on the off-chance they would secure an interview in the scramble for staff, succeeded. I saw examples of this including one deputy director ending-up as chief executive of one of the new authorities. However there was some attrition in the early days of the new councils and this particular individual was one of the losers. I was aware of a number of similar examples of staff surprising themselves with their success in this near lottery. Staff would also apply for a number of positions at the same time. Uncomfortable decisions would then have to be made when offered a job, whilst at the same time awaiting interviews for other positions that were even more desirable. Most staff got positions that seemed reasonable and reflected their capabilities, but there were casualties.

All this was a dilemma for me. The normal retiring age in local authorities was 65 and so at the time I had over nine years of service left after the winding up of the regional council. I would have served just over seven years in local government and one side of me said that was enough. If the Foreign Office has certain 'hardship' posts which count as double time, or whatever, in terms of years of earned pension rights, then I saw my years at Grampian as a hardship post, and I had had enough. Perhaps inadvisably and against my better judgement I applied for the chief executive vacancy in Moray, the smallest of the three new authorities in Grampian. There were already rumours that Aberdeen had their man marked out and that turned out to be correct. Aberdeenshire was less certain but it was unlikely I would get a look in there with my background. Incidentally, both these chief executive posts went to former Grampian Region officials. I did not get far with Moray. My application was ruled out of court because I had indicated that I would not be willing to move home to the Elgin area. The rejection of my application caused me little concern then and certainly not in retrospect.

With the Morayshire application out of the way I decided that local government had had enough of me and I of it. Immediately I sought a deal with my political masters that in return for a commitment to stay to the last day of the regional council I would be given an early retirement package. This was agreed with little problem and the deal was that I should retire with a pension that would include maximum 'added years'. This meant I would receive a pension on retirement commensurate with a retirement age of sixty-five, which was a very generous deal and made up the pension shortfall I was heading for, reflecting I did not start salaried employment until after my twenty-seventh birthday.

At the same time and contrary to my understanding of the implications of the deal I had no additional burdens during the wind-down of the region. During the last year the new councils were running in parallel to the old two-tier arrangements, in so far as there were elected councillors and senior management teams busy considering budgets and policy, but short of providing day-to-day services to the public. The region continued to be responsible for services up to the very last day of its existence. When a senior post became vacant as staff were hired by the new authorities, GRC tended to replace directors from the ranks of existing staff. This meant that the work I rather expected as one who had volunteered to help turn out the lights did not materialise. I had imagined that I would be asked to take on additional supervisory work for other departments. I think I was probably the only person who thought this would happen. Again it did not unduly worry me as I had a council committee blessed deal, along with the deputy chief executive who had a similar deal.

Even with just my own department to deal with life was busy enough during the last year of the council. I gave little thought to what I was going to do with my time after GRC, at least not until the beginning of 1996 and the four months leading to the demise of the council. One pointer to a new challenge awaiting around the corner was an invitation in December 1994 to join the board of governors of the Robert Gordon University. This came as a surprise and I guess was prompted by the then Principal, Dr David Kennedy. I did not know David all that well then and he was but one of many of the local 'movers and shakers' that I met regularly on the reception and 'cocktail' circuit (yes, there is a cocktail society in Aberdeen) and would often spend time chatting to him and his wife Audrey. I was already an admirer of what he had done for the university, and not least in fighting the former Robert Gordon Institute of Technology's corner in achieving university status, and in spite of some quite unpleasant locally inspired lobbying against. I was delighted to be joining him and the rest of the governors in at an exciting time for the still new university. I had a friend from student days who had been a member of the university court at UMIST in Manchester. I was always slightly envious of his appointment but never expected to to be asked to join an equivalent body, and in a slightly childish way I felt at last more his equal.

What I was even more unprepared for was an approach towards the end of 1996 to be the next Chairman of Governors. I could not have been more thrilled and honoured.

The lead-up year to April 1996 and the period of the parallel new councils rarely provided opportunities for individuals to show the best side of their character, and altruism and charity were uncommon assets amongst not only colleagues, but also the politicians. I have always worried about 'ambition' as an attribute and have seen it as, at best, a double-edged sword. This was a period where I could afford to enjoy my oft self-imposed role as the outsider looking in, as I had nothing to lose or gain. At the same time as officials were jockeying for position so were councillors, and once they had secured election to the new authorities many used their often dual membership of both the old and new authorities to their own ends.

One of the more bizarre episodes was the decision by the regional council's Liberal/SNP administration to sell off much of the large property empire that the council had assiduously built up over the previous twenty years. It was an ironic decision for me since one of my earliest run-ins with the then chief executive, Douglas Macnaughton, was over my challenging whether it was sensible to continue building the council's empire of industrial and commercial property. The point was not so much that we had a valuable property portfolio, thanks largely to a very astute Walter Murray, for many years the region's Director of Estates, but rather the assembly of the estate had no clear economic strategy. Councillors liked to feel they were significant commercial landlords and this no doubt imbued a sense of power. I would not deny it is sensible for any council to have a modest land-bank and this must be purchased at the opportune moment, which may be some years before it is needed for council purposes. However our council also had purchased large numbers of buildings, such as factory premises and often leased these back to the firm they were purchased from. This was a means of providing economic development assistance to growing firms, or often ailing firms, and getting around government controls on local authority capital expenditure. Such deals were considered as 'neutral' since they returned an income and did not use up the capital expenditure allowances. My argument was that much of the portfolio was unnecessary as the need could be met by the commercial sector and we should only intervene in the commercial market as the source of last resort. Macnaughton as chief executive and many of my colleagues, as well as councillors, enjoyed the position of banker and the influence and power wielded in the process, and when I challenged the policy and rationale of the property empire, all hell broke out. The issue continued to be a thorn in my side as the decision to engineer a 'purchase and lease-back' deal was supposed to be on the advice of my economic development officials but I found myself often undermined by a direct appeal to councillors by the property department. It was rare to talk the politicians out of the prospect of a purchase and lease-back deal, even if the deal reeked of lame duck and throwing good money after bad. The council made a speciality of lost causes in the textile industry. To be fair this became much more of a problem with Walter Murray's successor, who was directed to sell off this portfolio in the final days of the council.

In the final months of the council there was an atmosphere of a closing-down sale at some cut-price furniture store. The property portfolio was very successfully sold off and agreement reached on a formula to divide the spoils between the successor councils. Labour politicians due to transfer to the new Aberdeen city council were not entirely happy with the property sale since a lot of the estate was to be found within the city boundary and they were anxious to retain as much as possible for their new council.

One property snatch was more appropriate to an Ealing Studios comedy. The SNP group were anxious to retrieve for Morayshire a number of items they saw as looted from Moray during the time of the Labour led administration. These included some quite decent works of art and antiques that had been 'gathered in' by the Labour administration to adorn the convener's offices and private dining room. There were tales of a last minute and none too secret dash north to Moray with all the treasures in an SNP councillor's car and panic calls to the police to stop the 'looters'. There was certainly an element of truth in this almost Sexton Blake farce in that most of the articles did find their way home from whence they came.

My own mementoes of my time at GRC were my desk nameplate and the department's signboard from the visitor reception area. One last gift from the region was a retirement course that the interim chief executive had negotiated for us. This was aimed at all those who were taking early retirement. More retirement packages were offered in the closing weeks when the successor councils were beginning to count the cost of staff numbers and also were becoming more resistant to some staff allocations from the region. The snag with the course, which was contracted to an outside provider, was that it was aimed at all levels from the the clerical level to the likes of myself. However I found very little that was irrelevant, once I had got over my bout of intellectual snobbery. The only area where the gap was just too wide was advice on investment. The lectures from social workers, the voluntary sector and health advice were all good value, and although a lot was common sense, it does no harm to be reminded of the need, for example, to keep healthy and exercise. One of the best inputs was by a tax expert on setting up your own business and guidance on how beneficial running a business, even an unprofitable one, can be to your personal tax liability.

The advice on setting up one's own business encouraged me to think more about what I was going to do with so much time, or perhaps more importantly what Fiona was going to do with me if I had little to occupy my time at home. On retirement one tends to forget that partners have come to enjoy their peace and freedom with the other half safely away from the house for some twelve hours each day. For most of our married years Fiona did have her own job and latterly in Surrey a demanding one, but it was local to home and there was time to herself at the end the day. In Grampian she worked only part-time and I think my impending retirement was of concern, and she more than me wondered how we would get along together in the same place all day and every day.

I have always been conscious that as an administrator in public service I had a skill that was not very marketable in the 'outside' world. This was brought home to me when I started looking for a way out of the Civil Service. I realised that I could not include marketing and sales, legal expertise, accountancy, production systems or any of the other skills that advertisements list for jobs in the business world. The skills assembled over a Civil Service career as an administrator are real but they are rarely recognised outside the public sector. At the very top level Civil Servants do well on retirement, but many are recruited for their network of political and government contacts which are invaluable on the boards of large companies that will have to deal with government in one form or another. The fact that my alma mater, Glasgow University, has twice had ex-Scottish Office permanent secretaries as Principal in recent years in a way underline's my analysis of our skills. It was C. P. Snow's novel 'Corridors of Power' that drew strong parallels between life in an Oxbridge college and the Whitehall of the time. Whitehall has changed and Glasgow is no Oxford college, but there are 'good skills matches' as the personnel people would say.

I did as I was advised on the retirement course and drew up a 'SWOT' list, that is a list of my Strengths and Weaknesses, and foreseeable Threats and Opportunities. I was not much more optimistic at the end of this exercise but had decided my strengths were an innovative mind and an ability to deal with a large amount of confusing information, make sense out of chaos and present this in an attractive and user friendly form. Not surprisingly these are the essential skills of the good Civil Servant, although I am not sure about the relevance of the innovative mind.

I arranged also to meet an employment consultant or 'head hunter' based near Glasgow. This was an unsettling experience and did little for my confidence. She had my c.v. to hand and after about half an hour of discussion she concluded that I had little to offer "except a good brain" although did concede I had a good record of being innovative. In other words there was no way was I going to get onto her list of potential board appointments. Also I placed my name with a number of recruitment registers, including the Civil Service pool of names for 'quango' appointments. The retirement course prompted me to be more proactive and I decided to set up my own consultancy company, 'pi Solutions'. The Greek 'pi' was inspired by nothing more than a colleague from my research lab days in Glasgow who had the initials 'P.I.' and labelled all his lab glassware with a Greek 'pi'. I thought use of 'pi' would be memorable, prompt questions and provide a strong logo. There are lots of firms called 'alpha or delta something' or 'omega the other' and do use the Greek letters in their logo, but few use 'pi'. I tested the name on a successful local businessman and he was both mystified and irritated by the name. However, and likely unwisely, I stuck with it . Many years later I came across an advertisement for a recruitment agency in Aberdeen using the Greek letter 'pi' in the company title.

I drafted some copy as follows:

> "Over the years of close working with businesses it has been my experience that a firm's executive team often needs an unobtrusive helping hand, a sympathetic ear, an ideas person on tap (but not on top) and executive support available when it is most needed. A sort of just-in-time concept for management perhaps?
>
> To meet that need **pi solutions** has been set up to provide a personal, confidential and client directed executive support service, either on a retainer basis or confined to a specific project or assignment to address the client's particular needs.
>
> The service is aimed at those businesses and institutions that have necessarily slimmed down or maintained their executive team to levels that certainly meet day to day requirements, but at the same time may fall short in times of executive illness, crisis or duty absence. Many organisations are also finding that in meeting pressure to compete and to contain costs their hard pressed executives have less time to plan, to take the long view, to adequately consult and test their ideas, let alone keep up with the relevant legislation.
>
> Being in business at senior levels, be this in the private or public sector is, frankly, lonely. Such executives often would welcome an unbiased, experienced and confidential 'sounding

> board' for their ideas, rather than the formality of resorting to the more conventional consultancy firm or even public sector advisory agency. More useful would be access to somebody who has an uncluttered mind, can give a frank view and comes without all the baggage of being an employee. Particularly important is to have access to counsel when you are free, be that at the workplace, elsewhere or via that late night phone call. Perhaps the supreme attribute of such a service is that there is somebody to listen.
>
> **pi solutions** can provide all that. As Principal of **pi solutions** I have a very broad range of experience gained over 30 years of professional life with a track record of achievement and innovation in business related development."

I selected six local firms and ones that I judged had reached that size where the original founder was struggling to keep abreast of a company that is on the cusp of becoming a national, or even an international company rather than merely a successful family firm. I selected firms that I knew well and that knew me, and in all instances I was on first name terms with the managing director or the chairman. They were all household names and most would have been known well beyond our borders. I received only two replies.

To this day I cannot forgive the bad manners of those who did not even bother to lift a telephone to say nothing more than 'Thanks but no thanks'. The text books would have advised that I should have followed up my written approach with a phone call, but at the time I was so fed up with the initial response that my decision was a 'sod it', and I moved on. For the record the two individuals that had the courtesy to reply, and in more than civilised terms, were Gordon Baxter of the famous Fochabers based soup manufactures, and Jimmy Milne of the Balmoral oil services group. Both men are immensely successful and busy but still put emphasis on standards and the personal touch.

Happily, at about the time I was making these unsuccessful attempts to find work after GRC, I was approached to become Chairman of Governors at the Robert Gordon University. The appointment is normally for three years and my predecessor, accountant Ian Souter, was due to vacate the chair at the end of 1997. It was arranged that I should shadow him as vice-chairman for his last year. Suddenly my time immediately after retirement was beginning to look busy and I was pleased to drop all thought of pursuing a consultancy business. This did not stop me from applying to many advertisements for membership of quangos including Scottish Homes, Scottish Enterprise, the Scottish Higher Education Funding Council and even self-nomination to membership of the House of Lords. So unsuccessful was I that I got a friend to write to the Scottish Office Permanent Secretary to draw my talents to his attention. All that produced was the suggestion that I register my interest with the Scottish Executive's Public Appointments Unit. If the gentlemen had checked he would have found that I was already on the register of interest and had, a week or two before, updated my records at the Unit's request. I often wonder whether there was another reason that I was so unsuccessful on the quango job circuit. Was it because my experience was too broad, my talents never quite matched the job advertised or that somewhere there was a black mark of some sort on my records? It seems unlikely that I would be considered as a security risk as I have had good security clearance, if judged by the access I was given to secure information over my years in the Civil Service. I have a weakness for the conspiracy explanation of life's mysteries but in reality the explanation is often the simple one and here it could just be I did not measure up in the competitive field of government patronage. It did occur to me that my avoidance of political organisations could have been a cause for concern, especially to those that knew of my political leanings.

It was not just finding something challenging to occupy my time after retirement that was beginning to agitate but there was also the question whether we should, sooner rather than later, return to the south of England. It had never been our intention to stay in Grampian after the job had finished. However, the arrival of the university offer enabled us, conveniently, to delay this decision for another three years. At the time the assumption in the family was that we would, in due course, move south. Another consideration was responsibility for my parents. My father and mother, aged 94 and 84 respectably, still enjoyed life, living in accommodation next to us, and so any move of house immediately on retirement was not a practical option.

For the majority of the staff the last few days of the regional council were not as disturbing as they were for the likes of me where the process was linked to retirement. Most staff would say goodbye to GRC on the Friday and would turn up at the same office and to the same desk on the following Monday, with only new signage and note paper indicating life had changed. For the leavers like me it was not just the end of the council but the conclusion of a professional life. There were many small leaving parties but the interim chief executive, John Liddell, had wrested some funds from the politicians and had arranged for a large party, complete with lots of free booze and food, bands and decorations at the council owned Aberdeen Conference and Exhibition Centre. Whatever criticisms we might have made of John, he could organise the proverbial celebration in a brewery. It was a good 'do' and especially for the younger element. In fairness to him, he did a good job generally in keeping the show on the road once the previous chief executive had left to take up, most appropriately, that role at the new Aberdeenshire Council. John also organised a more formal farewell dinner at Woodhill House for all the remaining chief officers. This, including partners, was a very pleasant occasion. I made the speech on behalf of the leavers, and the convener's gift cupboard as well as the last of my Grampian Initiative goodies store were raided to provide prizes for some gentle parlour games. Fiona won the last bottle of Grampian Initiative labelled whisky, made at Aberdeenshire's Glengarioch distillery.

My own department also arranged a farewell presentation for me which was to coincide with the presentation of a cheque to a charity. The money had been collected as part of a dress 'casual for Friday' initiative, where one can dress down on a Friday for the price of a voluntary £1 contribution to a charity of the staff's choice. This was my idea where I had seen it successfully operated in Calgary's council, and although popular with most, my staff in the Grampian Initiative were hostile. With some staff it was often hard to spot the casual from the formal dresser anyway. Pleasant words were exchanged at the presentation but little more.

Margaret, my secretary, helped me load many pounds of paper records into my car on the final afternoon. I had been careful to keep good records at GRC, firstly with a view to writing about my time in public service but also because of the importance of good records should the need arise to defend one's corner, and not least I kept my own records because a decent filing regime was virtually non-existent. My emotions on leaving Woodhill House and Grampian Regional Council were very mixed. There is no doubt that the move to Grampian had changed our lives for the better. My job had provided me with the responsibility and satisfaction that was missing in my last years with the Civil Service. For Fiona it provided a real role in support of my position. She was not only included in social occasions involving the regional council as well as those of the many organisations and firms that my job brought me into contact with, but also she was involved as hostess in our own home where we entertained frequently in my capacity as Director. I should add that such home entertainment was all at my own expense. Many of our guests were from overseas and from countries where the regional council had pursued strategic alliance links. I remember how welcome a visit to an individual's home was when I made overseas visits, and not only as relief from the tedium of hotel life, but also as an insight to local culture. My overseas guests were very appreciative of the chance to see inside a Scottish home, although I am not aware that many of my colleagues followed our example. It was a lot of work for Fiona but we both much enjoyed such occasions and getting to know a wide variety of people and cultures. Some have become good friends.

I cannot deny that three or four councillors made life very difficult for me and to an extent that their hostile actions and reactions still colour my memory of GRC some years after. Two councillors in particular made it so much more difficult to manage senior staff and run my 130 strong department effectively, and gave rise to problems that I had never experienced in the Civil Service. I would not wish to give the impression that the seven years with the council were one long tussle, as they were not. Most of the staff were supportive and loyal, and some were superbly effective and would measure up to the very best I had experienced in the Civil Service. At the same time I would judge the quality of the average middle rank staff below that I was privileged to work with in DTI. It was difficult to motivate staff to improve, as for most of my time at the council there was no annual staff review and reporting system. There were some quite good training courses available but much was left to the enthusiasm of the individual. The style of senior management varied widely across the council, and the management of the constituent departments I inherited and that came together to form the Department of Economic Development and Planning were a good illustration of this. One part was rigourously controlled, with all correspondence, both in and out, monitored by the previous director even to the extent that the director signed himself most outgoing communications. There were numerous meetings with little real delegation. On the other hand my department also inherited a unit where the complete reverse applied. In this case there was almost no central direction and individuals acted with little supervision, which was particularly worrying for this unit had control over a significant budget. Of the two I felt more secure with the over-bureaucratic operation as this was more easily corrected.

At an early stage I realise that I had to allocate tasks and responsibilities that cut across the rigid organisational lines I inherited. This enabled me to better match the best staff to the task but also to avoid the one or two office 'politicians' that had little inclination to make it work and, happily, few of these had talents that I would miss using in front line tasks. At the same time I needed to deploy staff with some consideration of councillor interference with my direction of staff. On the whole I managed to neutralise most of this influence and only in one case did a politician seriously influence the efficiency of the department to the longer term detriment of the council.

Did I leave Woodhill House with a sense of achievement? Yes, very much so. Little worthwhile is achieved without some pain and my time at GRC was no different. I look back on seven years with the council with satisfaction. Much of what I did was new and innovative, and in many cases the legacy of my tenure can still be identified. The experience was often exhilarating and these heady moments far outweighed the moments of despair and disappointment. The question is often asked 'would you do it again?' The answer is yes, but with hindsight I would have looked more closely at the job description and terms of reference I was given at the start. Thanks to GRC, Fiona and I bettered our standard of living and quality of life in most respects.

Chapter 22

Dare to Struggle

The spring and summer that followed my retirement from the council in 1996 passed rapidly. I do not remember any withdrawal pangs and from the day I left Woodhill House behind I knew I had made the right decision. What did remain was the pressure to fill all spare waking moments, and although that has receded a little over the years I still have a slight feeling of guilt if I take a rest or read a book during what would have been work hours. However during that first summer there was so much to do around the property that the opportunity to 'slack' rarely occurred.

One of my first tasks was to buy and erect, with help from my son, a greenhouse in the garden. Thanks to father's generosity, for most of our years in Wonersh we had a greenhouse and raised from seed all the bedding plants as well as good crops of tomatoes. I had planned to continue this practice in Grampian but the pressures of the new job were always the excuses. I do wonder how I managed time in Wonersh to run a very large allotment, tend a garden and greenhouse to reasonable standards and be away from home for over twelve hours a day.

The 'lump sum' that I received as part of the retirement package was carefully guarded but we did pay off the small mortgage we had outstanding from a leading building society. It gave me a lot of satisfaction to break my links with this body as the staff had never been helpful or even friendly over the years since marriage and buying our first house. Whenever I had wanted their help they were unhelpful, and when I came to pay off my mortgage on retirement even this was a bureaucratic and none too efficient procedure. It was wonderfully liberating to know that no bastard in some distant office had control over your house, and by God we paid dearly for this over the years as our loan coincided with some of the highest interest rates in my lifetime.

We did indulge in one luxury, and that was the purchase of a new Land Rover 'Discovery' and so renewing our love affair with Land Rover, broken only when we moved to Grampian after seventeen happy years with a Series III. I am not sure whether sentiment rather than sense dictated a return to the Land Rover as after nearly fifty years of building essentially the same vehicle the build quality was still suspect. Undoubtedly a Mitsubishi or Nissan would have been a better buy in terms of build and reliability. It was a disappointment that the Germans via BMW did so little in this respect for Land Rover during their period of ownership. Let's hope that Ford, the new owners, can do the trick.

I was not due to take up the Vice-Chairman role at Robert Gordon University (RGU) until the beginning of 1997, but I was more than grateful that was the case as I envisaged that the role might be time-consuming and I had more than enough to do at home. That summer of 1996 was a happy time although there was an incident which seemed prescient. My father was 94 and still driving, albeit very slowly, and that continued to provide him and my mother with a degree of independence. Often we marvelled that my father did not have an accident and especially when motoring into Aberdeen. However in the spring of 1996 he lost control and badly damaged the car in the driveway to our property. I was at home and saw my mother and father literally walk away from the crash to their house next door. My father never did drive again and I think he was, secretly, rather glad to give up, although he much missed his independence. We thanked God that this episode did not take place in the car park at the busy local Tesco supermarket as surely someone would have been injured or killed. The car was repaired and Fiona became their chauffeur. My father never regained his self-confidence and the event coincided with or seemed to trigger a decline in his well-being.

In January of 1997 I took on the role of vice-chairman of Governors at RGU. My chairman, and only the second chair since it became a university, was Ian Souter, who was a partner in the accountancy firm of Ernst and Young. Ian was a pleasant and well-liked colleague and much respected in the local business community, although unwelcome professionally by most as his speciality was insolvency. His last year as chair coincided with the retirement of Dr David Kennedy as Principal and the task of recruiting David's replacement. The importance of finding the right person cannot be overstated and especially after David Kennedy's distinguished leadership. There was quite a heated board debate about who and how many should be on the committee set up to select and interview candidates and make a recommendation to the full board. I felt strongly that the process should not be restricted to a small inner 'cabinet' composed of the chairman and the chairs of the three main committees of the board, namely estates, finance and staff and student affairs, sometimes known as the 'Chairman's Committee' (later I was to make this committee redundant). One or two thought that the selection should be done by all lay governors, but there was a strong clique that wanted a very restricted selection board. The latter group tended to be dominated by board members with business backgrounds. I am sure that has something to say about the appropriateness of business methods to the public sector. I pressed for some compromise as did the majority, and the outcome was a larger selection committee with the additional member names chosen from a hat. I lost out but thought that as vice-chair I should have been involved in the process as I was going to be the new Principal's first chair of governors, bar a few weeks at the end of 1997.

One has to be realistic about how big a 'catch' applicants would judge the job at RGU to be. In UK terms it is but one of dozens of such new universities, and also one where we must take into consideration our fringe geographical location when it comes to the support of the candidate's family. So it was no surprise to have a number of Scottish-based candidates and indeed the job went to Bill Stevely from Paisley University. Bill was Vice-Principal at Paisley, a biochemistry graduate from Glasgow University with a doctorate from Oxford, but returning first to Glasgow and finally to Paisley.

In spite of the enlarged selection board there was still very little sense of a shared appointment, and in retrospect there was a lot to be said for involving all board members as did the former Grampian Region with fifty or so councillors. Some would say it was daunting for the candidate to be faced with a large selection team but as councillors at Grampian said in justification, 'if the candidate at this level cannot face the whole council, then he (or she) is likely not up to the job anyway'. I agree very much with the approach of Grampian's councillors. At RGU there would have been only twelve to fifteen people involved at most. This was hardly daunting when one considers the requirements of the post on offer. Because of the nature of the selection process I and one or two others felt very much excluded. We did have sight of the final shortlist and these gentlemen were paraded, in turn, at a lunchtime 'drinkies' occasion. I never saw the full applicant list although names have leaked out over the years. At least one of these names, in my view, should have been on the shortlist and interviewed. Rightly the then current Principal took no part in the proceedings, although I suspect that his advice should have been sought more than appears to have been the case.

The fact that as vice-chairman I played no part in the selection of the new Principal was a disappointment but also I regret how little opportunity I had to support the chair. I offered my help in drafting and representation but apart from attending two or three meetings of the groups representing Scottish and UK chairs of university governing bodies, I did little else. I attended all the meetings that were open to me to attend in an ex officio capacity and did learn a lot about the politics of the university, and more importantly the politics and dynamics of the governing body. Also I got to know some of the senior academics, which was to prove invaluable when I became chairman.

In the spring of 1997 my father's health deteriorated and he was admitted to hospital in Aberdeen in the May. The problem was prostrate cancer with metastasis into the bones. The diagnosis came as a bit of a shock as my mother had been hiding his symptoms from us for months. Chemotherapy slowed the disease and he was moved to Inverurie hospital. There reached a point where he seemed to have stabilised and we made arrangements that he should transfer to a nursing home in the nearby village of Kemnay. My father made no plea to be nursed at home and indeed quite the reverse. My mother had been giving him a hard time in the month or two before he went into hospital and he had actually asked me to arrange for him to go into a residential home even before he went into hospital. I think the years of nagging and brainwashing from my mother had finally got to him, and he longed for a little peace. However, days before he was due to move to the nursing home in August he died.

All funeral arrangements are difficult for the close family. Naturally my mother was distraught, but was always a survivor and she managed reasonably well in the circumstances. She was well enough to exploit the family tensions to her advantage and so causing me more problems than I needed once the funeral was over and all had returned to something like normal. Most of the arrangements for the funeral were taken out of my hands by my sister, with Mother's blessing. I did draft an obituary for the school magazine and managed to find a photograph of the three generations of Cranleighan Fishers, taken seven years earlier at the annual 'Old Boys' gathering at the school. My father had an eventful and long life and was always grateful for the values that Cranleigh instilled. My father's death was to affect me much more than my mother's. Even now, some years after, it is difficult to talk about it without tears welling. Strangely, the older I get the more I miss him.

I took over from Ian Souter as Chairman of the governing body of The Robert Gordon University in January 1998. I expected a lot of briefing and active files to come my way, but I received just three files of which one related to the Principal's pay review. Little did I realise it at the time that setting and negotiating the Principal's pay was to be one of the loneliest aspects of the job. The only briefing I had on taking up the role of chairman was a warning of the steep learning curve ahead of me. In fact that was never a problem as by the time I reached the position of chair I had assimilated most of the details of the university's finance, the dilemma of its scattered buildings and had a good idea of the politics of the institution.

What I was more worried about was the support I might expect from my lay governor colleagues. Although at the time I was unaware of any hostility to my appointment, elements of this were to shortly emerge. I had an early indication from one governor reporting that some in the local business community were critical of my lack of private sector experience. I was angry and not sure how or whether to respond, as I was anxious to begin my term as chair with smooth feathers all round. In the end I wrote him a conciliatory letter enclosing a copy of my CV which, hopefully, indicated a background broader and more varied than his and most of his colleagues. There were other straws including the reaction of one of the local grandees who I met on the main staircase at RGU's administrative offices. He asked casually what I was doing now, and when I said I was the new chair he could not even bring himself to say 'congratulations'. I later found out that he had vigorously opposed my appointment from behind the scenes. Happily I never rated the man, and so I did not lose much sleep on hearing about his opposition. He was not a member of my board and was well known for his contempt for public servants in general.

I should explain something of the history and setting of RGU. I had described it on occasions as the new university with the long history. The university takes its name from a merchant adventurer, Robert Gordon, born in 1688 who amassed a considerable fortune trading in the Baltic. On his death in 1731 he left his entire estate to build a hospital to educate scholars and this was opened in the summer of 1750. In 1881 the hospital became the Robert Gordon's College which provided commercial, technical and scientific education for clerks and apprentices. The College went on to incorporate the Aberdeen Mechanics Institute and this was key in the involvement and contribution of John Gray, a local industrialist. Gray was a Director of the Mechanics Institute as well as a Governor of Robert Gordon's College. Some would argue that Gray was the more significant founding father. In 1883 Gray offered to build, at his own expense, Gray's School of Science and Art. From 1885 Gray's School existed on the Schoolhill site in central Aberdeen until it was replaced in

1965 by a new building on a beautiful campus just west of the city centre by the River Dee, and donated by another generous local benefactor (and former student), Tommy Scott Sutherland. Gray's School of Art remains a prestigious and nationally recognised school of art and design within the current university.

The original Gray's School went on to incorporate pharmacy, and in 1903 to become a Scottish 'Central Institution' with central government funding, unlike the funding arrangements for similar institutions in England. In 1965 this now significant and growing institution became the Robert Gordon's Institute of Technology (RGIT), one of a number of Scottish 'central institutions', with degree-granting powers through the excellent CNAA grouping of higher educational facilities throughout the UK. The 1991 further and higher education Act of Parliament provided the opportunity for RGIT to become a university. This produced some strange splits in the city and its hinterland with many vehemently opposed to such a change, notwithstanding that the government had already agreed to confer university status on similar institutions in Scotland. I am not sure what motivated the objectors here in Aberdeen but that legacy lives on with at least two overt attempts to put the two Aberdeen-based universities together. The reality is that there is little overlap between them but this admission then opens the doors to those that perceive a 'synergy' in merger. The very mention of the word synergy in any corporate merger is usually the prelude to a disaster for both partners of such unions. During the last overt attempt at merger in 2002/3 a prominent member of the RGU senior management team said to me: " I cannot see the benefit (of merger). Here in RGU we have a mediocre new institution wishing to merge with a mediocre ancient university – and the result will be one larger mediocre institution. Where is the synergy?" Again I look for the motives of individuals behind the pressure for merger and in this particular case one can probably narrow the field to two or three and then I ask myself 'what is in it for them?'.

However at the time of writing RGU survives as an independent university and surviving rather well in the increasingly competitive higher education business. In the *Financial Times'* league tables of UK universities RGU is usually at the top of the list in terms of graduate placement. The fact that RGU became a university at all is largely down to the leadership of David Kennedy as Principal of RGIT, and subsequently the first Principal of the successor Robert Gordon University. David is a remarkable man in many ways. First and foremost he has a passion for education, but not just for the elite but for all, from the humblest to the privileged. Here is no ivory tower inhabiting and pompous academic, but rather a man of the people, a humble and caring man. David would be at home in teaching one-to-one adult literacy (which he does) or speaking to an audience of the country's intellectual elite. I have never seen David take a decision that was coloured by any personal ambition, gain or aggrandisement. When he came to RGIT in 1985 he turned around a sluggish and lacklustre institution and then shaped a new university that was to be seen as one of the best in its class. 'Inclusiveness' was the jargon slogan of the early Blair government and by this, I think, the politicians meant that higher education should be for all and not just the middle classes. David Kennedy here was years ahead of the politicians as he used RGU's new university status to provide students with a whole range of options to that final goal of a degree. The New Testament phrase 'In my Father's house are many mansions...' seems particularly apt as David encouraged the creation of alternative paths that included various sub-degree qualifications. Many similar institutions would turn up their noses at the very thought of a university soiling its hands on sub-degree awards. David was a pioneer of the nursing degree and saw it anomalous that this important profession had to make do with a 'registration' or similar qualification; a treatment akin to the separating of pupils with 'practical' skills into the former Secondary Modern schools after the '11 plus' examination. David Kennedy left a legacy at RGU and an institution that was respected not only in Scotland but throughout many parts of the world from the Middle East, India and the Far East to South America, as well as nearer home.

From my earliest days at the Regional Council I had heard much good talked of RGU and its Principal. The nub of comment was that RGU 'was the better' of the two universities in that it understood the world of commerce and 'you could deal with them'. So when I was asked to join the Board of Governors I was genuinely flattered and when the chairmanship of the board came my way I was honoured. The one minus was that I was not going to be working with David Kennedy. We are now good friends and perhaps it is no bad thing we did not have to accommodate each other as Principal and Chairman of Governors. If we had, I think we would have had our disagreements, but they would have been upfront and there would have been no hidden agendas. For sure, working together would have been a lively, stimulating and creative experience. David is a workaholic and it would have been hard keeping up with his outpourings of ideas and carefully crafted papers.

I took over the chairmanship of the governing body shortly after the appointment of the new Principal, Professor Bill Stevely. As had been my experience when I became vice-chair nobody bothered to see if I had secretarial facilities, there was no press announcement and indeed for some weeks the majority of university staff knew little of who had taken on the chairmanship. I had no base in town and so had nowhere to roost between meetings at the university. I put up with this for a while, using empty meeting rooms or going next door to Aberdeen's art gallery, until I found out that my opposite numbers in other universities were provided with offices. So I asked the Principal to provide me with an office or pied-à-terre on the Schoolhill city centre campus. This was forthcoming and I was provided, eventually, with a pleasant office in a quiet backwater of one of the engineering faculty's buildings .

The university official with formal responsibility for acting on behalf of the governors and the Board is the Secretary. It is the Secretary's responsibility to ensure the board acts within its powers and follow procedures. He should also advise the board on dealings with related companies or other entities in which the university has an interest. The Secretary has a responsibility to alert the board if any proposed action would be *ultra vires* or in breach of legislation to which the university is subject. So the role is an important one. However at the same time the Secretary's line manager at RGU is the Principal and so there is a potential split of loyalty. During my time as Chairman the Secretary had direct line responsibility for a number of functions including student services, marketing and publicity, and also sat on the board of a subsidiary company. This latter role was to cause me concern at a later date.

The role of the university Secretary was discussed by the forum that brings together all the chairs, or the equivalent, of UK university governing bodies, and that is the Committee of University Chairs (CUC). CUC used to meet twice a year and I found this an invaluable reference point. I was a member of a CUC sub-committee set up to look at university governance including the role of the Secretary. All recognised the dilemma of the unsatisfactory split in Secretaries' responsibilities and allegiances. A small minority of institutions did split the role of Secretary to the board from the other duties of a university Secretary, but this was difficult as the role of Secretary to the Board hardly warranted a full-time appointment. All the disadvantages of the combined roles were apparent at RGU and I was to personally experience the practical difficulties that can arise. This is one of many governance issues which I will return to later.

On arriving in Aberdeen in 1988 the then university Secretary was one of only two people that I had some information on, or 'SP' as they say in the racing world. We got on fine during the time I was a mere backbench member of the governing body, but as soon as I became chairman I began to experience the tensions that are inherent in a situation where there was 'split reporting' by functionaries, which is the dilemma of trying to serve two masters. There were pressing governance issues that I was eager to tackle and many which bore on the role of the Secretary, and indeed on the poorly defined role of chairman. I was anxious to see change and to restore a proper balance between the role of the governing body and the executive, which had drifted to a degree that in many areas the governors were, in effect, sidelined in a number of strategic decision processes that properly and constitutionally belonged to the board.

The relationship between chair of governors and Principal is a critical one. From the very first day I realised that I would have to work very hard at this. My prime objective was to be as supportive as possible and to try and offer the Principal a sounding board for his ideas. To that end I arranged that we meet, in private, every three weeks or so to discuss and review ongoing business, but I had hoped we could also use the occasions to discuss the development of broader and longer term strategy. Over the three years we kept more or less to the schedule and clocked forty-five such review meetings. The Principal provided a working agenda which I added to at the beginning of each meeting. This was nothing more than a checklist of subjects to be covered but was also a useful record. No minutes were taken but I made my own notes after each meeting, partly for archival reasons and it was difficult for an old Civil Servant not to have some records, for whatever reasons.

The meetings lasted about an hour and often took place over a light lunch in the Principal's office, which incidentally was far from grand and still reflected the low key and unpretentious environment in which Dr Kennedy carried out his role when Principal. All this and life in general at RGU was very far from the academic world portrayed by C.P. Snow in his '*Strangers and Brothers*' sequence of novels. Our sessions were correct and a tad on the formal side insofar as I never felt that Bill Stevely ever shared his inner thoughts about the university with me. It was as if I were a tame journalist, still to be treated with a healthy degree of suspicion.

During our regular meetings I cannot remember many instances when the Principal sought my advice and view on a matter of policy, apart from getting my formal blessing to his decisions on ongoing matters, where I would act more as a proxy vote of confidence on behalf of the board. My role in suggesting improvements to the regime or his stewardship required tremendous patience on my part. However more due to a process of drip feed and attrition than mutual agreement did I achieve most of the changes I wished to see.

Once a governor colleague asked me, mischievously, whether I thought I could do the Principal's job better than the Principal. What I am more certain of is that we had complementary skills, and we could have worked together more closely. On the other hand I would not have wished for a too cosy relationship as at the end of the day I represent the employer and all that means should disciplinary matters intrude. Whatever the pluses and minuses of our relationship the Principal was as correct as they come and in my wildest dreams I could never have imagined being dragged into the messes created for some of my opposite numbers by their respective Principals. However I do need a degree of shared passion and I work best where I feel I am on the same wavelength as my colleague.

The same mischievous colleague I refer to above would often press me as to whether I had an 'agenda' when I took up the role of chairman. Perhaps tellingly I was pressed to reveal my hand similarly at Grampian Region. Anybody who knew me would expect me to have an agenda, and indeed I had. My short period on the board and the year as vice-chair had given me plenty of time to see what was wrong but more importantly what I could hope to achieve bearing in mind the quality of individuals, both on the board, and within the university's senior management team.

In the handbook for governors, setting out the constitution and rules governing the university, there was a small section on the duties and responsibilities of the Chairman of Governors. It started with a statement that the chairman is responsible for the leadership of the governing body. There was a reference to the 'seven principles of public life' (as recommended by the Nolan Committee on Standards in Public Life) and the need for the chairman to be mindful of these on behalf of the governing body. Then there was very general guidance about ensuring the operation of the governing body in 'an effective manner'. There was very little about any delegated powers to the chairman to carry out these general responsibilities. The handbook acknowledged that the chair should agree the agenda for board meetings and has the power to call extraordinary general meetings. It did not deal with a number of other responsibilities such as setting and reviewing the Principal's performance targets, and keeping a check on the Principal's overseas trips as well his appointments out with the university. So there were very few specific powers and I was to experience the inadequacy of control mechanisms on a number of occasions. In exercising my role I was aware of the problems that erupted at two other universities at about the time of my period as chairman. In my view both were examples, although very different, where the governors had lost control over the executive and the normal checks and balances appear to have been ignored or overridden. Although the risks of similar occurrences were remote at RGU it was important that our system was transparent and necessary control mechanisms were in place. After all, at the end of the day the buck stopped with me. In any organisation spending some £50 million annually of largely public money, there must be very visible accountability at all levels.

The group dynamics of the governing body were probably like most of the many boards, advisory groups and committees I have served on during my professional life. My experience has been that the number of individuals on such bodies that are creative, visionary, and innovative are a rarity, and perhaps amounting to only ten per cent of the group. At the other end of the spectrum is an equally small number that are destructive and disruptive, but with, apparently, no real agenda. If this latter group were clearly intent on, say, doing away with the board or were politically motivated in some direction, then they would be easier to deal with and perhaps their enthusiasm, although destructive, could be turned to good use. As Chair the danger in handling this group is that one tends to paranoia and feels their negativity is directed at oneself. Somewhere between these two extremes is a soggy area with colleagues who rarely have their own ideas and will speak when they are confident they will not be isolated and when a bandwagon is rolling. With a bit of luck there will be a core that will regularly give a view and at least seem to have a mind of their own, however timidly put and hedged about are their contributions.

Our board consisted of nineteen members and pretty well adhered to the pattern I describe. My initial impression was of a board that was averse to much change and had a pronounced 'cringe' factor when it came to exercising their role of guidance and setting an overall strategy for the executive and the Principal. However, I know that David Kennedy, when he was Principal, found a small minority of the lay board members far from cringing when it came to dealing with their Principal. By the time I had reached the chair most of this element had gone. What I was left with was the rump of a tightly-knit bunch of Aberdeen business people, sometimes affectionately known as the 'mafia'. The 'mafia' could be difficult and had access to an extensive network of friends and allies. However this group was more often benign but on one or two occasions one got the feeling that the group were 'organised', in the trade union sense, and acted as a clique. Again, this might be my paranoia.

I had no say in the choice of my first vice-chairman. The vice-chair appointed was approaching his maximum number of years allowed as a governor and so had no chance of succeeding me. He was certainly a 'safe pair of hands' and it was the view of a senior member of the executive that he was made vice-chair to provide balance and some assurance to the rest of the board on the appointment of an 'unknown quantity' as chairman. My last two years as chair were shadowed by a vice-chair that was expected by the board to become the next chair of governors, and the appointment followed an election process. I was very much behind the decision that the post should be contested, as in effect we were appointing a chair-elect and as chair of the committee dealing with nominations I was unhappy with the powerful lobby for a particular candidate. I was also unhappy with the degree of involvement by the executive in the choice of candidates. The individuals that put themselves forward for election were a strange mixture of the unlikely and the obvious. Somewhere along the line I felt I had missed a trick. One surprise was the suggestion at the last minute that the election should be by single transferable vote. This was tabled at a meeting by the Secretary with no prior reference to me. The outcome was, in retrospect, predictable with a win for businessman John Milligan.

If there were ever two so different individuals, it was me and John Milligan. He was a successful and self-made businessman and used to the rough and tumble of the Scottish engineering and construction industry, and me, the lifelong public servant with a relatively privileged upbringing and with a training that was 'academic' in the broadest sense of the word. Our new relationship seemed to start well, and I welcomed John's promises of regular meetings with me and his wish to be supportive during my time as chairman. The reality was that we met once and never worked closely together. On his side I could fairly say that he had a lot more on his plate than I had, and on my side I suppose I was grateful to be spared what I thought would be a regular dose of the macho 'we in business know best and you in the public sector know nothing' that I had come to expect of successful businessmen. I shared with the former and colourful Conservative minister, Alan Clark, an aversion to the archetypal British businessman and his concern with status symbols and talk of money, golf and cars. However John was not archetypal but we were to later clash over the provision of information about one of the university's wholly owned subsidiaries.

My prime objective in the early days of the job as chair was that the governing body reclaim for the board the role of setting the broad strategy of the university. Over the years this had slipped away to the executive, but I suspect more from languor on behalf of lay governors than any plan by the executive to usurp the governors' rightful role. From what I was told by those with longer experience on the board than me, key members would spend too much time on the broader politics of appointments and internal wars rather than the stuff of university strategic plans.

The one area of policy that was well attended to by lay governors was the development of the university estate. There are a number of explanations for this which include the legitimate interests and experience of both executive and lay governors. A bit like Grampian Regional Council members enjoying their property role, so did my board colleagues. I suppose there was a similar satisfaction in dealing with the concrete rather than the more abstract of research policy (virtually non existent when I joined the board) for example. Then there is the satisfaction derived from decisions where the results are not only visible but often quite spectacular. There is a buzz to be gained from initiating a contract for a new building costing some twenty million pounds but less to be gained from getting one's head around a new pay framework for the staff.

Property matters were overseen by the Estates and Buildings Committee, one of three main committees of the board, with the others being Finance, and Staff and Student Affairs. I would not wish to give the impression that the Estates and Buildings Committee during my time at RGU was anything but professional and enthusiastic, and I would judge it as the most effective of all the board's committees. Indeed it was an example to other committees in the way that the lay governors and the various professionals, academic and non-academic, worked as a real team and with an obvious and shared enthusiasm. If only the main board could have adopted some of this team spirit and similarly put the turf wars aside.

The Estates Committee delivered two very successful new buildings (and more since) on the River Dee's banks at Garthdee and so changed the focus of the university from a sprawl of some twenty sites across the city to just two sites, the city centre Schoolhill site and now the main university campus at Garthdee. Both new buildings were brought in on time, although just a little over budget. The day-to-day supervision of the contracts was delegated to a Building Committee of the main Estates Committee. The first of these major developments was designed by the prestigious architect, Norman Foster. The decision to appoint Norman Foster was made before my period as chair, although the build took place largely during my tenure. I attended many of the Building Committee meetings with contractors and particularly with Bovis, the managing contractors. The academic in charge of this phase of development was Assistant Principal and Dean of the Faculty of Management, Professor Bill McIntosh. Here was an academic who was very practical in approach, and could be as pushy and combative as any site manager or foreman. Bill had a steep learning curve to climb but he did this quickly and with few mistakes. He was ably assisted by my governor colleague Bill Wyllie. If there were disagreements they did not let these show and their collaboration was a model to all us governors, and university staff from the Principal downwards. Bill Wyllie before retirement had run a very successful commercial nursery in Aberdeen. He was 'a man o' pairts' with good contacts in political and business circles and probably could be brigaded with the Aberdeen influential or so-called 'mafia'. Bill Wyllie was nobody's fool. He used a self-deprecating humour and wit to defuse most potentially difficult situations. Well before Bill was due to leave the board the Principal raised with me the Academic Council's wish to award Bill an honorary degree. Normally I was against serving governors receiving awards from the university as it tended to be divisive and also introduced an element of favour and reward and so potentially undermine the impartiality of the board. One such award was granted against my written objection. In the case of Bill Wyllie I saw no such risk. He had served well beyond the call of duty in his capacity as chair of the Estates Committee in nursing our Norman Foster building to birth, as well as playing a key role in selling part of our old estate to fund the second new building at Garthdee.

Very few governors put in as much time to the role as did Bill Wyllie. Even some of those that confessed to aspiring to higher office within the board were poor attenders at meetings and their contribution demonstrated that sufficient homework had not been put in before meetings. There is no doubt that many of my colleagues enjoyed the cachet that being a governor of a university brought but a few did not keep their side of the contract.

The Norman Foster building was to house the Management School, a new library, seemingly hundreds of computer terminals and a home for many other groups of academics who had previously been scattered around the university's numerous centres. It is a fine building and at just over £21 million was excellent value for money. For the next major development at Garthdee we plumped for a local firm of architects. I think that my input was decisive in coming to the choice of Fraser, Halliday and Munro of Aberdeen, and I am glad to say that none of us involved had any regrets, and especially as the new health sciences building took shape. I have to admit I have a slight twinge when I now look at the Foster and the Halliday, Fraser & Munro buildings side by side and am reminded how similar they appear. I find myself resorting to the arguments used by the Russians to explain why their supersonic passenger jet and the Anglo-French Concorde looked so similar. The Russians claimed 'convergent design' because the parameters were the same as worked to for Concorde and so inevitably the two aircraft would end up a similar shape. The same argument is often used by car designers to try and explain away why their products all look so alike. We did gain 'Brownie' points with local business and politicians for supporting a local firm, although this firm had made its name in designing supermarkets, and not academic buildings with all their complex and designated space requirements.

The board's handling of estates strategy apart, I was unhappy with the poor degree of board involvement in aspects of policy and strategy development. At the same time the lack of rigour on such matters within the executive left a lot to be desired. In some important areas, including research, marketing, overseas recruitment and fund-raising there was simply no policy, or where the executive claimed to have developed a clear policy it was rudimentary at best, and more often than not a rationalisation of an unsatisfactory situation. The 'quango' responsible for funding universities in Scotland, the Scottish Higher Education Funding Council (SHEFC) required all universities to submit to them every year a proforma-based return on the institution's 'strategic plans'. At RGU this would be circulated a day or two before a board meeting and governors would be asked to endorse it, there and then. There was only one description for this procedure and that was 'rubber stamping' by the board. This SHEFC return was, at the time, the only all-embracing strategy document that the university produced and was supposed to summarise all our priorities and strategy for the year ahead. It might have satisfied SHEFC, but I judged it woefully inadequate for internal needs and, more important, the needs of the board. How SHEFC found our return useful beyond compiling some doubtfully relevant statistical tables mystifies me to this day. More worrying is how my colleagues were content to agree a document on strategy that they had not had a chance to contribute to in any remotely sensible manner.

I expected and got resistance from some senior managers, but even more amazing was that one or two of my colleagues tried to argue that our role as governors was not to take an active role in devising and setting broad strategy. Naturally some of the senior academics jumped on this and insinuated that the likes of me were interfering and usurping a role more properly delegated to the Principal. Whilst the implementation of strategy is for the Principal, any board which shirks its responsibility for setting strategic guidelines is derelict in its duty. This lack of control by the board led to problems at an English university around about this period. Like so much at RGU it was a battle, but a battle that had to be won.

Colleagues I could really rely upon on the Board were few. I set out determined not to gather a clique around me, or to buy into an existing one. I decided that I would not lobby and pick off board members or establish any sort of kitchen cabinet. Academic institutions are notorious for gossip, back-stabbing and turf wars. I could see my board had enough cliques and I was not going to add to the total. I tried to play my role as straight as I could and project the image of 'what you see is what you get'. Entering into intrigues and behind the scenes deals might have been more stressful than the frustration of feeling the board was sometimes not wholly behind one. It was lonely. One way around this was to get out and about in the university and take the pulse of the organism myself.

Many of the senior staff were refreshingly honest and open with me. I hope I was able to return that candour without compromising the Principal. I got to know some of these people quite well and came to respect them. RGU had few people at the very top with a field marshal's baton in their knapsack. Indeed only two would I have seen as potential Principal material. My experience of RGU was that sharp intellect was relatively rare. I think it was Reichsmarschall Herman Goering who said something along the lines of, 'When I hear the word intellectual, I want to reach for my gun'. What RGU needed at this senior level was first and foremost good managers and not sharp intellectuals with an impressive list of publications behind them. It would have been a bonus to have both of course. The Principal was a believer in delegation, and this is as it should be, except the university was dangerously thin on good managerial talent. I was regularly reminding him of the need to address this shortcoming.

I would try and see all the Deans on a regular and one-to-one basis and then as many of the heads of departments and schools as I could. Not all were welcoming and some were suspicious. Most were won over when it was clear that I was not a mole for the Principal and they could talk freely. At the same time I did try and keep the Principal informed where I came across problems and where possible I 'aggregated' comment to protect my sources. Some individuals became quite good friends as well as useful sounding boards.

Although it was viewed at best unusual, on a number of important occasions I found it necessary to put my own papers to the governors. If I had relied on the normal channels of asking for some research and proposals from the executive I would have had to wait a long time, or the result would have likely been less than helpful in addressing what I judged to be the needs of the organisation, and certainly the needs of the board of governors. From the start I typed all my own material. Quite apart from any other reason, it was more efficient as I used home as my office and any use of the university secretarial facilities would have been clumsy.

About the only piece of advice that my predecessor gave on handing over to me was to take care to check the minutes of board meetings carefully. I assumed he meant checking for omissions and typographical errors rather than for any other reason. From years of experience in the Civil Service I knew the power of the minute-taker, and especially if he or she is trying to meet the demands of someone other than the chair of the meeting. At RGU the board minutes were taken and written up by a senior member of the Academic Affairs Department, but were also seen by the Secretary and the Principal, and likely to be amended on the way to me as chairman. That was fine, but what I objected to in the early months was that minutes were amended after my agreement to the draft. I soon put a stop to this but even then I found I had to be on my toes and crawl through every line and phrase to ensure what was agreed was recorded without a subtle change of nuance, usually to the benefit of the executive. By the last year I had an admirable lady in charge of the minutes. She was not only an excellent drafter of minutes (a real skill that few people have or recognise) but she knew and respected my rules and any changes would be checked with me.

One question that I often used to ask myself was where does real power lie in the university. Constitutionally it should firstly lie with the board of governors which is charged with setting the broad strategy of the institution and appoints, and dismisses, the Principal. Within the executive one might think that power lies with the Principal. In an odd way whereas even a weak Principal can exercise a measure of control over his board of governors, a strong Principal often finds it difficult to take on and control his senior academic and professional colleagues, and even less the rank and file staff. The odds are stacked against the Principal for a number of reasons. Rarely do universities have good management information systems to measure staff by and call them to account, and then if staff terms and conditions of service are threatened there is a tough battle with powerful and very effective academic trade unions such as the

Association of University Teachers (AUT) or at RGU the schoolteachers' union, the EIS. Also the concept of academic independence runs deep, and spreads much wider than mere scholarship and research. Theoretically, it would be difficult to conceive a more 'stroppy' set of employees, and at the same time here is a group that is exceedingly articulate and that revels in office 'games'. If there is a focus of power then, In my view, it is the Deans and Vice-Principals. They run large empires, and staff are likely more amenable in that they know the Deans control access to research funding and the architecture of the complex and interrelated courses that make up the teaching programme. So the Deans have some leverage, but the Principal has little leverage over his Deans. One Scottish university Principal at the time I was with RGU was widely reported to be 'the prisoner of his Vice-Principals and Deans'. I suspect this is more common than one imagines. Some Principals almost opt out and seek acknowledgement in numerous representative organisations leaving the running of the university, in practice, to this powerful second tier.

There are many aspects of life at RGU to be found in the above brief analysis. As a colleague once reminded me – 'these institutions have been around for hundreds of years and hold all the records for corporate survival, and so nothing you can do will change them'. Although RGU, in some senses, is a young institution already it had acquired all the accretions to ensure its survival, and that may include the ability to morph into something that suits the political climate of the time.

Chapter 23

Allowing the future to be born

The finance committee of any organisation is perhaps the most important in exercising control. We had a series of good chairs of finance at Robert Gordon University and one, a former senior banker in the region, stands out. This man's best attribute was not just his ability to read a balance sheet, which one would expect as a minimum qualification, but his ability to get into the detail and so keep the university finance department on its toes. Some might describe him as the supreme nit-picker, but that tends to indicate a person who takes pride in catching out his colleagues on often inconsequential matters and perhaps more for the sake of irritation than any real need. This was not the case. His questions, although often in the detail, were always relevant and to the point. I know that his advice and eye for detail was appreciated by the university's director of finance and the very last thing this excellent lady wanted was some sort of 'yes man' as her chairman. The two worked extremely well together and kept the university finances in a state that many of our competitors would envy. I think this finance chairman was universally respected by his colleagues on the board, including myself. However I am not sure that he felt quite the same about me.

The finance committee was very good at looking after the accounts but what neither it nor the main board was doing was looking at the policy and strategy issues behind the figures. My concern here was echoed in a discussion at one of the meetings of the Committee of University Chairmen I attended where we debated the possibility that an institution can have a good record in terms of out turn but at the same time have a weak board and poor governance. This can work well until a major internal failing is missed or outside events shift the goal posts. The result then could be a sudden collapse or catastrophe at the institution. In other words the absence of a strong lead by the board, with all the checks and balances that implies will sooner or later lead to problems for the institution and its performance. I saw parallels to this situation at RGU. The university was doing well in terms of financial out turn but at the same time the board, in my view, was not on top of the situation. I am not in any way suggesting that we were missing any wrongdoing in the university but more we were not sufficiently involved in setting key strategies for the Principal and the executive to work from. In some areas the board's knowledge was minimal, either of a particular area of strategy or of whether a strategy existed at all. Unfortunately, in some policy areas the latter was the case, where the executive had little in the way of considered strategy at all, but for many lay members on the board ignorance seemed to be bliss.

I spent a considerable amount of personal time in researching and writing papers drawing these inadequacies to my colleagues' attention. Games were played by colleagues to fudge or bury issues by using standard bureaucratic ploys such as allocating responsibilities to committees that would likely not have the time, inclination or skills to deal with the problem. A variation on this was to refer anything that did not fit into 'estates' or 'staff and student affairs' to the finance committee. However I did make headway through a new subcommittee on governance where I was in the chair and so could, to a large degree, set the agenda. A further useful vehicle was the annual 'away day' seminar session for the board. The executive would often try and fill these days with 'interesting' presentations by staff members so minimising the time for the board's own discussions. As chair I was able to head off most of this 'agenda stuffing' and allow colleagues to focus on more important and more strategic thought. It was a useful Trojan horse and by careful control of the summary of the sessions I would ensure the conclusions were couched in terms of succinct and specific actions. Armed with these I was able to confront the Principal and his senior managers with the clear and recorded will of governors.

Sometimes the process was a long and tedious one. One example was a simple suggestion that the executive and the board should set up a joint group to look at the long-term development of the university. At the time there was no forum in which the senior management could discuss long-term vision, although some would have welcomed this. The board of governors were certainly not doing this, apart from the long term implications of board decisions concerning the university's physical estate. The idea of a joint brainstorming group seemed sensible enough. I engineered one of the brighter academics with a flair for lateral thought to address the governors. This went down quite well but it took the executive three years to arrive at the very same idea. I would like to think that the cause of delay was the 'not invented here' syndrome, but I cannot help recall how nebulous the Principal was when I pressed for his views on the long-term game plan for the university. The best vision I could elicit from him in one 'blue sky' session was that his goal was to see the university as a Scottish edition of Oxford's Brookes University. Brookes is certainly a very successful new university but not a good comparator for RGU for a number of reasons, and not least its location in Oxford.

There was only the one occasion where my frustrations almost boiled over and risked a more public row and that concerned access to the business plans of the then wholly owned subsidiary company, RGIT Ltd. This company had been set up in 1989 in the days when the university was the Robert Gordon Institute of Technology and provided survival training for oil staff working offshore, amongst other training roles. All personnel working on rigs in the North Sea had to undergo regular survival training and this included helicopter escape training should a sea 'ditch' be necessary on the journey to oil exploration and production platforms. RGIT Ltd had a large indoor pool to this end and a training shell of a helicopter cabin, designed and built by RGIT, which could be submerged and rotated to simulate the disorientation of a helicopter cabin turning under water would cause. Even the training can be a pretty frightening experience and after watching a class being processed I declined the opportunity to experience the training first hand. However I did make a couple of trips offshore by helicopter and it is fair to say that it is probably the most unpleasant and uncomfortable form of air transport. Somewhere between the Scottish mainland and Shetland I would wish I had the benefit of the survival training. Thousands of offshore staff passed through the university-owned establishment and it was a very profitable operation for many years. However with the downturn in numbers working offshore (partly as a result of new technology) and the pressures on the oil and oil service companies to cut costs RGIT Ltd's fortunes began to sag during the period I was chair of governors. There was also new competition from a Norwegian firm and so some sort of rescue operation was imminent for the university's training company

Appropriate skills were drafted on to the subsidiary board of the survival training company and sensible options were addressed. At the same time the subsidiary was making demands on the university and there were implications for the university's estate. My problems started when I asked to see a draft copy of the company's business plan. My initial request was through the university Secretary, who was also on the board of the subsidiary company, which I indicated as somewhat unwise from a governance view point. I made approaches to the Principal who was also on the board of the subsidiary, as was my vice-chair. All my requests were side-stepped. The Secretary sought advice from the university's local solicitors which did little to justify the case for denying the chair of governors access to the business plan of RGIT Ltd. One member of the subsidiary board used the excuse of commercial confidentiality, which was rich when the chairman of RGIT Ltd (and also was my vice-chair of governors) had previously owned an oil service company, whereas I had no links with the oil or survival training industry whatsoever. At one early stage in my battle I was asked down to the training facilities on Aberdeen's King Street and given little more than a child's guided tour. After the tour the opportunity came to ask some questions to RGIT Ltd's chair and the chief executive about policy and strategy but the discussion was abruptly halted when we got beyond the banal. In spite of repeated requests over some weeks I got nowhere, and at this stage I spent most of a weekend drafting a letter to the Scottish Higher Education Funding Council as I thought there was a serious breach of the governance guidelines for public bodies. I am not suggesting in any way at all that I had grounds to suspect anything was untoward but more a proper flow of information was being denied to the chairman of governors, and in that role the representative of the university as the sole shareholder. I was within a day or two of sending this off, when the university's auditors produced a report totally vindicating the stance I had taken, and advising that far more information on subsidiary companies should be made available to the board. I never got a real apology from any of those that frustrated my proper access to information on subsidiary companies.

It was an important personal battle but also an important battle on behalf of the board, although I was unaware of much support from colleagues at the time. In areas of governance like this there is a very different approach by the private sector and so a genuine puzzlement by my board colleagues from the private sector as to why I should make so much fuss about this. Their approach, and I can understand this, was to focus almost exclusively on the outcome, and the process was almost incidental. When public money is involved the process is important, and important that it is as transparent as possible. There is, and has to be, a difference in approach between running a large commercial operation and a large public sector body such as a university. There are crossovers and lessons to be learnt from both sides, but the two types of body are distinct and the management ethos must too be distinct. It was this battle that brought home to me how far the public sector ethos had been eroded over the years since Margaret Thatcher became prime minister. I took this theme for my address to new graduates after receiving my honorary degree from the university in November 2001.

The chair of governors was the main link between the board members and the executive that is responsible for the day-to-day running of the university. Normally the governors met only four times a year, but each governor was expected to join one of the three main subsidiary committees of the board, with a parallel frequency of meetings. For many lay governors there was little contact with the university outwith the formality of some eight meetings a year, and RGU, unlike our neighbour institution in Aberdeen, had little tradition of social occasions where governors might meet senior staff, such as university receptions or hospitality offered by the Principal. However, the role of the chairs of the three subsidiary committees to the main board was more demanding and especially that of the chair of the estates committee, with the university's ongoing multi-million development programme. Also the chair of finance would normally have regular contact with the finance director between formal meetings of the finance committee. So the chair of governors was the only lay governor with the opportunity to take an overview of the university on a day-to-day basis. More importantly he was the only board member able to monitor effectively the Principal's performance.

I touched earlier on my relationship with the Principal and the importance that it should be 'correct' and not too familiar. There was no risk of over-familiarity in our relationship and this made the job of undertaking the Principal's annual performance review slightly easier. He was first to raise that he welcomed such a review process although this was high on my agenda on taking on the chairman's role. An added incentive for the Principal then, and indeed for all his senior colleagues at the time, was a link between performance and bonus payments. Together we agreed performance indicators and each year I produced a written appraisal of the Principal's performance, reflecting performance measured against targets, as well as setting new targets for the year ahead. Where there was criticism this was recorded alongside praise. I gave the Principal sight of my report to allow him to comment before this was put to a small remunerations committee (which I chaired). There were rarely any substantive comments from the Principal and so I hope I produced an appraisal that was fair. This was the first time that such a formal and written annual report had been produced on the Principal's performance. In my view the review of the Principal's performance should have been circulated to all the lay governors, that is all except university staff or student members of the governing body. Armed with my report and advice the Remuneration Committee then made a recommendation on the Principal's salary for the year ahead, as well as his bonus for the year past. In setting his salary level I had access to the supposedly confidential comparator statistics of the pay and bonuses for all UK university Principals, prepared by the Committee of University Chairmen. We tracked all this information, but in more detail a list of comparable institutions and particularly those in Scotland. The setting of the bonus was more tricky.

We scrapped the bonus arrangement for senior staff towards the second half of my chairmanship but not only was the changeover tiresome, but I am not sure that we ended up with a system that was much better in terms of getting the best from our senior staff. Quite apart from any other consideration I was unhappy with a system that offered incentives to only the very senior staff, and nothing to the rest of the staff but the scale incremental increase, plus the annual increase negotiated with the unions centrally to reflect inflation and cost-of-living increases. Another disadvantage of our bonus system was that it tended to become institutionalised and more or less automatic and so the link between effectiveness and the bonus amount became obscure. In one instance I thought an individual's work had been less than satisfactory and I recommended the bonus should be withheld. I was outvoted and the individual was rewarded 'as usual'.

I said that annual cost-of-living increases for university staff were negotiated centrally, but in reality the process was a lot more complicated with, then, separate negotiating machinery for the Scottish older universities, that is the four ancient ones as well as those established in the 1960s such as Strathclyde and Stirling. For the later clutch of new universities including Abertay, Paisley, Napier, Glasgow Caledonian and Robert Gordon the staff employment terms and conditions were quite different, reflecting the somewhat different history of this group. The new universities had their origins in polytechnic institutions or better known as 'central institutions' in Scotland. Staff in these institutions had different union membership to those in the ancient and older universities, with the schoolteachers union, the Educational Institute of Scotland or the 'EIS' predominating, with a minority (and particularly at Dundee's Abertay University) with Association of University Teachers' membership, the main union in the older universities. I was to become very involved in the politics that led to a stand to bring the employment terms and conditions of the Scottish central institutions more in line with university mainstream, both in Scotland and the rest of the UK.

Negotiations on pay, terms and conditions for the newer universities in Scotland were co-ordinated by a representative body known as 'Conference', or more fully the Conference of Scottish Centrally Funded Colleges. The title underscores the origins of the group and included higher education institutions like the prestigious Glasgow School of Art, Queen Margaret University College and the Northern College of Education, as well as my own university and others of that ilk. One of my roles as vice-chair was to attend 'Conference' with the then Principal, David Kennedy. Conference was one of the few university representatives bodies that included both lay governors and academics, or non-executives and executive representatives of the institutions involved, although both 'sides' also had their separate representative forums. It was an opportunitiy to see our Principal operating and negotiating with his colleagues.

My early experience of 'Conference' was of meetings dominated by much hand-wringing over the situation we all found ourselves in, not so much over pay, but rather the now indefensible and excessively favourable conditions of service that our respective staff enjoyed. The nub of our concern was that our staff saw their conditions as paralleling those of school teachers rather than those found in the UK university mainstream. These terms and conditions dated from a 1988 agreement known as 'FE 64'. The agreement provided for 62 days holiday and that excluded public holidays, but there were many other sacrosanct practices that were incompatible with running a modern university. At each meeting the hand-wringing continued and nobody suggested grasping the nettle.

Eventually I got exasperated and pressed for some action and got some support from the non-academic element. However RGU under David Kennedy's guidance had already taken the bull by the horns and had introduced a new staff contract that was a vast improvement on the conditions set out in the 'FE64' deal that others were clinging to. This had been challenged by the union but RGU successfully resisted and was being implemented for new staff and any other staff wishing to take up the new contract. In practice the keener staff were already working along the more flexible lines sought by David Kennedy, and as far as annual leave was concerned few of these motivated staff ever took the long holidays provided for by the union-blessed contract.

Another straw suggesting a new will to break the deadlock was an informal meeting called by the Principal of Paisley University. This was a pleasant social occasion held at Paisley but it did move forward the debate with a clear indication from most that something 'needed to be done'. As a result of that meeting I drafted one of those simple eight or ten point plans which stated quite baldly what we should be doing and put this to the Principal at Paisley. Nothing happened as a result, but meanwhile the 'Conference' meetings about annual pay awards were becoming more and more restless, and I continued to press for some action. Two events contributed to the breaking of the deadlock. First was the arrival of Ian Johnston as the new Principal at the war-torn Glasgow Caledonian University. Ian had been the senior man at the Department of Employment office in Sheffield and part of his portfolio had involved detailed knowledge of the government conciliation and arbitration service, ACAS. He stiffened sinews by advising us all that in any industrial dispute, key is the will to win, although when we later faced a strike Ian Johnston's role was central in reaching a compromise that led to a settlement. The other change at the time was the secondment of a senior academic from Queen Margaret College to review the the whole question of staff pay and conditions in 'Conference' institutions.

In July 1999 I was asked to take on the chairmanship of the 'Conference' Salaries Committee, and no doubt because I had had plenty to say on the subject in the preceding months. This was a daunting role but I was thrilled to have been offered the responsibility. Back in my own institution this news was greeted by the director of human relations and the Principal, now Professor Stevely after David Kennedy's retirement, with a distinct lack of enthusiasm, to say the least. Whether they had no confidence in me or whether they thought that lay folk should keep their noses out of such matters I am not sure.

It took until the end of April 2000, after eight years of prevarication by the 'Conference' institutions, to reach a new pay and conditions deal with the unions (EIS and AUT, but mainly EIS). However this was not before a strike by the EIS union. It was strange to be leading an employers' side into negotiations with the unions and to be firmly in the management camp. My last involvement in strike activity had been in the Civil Service where I spent many an hour on a picket line. On this occasion I had to cross our own university picket line outside the Schoolhill administrative building and chat to the EIS branch chairman in so doing. It was all very civilised, but the EIS in particular were worthy opponents and were no push over.

The strike was key in softening up my colleagues, some of which came under pressure from their governing bodies and some were concerned about the real possibility of students affected taking a breach of contract case against their university authorities. The changes in student funding had certainly sharpened both student and university management attitudes to student rights as paying customers, and all that might mean in contractual terms. We never got to the point of testing these in the courts but the EIS-led strike of staff did panic many of my Principal colleagues on the Salaries Committee. Some of the most vociferous became circumspect and hesitant. Again, the nerve of governor representatives was stronger but I suppose I and my lay and non-executive colleagues had less to lose by way of careers.

I was in a bit of a difficult situation as regards the interests of my own university as any agreement was likely to make null and void the headway we had made under Dr Kennedy's leadership when he was Principal. What we wished to avoid was a settlement less rigourous than the one we had already 'imposed' unilaterally. At an early stage my colleagues in the other institutions made it plain that they were willing to settle for a lot less and particularly on annual leave or holidays. Much of the early preparative work on drawing up the proposal to put to the unions was undertaken by RGU's excellent director of human resources, and together with the Salaries Committee's industrial relations adviser from Queen Margaret College we were able to put the first succinct proposal to the unions in August 1999 under the banner of partnership – 'Partnership 2000'.

One can be (and I have been) very cynical about the term 'partnership' emanating from any management side of negotiations, as the last thing that is usually on offer is a partnership in any sense of the word. Although I would not claim that our approach was either altruistic or totally even handed, we had gone a long way to meet the concerns of staff, and indeed further than I would have done myself in the circumstances. We were also encouraged by hints from the trade unions that they were also ready for a change. Again, I would not have expected any trade union, let alone the EIS, to roll over and say words to the effect 'It's a fair cop and it is time we gave up these ridiculous holidays'. One can only guess what was behind the EIS union's apparent wish to now move forward. One or two of us spent some time puzzling this and the view we arrived at was that the EIS saw the two types of universities in Scotland moving closer together in terms of practices, terms and conditions of service including pay, where the staff in the older group of Scottish universities often had better pay scales. At the same time EIS could see its membership base at risk to the mainstream university union, the Association of University Teachers and may well have taken the view that it would lose out in a long war of attrition and its members would drift away to the AUT, a union that likely had more muscle in the longer term. There was also the issue of academic snobbery where 'real' university staff would see membership of the EIS as very much second division, being the main schoolteachers' union in Scotland. However all this is supposition, although there had to be a reason why at the very early stages in our negotiations the EIS gave clear indications that it was seeking a deal and the 'time was ripe'.

If any of us thought that the gates were wide open and the negotiations were going to be easy, then we were to learn quickly how rather good and professional the EIS was. I am not sure we expected the union to use the strike weapon, but equally I was not expecting some of my colleagues to roll over quite so quickly. Some of the hitherto strongest voices amongst my Principal colleagues buckled after the first day of the industrial action. Partly because we had already achieved a deal which we did not want undermined, RGU remained one of the hawks in the discussions on the Salaries Committee and in the full committee of 'Conference'. From the early stages of the negotiations with the trade unions I think the industrial relations adviser saw it as a personal test of his abilities to achieve a deal, although just short of a deal at any cost. I guess the waverers, and they were in the majority, had made it clear that a deal and a quick deal was what they and their governing bodies wanted. This put me in a difficult position, not just with my own people, but my role as chair of the Salaries Committee was being undermined. I was aware discussions were taking place bilaterally with the industrial relations adviser and meetings were being called with agendas and participants agreed without clearing with me. I would not have objected to any bilateral or informal contact had I been consulted, as from the first day as Salaries Committee chair I had adopted very much a 'real politik' stance. So, towards the end of the process I stepped aside and left the adviser to deal with us all, but informally led by the Principal of the institution that had become, by that stage of the game, the most compliant of the 'Conference' group. I had some sympathy with the Principal in question as he claimed, and with some justification, 'trouble at t'mill', although not his phrasing.

It is pointless to speculate what additional ground we could have gained if we had weathered a few more days of strike action. In the end both parties wanted to settle and I belief that the trade union side were happy to bring their members' contracts in line with the main stream of the university sector, not just in Scotland but also in the UK as a whole. It will be interesting to see how the EIS is able to hold onto its university membership in Scotland in the years ahead.

With a settlement on 30 May 2000 that covered much besides holidays and pay there was little point in maintaining 'Conference' as an institution, as its main justification was as a body to fix the pay (and at last the more important 'conditions') of the staff at member institutions. Individual 'Conference' institutions then joined the main UK negotiating body, the London-based University and Colleges Employers Association, with the inevitable Scottish sub-committee.

I much enjoyed my time as Salaries Committee chair and not only the chance to experience an industrial dispute from the other side of the fence, but also the chance to get to know most of the Principals and many of my opposite numbers on the respective governing bodies. As one would expect a minority, perhaps two or just possibly three were quite impressive, but the rest were run of the mill. At the same time I acted as a liaison channel to the club-like body that linked all the Scottish universities chairs of governors, university courts, or their equivalent. In many ways I regret I was not to be around to develop these contacts, as over three years this group of university chairmen had given me more encouragement than they might realise to pursue some of the blatant nonsense that frustrated me at my own institution. At the same time I found my membership of the Committee of University Chairmen (covering all UK universities) and its governance working party not only interesting but similarly comforting, with the opportunity to compare notes with a wide range of institutions across the UK, including Exeter, West of England, Glamorgan, Middlesex, East London and London's Goldsmiths universities. Amongst fellow chairmen was a former British Overseas Trade Board chair, Lord Pat Limerick, who preceded Lord Jellicoe at the BOTB. Lord Limerick was a popular British Overseas Trade Board chair with us officials and it was good to meet him again. As chair of the governing body of Goldsmith's College his role was far more prestigious than mine in Aberdeen.

The three years as university chair were busy ones. On average it took about two and a half days a week of my time. This included many meetings at the university, including appointments boards, meetings with staff, the Principal and individual governors, attendance at the main subsidiary committees of the board, the meetings of the board itself, as well time in my office at Schoolhill but mainly at home spent in preparation, dealing with correspondence, researching and writing a number of key papers for the board. Progress-chasing occupied too much of my time. Thankfully the targets of my chivvying amongst the university executive numbered less than the fingers on one hand but these individuals were particularly tiresome. On balance staff were more than helpful and some were outstanding in their willingness to co-operate and meet my requirements.

An article on university governance in the *Times Higher Supplement* of

18 December 1998 reports the retiring chair of Coventry University, Patrick Lister, as saying that being retired was integral to being a good chair, because of the necessary time commitments. At the same time governors and their chair must be in touch with the world around. A balance needs to be struck, with the ideal board containing a mix of skills and professions, and a mix of those who remain professionally active with a proportion that are 'retired', in the sense that they do not have the commitment of a demanding '9 to 5' job. However the majority of my contemporaries as chairmen of governors at Scottish universities were retired in the formal sense, although most had a portfolio of commitments and often these included other non-executive board appointments on public sector bodies or private companies. If the Committee of University Chairmen governance working party I served on was representative then the chairs of the majority of the English universities would likely be similarly 'retired'.

However there were occasions at Robert Gordon where I thought that some of the university officers would rather I was less visible and less committed. The chairman is the best placed of the governing body to spot not only irregularities but to spot the insidious drift away from policy set by the board, or in my experience the problem was more that the board was not adequately fulfilling its role in setting policy in the first place. The setting of broad strategy should be the responsibility of the governing body and in my view the surrender of responsibility to the executive had gone too far, and the annual process of drawing up and agreeing the strategic plan was central to my concern. One of my first priorities on becoming chair was to recover the board's responsibility for setting the university's strategic targets. In many instances my board colleagues had to be subtly bullied to address their responsibilities. This neither endeared me to those colleagues or to a number senior members of the university.

The potential to play 'games' by and between both governors and staff in the circumstances was considerable, and on occasions there was clear evidence of such. I referred earlier to the lack of any forum in the university to look at the long term future of the institution, say some ten or fifteen years down the line. I used the annual 'awaydays' to get the board to address where the university should be heading, and against the background of a market that was crowded and where our geography did not help. This exercise was not wholly supported by some senior academics, even though there was no provision for the senior management to undertake such a visioning exercise themselves. I cannot help but see a link between the attempts (in the event unsuccessful) at merger with Aberdeen University immediately after I had left the board, and the resistance I met during my tenure as chair to addressing the long term future of the university. Although I and colleagues always urged closer co-operation with our neighbouring academic institutions, including the further education colleges, there was never a hint in board discussions that we should be re-examining merger. There was one straw and that was gleaned from the businessman who took over the equivalent role to mine at Aberdeen University. Of course there were still those in the town that always opposed RGU obtaining university status, and some of these were graduates of Aberdeen University. This group had influence in some of the local key business forums and through their links to various government 'quangos'. My own views were well known to be against any renewed talks on a full merger and this was, as far as I was aware, the view of most of my board colleagues at the time.

It would be wrong to give the impression that all academic minds were closed to addressing the long-term future of the university. In my discussions with 'middle management', that is heads of small departments at senior lecturer level and above, there was often confusion as to what the university was about and where it was heading. For example were we, as were so many of the last batch of universities created, going to ape the older institutions and compete for scarce research funding from the government and its various agencies, or were we content to remain a largely vocational university and become even better at that role. At the same time research is a valuable part of scholarship and a good record in research attracts some of the best staff, or at least staff that have published successfully in academic journals, which is not always the same as staff that are good at teaching undergraduates. We were not helped in the debate by having, at that time, anything that might be described as a considered research strategy, even as part of the overall strategic plan. Again it was pressure from me as chair that eventually drew forth a focussed research strategy, although this remained a little on the thin side. I remember one relatively junior staff member saying to me "When we were RGIT I knew we were the best, but now we are RGU I am not sure". I felt rather the same as 'not being sure' where we were heading, and as the years passed the inheritance left by the previous Principal, David Kennedy, was waning. If as chair I was confused, then God help the rank and file.

In 1998 I suggested, in a paper to the board's Governance Working Party, that we should establish a new joint working group of governors and university staff to "look at long-term issues". This proposal was rejected by both sets of colleagues with a preference for the status quo, with the current committee structure of the board seen as adequate. However after nearly three years such a body was set up. It does remind one of the strap line that so epitomised old British Rail – 'We are getting there'. I always look for the reasons why an organisation or individual behaves in a certain way. Often the 'cock-up' theory is more likely to be correct than the conspiracy alternative. In this case there was no cock-up and the most charitable explanation might be 'the not invented here' obstacle that is so common in office politics.

An informal group of enthusiasts did come together to pursue the prospect of a special relationship with a large international bank. We looked at the mundane links a university might have with a bank but two or three of us were searching for a relationship that proved to be step too far for many. We were grappling towards an entirely new concept that was neither a private sector university nor an arrangement where the university merely entered into a contract to provide training for the bank's staff. We were beginning to explore the idea of a new hybrid between a commercial firm and a university. A number of large firms had already set up so-called 'universities', for example Motorola. At about the same time Microsoft had decided to invest eighty million dollars in a new computer science laboratory at Cambridge University. Such firms see themselves increasingly as creators, disseminators and users of knowledge, like universities. Many have created in-house training facilities which mirror, to a lesser or greater degree, universities. Some have contracted this to an external university, and even a Grampian-based firm has such a special relationship with an English university. RGU, in line with many other such institutions, has set up a virtual campus to provide degrees by distant learning, and although not a new idea it is further facilitated by new communications technology. Larger commercial firms are also establishing such distance learning facilities for staff and here again the gap between universities such as RGU and large commercial corporations is narrowing. There have been press articles over the years, including one in *The Economist* (4 October 1997) commenting that the future university will come to consist of 'a diminished core and a cloud of external relationships'. A key question is what would that core consist of? All these thoughts were much in mind as we groped our way towards formulating a proposal to the bank we were talking to. This time there was an element, for sure, of 'not invented here' by some university staff. The result was we wasted and lost the inside track we had to very senior levels in the bank, and RGU lost an important opportunity to rise above the competition. We were also hampered by not having a champion of sufficient status amongst the senior academic staff. Such ideas demand a lot of imagination, intellect and above all leadership if they are to fly.

I continued to think about the options open to the university and shared these whenever I could with the Principal and his staff. One such option that I peddled was that there was room for a vocational university that committed itself to serving the welfare state. With so many of our staff tied up in the provision of training for the nursing and other professions allied to medicine and social work, as well as all the courses linked to the built environment such as construction, architecture and design, there was a case that RGU could become a 'people's university'. As such we might commit ourselves to providing specialised training and contract research to the National Health Service, the employment departments, and local authority social work departments. Our engineering and pharmacy departments could contribute as could even the business school to a reorientation of the main focus of the university. Such a proposal, well worked up and packaged, should surely attract support from at least Scottish Executive ministers. This could be integral to reforms of the public service. Perhaps all this was too rich, too idealistic, too impractical or just too political. My ideas may have been way off beam but what I wanted more was to encourage some debate. As one senior academic colleague said later a merger with Aberdeen University was the easier option.

I was not against RGU merging with another university as such, but more appropriate I thought was a link with a university at the other end of the UK or in North America. I had suggested to the Principal a link with Surrey University, if for no other reason at the time than the geography was right and the development of a binary university with Surrey would provide genuine synergy, and particularly in marketing the resulting two campus university to overseas students, who could split their time between two very different locations. To my knowledge no approaches were made to Surrey.

A number of years earlier David Kennedy and I had looked at Memorial University in St John's, Newfoundland with similar ideas in mind, although at a very embryonic stage of thought. We signed a declaration of intent with Memorial in 1995 but all such agreements need a champion and without one at RGU the subsequent links were minimal.

A few years before our trip to St John's together I remember that I had arranged for David Kennedy to meet a business consultant that I had contracted to advise Grampian Regional Council on the development of new industries in the region. The gentleman concerned was a tough and in-your-face American. After a few minutes of chat he asked David would he be prepared to sell the intellectual rights of one of the university's schools to a large corporation in return for a massive injection of cash towards facilities and equipment at the school. David was not shocked at the suggestion, but thought for a number of seconds before replying "Yes". That directness is what I came to admire about David. It was this meeting that started me thinking more widely about options were open to the university to ensure its long term success. Never at the time did I imagine I would end up so closely involved with the university.

My three years as chairman passed remarkably quickly. During the last year I began to consider what I should do at the end of my term. I had the option to stay on the board for another three years, but not as chair. I took the early decision to resign from the board when my time was up as chairman and indicated this to colleagues in July 2000, with my last board meeting in the December of that year. The response was mixed, but overall I was left with the distinct impression that colleagues thought I was in some way dissatisfied or even disloyal in leaving ahead of the maximum permitted time allowed to be a governor. I explained that nobody welcomed yesterday's men with their tendency to offer unsolicited advice and it was best that ex-chairs got out of the way and left their successors a free hand. It was thought somewhat odd, at least, by most. However I suppose that I was less than honest, but at the same time necessarily diplomatic, in holding back some of the other reasons that contributed to my decision. Frankly I had, by then, had my fill of the frustrations of bringing about necessary change at the university. I am not the sort of person that could have taken a back seat and sat on my hands for the next three years. This would have been more frustrating than being chairman since as a back bencher I would have had even less chance of influencing affairs.

A few months before leaving the board I had suggested to the university that they should second a staff member to the city council to provide the leader of the council with a research capability. This idea had arisen when I had pressed the university to offer some leadership to the local community and had been challenged to be more specific. I put forward a number of ideas including initiatives that would enhance the university's ability to influence the thinking and strategy of local councils. I had in mind particularly our ability to influence the long term economic development strategy for the region. The university had the expertise within its business school to provide the council with the necessary research input to better frame future strategy. Preliminary discussion with the leader of the council, Councillor Len Ironside, indicated that this RGU input would be very welcome, although the funds would not be available to purchase such research. I saw that such an offer would be in both parties' interests. The city council would get a valuable academic research input and the university would receive in return a better insight to city thinking, as well as some experience that might contribute towards a research degree.

The idea lay on the table for almost a year and was used, unsuccessfully, by one university department as a lever to obtain an increase in their research budget allocation. Just before I retired from the board I managed to get the idea back on course although it was some nine months after I retired that the idea at last started to become a reality. It was some further months later I found out that a staff member of RGU had been assigned on a very part-time basis to the leader of Aberdeen Council. When it was later reported this arrangement was not working out too well I decided to offer my own services to Councillor Ironside.

I had worked with Len Ironside for a number of years when I was the planning and economic development director at Grampian Regional Council and he was then chairman of the Grampian Initiative. On the whole we got on well, at least when we were able to keep our respective mischief-making colleagues at bay. The proposal I put to him at the beginning of 2002 was quite simple: I would become his personal researcher to support his role as leader of Aberdeen Council to enable him and his colleagues to be better briefed on policy options open to the council. I would require from the council access to an office and all the normal information services open to council staff. I asked also that I had access to his discussions with his political colleagues and advisers. There would be no cost to the city council, and my time and services should be considered as the university's resource contribution to the community as represented by the council. I asked that the university provided me with all the services of a staff member, such as access to the library and computer services, as well as access to academic colleagues in a relevant department. I would provide my services free of charge, except for travelling expenses (which I decided not to claim), and all this in return for the title and status of visiting professor of public policy.

This was agreed by the Principal in June 2002 when I was formally offered an honorary visiting professorship in the School of Public Administration and Law, for three years in the first instance (subsequently renewed for a further three years in 2005). So my new role as, in essence, a political researcher began in the summer of that year. Because the university is a publicly funded body, my services were, in theory, available to all political parties within the council, although in practice my work was to the Leader of the Labour led administration. The chief executive of the council was informed and it was for him to clear any internal complications. As far as I was concerned there were no problems and as soon as I had received a staff security pass I was to bump into many members of the opposition parties, and a fair number of these I knew as they had served as councillors on the former regional council. None seemed to raise an eyebrow when I explained what I was doing. I was received with politeness, and actually quite enjoyed meeting old colleagues again, both elected members and officials.

The experience was to be a short one as the following April (2003) the Labour group lost its control of Aberdeen council which meant the end of my role. The university did ask whether I wished to continue my research role with the new Liberal Democrat-led administration, although I had no idea whether that administration would welcome such an arrangement. That Labour lost control was no surprise and indeed I had warned Len Ironside some months earlier of a likely collapse of the Labour vote.

I would not have missed the experience of working with the council, although it was not nearly as rewarding as I had hoped it would be. I received no further contact from the university department I was attached to after an initial introduction. This was not of particular concern to me as it had been the Principal who had pressed me to play a parallel role with the university department and to contribute to departmental policy and undertake the odd lecture. I was concerned that this additional commitment might take up too much of my time, and especially as the university would get my time for nothing. However, I need not have worried as they never bothered me and this allowed me to focus on my role in support of the council leader. Secondly, the research role proved to be more tiresome than I expected. It was not that it was in any way demanding, but more my political boss was difficult to access and I feel he had underestimated the amount of input he had to make to ensure that I was gainfully employed. I would produce a paper on a subject agreed with him but then weeks would elapse before I got any feedback and then often only after I had left messages on his answerphone or with officials in the council. I would have welcomed comment that the ideas were impracticable. When we met, Len was fine and I enjoyed working with him, but there simply was not enough close working to give me the links

I needed. The arrangement did not allow him to get the best out of me, and certainly I was not getting the job satisfaction that I needed as a 'volunteer'.

The period was not entirely unproductive. I did some work on vagrants, an assessment of the Aberdeen bypass, and produced with Len a radical proposal to reorganise the council. This was put to the Labour group and was promptly leaked to the local evening newspaper — the *Evening Express* of 28 November 2002. However in political terms the leak may have been an unexpected bonus as Len and the proposals received front page and two additional inside pages of coverage. Unfortunately this was all too late for the Labour group. The leak also included my warning that the writing was on the wall and we approached the April elections 'with a sense of foreboding'. The leak may have come from within the Labour group as all members were circulated a copy of the then confidential proposals. It brought home to me again that I did not have a sufficiently thick skin to be a successful professional politician, rather than the politician *manqué* that in my less temperate moments I sometimes see myself as. There have been many public servants cross the divide and become successful politicians, although most of the examples I can think of are those where the individual spent only a relatively short time as the official, for example former prime minister Harold Wilson. For most people I think the two types of public service vocation are so different as to make the successful transition from one to the other difficult. During my period at Grampian Regional Council a former Director of Roads was elected as a Liberal Democrat to the same council he had recently retired from. I know he found the transition difficult. As an elected councillor he was unhappy making concessions on the promises that he had made in his election manifesto. As a very honest and straight man he found the nip and tuck of real politik too rich and resigned. I think I would rail against party discipline and whip control, but I still would like to have been a professional politician. My problem now would be to chose a party that I would feel comfortable in.

I chaired my last board of governors meeting at the university in December 2000. The agenda seemed a long one and it was not until the end of the meeting that we reached my report on my period as chairman. I had spent a long time in preparing this as I was anxious to avoid one of those occasions when the retiring person reports all through rose-tinted spectacles. I was happy to leave that to the 'PR' brochures, and besides the board was a tad too well practised at patting itself on the back, in line with the prevailing Aberdonian culture. At the time I had just read John

Campbell's biography of Nye Bevan and one of Bevan's favourite phrases quoted was 'to allow the future to be born'. These words seemed to sum up my struggle with RGU over the preceding three years. Behind Bevan's phrase was his belief that society depended on leaders unafraid. Where my final report was critical I tried to couch such criticism in as constructive terms as possible. I had hoped, perhaps very naively, that I might give some pointers to my successor whilst taking a gentle swipe at what I saw as the too often self-satisfied and complacent nature of most of my board colleagues. There was no time to discuss my valedictory paper but this was perhaps as well. The only comment I got was from one of our more quiescent female board members, who said she found my thoughts 'so depressing'. I did clear the paper with the Principal to see if he objected to any of the points raised. He did not, but that is quite distinct from indicating any agreement.

My approach to the period as chair was to be informal, as indeed has always been my style of 'management' of people, but what jarred, I suspect, with many colleagues was my belief in a degree of pressure to achieve change. At about the same time the retiring CEO of the chemical company ICI, Brandon O'Neill, was reported in *Chemistry in Britain* as liking to work with people 'who are passionate about what they are doing', and valuing 'passion and commitment a little more than intellect at times'. I can identify closely with that approach, but throughout my career this has often caused me more problems than it it has solved. My experience at RGU was no different.

The university were very kind to me on leaving. Within the year I was offered the honorary degree of Doctor of Business Administration. I cannot pretend this was a great surprise as my predecessor as chairman had received a similar degree, but I was genuinely honoured and, yes, thrilled. My graduation day was a memorable occasion, as was the dinner arranged for me and Fiona at the Marcliffe Hotel the previous evening, hosted by Bill Stevely, the Principal. What was unexpected was that the Principal asked me to give the address to fellow graduates at the ceremony held in Aberdeen's 'Music Hall'.

I was free to speak on any topic although speeches on such occasions must be brief and must be suitably uplifting in one way or another. I chose to speak on public service as a worthwhile career. I set out to right the balance in the debate between public and private sectors by a number, of what I hoped, were amusing anecdotes. One such story concerned a young friend of mine in the investment management business and my attempts to convince her that peer group respect and loyalty were as important as money to an employee. She was unconvinced and said "Howard, if you want loyalty, buy a dog". On a more serious note I referred to the rewards to be had in sharing in the public service ethos with its strong emphasis on commitment but also a code of care, compassion and loyalty. I finished my address with a number of tips to a successful career in public service. I think the message went down well enough as a number of university colleagues in the weeks that followed commented to the effect that it was about time the balance between the public sector and business was redressed and welcomed my attempts to do this at the graduation ceremony.

My long friend Roy Cunningham was able to be present at the ceremony as was David Kennedy and my family. It was an emotional day and one I will never forget.

As an honorary graduate one is able to return to all subsequent graduations. It is a chance to dress up in the splendid red robes of the university's honorary graduates and join the academic procession onto the platform. I attended many graduations in my capacity as a board member, and each is always an uplifting experience. To witness so many young (and a few older) graduates reap the rewards of three or more years of hard work and see, not only their faces, but also the faces of many proud parents and relations is a happy occasion that is difficult to equal.

My public service involvement continued after my period as chair of governors, but it was not until the local authority elections in April 2003 and the termination of my role as adviser to the leader of Aberdeen Council that my links with public service really came to an end. I continued to serve on a number of charities which depended on public funding to a large extent, including one dealing with mental health. In all these I was able to pass on my experience in dealing with public sector bodies but I was not able to get the satisfaction from these roles that I had hoped. This may be something to do with the fact that the element of passion was missing or, perhaps more disturbing, it had died a little within me. I remain a radical but perhaps the flames need more of an catalyst than before. I feel I need time for reflection, and am even somewhat disillusioned.

Chapter 24

Nunc dimittis [1]

I have tried to examine my motives in wishing to write a book about my working life. Has it been a bout of colossal arrogance to think that anyone would wish to read about the life of a very ordinary and scarcely known individual? I have often thrown down my newspaper in exasperation on reading of the publication of yet another biography or autobiography of some 'C' category show business or sports personality and wonder who would be interested. The test is often the speed with which such biographies of 'celebrities' turn up on the remaindered counter at the local book shop. Surely that should be enough to deter anyone like me from writing an autobiography.

Then there is the difficulty or almost impossibility of finding a publisher when one is totally unknown as a writer or a 'personality'. There have been a number of books recently by public servants, including the more notorious such as the former MI5 agent David Shaylor and the slightly less glamorous Clive Ponting, and not least the memoirs of the former MI5 head, Stella Rimington. It was Civil Servant Ponting who blew the whistle on aspects of the sinking by the British of the Argentine naval vessel the *Belgrano* during the Falklands war. He was tried and acquitted at the Old Bailey under Section 2 of the Official Secrets Act for passing documents to Labour MP, Tam Dalyell. I suspect finding a publisher for a book on his role in the affair was not too difficult. However Clive Ponting has published subsequently other books. I enjoyed and would recommend his analysis of Civil Service life in his book "Whitehall: Tragedy and Farce" (1986). There have been one or two books by former so-called 'mandarins', that is by those at the pinnacle of the Whitehall machine. In that context it is interesting to compare the recall by a senior official of the same event with that of a Minister. I have enjoyed reading books by those whose actions I brushed against as a middle-ranking official in DTI. Here I would particularly mention Ian MacGregor's book "The Enemies Within", which is the account of his time as Chairman of the National Coal Board during the 1984-85 miners' strike. This is nicely complemented by Bill Sirs' record of that period in his book "Hard Labour" when he was General Secretary to the

Iron and Steel Trades Confederation. Morrison Halcrow's biography of Sir Keith Joseph, the architect of much of the political theory that underlined Thatcherism and who was one of a long parade of ministers to be in charge of DTI or one of the DTI family of ministries during my time at the department, is a sensitive and important insight to a man who was misunderstood by many, including myself at the time. Most delicious of all was reading Alan Clark's indiscreet diaries which also covered the period when we were both at DTI. Clark was as scathing of some civil servants as he was of many businessmen and of course his colleagues in the Tory party. His private office came out reasonably well although maybe some of the staff were not to meet all his requirements. At the time he was a DTI minister I used to hear stories from colleagues who accompanied Clark on his official overseas trips, but it was not until I had read the diaries that the stories and description of his behaviour made any sense. Although our respective lives and experiences have almost nothing in common I have now a sense of fellow-feeling with Clark and share some of his many prejudices, although short of moving from the opposite end of the political spectrum at which I have always found myself.

All the authors and individuals I refer to are well known and have an interesting story to tell. I ask myself, constantly, what have I got to offer a prospective reader with a story about a professional life that only rarely rose above the mediocre and the humdrum?

Arising more from frustration I started to think about writing a book about my time in the Civil Service during my last two years in DTI when I was, from 1985 to 1988, Director of Exports for the south-east region of England. I had not kept a detailed diary but since about 1980 I had begun to keep newspaper cuttings and photographs and one or two notes with a book in mind. It was not until the end of my time at Grampian Regional Council that I started to seriously think about what sort of story I had to tell. I toyed with writing a collection of amusing anecdotes about public service, somewhat similar to the format of the tales of Yorkshire vet James Herriot. However I felt I had too much anger to dissipate to emulate the Herriot approach and after nearly seven years with a local authority at senior level I saw a niche to write about my public service experience. Few individuals have extensive experience in both central and local government. Then after retirement from local authority work in 1996 I was fortunate to experience yet another facet of public service, through my involvement in academic administration. This last role finally convinced me that I had a story to tell. My approach has been not to reveal secrets or whistle-blow but more to relate the frustrations, as well as a fair amount of joy and satisfaction, to be found in public service. I was senior enough to see a wide range of tasks and people but not senior enough to lose touch with the rank and file. I feel both my character and career enable me to give an insight to what public service is really like, and with no need to be shy of describing the warts.

An important part of the initial motivation to write about my Civil Service experiences was the change in the standing and status of the public servant wrought during the years of the Thatcher government. This corrosive influence has continued unabated through a Labour government under Blair. I was not foolish enough to believe that a change to a Labour government would suddenly reverse government and business attitudes to public service. However I did think that there would at least be a line drawn under the assumption at the heart of so much government 'spin' that 'private sector' or business equals 'good', and public sector is synonymous with waste, inefficiency and fecklessness. If anything New Labour has been worse in the sense that they are less honest than the Tories and so much is wrapped up in weasel wording. There were many good things about Margaret Thatcher and one was that all knew exactly where they stood, and she did exactly as it said on the packet. Putting aside political belief and dogma I would rather have an 'enemy' the likes of Mrs Thatcher than a 'friend' the likes of Prime Minister Tony Blair.

Underpinning my need to get something down for posterity is the fact that I know so little about the events and pressures that took my father into the building trade. Both father and mother, if not secretive, were sparing in releasing information on events that shaped their early life. Much of mother's childhood remains a mystery with only a few glimpses presenting themselves since her death in 2002, and then when I was already into my sixties. Both parents operated on a 'need to know' basis and not always then as my mother's birth certificate came to light some months after my registration of her death. Consequently she is registered as being born in Aberystwyth and not, as was the case, Leyton in east London Essex. In trying to find out a little more about the Fisher side of the family my second cousins let me have a few pages written at a very late stage by their father, Jack Fisher (my father's first cousin), about his young life. This small shred of Fisher history influenced me to take steps to ensure my children had a better record to pass on to the family than was available to me. I have always maintained tidy records but since my father's death I have been almost possessed in maintaining photographic and other archives. I inherited many photographs of father's relatives from Victorian and Edwardian times but very few are labelled and the identity of those photographed is lost for ever. Our family is small with just two first cousins via my father's sister and the two second cousins being the children of the Uncle Jack I refer to above. Getting old also prompts obsession with 'getting one's affairs in order' and no doubt this made a contribution to my decision to write about my life in public service.

With no Civil Service tradition in the family, including family acquired through marriage, a constant question asked was 'What do you actually do?', with always the emphasis on the 'do', as if the suspicion was that I did very little as a civil servant. This has irritated me over the years and was not helped by the 'Yes, Minister' television series. It was not only that my life in Whitehall had little in common with the the television series but more that it made the role of a civil servant looks even more useless than some might have believed before the series. Like most, I hugely enjoyed the adventures of Jim Hacker and his chums and concede that in the humour, as with all good humour, there was some, and necessarily cruel, truth. To really appreciate the funny side of 'Yes, Minister' it helped to have some understanding of life at the top in Whitehall. Few of my friends and relatives had this basic understanding and hence the recurring question as to what I actually did.

I would like to claim that I joined the Civil Service for a life of dedication to my fellow citizens and that the motivation was the opportunity and privilege of service. I cannot claim any such 'calling' or vocation. I had long decided not to follow my father into his business, although I know this was a disappointment to him. By the time I was finishing my research degree I was already hostile to big business although I did attend one or two of the 'milk round' interviews with the likes of ICI, but more with a view to testing the market than any remote wish to join a large agro-chemicals firm. I felt, perhaps wrongly at the time, that I would be required to sell my soul in some way as part of the expectation by such employers that I should become a 'company man'. What I am quite sure of now and forty years later is that I would have been a disaster in a large commercial company where one has to toe the line somewhat if any career progress is to be achieved. Part of my problem is I have never been a 'company man' or indeed anyone's man. Team-playing in the conventional sense, where authority and direction has to be respected and acceded to, has always been a difficult role for me. My parting with office in my Civil Service trade union was because I refused to accept direction to a particular committee, although if it had been discussed with me I am sure I would have reached a compromise with the national branch secretary. I am not sure even at this late stage whether I choose and enjoy being the outsider looking in or whether I am the victim in the sense of accepting some sort of self-imposed 'Coventry'.

For better or worse it was an advertisement in the *Observer* that brought me to public service and for perhaps the wrong and misguided reason that I thought it would be glamorous and, perhaps oddly, I found life as a research chemist lonely. Although never a 'joiner' I am not a 'loner' and welcomed the opportunity that the Civil Service would provide for meeting a new range of people and those that were intellectually stimulating. Neither school, nor university had provided me with the stimulation that I needed to give of my best. Much of the antagonism I generated in colleagues at school was as much to do with stirring up debate than any wish to alienate, and the same goes for colleagues I met during my initial degree in agriculture. It was this desire for the new and unexplored that prompted me to answer the advertisement for the Civil Service's then 'Administrative Class'. At the same time there was little sense of ambition, and one certainly does not join the Service to become rich. I did not see the Civil Service as key to a different life style in the social or class sense, as I was no working class lad with an eye to a better accent and the right friends. In a way I had no need for all this, thanks to the family and my education, although as I have said the family, although middle class, was odd.

The Civil Service at the time I joined still shared much of a tradition that stretched back to the 1940s and the Administrative Class perceived itself as the officer and the gentleman cadre, and along with this tradition there was an all-pervasive and deep sense of public duty. However I quickly found out that the public service ethos was as strong amongst the executive and clerical ranks as it was in the officer class. I found all this very comforting as I needed an 'heroic dream of betterness' and I have sought that grail since. However, with respect to what the Civil Service was looking for in its young Assistant Principals, my initial assessment of my new career was misplaced to say the least. Many years later when trying to explain to a friend and former Whitehall warrior of my need for an element of passion in my job, it was obvious from his response that this was just about the worst thing I could have sought if I was to have made significant progress in the service. What was wanted was the laid-back and languid disinterest of the archetypal Old Etonian, where the chase was more interesting and important than the outcome. I did get a perverse pleasure in acquiring the ability to draft a brief for one government and then redraft it to the requirements of a new government of a totally different political persuasion the next day.

Nonetheless as far as job satisfaction was concerned I was happier working in policy areas where at least I had an element of sympathy with the policy pursued, which is not the same as political agreement. However if the team I worked with had a degree of shared enthusiasm and had good leadership I could come to terms with most jobs. Unfortunately I had a number of postings within DTI where there was poor staff leadership, where I was underemployed and where the subject matter failed to arouse any passion at all. These postings proved somewhat of a disaster for me.

King George VI described leadership as the gift of vision and a desire to leave the world a better place. Very few of my bosses, at whatever grade, met that description of leadership. If they had I am sure I would have been both happier and more effective. Leadership of men in the context used in the armed forces was a rare commodity in my Civil Service experience. Some of the best people I came across had made the transfer from the armed forces to the Civil Service at that level where promotion becomes very difficult in the armed services. These ex-officers did have good man-management skills and one of my best bosses was such an ex-naval officer. Like any good leader he did not need to resort to the disciplinary apparatus or use the threat of a poor performance marking in the annual report to get the best from his team. At the same time he did have passion for the job.

Over the years I saw a slow decline in the commitment of the executive staff and then amongst the ranks of Principal (later to be termed Grade 7), and especially those who had not been picked as fast track material. It was made clear to many of the latter that promotion avenues would be very restricted and so there was a strong element of demotivation. Sometimes this was made clear by denial of certain in-service training courses and in other instances many were told, bluntly, that was as far as they were going in terms of promotion. A more subtle approach by 'management' was to keep people in the same jobs for long periods, that is five and more years, on the pretext that the department wished to develop more staff specialism. At the same time we all knew that those destined for greater things rarely spent more than three years in the same job, as was the pattern of postings and career development in the former Administrative Class. All this coincided with the Thatcher years when there was great pressure from government to reduce the size of the Civil Service. Reductions in numbers were achieved by the creation of a plethora of government agencies or 'next steps agencies' and the staff transferred to these agencies ceased to be counted towards the Civil Service total. There was a surge in early retirement with some very good packages on offer. As often happens in such circumstances it is not always the staff you wish to shed that volunteer.

Such was the pressure at the time, combined with the attractiveness of the severance deal, that I suspect the government rather overdid the slimming operation. The evidence for this was the need to buy back some of these skills through the use of consultants and in some cases the use as consultants of the very same civil servants that had taken the severance deal and left the service. This happened to a friend of mine. He was a bright Assistant Secretary and through some inept management had become disillusioned and had taken the early retirement package. Aged fifty and with a pension enhancement of something like six and two thirds years it was an attractive deal, and fitted my friend's personal circumstances. For the next nine years he has made a respectable supplement to his pension by selling his services back to the Civil Service.

There was no single cause for my disillusionment with the service but my perception that the public service ethos was being rapidly eroded was a key factor. The service I left in 1988 was a different creature to the one I joined in 1967. The Thatcher years saw the curse of the management culture upon us. In my last job I spent hours defining objectives and ensuring we had an imitation, although somewhat pale, of the deadly apparatus of business management. It is not that I am against an efficient delivery of public services and would not deny there are lessons to be learnt from the private sector, but the two types of business are very different animals. This was to be brought home further to me when I was involved with Robert Gordon University and also in the administration of a local charity. Businessmen were involved in both and tried to insensitively transfer their business management skills to public administration. In both cases the business people had failed to grasp the nature of the public sector, and particularly its need for much more transparent accountability. I spent a lot of time during my last three years at DTI implementing centrally required reporting systems where the philosophy was 'if you cannot measure it then you cannot manage it'. Again, in some sorts of business, there is a lot to be said for the approach and there are even some aspects of the public service where the approach could be helpful. But like so many management fads borrowed from industry at the time, the good aspects were lost by the excessive zeal of the convert and a failure to adapt the best attributes sensitively to the very different needs of public service.

It was not so many years later when I was at Grampian Regional Council that I was able to apply some of the lessons learnt at DTI, although in a negative sense I fear. In a misguided attempt to impose what councillors deemed as a tighter financial discipline a whole series of targets were set and regularly reviewed by a committee of elected members. Each departmental director was called to account and to explain any shortfall or shortcomings in meeting the targets set for the department. Some of these targets were financial but many were measurements of service provision such as telephone and letter response time or number of 'customers' serviced, be that an internal or external customer. The problem for councillors was their relative lack of knowledge of the system and the services provided and so it was very easy to produce data, often spurious, that met their needs. In a perverse way I rather enjoyed these star chamber sessions. It was very rare for me or my colleagues from other departments to be wrong-footed, although all relished the sense of theatre when a hawkish councillor seemed to be on to a winner in cross examination of the official concerned. So, there was an element of sport about these regular performance review sessions. Spice was added when for some elected members of the council it became 'personal' and the exchange became more like an inquisition. Happily this rarely happened to me although a number of councillors had me in their sights.

The idea of performance review was good in principle, but not enough thought had been put into the exercise to ensure the targets set were meaningful or realistic in terms of measuring the effectiveness or the efficiency of the service concerned. By that stage in my career I was an old hand at the numbers game, and was aware that such poorly devised exercises contributed very little to the efficiency of the service, and had learnt in the Civil Service that anybody with half a brain could meet the misguided objectives of 'management' with not too much distraction from the real job in hand. In no way was I hostile to performance measurement and indeed would have welcomed political support in improving the performance of my own staff, but I was against reporting systems that took up a lot of staff time and caused my staff to become cynical about all performance measurement, good and bad. The control systems implemented during my time at Grampian Region just irritated staff, who quickly saw the irrelevancies of the counting procedures they were directed to implement. So cynical was one senior member of my staff that he, unbeknown to me for some months, made up his own and entirely fictitious returns. Unfortunately he was not sufficiently imaginative and I became suspicious of the often 100% performance returns and asked to see the disaggregated data. There was no such data.

To some extent in all this I was hoisted by my own petard as it was me in a recommendation in my "Together to the Future" economic strategy that introduced the concept of total quality management to the council. This was seized upon by the incoming Labour-led administration as a way of improving the council's efficiency, although I suspect it was more about control for control's sake and control of officials in particular. The Convener of the council and a few others of influence in that Labour administration were often motivated in their relationship with senior officials more by resentment and envy than by any altruistic drive for a better return on the taxpayer's money.

There was a parallel between my experiences with Labour politicians in local government and the behaviour of the subsequent 'New Labour' of the Blair administration. Both had a love /hate relationship with big business and wealth, although in the Blair case it was more an undiluted and undying devotion to big business. At least Labour politicians in Grampian were occasionally apologetic and carried some guilt as in reality many of our Labour members were old-fashioned Labour and use of the word 'socialist' was not an embarrassment, with lip service only paid to Labour headquarters in Glasgow. We had also a fellow-traveller or two with roots in what the press call the 'hard left'.

Part of the reason why the big oil corporations got an easy ride from local politicians in Scotland and particularly Grampian was the ease with which local goodwill was bought. I am not suggesting that our politicians were susceptible to the lure of brown envelopes. It was more that our politicians seemed mesmerised or even cowed by the enormous power and wealth of the oil corporations. On many occasions I wanted to question the return that Grampian had received from North Sea oil, over and above the employment of its labour and the purchase of other goods and services by the oil companies. Only little Shetland had been bold enough to seek compensation for the community via a 'disturbance' charge on the oil companies, and this was to be used to contribute to a future for the islands once the oil caravan had moved on. The excuse given for our more submissive stance in Grampian was that we were in a competitive market and there was always the opportunity for the oil industry to place their business with more compliant communities such as Dundee or Montrose. In reality Aberdeen had little competition in becoming the nation's offshore oil capital, notwithstanding that Glasgow had attracted the transient Britoil operation. Happily for Aberdeen nature had placed the oil on the east side of the country and never was Glasgow going to be the exploration and exploitation servicing centre for the North Sea oil fields. Newcastle had all the benefits of a skills base with a good air and sea ports but the helicopter trips to the offshore rigs would have been too long and expensive. Nonetheless there remains, even at the time of writing, a local self-imposed censorship on criticism of the oil companies.

The oil 'majors' spent the minimum needed to keep locals in Grampian 'sweet'. Indeed the oil companies here got away with less than would be expected by communities in the United States where there is a stronger tradition of corporations reinvesting in their host communities. On my many trips to both the United States and Canada I took the opportunity of talking to senior managers of some of the same companies that operated in the North Sea. There was a noticeable difference in approach to investment in the host community by these same companies when operating in the United States, and whether they were 'British' in origin or US made no difference. In the US there seemed to be more of a tradition of support for the local community, over and above the purchase of the companies' immediate needs. US companies made the link between self-interest and return to the community they relied upon for the profitability of their business. In Grampian and also, oddly perhaps, in Canada, 'putting something back' was equated with tiresome requests for charitable donations, and the challenge was handling this pressure with the minimum input.

We might expect American based colleagues to adopt a more gung-ho exploitative approach to communities but I did not find this the case. There is a stronger tradition of charitable giving in the US at the level of the individual than is the case in the UK and especially by the more privileged sector of society. When I pressed senior oil executives here on putting more back into the community that was the source of their wealth their response was 'why should we be different from any other sector, and anyway we pay enough in taxes' etc. Of course there are many modern UK examples of corporate investment in 'their' community, for example Boots, Moores and Clarks but I fear they are the exception rather than the rule.

It never ceased to amaze me how an invitation to lunch or the theatre from an oil company was sufficient to silence most of Grampian's local politicians, and any attempt that I made to seek a better deal for the community from the oil companies was met with an agitated request 'not to rock the boat'. Just before leaving local government I did manage to arrange for a critical article to be printed in the *Press and Journal* (6 September 1995). Although my Scottish Nationalist committee chairman was encouraging I got very little support from other members of the council, as had been the case on earlier occasions on raising the question about what the oil companies had done for us, over and above buying our goods and services. Clearly, Grampian had been good for the oil companies.

I hate the concept of studied personal networking as this seems a devious and contrived approach to making friends and winning respect, and so I never have had a wide array of regular contacts. This has made it difficult for me to say with any degree of certainty whether my views on public service are representative of my contemporaries in the same line of work. I believe there has been a distinct retreat from the public service ethos over the years since Margaret Thatcher became Prime Minister. There is some support for this view from a few close friends. However in very recent years this view has gathered support in press articles and books, including Anthony Sampson's 'Anatomy of Britain in the 21st Century'. It has been comforting to find that I was not in a small minority made up of discontents and 'the usual suspects' in detecting a wide spread loss of staff morale in my last few years in the Civil Service. For some reason this was harder to detect amongst local authority staff. Paralleling this change has been the steady insinuation of business influence and business 'ethics' into every aspect of public life. A key goal has been to indoctrinate our youth and one of the more insidious weapons has been the introduction of 'entrepreneurial studies' to school and college courses.

Part of this loss of morale must be attributed to the regular and odious comparisons made of the public sector with the world of commerce and industry and how much business had to teach us in the public service in terms of efficiency. New Labour has encouraged and continued this unfavourable comparison with constant talk of 'reform' of the public services. The absence of much detail as to what exactly Blair and his Ministers wish by way of 'reform' only adds to suspicion that 'reform' is merely a code for the introduction of more business methods. If only British business was that efficient! My own experiences over recent years and together with press reports of the goings-on in some of our larger corporations indicate there is limited opportunity for our private sector to act as a role model to their public service counterparts. What we all see more clearly now is a business ethos where self-interest, greed and deception take priority over responsibility to the shareholders, good treatment of staff and a respect for the customer. It was no surprise to me that a 'British' oil company has been found misleading shareholders and the stock market as to the true size of its oil reserves. If there is one weak thread that runs through post-war Britain it is the quality of our business managers. The collapse of our motor manufacturing industry can be laid more at the door of incompetent management than any trade union practice or 'unfair' Asian competition.

If we are to retain a public service that even measures up to that of our neighbours in France, let alone return to a situation where we have a public service the envy of the world, Governments of what ever political persuasion must act quickly to restore morale and start once again to extol the virtues of selfless public service. Rewards such as pay and a pension are important, and not just for those at the top, but as important is that public servants feel valued and are seen to be valued by their employer. Happily, the public at large has never entirely lost that respect for its servants, be they employed at the local post office, in the classroom, or at the local health centre. What is also disappearing, and more worrying, is public servant self-esteem.

We British see ourselves as a fair-minded people, and see our public servants similarly so and also incorruptible. Do we trade this image of our public servants for one closer to that of the current perception of big business, where directors' performance bonuses and share options, and company profit margins become central in a new public service morality? We do this at our nation's peril.

After a bumpy and sometimes far from comfortable experience of the public sector at a working level I remain committed to the ethos of public service. I have been privileged to work with colleagues where the majority shared that commitment to public service. It sounds pompous but I have enjoyed the opportunity to contribute in a little way to what might be described as the public good. I was rewarded fairly for this and my lifestyle has been comfortable, although not lavish. I have had a far more varied career than many in the private sector and this has been part of the reward as far as I am concerned. I know I would have been bored if I had pursued my initial training and joined one of the large chemical companies. More importantly I know also I would have been a failure as 'corporate man' and no business employer would have been as patient with me as have been my various bosses in public service. I remain grateful to DTI in it's various guises and to Grampian Regional Council for giving me that opportunity to serve.

I remember an old television advertisement for the London Metropolitan Police which went something like: 'The Met, dull it isn't.'

For me, dull it wasn't.

December 2005

[1] 'Nunc dimittis' is traditionally sung at Church of England Evensong service and begins 'Lord, now lettest thou thy servant depart in peace...'

Glossary

Agrichem – Agricultural Chemistry Department at Glasgow University
AP – Assistant Principal
ASTMS – Association of Scientific, Technical and Managerial Staff
AUT – Association of University Teachers
A/V – Audio visual presentation
BA – Buenos Aires, Argentina
BAEC – British Agricultural Export Council
BISPA – British Iron and Steel Producers Association
BOTB – British Overseas Trade Board
BSC – British Steel Corporation
BSE – Bovine Spongiform Encephalopathy
BT – British Telecom
CA – Clerical Assistant
CCF – Combined Cadet Force
CCT – Common Customs Tariff of the European Union
CEDA – Calgary Economic Development Authority
CIA – Central Intelligence Agency
CIU – Clubs and Institutes Union
CJD – Creutzfeldt Jacobs Disease
CNAA – Council for National Academic Awards
CO – Clerical Officer
C of E – Church of England
COI – Central Office of Information
CP – Communist Party of Great Britain
CPSA – Clerical and Professional Staff Association
CQMS – Company Quarter Master Sergeant
CRE – Commercial Relations and Exports Division of DTI
CRE2 – Branch 2 of CRE Division of DTI
CSSB – Civil Service Selection Board
CUC – Committee of University Chairmen
DHSS – Department of Health and Social Security
DIY – Do-it-yourself
DNA – Deoxyribonucleic acid
DoE – Department of the Environment
DSIR – Department of Scientific and Industrial Research
DTI – Department of Trade and Industry
ECGD – Export Credit Guarantee Department

EDP – Economic Development and Planning Department –GRC
EEB – Exports to Europe Branch of DTI
EFTA – European Free Trade Area
EIS – Educational Institute for Scotland – trade union
EO – Executive Officer
E Division – Establishments Division of Ministry of Technology then DTI
FDA – First Division Association – trade union
FCO – Foreign and Commonwealth Office
G Division – General Division of DTI
GATT – General Agreement on Tariffs and Trade
GCHQ – Government Communications Headquarters
GEDAC – Grampian Economic Development Advisory Council
GEL or Gel – Grampian Enterprise Limited
GLC – Greater London Council
GMWU – General and Municipal Workers Union
GNP – Gross National Product
GRC – Grampian Regional Council
HARC – Houston Advanced Research Centre
HEO – Higher Executive Officer
HMG – Her Majesty's Government
HMI – Her Majesty's Inspectorate
IC – Industrial and Commercial Policy Division of DTI
ICI – Imperial Chemical Industries
IP – Industrial Policy Division of Ministry of Technology
IS – Iron and Steel Division of DTI
ISTC – Iron and Steel Trades Confederation - trade union
Quango – Quasi autonomous nongovernmental organisation
LGC – Laboratory of the Government Chemist
MAFF – Ministry of Agriculture, Fisheries and Food
M&S – Marks and Spencer
Mintech – Ministry of Technology
MI6 – Secret Intelligence Service
MOD – Ministry of Defence
MOU – Memorandum of Understanding
NESDA – North East of Scotland Development Agency
NHS – National Health Service
OC – Old Cranleighan
OECD – Organisation for Economic Co-operation and Development
OTC – Offshore Technology Conference – Houston, Texas

PCB – Polychlorinated biphenyl
PQ – Parliamentary Question
PR – Public relations
P&R – Policy Resources Committee of Grampian Council
prep – After school study or homework
Prep school – Primary school leading to 'public' school entrance
PhD – Doctor of Philosophy – research degree
PRT – Petroleum Revenue Tax
RGIT – Robert Gordon Institute of Technology
RGU – The Robert Gordon University, Aberdeen
RNA – Ribonucleic acid
SCPS – Society of Civil and Public Servants – trade union
SDA – Scottish Development Agency
SEG – Scottish Enterprise Grampian – see GEL above
SEO – Senior Executive Officer
SERO – South East Regional Office of DTI
SET – Selective Employment Tax
SHEFC – Scottish Higher Education Funding Council
SNP – Scottish National Party
SP – Starting price – racing term
TQM – Total Quality Management
UKAEA – United Kingdom Atomic Energy Authority
USD – State University of South Dakota
UMIST – University of Manchester Institute of Science & Technology
UV – Ultra violet light
WEC – World Energy Cities

List of publications referred to

A History of Cranleigh School – Alan J Megahey, Collins, 1983
The Lost Continent – Travels in Small Town America – Bill Bryson, Abacus 1990
Collins Field Guide to Archaeology in Britain – Eric Wood
The Ragged Trousered Philanthropist – Robert Tressel
A Walk in the Hindu Kush – Eric Newby
Scottish planning Law and Procedure – Eric Young, Jeremy Rowan-Robinson, William Hodge & Co Ltd, 1985
Whitehall Tragedy and Farce – Clive Ponting, Hamish Hamilton Ltd, 1986
The Enemies Within – Ian MacGregor, Collins 1986
Hard Labour – Bill Sirs, Sidgwick & Jackson 1985
Keith Joseph – A Single Mind – Morrison Halcrow, Macmillan, 1989
Alan Clark Diaries – In Power 1983-1992 – Phoenix 1994
Who Runs this Place – Anatomy of Britain in the 21st Century – Anthony Sampson, John Murray, 2004
Nye Bevan – A Biography – John Campbell, Richard Cohen Books, 1997
Press & Journal – newspaper published by Aberdeen Journals

Cover Design: The Digital Canvas Company
Forres
Scotland
bookcovers@digican.co.uk

Layout: Stephen Young
touv@mac.com

Fonts: Adobe Garamond (11pt)
FranklinGothicEF-Book (10pt)

Copies of this book can be ordered via the Internet:

www.librario.com

or from:

Librario Publishing Ltd
Brough House
Milton Brodie
Kinloss
Moray IV36 2UA
Tel /Fax No 01343 850 617